Required Reading

Required Reading

Literature in Australian Schools since 1945

Edited by Tim Dolin, Jo Jones and Patricia Dowsett

Foreword by Rod Quin

© Copyright 2017

© Copyright of this collection in its entirety is held by the editors, Tim Dolin, Jo Jones and Patricia Dowsett.

© Copyright of the individual chapters is held by the respective authors.

All rights reserved. Apart from any uses permitted by Australia's Copyright Act 1968, no part of this book may be reproduced by any process without prior written permission from the copyright owners. Inquiries should be directed to the publisher.

Monash University Publishing
Matheson Library and Information Services Building
40 Exhibition Walk
Monash University
Clayton, Victoria 3800, Australia
www.publishing.monash.edu

Monash University Publishing brings to the world publications which advance the best traditions of humane and enlightened thought.

Monash University Publishing titles pass through a rigorous process of independent peer review.

www.publishing.monash.edu/books/rr-9781925495577.html

Series: Literary Studies

Design: Les Thomas

National Library of Australia Cataloguing-in-Publication entry:
Title: Required reading : literature in Australian schools since 1945 / edited by Tim Dolin, Joanne Jones, Patricia Dowsett.
ISBN: 9781925495577 (paperback)
Subjects: Reading (Secondary)
Literature--Study and teaching (Secondary)
Australian literature--Study and teaching (Secondary)
Other Creators/Contributors:
Dolin, Tim, 1959- editor.
Jones, Joanne, editor.
Dowsett, Patricia, editor.

Printed in Australia by Griffin Press an Accredited ISO AS/NZS 14001:2004 Environmental Management System printer.

The paper this book is printed on is certified against the Forest Stewardship Council ® Standards. Griffin Press holds FSC chain of custody certification SGS-COC-005088. FSC promotes environmentally responsible, socially beneficial and economically viable management of the world's forests.

CONTENTS

About the Contributors ix
Foreword xv

PART I: INTRODUCTION 1

Chapter One
Conditional assent: Literary value and the value of English as a subject. . . . 3
Tim Dolin, Jo Jones and Patricia Dowsett

Chapter Two
An overview of the ALIAS data and findings 19
John Yiannakis

Chapter Three
Discipline and subject: Academic literary studies and school English
in Australia since 1945 38
Tim Dolin, Jo Jones and Patricia Dowsett

PART II: HISTORIES 59

Chapter Four
Framing the Literature curriculum 61
Ian Reid

Chapter Five
Inscribing culture: The history of prescribed text lists in senior secondary
English in NSW, 1945–1964 78
Jacqueline Manuel and Don Carter

Chapter Six
Provenance and transformation: The history of prescribed text lists in senior secondary English in NSW, 1965–2005 106
   Jacqueline Manuel and Don Carter

Chapter Seven
Literature at school in NSW: Some recent history 137
   Wayne Sawyer

Chapter Eight
Turning around English: Distant reading and rapid subject change from 1980 to 1995 158
   Jo Jones

Chapter Nine
Changing the subject: Text selection and curriculum development in VCE English 1990 174
   Larissa McLean Davies and Brenton Doecke
   with Prue Gill and Terry Hayes

Chapter Ten
Carnivalesque canons: "Professors" and text selection in secondary English syllabuses in Western Australia, 1945–1975 196
   Patricia Dowsett

PART III: TEXTS, AUTHORS, PERIODS, THEORIES 223

Chapter Eleven
Shakespeare and the conditions of dissent 225
   Jenny de Reuck

Chapter Twelve
What the Dickens?: Exploring the role of canonical texts in mediating subject English in Australia 238
   Susan K. Martin and Larissa McLean Davies

Chapter Thirteen
Growing up with *Tess*: Contexts, close reading and theoretical analysis . . . 261
   Tully Barnett, Kate Douglas, Alice Healy-Ingram

Chapter Fourteen
Modernism and modernist criticism in Australian senior secondary English 285
   Tim Dolin

Chapter Fifteen
"One of the worst things you can do to it": The teaching of Judith Wright's poetry 310
   Georgina Arnott

Chapter Sixteen
The conditions of assent and ascent: *Cloudstreet* as classroom classic . . . 327
   Claire Jones

Chapter Seventeen
Literature's ghosts: Cultural heritage and cultural analysis in subject English 339
   Tim Dolin

Index 359

ABOUT THE CONTRIBUTORS

Georgina Arnott is a researcher in the History program at Monash University. In 2013 she received a doctorate in History from the University of Melbourne for her study of the life of Judith Wright. She holds a Masters in Literary Studies, has taught in that field at Swinburne and Victoria Universities, and has had a number of articles and book reviews published in Australian literary journals. Her first book, *The Unknown Judith Wright*, was published by UWA Publishing in 2016.

Tully Barnett is a Research Fellow in the School of Humanities and Creative Arts at Flinders University, South Australia, researching methods for determining the non-economic value of arts and culture. She contributed to the project Building Reading Resilience: Developing a Skills-Based Approach to Literary Studies, funded by the Office for Learning and Teaching, and researches the digital impacts of reading cultures in and out of the tertiary classroom.

Don Carter is Senior Lecturer in the School of Education at the University of Technology, Sydney where he is the co-ordinator for English education. Don has also held numerous senior positions including: Inspector (English) and Inspector (Registration & Accreditation) at the Board of Studies, Teaching & Educational Standards (BOSTES); and Consultant for K–12 English as a Second Language/Multicultural Education for the NSW Department of Education and Training (DET). He has extensive experience in the teaching of English (head teacher) and has been a senior marker and an assessor of English examinations for the NSW HSC. Don has also developed curriculum materials for English in NSW and was responsible for the development of the new K–10 English Syllabus and the Stage 6 English Studies course.

Jenny de Reuck is an Associate Professor at Murdoch University with practice-led and traditional research interests in Renaissance and Early Modern studies as well as in theatre in education. She has published articles on same-sex performance and her adaptations of Shakespeare have been produced in Western Australia and Malaysia. Her most recent publication in the field is a dramaturgical critique of Webster's *The Duchess of Malfi*.

Brenton Doecke is an Honorary Professor in the School of Education at Deakin University. He has published widely in the fields of teacher education and English curriculum and pedagogy. His research has involved a sustained focus on the professional learning and identity of teachers within a policy context shaped by standards-based reforms, including his work on the Standards for Teachers of English Language and Literacy in Australia (STELLA), and many other projects. He is currently engaged (with Larissa McLean Davies, Philip Mead, Wayne Sawyer and Lyn Yates) in a major Australian Research Council Project on the role that literary knowledge might play in the professional learning and practice of early career English teachers. He is an Honorary Life Member of both the Victorian Association for the Teaching of English and the Australian Association for the Teaching of English, and is a former editor of English in Australia, and co-editor (with Jennifer Rennie and Annette Patterson) of *The Australian Journal of Language and Literacy*.

Tim Dolin is Professor of Literary Studies at Curtin University. He is a member of the editorial board of the Cambridge Edition of the Novels and Stories of Thomas Hardy, for which he is preparing a critical edition of *The Return of the Native*. He has written numerous essays and chapters on the nineteenth-century novel for international journals and books, and has edited novels by Hardy, Charlotte Brontë and Elizabeth Gaskell. He is also completing *The Irony of Distance*, about British novels in nineteenth- and early twentieth-century Australia, based on data collected and stored on the Australian Common Reader website.

Kate Douglas is an Associate Professor in the School of Humanities at Flinders University. She is the author of *Contesting Childhood: Autobiography, memory, trauma* (Rutgers 2010) and (with Anna Poletti) *Life Narratives and Youth Culture: Representation, agency and participation* (Palgrave 2016). Her scholarship of teaching has been published in *Arts and Humanities in Higher Education*, *HERD* and the MLA Options for Teaching series.

Patricia Dowsett is a teacher of English and Literature who has taught at both the secondary and tertiary levels in Western Australia. In 2016 Trish completed a PhD at the University of Western Australia. Her research examined 'The History of Curricular Control: Literary Education in Western Australia, 1912–2012', a reflection of her interests in subject histories,

About the Contributors

English Studies and Australian literary history. With Bill Green and Brenton Doecke, Trish co-edited a special issue of the AATE journal *English in Australia*, dedicated to reading the impact of the 1966 Dartmouth Seminar upon the teaching of English and interrogating its central question, 'What is English?'.

Alice Healy-Ingram is Lecturer in Australian Studies at Flinders University. Her main research interests are novel-to-film adaptation, literature in education and historical writing. She was co-director on the ALTC-funded project, "Teaching Australian Literature" with Philip Mead and Kerry Kilner, completed in 2010. She is co-managing editor of the journal *New Scholar: An International Journal of the Humanities, Creative Arts and Social Science*s with Bridie McCarthy.

Claire Jones is in the final stages of completing a PhD in the School of English and Cultural Studies at the University of Western Australia titled "The national subject: deconstructing the Australian *Bildung* project". Her areas of interest include Australian literature, world literature and post-national studies. She is currently the president of the English Teachers Association of Western Australia and has been a secondary English teacher, Head of English, and served as the examiner for both the Year 12 English and Literature courses in Western Australia.

Jo Jones is Lecturer in English Studies in the Faculty of Education, University of Tasmania. She has a PhD in Australian colonial historical novels and has taught extensively at Curtin University and the University of Western Australia. Jo has a forthcoming monograph, *Dark Times: Australian historical novels and the history wars* (UWA Publishing), and is currently undertaking studies of the Gothic and its reception in Tasmanian schools.

Jacqueline Manuel is Associate Professor of English Education in the Faculty of Education and Social Work at the University of Sydney. She holds a BA (Hons) in English, a Dip Ed and a PhD in English Literature from the University of New England. She is Program Director of the Master of Teaching (Secondary) and Secondary English curriculum co-ordinator in the Faculty. Jackie's teaching and research interests include teenagers' reading; creative pedagogies in secondary English; pre-service English teacher motivation; early-career teacher experience; and English curriculum history.

Susan K. Martin is a Professor of English, and Associate Pro Vice-Chancellor (Research) for the College of Arts, Social Sciences and Commerce, at La Trobe University, Melbourne, Australia. She is currently working with Larissa McLean Davies on a project exploring the ways in which teachers select Australian teaching texts. She has published widely on Australian and British literature and culture. Her books include *Colonial Dickens* with Kylie Mirmohamadi (Australian Scholarly Publishing, 2012) and *Sensational Melbourne* (ASP, 2012), *Reading the Garden: the settlement of Australia* with Katie Holmes and Kylie Mirmohamadi, (MUP, 2008), and *Women and Empire* (Routledge, 2009: about to be republished in digital form).

Larissa McLean Davies is an Associate Professor in Language and Literacy, and Associate Dean, Teacher Education Research in the Melbourne Graduate School of Education at the University of Melbourne. Prior to commencing work in the tertiary sector, Larissa was a Secondary English and Literature Teacher in a range of Victorian schools. Larissa's current research is concerned with the way in which English teachers conceptualise and account for literature and its role in subject English, and the way these understandings impact on their practices. To this end, she is lead Chief Investigator, with fellow CIs Wayne Sawyer, Philip Mead, Lyn Yates and Brenton Doecke, on the Australian Research Council funded project 'Investigating Literary Knowledge in the Making of English Teachers' (DP160101084 2016-2019), and is working with Susan K. Martin on a Copyright Agency Limited funded project titled 'Teaching Australia', which is concerned with the resourcing of the teaching of national literatures.

Ian Reid, an Adjunct Professor in Humanities at The University of Western Australia, has published on various topics including literary theory, education policy and history, and English teaching. He has a dozen books to his name – fiction, non-fiction and poetry – along with hundreds of articles in magazines, newspapers and periodicals. AATE issued his influential book *The Making of Literature: Texts, Context and Classroom Practices* in 1984 and he continues to publish in the field of English education, having contributed chapters to the AATE books *English Teachers at Work* and *Teaching Australian Literature* and articles to journals such as *Changing English* and *English in Australia*. His writings, some of which have been translated into several languages and won international awards, include three historical novels, *The End of Longing*, *That Untravelled World* and *The Mind's Own Place*.

Wayne Sawyer is Professor of Education and Director of Research in the School of Education at the University of Western Sydney. His doctoral thesis was on English in New South Wales in the late twentieth century. He has written on the place of literature in the national curriculum and on the roles of literature and language in the history of school English.

John Yiannakis OAM has a strong and diverse research and publication record. For many years, he lectured in Modern and Ancient History at Tuart College, and was Head of the Social Sciences Department. More recently, he has worked as a Research Fellow at Curtin and Murdoch Universities.

FOREWORD

Teachers who lack an adequate understanding of the history of their discipline are in danger of suffering from what British educational theorist G. H. Bantock referred to as the parochialism of the present.[1] Without such an understanding we are inclined to see current educational policies and practices as the natural and perhaps only possible way of doing things. We are also likely to fall prey to prevailing educational fads and academic theories unthinkingly and to meekly fall into line with new bureaucratic dicta because we lack an adequate framework for evaluating these developments.

An understanding of the history of our discipline allows us to question, critique and evaluate not just the past but the present, and to think about possible futures. In presenting us with some insights into the teaching of literature in Australian schools since 1945, *Required Reading* presents all those interested in the subject with a timely reminder of the value of an historical perspective.

However, historical perspectives can offer at least two potential traps. The first is post-lapsarianism – the view of the past as a golden age against which the present can only be seen as a period of loss and decline. *Required Reading* helps us to avoid falling into this trap by documenting the manner in which the study of literature since 1945 has become more broadly inclusive and thus much richer in terms of the authors and texts studied. Literature has clearly moved from being simply a colonial outpost of British culture to a subject that offers students the opportunity to experience and interact with diverse voices from around the world.

The other potential danger of a historical perspective is to fall into the trap of what British historian Herbert Butterfield once called the Whig interpretation of history.[2] In this view, history is seen as a continual march of progress from an unenlightened past through a better present to a brighter future. *Required Reading* prevents us from also falling into this trap.

A number of the essays ask us to consider whether in recent decades we teachers of literature have lost focus on certain important aspects of literary study. In particular, some chapters ask, has the influence of cultural studies

---

1   *The Parochialism of the Present*. London: Routledge & Kegan Paul, 1981.
2   *The Whig Interpretation of History*. London: W.W. Norton and Co., 1965 (originally published 1931).

and what Terry Eagleton called political criticism,[3] with their interest in the social function of literature and the relationship between texts and contexts, led to a neglect of the aesthetic in the study of literature?

Joyce Carol Oates, in discussing the adaptation of her short story 'Where Are You Going? Where Have You Been?' (which, by the way, would have made a good sub-title for *Required Reading*) into the film *Smooth Talk*, has this to say:

> All writers know that Language is their subject; quirky word choices, patterns of rhythm, enigmatic pauses, punctuation marks ... Of course we all have 'real' subjects and we will fight to the death to defend those subjects but beneath the tale-telling it is the tale-telling that grips us so very fiercely.[4]

Of course language is a social and political practice, but, especially in literature, it is also an aesthetic practice. Like other forms of aesthetic practice, the best literature has the capacity to transcend the concerns of a particular time and place. Some chapters of *Required Reading* ask us to consider whether in our attempts to make the study of literature relevant to the here and now and in the over-privileging of context in the study of literature we are in danger of neglecting those aspects of literary works that transcend specific contexts.

A number of the essays in *Required Reading* encourage us to avoid both the post-lapsarian and Whig views of the history of literature by reminding us of the persistence of certain challenges teachers have always faced and continue to face in the teaching of literature. I refer specifically to the obstacles that rigid syllabuses and external examinations pose for those of us who wish more than anything for our students to be gripped 'so very fiercely', in Joyce Carol Oates words, by the 'tale-telling' of literature.

In asking us to think about where we have been, where we are going and, most importantly, where we wish to go, *Required Reading* should be required reading for all teachers of literature.

Rod Quin

---

3 In *Literary Theory: An Introduction*. Basil Blackwell, Oxford, 198.
4 'Smooth Talk: Short Story into Film'. *New York Times*, March 23, 1986.

Part I

Introduction

Chapter One

CONDITIONAL ASSENT

Literary value and the value of English as a subject

Tim Dolin, Jo Jones and Patricia Dowsett

Literature, Roland Barthes famously wrote, is "what gets taught". But what has been taught as literature in Australian senior secondary school English programs since 1945? No large-scale study of the texts set on English syllabuses in Australia has been undertaken before now, partly because "what gets taught" also means "What assumptions about literature get taught?", "What approaches to literary studies get taught?", "What else is the school English curriculum required to teach?" and so forth. You cannot isolate syllabus lists from the written and enacted curricula of which those lists were a part, and cultural critics would argue in any case that such lists tell us nothing about the regimes of reading that regulated the use of these texts.[1] As a result, the lists themselves, the works themselves, have not been investigated systematically. We all seem confident about what counted as literature in Australian classrooms in the past (and what that section of the syllabus devoted to literature study used to look like), and yet few studies in

---

1   Frow defines the literary regime as a semiotic and social apparatus "that inspires and regulates practices of valuation and interpretation, connecting people to textual objects and processes by means of normative patterns of value and disvalue" (Frow 51). It operates through "the structured articulation of a set of knowledge institutions (the school, the church, the theater), a more or less professional custodianship of literary knowledge, a designated set of proper social uses, and a more or less supportive relation to hierarchies of caste or class, of gender, of ethnicity, and so on … the literary regime in this broader sense is composed at once of codes, practices, organized bodies of texts, physical spaces (libraries, bookshops, bedrooms), modes of authority, and people and things interacting (all at once) physically, semiotically, and socially. … [It is] a regulatory manifold which makes possible the free exercise of judgement within a limited but disparate range of interpretive possibilities" (52).

curriculum history or the history of literary studies in Australia appear to have tested their assumptions against the historical record.

This book is one outcome of a project aimed at remedying that situation by establishing as definitively as possible what texts have been set as literature in upper-secondary schools in Australia since the end of World War Two. The primary documentary sources used in the project are text lists and English syllabuses, many of which are preserved in archives around the country (see Yiannakis here). Taken together these sources offer a broad and comprehensive picture of the written culture set in the Year 11 and 12 subjects variously called "English" and "English Literature". Although such evidence can never by itself conclusively show what most Australians actually read or were required to read in upper-school, let alone what it meant for them to read it, study it and be examined in it – as Ian Reid argued forcefully in 1984 (and again here), a curriculum is not "simply a programme of things-to-be-studied" (1984, 7) – the evidence does afford us new insights into what is widely agreed to be one of the most important "apparatuses of canonicity" (Berubé 458).

The chapters that follow do the vital work of reconnecting the raw data in the text lists, collated in a database called ALIAS (Analysis of Literature in Australian Schools),[2] with the archives of curriculum histories, theories and practices of teaching, and histories of literary criticism and theory. The book's objective is to take this newly assembled, relatively comprehensive information about set texts and carry it back to the long-running debates about the history of English and the successive waves of modernisation in upper-school English. The contributors are variously (and sometimes both) curriculum historians and literary critics, and what we have attempted here is to bring together the methods of curriculum history and literary studies to overcome what is (borrowing from John Sutherland) a hole at the centre of curriculum history and at the centre of the history of English: evidence showing *exactly* what was set – when, where, how, and in which disciplinary, institutional, socio-historical and pedagogical contexts. The database tells us that there was a rich and unexpected diversity in what was to be studied in different states in Australia at different times and the text lists never amount to predictably representative subsets of any recognisable "literary canon" at any given historical moment. Rather, they appear to absorb into the category of the literary a varied range of high literary, middlebrow and popular texts, British and non-British texts, local and national texts,

---

2   www.australiancommonreader.com/syllabus. Username = tim; password = tim2010.

and book and non-book texts, in ways that are so highly distinctive as to demand explanation.

How confident can we be, then, that these multiple pedagogic canons produced the "shared competencies, norms, and values that govern how we read and the kinds of value we attach to books" (Frow 139–140), given that they did not always share the same assumptions about the literary? If, as John Guillory argues, "the process of canon formation has an institutional context, the school, and it is this institution which is responsible for the systematic regulation of reading and writing as social practices" (45), why do these canons appear to be at once narrower than expected – they are strikingly local, even parochial – and much wider, unpredictably breaking away from national and imperial models? Nor is it obvious that pedagogic canons are or have historically been committed to the transmission of cultural capital (at least it is not always obvious what counted as cultural capital).

By the term "literary canon" we mean that "body of literary works traditionally regarded as the most important, significant, and worthy of study; those works of especially Western literature considered to be established as being of the highest quality and most enduring value; the classics" (OED). As Guillory has influentially argued, however, canons are not collections of texts so much as clusters of values. Works are not individually canonical, that is to say, but take on canonical status as part of a literary system that seeks to promote certain values (Guillory, *Cultural Capital*). Put differently, in Stanley Fish's classic formulation, "literature […] is the product of a way of reading, of a community agreement about what will count as literature, which leads the members of the community to pay a certain kind of attention and thereby *create* literature" (Fish 97). In practice there is not, therefore, "an abstract, hypostatized 'Canon'", but multiple canons, and it becomes necessary to "explore the circulation and function of [those] actual historical canons in specific communities, institutions, and individual critical careers" (Gorak ix).

Canons might also be described as sets of instructions for the constitution and maintenance of the category of the literary, so that school English syllabuses are not properly collections of texts (canonical or otherwise) either, but sets of instructions for the proper uses of the literary: in the constitution and maintenance of social and cultural subjectivities and values, and in the constitution and maintenance of English as the foundational subject in the entire school curriculum. To become canonical, a work must be reproduced "by being taught over and over again" (Eaton 306) and undoubtedly, pedagogical canons do perform the central reproductive role of educational institutions in the consecration and preservation of symbolic goods. Yet the evidence of the syllabuses suggests that schools reproduce legitimate modes of consumption (Bourdieu 37) – the knowledge to recognise and respond to literary works – in an environment in which they are engaged in a ceaseless struggle for the "monopoly of legitimate discourse" (36) about the world, which is a disciplinary struggle for institutional authority. As Franklin Court argues with regard to academic literary studies:

> The record of the genesis of English literary study is in part a record of major institutional commitments, of the publication of definitive critical tomes, of the shaping and projection of a teachable canon of literary works, and of the vibrant and colorful personalities who left their marks on generations of highly impressionable students. But the full record of the genesis of the discipline also includes other traces of the past: salary disputes, professional conflicts, highly problematic programmatic needs and demands, conflicting pedagogical visions, territorial rifts, professional threats and jealousies, the rising awareness of British racial distinctions and British imperial power, the question of institutional credibility, economic constraints, the marketing of books, the idiosyncracies of committee formulations, unwritten committee and department agendas, degree requirements, academic factionalism, political demagoguery, pressures from privileged social and religious sectors, colonialism, campaigns for national literacy, academic one-upmanship. (Court 3)

In schools, literary studies is embedded in subjects – most commonly "English" – that originated in, and take part in, a completely different set of institutional commitments and struggles. School subjects are specialised "social systems" which do not reproduce the ideological and professional dynamics of the disciplinary field but convert them into a dynamics of the scholastic field. It goes without saying that school subjects are social systems competing "for power, prestige, recognition and reward within the secondary or high school situation" (Hargreaves 56). What constitutes "literary value" inside these social systems is therefore quite different from what constitutes it in other literary cultures, fields or social systems. In the school classroom (and differently in the university classroom), "belief in the value of the work" (Bourdieu in Johnson) must be negotiated with belief in the value of the subject.

So what does the historical development of English literary study in Australia look like when viewed from the school syllabus? Take the history of Australian literary studies as an example. As David Carter reminds us, Australian literature was part of the school curriculum long before it was accepted into the university (Carter 25): that is to say, a crude populist version of the radical nationalist canon (exemplified, let's say, by Dorothea Mackellar) had ideological work to perform in the classroom long before the professionalisation of academic Australian literary studies called for a national canon with "the authority to speak for the universal rather than the merely local" (30). At length, of course, Australian literature in schools *was* modernised in line with the developing "metaphysical" canon (Docker). Its curricular exemplar here was Patrick White's *The Tree of Man*, its critical exemplars Leonie Kramer, A.D. Hope and James McAuley. This approach to Australian literature was quickly discredited, however, and the newly valorised national canon collapsed under the weight of postcolonial revisionism, multicultural critique, the decline of nation-making as a symbolic function for literary history, and the canon wars.[3] English teachers joined in (indeed, no institution has demonised canonicity quite as energetically as the school), yet ironically the age of ideological critique had a somewhat "reversing" effect on the study of Australian literature. Where once we celebrated our distinctive sunburnt Australian-ness, we now teach our children that Australian literatures – including Indigenous oral and inscriptional narrative traditions – are valued primarily as spaces in which readers can engage imaginatively and critically with the "variety of cultural, social, and ethical interests and responsibilities" that have arisen from Australia's "evolving ethnic composition" and its geographic location in the Asia-Pacific, and with "the collective cultural memories that have accumulated around" these interests and responsibilities (National Curriculum Board 8). It has been the special fate of Australian literature to thrive in the school system, where it can never altogether escape from the cultural nationalism that first defined it. Textual critique is social ethics is civic education is national subject formation *is* school English.

All of which leads us to ask: can we claim that Australian literature is even the *same thing* inside and outside the school system? How was Australian literature positioned in schools in relation to other literatures (pre-eminently

---

3   Nearly three decades on from the heady days of the "canon wars" (Lauter; Hirsch, Graff), school English and English literature are still the focus of heated controversy in Australia and literary scholars everywhere remain concerned with questions of canonicity (Insko; Gluzman; Low and Wynne-Davies; Bérubé).

British and American literatures, and postcolonial literatures), themselves represented by different authors and works at different times and levels in different states? How was it positioned in relation to changing curricula and differing rates and kinds of curriculum change? These questions don't just concern the changing nature of literature and literary value in a complex nationwide school system, then – they're not just questions about the creation of a national literature within a federated structure of knowledge institutions. They also concern the fundamentally different *nature* of literature and literary value inside the classroom. Literature does not name something stably knowable, but a continuous process: the coming-into-being of the literary within determinative but always changing structures of social and cultural relations that regulate the experiences of writing and reading. In particular, literature is the name we give to certain modes of readerly *attentiveness*, and to certain vocabularies we mobilise in our reading – linguistic vocabularies (of tropes, discourses, genres, styles), bibliographical vocabularies (of production and circulation) and symbolic vocabularies (of use and value). A "text" is thus "not a 'material thing' but a material set of events, a point in time (or a moment in space) where certain communicative interchanges are being practiced" (McGann 21); and "literature" is actualised in those communicative interchanges, its meanings always "given in part by the social field into which it is incorporated" (Hall 293).

So, yes, school syllabuses are apparatuses of canonicity, but not in the usual narrow sense of the word canon, which signifies the disposition of cultural capital across a hierarchy of texts and a field of social power relations. The evidence suggests that the institutional preservation of certain written works reflects a much more complex dynamics of inclusion and omission, as well as a more mundane mechanics, and that the discourse of canonicity as we commonly use it is too exclusively concerned with "credentialising functions" of the canon (Carter 25). This is not to deny that the school system has participated in the wider project of producing a body of Australian imaginative writing worthy of being denoted "literature", especially when "canonisation in traditional ethico-aesthetic terms" (28) gave way to canonisation on the grounds of ideological critique and subversiveness. Nor is it to deny, on the other hand, that the school canon can tell us little about the shifting canonical status of Australian literature, since the school is ranked relatively low in the system of cultural legitimisation, as David Carter observes.

Perhaps "canon" simply isn't the right word to describe those clusters of texts and patterns of use that become evident when we take a synoptic view of historical syllabuses using a relational database. But what other term would do? Classroom canons are constituted and maintained according to criteria of symbolic value: it's just that those criteria do not only, or even principally, serve ethico-aesthetic practices or ethico-political practices. That doesn't mean, however, that they do not extend beyond the classroom. To begin with, schools produce powerful and enduring *sentimental canons* that influence whole generations of readers. We might also call these middlebrow canons. *To Kill a Mockingbird*, *Snow Falling on Cedars*, *Pride and Prejudice* and *The Great Gatsby* are among the most notable examples of works that become our "best-loved" books. Along with their Australian counterparts – *Cloudstreet*, *My Brother Jack*, *The Fortunes of Richard Mahony* and *My Place* – these books are canonised by literary institutions for reasons that have little or nothing to do with either their ethico-aesthetic autonomy or even their nationalist ideology: they are valued instead for a kind of affective universality – a feelgood moral seriousness in line with the popular-commercial media's idea of literary value.

This is evidence that the school literary system promotes certain forms of symbolic value in which the autonomy of the literary is sometimes greatly weakened. But it doesn't stop there, for the school system will simultaneously mobilise many different criteria of value – nation-making, the assertion of locality and region, civic multiculturalism, modernist polysemy, political dissension, and so on – and often simultaneously for the same texts, which might sit in a number of separate but overlapping canonical groupings. There are plain structural reasons for this. The most important change to happen to literature in Australian curricula in the period of our study was the nearly synchronous nationwide partition of upper-school English into "General English" (or "English Expression") and "English Literature" (or "Literature") in the late 1960s. This change complicates the data analysis we're doing somewhat, although to good purpose, for it inaugurates two or more parallel sets of framing conditions for the reading of many of the same texts in each state, according them different uses and values. This can tell us a great deal, and in very great detail, about the moveable boundaries of the literary during a time when profound disciplinary unity and stability gave way to massive cultural and disciplinary upheaval.

Nor are school canons always the product of straightforward value judgements. To begin with, what is set on syllabuses almost never corresponds exactly to what is taught. Teachers had some small degree of choice even in the 1940s and 50s, when the syllabus was tightly prescriptive, and only examination scripts or statistical and anecdotal details from examiners' reports (which do exist for some states in some recent years) can recover reliable information about what was taught and how it was taught. Yet we can much more safely infer what constituted the literary from a syllabus of, say, five texts or authors in each genre, than we can after the 1970s, when most syllabus lists, afraid of their own canonicity, grew larger and larger, and are accordingly much less indicative of the taught curriculum. In addition, syllabuses are subject to the availability of books in print; school syllabuses are additionally subject to what is available in box-sets in the book-room. The same plays, poems and novels get taught every year, which puts pressure on syllabus committees to ensure that the canon is only minimally disturbed from year to year. Even when text lists grow uncontrollably (as in Western Australia), or are dispensed with entirely (as in Queensland), this can be used as a tactic to deter change, since it allows the real number of texts taught to remain moderately compact and stable from year to year, even decade to decade, as new teachers come into the system and teach the books they were taught as students. Consider Arthur Miller's *A View from the Bridge*. This play was a set text in 1990 and 1992 in Tasmania, and 2005 in Victoria, but nowhere else in Australia except Western Australia, where it was set from 1973–76, 1983–85, and 1998–2005. These are unique conditions, one might think, for the functioning of what Tony Bennett calls "iterability". Long-haul syllabus texts are "constantly brought into connection or articulated with new texts, socially and politically mobilised in different ways within different class practices or educational, cultural and linguistic institutions". In this book we hope to show how "historically concrete, variable and incessantly changing determinations – determinations which so press in upon a text as fundamentally to modify its very mode of being" (Bennett 224–25) – affected the meanings of texts like Miller's play.

School Literature subjects in Australia have generally followed the discipline's rotations between dominantly formalist and dominantly historicist text-worldviews. The academic discipline, on the other hand, has been only intermittently concerned with literature's ethical function – its capacity to help us "make sense of the here and now" (Kermode 39). One thinks of the Leavisite ascendancy of the first half of the twentieth century,[4] and more recently the various critical paradigms shaped by ideology politics and

---

4 F. R. Leavis (1895-1978) was a British literary and cultural critic whose major works, including *New Bearings in English Poetry* (1932), *The Great Tradition* (1948), and *The Common Pursuit* (1952), along with his journal, *Scrutiny*, had a profound influence on school literary study in Britain and Australia.

cultural materialism: the politics of class, gender and sexuality, ethnicity, colour and colonialism, ecological politics, non-human animals and so on. In schools, however, the ethical imperative has always been foremost in literary study, and literary texts there have always been, in Frank Kermode's words, pre-eminently "for finding things out" about ourselves (Kermode 39), not for preserving the heritage of the cultural past (see the final chapter of this collection). Canons were formed – texts have remained on a list for years, even decades, as we noted – but they are canons that do not always submit to the myth of the canon; not, at least, in Kermode's sense of myth as absolute assent in "things as they are and were" (Kermode 39). School text lists are evidence rather of a "conditional assent": assent to the power of imaginative writing on condition that it serves the always changing needs and purposes at hand. This book is primarily concerned with recovering those needs and purposes: what we might call, borrowing from Kermode, the historical conditions of assent. Why, in the here and now, are certain texts valued and endorsed over and above others? And what was it that earlier generations were trying to make sense of in their presents? *Required Reading* challenges enduring myths about literary study using the primary evidence and scholarly literature of curriculum history, the history of literary studies, critical theory and cultural studies.

The contributors to *Required Reading* contextualise this primary evidence in a variety of ways and the collection is accordingly structured into four sections. In Part I, opening chapters provide an overview of the project and offer ways of thinking about text lists and their significance within a range of broader contexts. In the following chapter John Yiannakis presents a summary of the ALIAS project and the processes of data collection and analysis, and outlines the findings in broad terms, setting the scene for the more detailed and critical analyses of later chapters. Surveying the Literature reading lists for English courses in five Australian states between 1945 and 2005 (the data is restricted to states conducting public examinations at the end of Year 12), Yiannakis reviews the changing (and persisting) titles, forms of work and writers appearing on the syllabuses over time. He identifies general tendencies and patterns of change, paving the way for the closer historical investigations of text selection processes, syllabus enactments and discipline-subject dynamics in the chapters that follow.

A third introductory chapter considers an array of issues provoked by ALIAS around the relations between the academic discipline of literary studies and upper-school subject English. It is divided into three broad periods: 1945–65, 1965–82 and 1982 to the present.

With the national curriculum framework now in place, state-based historical studies of literature and schooling are more important than ever in informing curriculum design, text choice, and teaching and examination practices in upper-secondary English in Australia. In this context Part II offers a timely examination of state curriculum histories and the ways in which cultural texts, meanings, values and reading practices have been shaped and authorised by the choices of texts for classroom English teaching.

As always, Ian Reid provides an elegant and challenging argument for the construction of literary knowledge as an effect of framing. Reid's overview of ways of reading syllabuses stands as a critical and complex discussion of the nature of curriculum itself and how we "read" it. His chapter argues that while a list of set texts such as ALIAS does not constitute a curriculum in literary studies, it may serve as a useful starting point for considering what does. Its usefulness, however, depends on other information, less readily available for analysis. This includes information about several circumtextual factors that "frame" the curriculum. Reid focuses on some of the ways in which the curriculum for literary studies has been framed in senior secondary Australian classrooms, with particular reference to the Literature Study Design and associated Course Development Support Material initially devised in the late 1980s for the innovative Victorian Certificate of Education.

Jacqueline Manuel and Don Carter offer a comprehensive state curriculum history of New South Wales. They contend that, of all the Australian state and territory versions of senior secondary English, the identity of the subject in New South Wales has been the one most obviously regulating and examining not only the kinds of texts that students will encounter in English, but also the ways in which those texts are to be read and experienced. Through chronologically analysing the "what and how" of literary study revealed in these lists, Manuel and Carter's rich and detailed chapters critically examine the senior secondary English text lists in New South Wales from 1945 to 2014. They discuss the extent to which these lists inscribe and perpetuate certain cultural values and discourses, and weigh the implications of such historically informed insights for the present and future conceptualisations of senior secondary English curriculum and the quality of students' experience of the subject in schools.

Also providing a New South Wales curriculum history, Wayne Sawyer's chapter offers a case study of "the culture of school literature" via a personal history of classroom practice recovered from teaching notes through the 1980s and 1990s. Sawyer examines how the study of literature was defined in

New South Wales in time and place for the years 1980, 1988, 1992, and 1993. In each of these years, a significant professional text ("method" book) dealing with the teaching of literature was published by an Australian professional English teaching association, and these years mark key points in the professional discourse of the subject "English". Sawyer's discussion of theorised experiences joins the abstraction of curriculum and syllabus to the more human shapes of secondary English.

Jo Jones's chapter "Turning around English: distant reading and rapid subject change from 1980 to 1995" discerns thematic and formal trends on the most included texts in English syllabuses over 25 years – 1980–85, 1985–90, 1990–95, 1995–2000 and 2000-05. The twofold approach considers each five-year span observed "from afar", according to Franco Moretti's process of distant reading. English is the course that changes its text inclusions often in order to remain immediate and relevant. Jones claims that there are fascinating patterns of inclusions that reflect historical and social preoccupations and, indeed, reinforce the course's status as au courant. ALIAS data, however, also reveal overwhelmingly strong trends in the thematic content of popular text inclusions that raise questions about English's taken-for-granted status as a radical and democratising course.

Larissa McLean Davies and Brenton Doecke analyse text selection data and curriculum in Victoria between 1990 and 2005, a key time of innovation and transition heralded by the introduction of the Victorian Certificate of Education (VCE). This chapter presents a history of the VCE since 1990, asking how such "a brave and imaginative attempt" to develop an equitable and socially responsible English curriculum failed so badly in its aspirations. At the core of the discussion is the effort of the VCE curriculum writers to give far more students "access" to literature, and an argument about how the text list was broadened to cater "for a diverse range of interests". The chapter draws on the ALIAS data to show exactly how this concern with access played out. McLean Davies and Doecke approach the data from the curriculum history point of view, rightly arguing that "texts do not function in isolation and cannot be separated from the institutional and curricular ideologies which constrain them" (193). In so doing, this chapter reminds us that the VCE was born in the front line of the canon wars of the 1980s, demonstrating how significant anti-discriminatory discourse (of "access to literature") was to the transformation of literary studies in schools.

The final chapter of the "Histories" section is Patricia Dowsett's study of "Carnivalesque canons" at the University of Western Australia from 1945 to

1975. During these decades, (William) Allan Edwards was the state's only Professor of English. This chapter historicises subject English in Western Australia in terms of biography because Edwards was the sole director of English syllabuses and examinations in the state. It follows, Dowsett contends, that his text selection and educational and cultural experiences shaped the version of English that emerged during this period. Dowsett argues that Edwards imported a version of "Cambridge English" marked by literary study, practical criticism and the Leavisism which was to influence English across Australia in the 1960s; yet beneath this surface of traditional canonicity there was a distinctive way in which university staff engaged with literary study. The inclusions of professors' books, and the creative practice, theatrical engagement and "carnivalesque" approach to texts, suggest not only the significance of institutions and personnel at a local level, but also the intimacy and intricacy of many curriculum decisions made in the teaching of English at both the tertiary and secondary levels of education.

Part III of the collection turns to analyses of the data based upon specific texts, authors, theories or periods, beginning with William Shakespeare. Jenny de Reuck argues that the sustained popularity of Shakespeare's plays on secondary text lists is a product of their openness – their "epistemic instability" and their "assertion of the right to dissent". In this way and with particular reference to *Hamlet*, de Reuck attributes Shakespeare's appeal and occupation of the text lists throughout the decades of the ALIAS project to the way in which Shakespeare celebrates humanity without socio-historical tendencies or contextual constraints.

Larissa McLean Davies and Susan K. Martin investigate the changing role of Dickens's novels in Australian versions of subject English. They explore the ways in which Dickens's canonical texts were increasingly placed alongside Australian texts in subject English over time, and the ways in which the texts can be seen as contributing to and/or ameliorating negotiations of national identity that are brokered by the intended English curricula in different places. Mapping the uses of *Great Expectations* in Western Australia and South Australia in particular, McLean Davies and Martin consider the shifting values of the texts as carriers of cultural value and national and international meaning, and their circulation in the field or economy of the school curricular and the national marketplace.

Tully Barnett, Kate Douglas and Alice Healy-Ingram share their experiences of "growing up with" Thomas Hardy's *Tess of the d'Urbervilles*. They use personal reflection and secondary material to examine the ways in which close, contextual and theoretical readings necessarily change even when texts do not. From this, the chapter connects *Tess* in a classroom context to its interpretive framing and different interpretations. Barnett, Douglas and Healy-Ingram argue that the novel illuminates some of the fascinating trajectories and tensions emerging from the movement of studying a literary text from high school to university level English. For example, what are the limits of a feminist literary analysis at high school level? What ground might be gained in employing such an analysis at university level? How does school context affect teaching and reception of the work?

Tim Dolin's chapter re-examines historical narratives of modernism and modernist criticism in Australia, and traces out some barely perceptible lines of influence between European modernism and Australian school English. Historical evidence suggests that school English does not embrace modernism until the second half of the 1960s, when many of the leading modernist texts (and especially Australian modernist texts) first appeared on upper-school syllabuses, and the critical practices of Leavisism and American New Criticism began filtering down from the universities. The chapter contests this, arguing that an early examination paper from New South Wales gives us reason to think about modernist criticism/s in the plural, in the same way that we now think about multiple modernisms.

Returning to an author study, Georgina Arnott's chapter on the works and attitudes of Australian poet, Judith Wright, contends that "context matters in the process of canonising poems". The chapter begins with an informed consideration of some of Kermode's key propositions in *The Sense of an Ending*, which are brought to bear on Wright's oeuvre before discussing the substantial presence of her poetry in Australian literary educative systems and, relatedly, in the ALIAS database. Wright's forcibly negative views of the use of her work in pedagogical contexts are considered through a detailed discussion of her early experiences of formal education. Arnott then moves on to discuss Wright's impassioned claims about the formal teaching of poetry. In a radical rejection of creative texts being used pedagogically, and even of the premise of much literary criticism, Wright said that "It's the individual response that counts". Arnott examines this argument for the removal of poetry from curricula in light of how Wright's work was included within Australian curricula; the objectives of curriculum boards, as implied by such a history of inclusion; the relationship between such objectives and broader social change; the influence of this history of inclusion on the publication of Wright's work, especially in collected editions; and the attempt by Wright to assert some authorial control over the teaching of her work by removing 'Bullocky' from future publications.

Every year in Australia readers are invited to vote on their favourite book, and every year these popular canons reveal the extent to which Australian culture has been shaped by the books that Australians were required to read in English at school. Claire Jones's chapter on "The conditions of assent and ascent: *Cloudstreet* as classroom classic" argues that popularity and canonicity can, at certain cultural moments, be closely connected. In fact, Jones argues, the sustained popularity of *Cloudstreet* on secondary text lists was one way to ensure continuation of a bicentennial cultural project that was in danger of being overlooked. This chapter explores the way Winton's nationalist myths provided a stable platform for conservative Australia that has been embraced by educational institutions throughout the decades.

The final chapter in the book, Tim Dolin's "Literature's ghosts: cultural heritage and cultural analysis in subject English", examines the return of the aesthetic in the Australian curriculum. It shows how in state syllabuses (in this case the Western Australian WACE) the aesthetic is awkwardly reconciled with the dominant values and attitudes of the course – values and attitudes that may be broadly described as left-liberal: tolerant, pluralistic, inclusive. There is a prevailing uneasiness with the place of the aesthetic in a tradition that has long since distanced itself from ideas of literature as aesthetic practice, because of their powerful historical associations with contrary values and attitudes (exclusiveness, inequality, literature as a form of cultural power). Through a discussion of *Wuthering Heights*, the chapter explores the long-time association of aesthetic reading practices with the term "cultural heritage", and political reading practices with cultural analysis, a distinction that goes back to the UK Cox Report in the 1980s. It concludes by suggesting that the rejection of Cultural Heritage approaches to literary study in Australian schools represents a renunciation of responsibility for the future.

Works Cited

Arac, Jonathan. "Why does no one care about the aesthetic value of *Huckleberry Finn*?" *New Literary History* 30. 769–784 (1999). Print.
Analysis of Literature in Australian Schools Database (ALIAS). www.australiancommonreader.com/syllabus. Web. 17 May 2016.
Baldick, Chris. *The Social Mission of English Criticism, 1848–1932*. Oxford and New York: Clarendon Press, 1983. Print.
Bennett, Tony. "Text and history". *Re-reading English*. Ed. Peter Widdowson. London: Methuen, 1982: 223–36. Print.
Bérubé, Michael. *"Canons and Contexts* in context". *American Literary History* 20.3 (2008): 457–64. Print.
Bourdieu, Pierre and Jean-Claude Passeron. *Reproduction in Education, Society, and Culture*. Trans. Richard Nice. Theory, Culture and Society. London; Newbury Park, Calif.: Sage, 1990. Print.
Bourdieu, Pierre. *The Field of Cultural Production: Essays on art and literature*. Ed. Randal Johnson. Polity Press, 1993. Print.
Brock, Paul. "The role of the University of Sydney in the construction and distortion of the New South Wales secondary English curriculum, 1951–1965". *Education Research and Perspectives* 16.2 (Dec 1989): 12–21. Print.
Carter, David. "Literary canons and literary institutions". *CanonOZities: The Making of Literary Reputations in Australia*. Ed. Delys Bird et al. Spec. Issue of *Southerly* 57.3 (1997): 16–37. Print.
Court, Franklin E. *Institutionalizing English Literature: The culture and politics of literary study, 1750–1900*. Stanford, Calif.: Stanford University Press, 1992. Print.
Docker, John. *In a Critical Condition: Reading Australian literature*. Ringwood, Vic.: Penguin, 1984. Print.
During, Simon. "Transporting literature". *Shakespeare's Books*. Ed. Phillip Mead and Marion Campbell. Melbourne: Literary and Cultural Studies, University of Melbourne, 1993. 50–78. Print.
Eagleton, Terry. *Literary Theory: An introduction*. Oxford: Blackwell, 1983. Print.
Eaton, Mark E. "The cultural capital of imaginary versus pedagogical canons". *Pedagogy* I (2001): 305–315. Print.
Fish, Stanley. *Is There a Text in This Class?: The authority of interpretive communities*. Cambridge: Harvard U P, 1980. Print.
Frow, John. *Genre*. The New Critical Idiom. London; New York: Routledge, 2006. Print.
Gallagher, Susan Van Zanten. "Contingencies and intersections: The formation of pedagogical canons". *Pedagogy* I (2001): 53-57. Print.
Gluzman, Michael. *The Politics of Canonicity: Lines of resistance in modernist Hebrew poetry*. Contraversions. Stanford, Calif.: Stanford University Press, 2003. Print.
Gorak, Jan. *The Making of the Modern Canon: Genesis and crisis of a literary idea*. Vision, Division, and Revision. London; Atlantic Heights, NJ: Athlone, 1991. Print.
Gossman, Lionel. "Literature and education". *New Literary History* 13.2 (1982): 341–71. Print.
Graff, Gerald. *Beyond the Culture Wars: How teaching the conflicts can revitalize American education*. New York: W.W. Norton, 1992. Print.
Green, Bill and Catherine Beavis, eds. *Teaching the English Subjects: Essays on English curriculum history and Australian schooling*. Geelong, Vic.: Deakin University Press, 1996. Print.
—— and Phil Cormack. "Curriculum history, 'English' and the new education: Or, installing the Empire of English?" *Pedagogy, Culture and Society* 16.3 (2008): 253–57. Print.

———, John Hodges, and Allan Luke. *Debating Literacy in Australia: A documentary history, 1945–1994.* Melbourne: Australian Literacy Federation, 1994. Print.

Guillory, John. "Canon, syllabus, list: A note on the pedagogic imaginary". *Transition* 52 (1991): 36–54. Print.

———. *Cultural Capital: The problem of literary canon formation.* Chicago and London: University of Chicago Press, 1993. Print.

Hall, Stuart. "Notes on deconstructing 'The Popular'". *People's History and Socialist Theory.* History Workshop Series. London: Routledge and Kegan Paul, 1981. Print.

Hargreaves, A. *Communicative and assessment reform.* Milton Keynes: Open University Press, 1989. Print.

Hay, John. "Canonical and colonial texts: English appropriations and misappropriations". *A Sense of Exile: Essays in the literature of the Asia-Pacific region.* Ed. Bruce Bennett. Nedlands: Centre for Studies in Australian Literature, 1988. 18. Print.

Healy, J.J. "The poem and the professing of English in Australia: The La Trobe debate and *Australian Poems in Perspective*". *World Literature Written in English* 20 (1981): 254–73. Print.

Hirsch, E.D. *Cultural Literacy: What every American needs to know.* Boston: Houghton Mifflin, 1987. Print.

Hunter, Ian. *Culture and Government: The emergence of literary education.* Houndmills, Basingstoke, Hampshire: Macmillan Press, 1988. Print.

———. "English in Australia". *Meanjin* 47 (1988): 723–38. Print.

Insko, Jeffrey. "Generational canons". *Pedagogy* 3.3 (2003): 341–58. Print.

Lauter, Paul. *Canons and Contexts.* New York: Oxford University Press, 1991. Print.

Levine, Lawrence W. *The Opening of the American Mind: Canons, culture, and history.* Boston: Beacon, 1996. Print.

Low, Gail and Marion Wynne-Davies, eds. *A Black British Canon?* Houndmills, Basingstoke, Hampshire; New York, N.Y.: Palgrave Macmillan, 2006. Print.

McGann, Jerome J. *The Textual Condition.* Princeton: Princeton University Press, 1991. Print.

Michaels, W.F. "The constitution of the subject English in New South Wales senior English syllabus documents, 1953–1994". PhD thesis. North Ryde NSW: Macquarie University, 2001.

Moretti, Franco. "Conjectures on world literature". *New Left Review* 1 (n.d.): 54–68. *Arts & Humanities Citation Index.* Web. 26 Apr. 2016.

National Curriculum Board. Shape of the Australian Curriculum: English. Barton, ACT: Commonwealth of Australia, 2009. Web. 3 July 2016. <http://www.acara.edu.au/_resources/Australian_Curriculum_-_English.pdf>

Peel, Robin, Annette Patterson, and Jeanne Gerlach. *Questions of English: Ethics, aesthetics, rhetoric, and the formation of the subject in England, Australia, and the United States.* London; New York: Routledge, 2000. Print.

Putnis, Peter. "Shakespeare and the direction of state schooling in Queensland". *History of Education Review* 15.1 (1986): 49–66. Print.

Reid, Ian. *The Making of Literature.* Norwood, SA: Australian Association for the Teaching of English, 1984. Print.

———. *Wordsworth and the Formation of English Studies.* Burlington, Vt.: Ashgate, 2003. Print.

Showalter, Elaine. *Teaching Literature.* Oxford: Blackwell, 2003. Print.

Spaulding, Ralph. "Poetry's 'formative power': Teaching poetry in Tasmania, 1900–1950". *Australian Literary Studies* 22.2 (2005): 175–91. Print.

Chapter Two

AN OVERVIEW OF THE ALIAS DATA AND FINDINGS[1]

John Yiannakis

Background

Across Australia there are eight state and territory jurisdictions, each responsible for its own English (and other subject) courses. Before the implementation of the national curriculum, each determined its own curriculum, syllabus, subject reference and reading lists, as well as assessment and reporting procedures, including the administration of the public examinations held in the final year of schooling. English, or a variant of the subject, remains the only course most jurisdictions require students to study in order to "matriculate" or achieve a tertiary entrance score, now known as an Australian Tertiary Admissions Rank (ATAR).

Beyond providing literacy competencies that assist learners to navigate university or further training expectations, subject English, from its beginnings, has been "central to the curriculum as a principal means by which students explored their expressive, creative, imaginative and ethical selves, either through their own writing or through an encounter with literary texts" (Macintyre 4). In the first half of the twentieth century, English in senior secondary schooling around Australia had been a literature-based course; a subject conceived as essentially being the "close study of literary works and the nurturing of students' responses to them" (Rosser 91). In the postwar world, however, the school curricula for English began to slowly

---

[1] A version of this chapter was previously published in *Issues in Educational Research* 24.1 (2014): 98–113.

engage more with the life and language of students, which in effect meant engaging with popular culture and its media. Thus, in the 1960s and 1970s, to the joy of some and the alarm of others, the civilising mission of English began to give way to personal encounters with the worlds of texts: the so-called "new English". "In schools, the certainties of the literary and linguistic heritage now had to compete increasingly with the incursions of popular culture: radio, comics and television" (Beavis). Historically, therefore, English has not been as stable or as singular as sometimes assumed, particularly given that the aims and content of the subject are continually contested (Cormack 1).

English has undergone a significant shift over the past four decades, from a "study of culture" to "cultural studies" (Patterson, "Literature"). Beginning in the 1960s, English changed and split into two, three or even four separate courses as cultural studies reshaped what and how texts would be studied. Thus, each state offered a range of English subjects, each with a different title (see Appendix). Varying from state to state, literature-based courses became known as English or Literature or English Literature. The focus of this chapter is these specialised literature courses: that is, courses which emphasise literary texts, not those courses that are broader in nature and content, such as English Expression, English Communications, Alternative English or Senior English.

What this chapter sets out to do is to introduce the ALIAS study and its methods, and lay the groundwork for what follows in this collection by providing a brief descriptive outline of the variations and changes in the titles of works that appeared on the reading lists of the different Australian states in their English literature-based course(s) between 1945 and 2005. Its focus will be the decade after 1945, and the 15 years prior to 2005. This chronology allows for the comparing and contrasting of texts identified by different educational authorities as worthy of students' study at the Year 12 level.

The states that offered a set of public examinations at the end of Year 12, designed to help identify and rank students suitable for university admissions, were considered in the ALIAS study. As a result, data from Queensland, which abandoned public examinations in 1972, is not included. Nor is data from the Northern Territory (NT) or the Australian Capital Territory (ACT), as each territory relied on the education system of a neighbouring state for their upper-school courses and examinations (ACT and New South Wales until 1973 and NT and South Australia until 1984). Furthermore, I leave discussion of the determinants and processes by which senior secondary school English curricula and reading lists were constructed to the chapters that follow (and to previous studies: see e.g. Nay-Brock, *Who's Doing What?*). This chapter principally provides a chronological frequency count to inform the interested reader of what and who appears on reading lists around the country at different times, accompanied by a short account of some of the broad social and cultural factors lying behind those lists.

To be able to undertake such an analysis, an extensive single database was created, recording all the reading material listed in the syllabuses of every publicly examined English subject for each year and every state from 1945 to 2005. Called ALIAS (Analysis of Literature in Australian Schools) this robust tool was created during 2010 and 2011.[2] A purpose-specific platform was designed by a programmer. Strings and codes were added as the research data was input and questions were asked of the information, building a sophisticated data-mining tool. Significantly, ALIAS also has the potential to serve as a valuable template or tool for similar investigations in other subject areas. Currently, and for reasons beyond the author's control, open access to the ALIAS site is unavailable (username and password access is given in Chapter One).

ALIAS allows for the tracking and better understanding of the changes in senior secondary school English courses around the country. Types of empirical data input included the form of work, author details (including nationality), the year of publication, and year of inclusion on a reading list for publicly examined English subjects. All the available syllabus manuals, handbooks and reading lists from the five remaining Australian states for 1945 to 2005 were scrutinised for data to be recorded. Digital images of each source were taken and thousands of pages stored to be made available to researchers in the future. This baseline database could potentially help researchers fill the historical gap that Annette Patterson believes exists in English pedagogy in Australia, and which Wayne Sawyer identified in a 2003 editorial for *English in Australia* (Patterson, "English" 6).

Questions under consideration in this chapter include: What similarities and differences existed in reading lists around the country at the matriculation level for Literature, or subject English as it was called in some states,

---

[2] ALIAS was created by Tim Dolin and John Yiannakis, with technical assistance from Joko Wong. It is based on all available syllabuses, reading lists, examination papers and subject manuals and/or handbooks from 1945–2005 for Western Australia, New South Wales, South Australia, Tasmania and Victoria. The website is currently temporarily housed as part of the Australian Common Reader website (www.australiancommonreader.com). In the future it will be hosted by the Australian National University, Canberra.

prior to the late 1950s and then at the start of the twenty-first century? What forms of work have gained or lost popularity over time? Which texts remained popular and which didn't? Was there any significant state variation in this regard? Was there any diversification in the nationalities of writers on reading lists? This chapter seeks only to outline what the reading lists show and what trends appear in terms of text and author consistency over the years, and from state to state, so as to ascertain frequency patterns and the endurance of texts and authors. Such data can, however, make an important contribution to debates about schooling and the literary canon. For teachers of English, beyond the general interest that the trends identified below may generate, the changes to reading lists signify more than just the varying of titles. Literary legitimacy, cultural capital, notions of nationhood, canon fluidity and even classroom practice are being affected.

Furthermore, at a time when English curricula across the country, including the new national curriculum, are condemned for allegedly being dumbed-down in terms of content and in a context of falling standards, the ALIAS database can help test the validity of such criticisms. The data presented can help identify a historical curriculum overview across time and place, while making possible the identification of consistent writers and works. This, in turn, can inform the content and standards debate and assist in any curriculum review. Given the ongoing controversy about the national curriculum, this research has added significance. The implications of this work and model also have relevance to other courses where there is contestability about what is taught, such as history and biology. Compared with the past, for instance, is there less reference to ANZACs in the new history curriculum? Are there courses overly laden with the "cross-curriculum priorities" of Indigenous awareness, engagement with Asia and sustainability when compared with the past? A similar database tool to ALIAS could help test such claims.

1945

The data analysis begins with the final year of the Second World War, where both differences and similarities were evident in the reading lists for literature-based English courses being studied in the final year of school in the various Australian states (except for Queensland). The greatest choice available in what could be studied was in Western Australia (WA). In 1945, one Shakespearean play from among *Coriolanus, King Lear, Henry IV* or *Much Ado about Nothing* had to be read, as well as one novel from a selection of nine, which included works by Charles Dickens, Thomas Hardy, Joseph Conrad and Robert Louis Stevenson. There was one Australian piece of prose in the collection, Ion Idriess's *Flynn of the Inland*. Geoffrey Chaucer's *Prologue to The Canterbury Tales* was compulsory reading in Western Australia, as it was in Victoria. WA teachers had a choice of one from four essay collections and four poetry anthologies, including *The Golden Book of Modern Poetry* and *English Verse: Old and New*, but there was only one short story collection to be studied. By contrast the similar level New South Wales course for the same year was much more prescribed and limited in choice. There was one play, Shakespeare's *Macbeth*, one collection of essays and one of short stories, plus the poetry anthology *English Verse: Old and New*, and only one novel to be read: Dickens's *David Copperfield*.

The syllabus offerings in Tasmania were even fewer than New South Wales, while the choice available in Victoria and South Australia was somewhere between that of Western Australia and New South Wales, with each of these states requiring students to study at least one Shakespearean play from a short list, *Macbeth* and *King Lear* being the most popular. Tasmania had no novel on its 1945 reading list while South Australia (SA) had a choice of seven, including works by Dickens, Hardy and Conrad, as well the American author Edgar Allan Poe. Furthermore, one of the following biographies had to be studied in South Australia: *(The Life of) Madame Curie*, *South with Scott*, or *Everest, 1933*. Poetry anthologies and essay collections were popular across the country in 1945. All 33 writers and editors recorded for this year, with the exception of George Eliot, Gordon Daviot (Josephine Tey) and Eve Curie, were male, and just over 75 per cent of them English (of the authors listed only three were not from England or Scotland: Curie, Idriess and Poe).

What is evident from an examination of the data for Literature courses across the country in 1945 is that while certain writers, notably Shakespeare, Conrad, Dickens and Hardy, were commonplace, others, for example, Daviot, Eliot and Rudyard Kipling, were not. With the days of Empire and colonialism coming to an end, works such as Kipling's may have been seen as anachronistic in some jurisdictions. Additionally, the works studied varied and there is breadth and difference in the range and form of work available for study from state to state. In Western Australia and South Australia, non-British writers could be read and, beyond the essayists who were popular in every state, non-fiction works appeared, while in Tasmania no novel is even listed. An examination of the reading lists from a number of chosen subsequent decades will further highlight state differences and at the same time reveal a commonality of reading material.

Post-World War Two

In the aftermath of the Second World War, state governments gradually introduced universal secondary schooling to at least third-year high school (either Year 9 or 10, depending on the state). Yet, teaching activities within secondary schools changed little until the late 1960s. Many of the English texts under consideration by students of that time would have been familiar to their parents, despite the changes Australia was undergoing.

While Chifley's Labor Party lost the 1949 federal election to Robert Menzies and his recently formed Liberal Party, the postwar migration scheme they established in 1947 continued. This scheme brought to Australia a great influx of European migrants who would help transform the country economically, socially, politically and demographically. The last remnants of war rationing and austerity also ended with Chifley's defeat, heralding for most Australians a more affluent future. Australia experienced an industrial revolution in the 1950s, with high export prices helping to improve living standards (as did a mining boom in the 1960s). For all the political opportunism and alleged inertia of the Menzies government (1949–1966), it helped deliver prosperity and stability to Australia. There was a great, if ad hoc, expansion in social services and increases in government spending on education.

The geo-political divide of the era had a gradual but deep impact on Australia. Though somewhat isolated and insular, the menace of the outside world was making itself felt. In particular, the fear of communism shaped decision-making, climaxing in the 1954 Petrov Affair and, in the following decade, with Australia committing troops to halt the spread of communism and the "domino theory" by supporting the United States in the Vietnam conflict (Laidlaw 263–264, 270).

Additionally, Australia began to feel the ever-increasing cultural impact of the United States. Film, music, fashion, cuisine, aspirations and lifestyle were being altered and those most heavily affected were the young. The influence of television in this regard cannot be underestimated. On the other hand, there was a desire for a return to "normalcy" after the war, as demonstrated by the enthusiasm associated with Queen Elizabeth's 1954 tour of Australia. The first visit to Australia by a reigning monarch triggered an outpouring of nostalgic affection for the past and the "mother country". Described by one social commentator as being "bigger than the Beatles" (Adams), it is estimated that one in three Australians saw the Queen at least once on her first visit.

However, many Australians sensed that the world and their country were changing and that there were new national and global tensions, primarily associated with the Cold War, which called for change and a re-assessment of Australia's place in the world (Rickard). Censorship, political and otherwise, was not relaxed during this decade, while the suspicion of intellectualism and a cultural cringe remained. Combined with growing student numbers and the need for more schools to be built, these developments would eventually impact on school curricula and English reading lists.

Yet, ten years after the conclusion of the Second World War, school systems remained, by and large, comfortable with their established English or Literature reading lists. This steadiness "was despite the dramatic increases in the demand for secondary education and escalating cultural change" (Beavis 25). Some variations existed and a few changes had crept in to the reading material, but fundamentally the syllabuses of 1945 were still very much the foundation of what was operational in 1955. For instance, New South Wales had seen works by writers such as Conrad, Eliot, Hardy and Stevenson come and go from the reading list, but the number of novels to be studied remained at one. The inclusion of works by female writers – Jane Austen's *Emma* and *Pride and Prejudice*, and Emily Brontë's *Wuthering Heights* – were noteworthy changes. So too was the inclusion in 1949 and 1954 of George Mackaness's Australian anthology, *The Wide Brown Land*, and, in 1954, *Australia Felix* by Henry Handel Richardson. Shakespeare still dominated the drama category during the decade after the war, though different Shakespearean plays were on offer each year, for example, *Hamlet*, *Julius Caesar*, *Othello* and *Twelfth Night*. The opportunity to study poets like John Keats, Samuel Taylor Coleridge, Alfred Tennyson and William Wordsworth gave the syllabus further breadth, even though they were all Englishmen. Ultimately in 1955, as in 1945, teachers and students in New South Wales had a choice of one play, one novel, a poetry anthology and a collection of essays.

For a time in the late 1940s, South Australia witnessed a slight expansion in the choices available for study, but by 1955 the reading list had reverted to a number similar to 1945, even though many titles had changed. Dickens, Charlotte Brontë and HG Wells were on the reading list, along with dramatists Richard Brinsley Sheridan, Oliver Goldsmith and Shakespeare. The poetry anthology was Ernest Parker's *A Pageant of English Verse*. Works by American writers Poe (*Tales of Mystery and Imagination*) and Herman Melville (*Moby Dick*), along with Rolf Boldrewood's Australian tale, *Robbery under Arms*, which had all been regulars on the reading lists of the late 1940s, no longer appeared. The category of biography had also been removed from the syllabus by the early 1950s.

In Tasmania, the reading list for English, known from 1947 as English Literature, remained the smallest in the country. By 1955 it had contracted to one anthology of poems, *A Pageant of English Verse*, a collection of short stories and Shakespeare's *Hamlet*. No novels were to be studied, even though in 1954 a choice from four had been available (all English writers including Dickens and Thackeray).

It was in Victoria and Western Australia that the greatest expansion of reading options took place during the postwar decade. The Victorian reading list for English Literature expanded from just William Thackeray's *Henry Esmond* to nine novels, including works by Dickens, Hardy, Homer, Richardson and Jane Austen. Along with Shakespeare, plays by George Bernard Shaw (*Saint Joan* and *Caesar and Cleopatra*), T. S. Eliot (*Murder in the Cathedral*) and Henrik Ibsen (*An Enemy of the People*) were on offer, plus, in poetry, Chaucer's *Prologue*. In New South Wales, South Australia and Tasmania Chaucer's work did not appear.

The already expansive Western Australian syllabus remained, though the emphasis changed. By the early 1950s novels were no longer as dominant a reading item as they had been in 1945. Drama and poetry in particular offered more alternatives for study. By 1955, only three novels were on offer: Austen's *Persuasion*; Eleanor Dark's *The Timeless Land* and, for the first time, Mark Twain's *The Adventures of Huckleberry Finn*. A clear choice between authors from different national backgrounds appeared on the reading list with an English, Australian and American writer. Shaw (*Arms and the Man* and *The Devil's Disciple*) and Shakespeare (*Richard II* and *Julius Caesar*) were the choices in drama, while four poetry anthologies and poems by the Victorian era poets Matthew Arnold, Alfred Tennyson and Robert Frost, as well as Chaucer, were available for study. The short story collection was Australian: Walter Murdoch and Henrietta Drake-Brockman's *Australian Short Stories*. In New South Wales, it would not be until several years after the tabling of the *Wyndham Report* into secondary education that the inclusion of Australian and American literature in English courses was recommended (van Straalen 63).[3] The cultural changes Australia was undergoing were finally being recognised in New South Wales. While a handful of Australian writers had sporadically

---

3   The Wyndham Report was concluded in 1957. The suggested reforms were approved by Parliament in 1961 and the changes initially appeared on reading lists by 1965.

appeared on New South Wales reading lists pre-1957, no American did so.[4]

During the 1946–1955 period, the three most popular works listed on the relevant reading lists around the country were Shakespeare's *Macbeth* and *Hamlet*, and Chaucer's *Prologue to the Canterbury Tales*; all appearing 15 times. The plays of Shakespeare were universal across Australian state curricula. His plays such as *Julius Caesar, Richard II* and *The Tempest* were common listings. Drama constituted approximately 25 per cent of all forms of work for study on relevant English Literature syllabuses. The most popular novel was Stevenson's *The Master of Ballantrae* with 14 listings. *Pride and Prejudice* and *Jane Eyre* were the most popular works by females: Austen's work appearing 12 times and Brontë's novel 11. Female writers contributed just over ten per cent of the works listed between 1946 and 1955.

The most popular writer in upper-secondary school Literature courses across Australia during this period was Shakespeare (103 entries), appearing three times more than the next most commonly listed writer (Chaucer, with 30). Of the 20 most prevalent writers recorded, all but one was from England, namely Stevenson from Scotland. The list also included two Australian anthologists, Alick Merson, who edited a collection of non-Australian essays called *Still Lighter Essays*, and poet and essayist Douglas Stewart. Norman Corwin, who contributed a play to the collection *Five Radio Plays*, which was listed on six occasions, was the most frequently included American writer, while Homer (six listings) was the most commonly included non-English writer. Eleanor Dark's *The Timeless Land* was the most frequently listed novel by an Australian.

Sixty-two (48 per cent) of the 129 writers listed in the syllabuses throughout Australia came from England. A little more than 16 per cent of the writers were Australian, with approximately 6 per cent from the United States and 5 per cent from Ireland respectively. Of the 226 works in the syllabuses, a little more than 64 per cent were from England. What this suggests is, firstly, that at Leaving or Year 12 level (or its equivalent) in the decade after World War Two, the literature that mattered still came from England and secondly, that a school literary canon did seem to exist: though works may have varied, the writers under consideration did not.

In the meantime, steady improvements in housing, transport, education, and health care accelerated. Living standards reached new levels in the

---

4 According to Paul K. Nay-Brock (1984, p. 55), it is not until 1962 that there is a "notable ... American influence in a NSW English Syllabus in the section on reading."

1960s, though some people were struggling to make ends meet. Consumerism took hold in Australia, as it did elsewhere in the Western world during this decade, and as a sustained period of postwar economic prosperity (the "long boom") spread, Australians sought mass-produced, mass-marketed, labour-saving devices and consumables. The austerity of the immediate postwar world was by now over and there were many more options available in the new and expanding supermarkets, department stores and car yards. Australian cities grew rapidly and sprawled in this decade, as the nation's population quickly expanded. Disputation over dress, music, sexuality, politics, art and relationships punctuated the decade. Through film, music and television, foreign policy, political and economic engagement, American influence in Australia grew further.

A new way for WA (and Australia)

As early as 1961 (WA Policy Committee of the Public Examinations Board) there was debate in Western Australia about "the experiment of dividing English into two subjects" (Minutes of Public Examination Board for English, 7 July, 1961). Members of both the Public Examinations Board English Committee and the Policy Committee of the Public Examinations Board opposed any such division. They believed it to be subject self-aggrandisement, based on the simplistic view that English was just about students being able to express themselves, and that the push for division was merely following trends emerging in universities (where English was divided into Language and Literature).

By 1969, every Australian state had chosen to split the subject English in to a literature course, along the lines of the existing subject English, and another, loosely defined as English expression (see Appendix). Later, the emphasis in studying English shifted to an engagement with real-world issues and a focus on social and cultural contexts, while Literature remained an "old school" literary subject. In 1964, Dr J.A. Petch was invited by the University of Western Australia to report on the Western Australia public examinations system. Petch was critical of the Year 10 Junior Certificate and recommended splitting both Year 10 and Year 12 English into Expression and Literature. Much debate followed the Petch Report release, notably about what form the two English offerings at Year 12 level would take. When debate settled on this occasion, though not to everyone's satisfaction, English was to be a wide-ranging course of predominantly contemporary fiction and non-fiction, with a choice of texts recommended rather than prescribed. Textual knowledge was not examined for its own sake; understanding and appreciation were (Corby). Literature was unchanged from the existing course except for having a wider reading list. The other states made similar decisions soon after Western Australia authorities, but implemented them earlier than 1969. This was a momentous change to Australian curricula; the nearly synchronous nationwide partition of upper-school English into "English" (or "English Expression" or some similar name and/or level) and "English Literature" (or, as in New South Wales, it remained literature-based "English" with differentiating levels or "Literature" or something akin) in the late 1960s.[5] Literary works were studied in English and such courses remained publicly examined. The non-examinable English courses were still several years away and are not part of this study.

Western Australia was the last state to divide English into more than one examinable secondary school course (Literature and English), in 1968 for Year 11 and 1969 for Year 12. In South Australia this division occurred in 1966; in New South Wales the new HSC courses were formulated in 1965 and examined in 1967; Victoria, initially in 1957 and then again in 1968; and in Tasmania in 1969. According to the 1969 WA Syllabus Manual for English:

> The prescribed texts are to be studied as a means to an end, and not as an end in themselves. The aims of the reading course are to extend the interest of candidates; to interest candidates in techniques of writing; to promote an attitude of critical awareness in candidates when they read. The prescribed texts have not been chosen as models to be imitated, or as examples of literature to be studied in detail.

---

[5] This division complicates the data analysis. More recently in NSW the following distinction between types of English has been made: While English (Advanced and Standard) is designed for students to improve their English "in order to enhance their personal, social and vocational lives", the non-examinable Fundamentals of English "addresses the literacy needs of students undertaking the course and assists students to use the English language effectively in their study and for vocational and other purposes." <www.boardofstudies.nsw.edu.au/syllabus_hsc/pdf_doc/english-syllabus-from2010.pdf>

In Western Australia the division of both examinable subjects is thus: "Through the study of Literature, students create readings of literary texts and develop the skills necessary to better understand their world." In English, "through the use of oral, written and visual communication texts, students examine the relationship between language and power, and learn how to become competent, reflective, adaptable and critical users of language." <www.scsa.wa.edu.au/internet/Senior_Secondary/Courses>

However, when a sample paper for the new subject (Leaving) Literature was forwarded to schools in 1968, the texts to be studied remained what they had been for many years and included Chaucer, Shakespeare, Austen, Dickens, John Milton and D.H. Lawrence – all members of the English literary studies establishment (van Straalen 70). Poetry dominated the paper. Furthermore, the 1969 reading list for the subject revealed that most texts were by English writers.

The division of traditional English into distinct Literature and Expression subjects (though the nomenclature did vary from state to state) by the late 1960s resulted in a different emphasis being given to the forms of work being studied in each area of study. For Literature, 1970 saw poetry; drama and the novel (in that order) make up 91 per cent of the work listed on syllabuses Australia-wide. For the same year, the novel, drama and non-fiction prose were the main forms of work listed on the reading lists of the English expression-type courses, making up approximately 69 per cent. Poetry constituted less than 11 per cent of the works identified for English, whereas for Literature it was the most popular form of work on offer at 42 per cent. Short stories still had a place in general English courses, as did the essay, but they had all but disappeared from the Literature courses.

With the growth in the number of English courses on offer during the 1970s, and a shift from prescribed to recommended texts, the choices available to teachers grew dramatically. There was a fear in some quarters that the limited reading list of the past could be perceived as a literary canon in its own right. This concern helped to prompt an expansion in the works offered on reading lists, notably in general English courses, across the country in subsequent decades.

The emphasis on Australian cultural nationalism during the prime ministerial terms of John Gorton and Gough Whitlam would see further changes in the works on offer. The impact of multiculturalism, women's liberation and Indigenous rights filtered through to educational authorities and practitioners, influencing decision-makers in what would be included on reading lists. Technological change also altered offerings and the delivery of subject matter with the advent of video and DVD.

Another consideration in the expansion of school reading lists was the extent to which reduced university influence on syllabuses liberated courses. For decades, education in Australian high schools had been heavily influenced by tertiary selection requirements. In Western Australia, for example, complaints about the nature and extent of that influence led to a variety of investigations and reforms, such as the Dettman (1972), Beazley (1984),

McGaw (1984) and Andrich (2006) Reports. Course and assessment structures were altered, as was the composition of syllabus and examination committees. Educational objectives also became broader to cope with the ever-increasing number of non university-bound Year 12 students.

The 1988 Western Australian Examiners' Report for Literature also throws light on the changes and continuities of "traditional" works. Wilfred Owen and Australian Bruce Dawe were the most popular poets studied, far more than Keats and the metaphysical poets. Tennessee Williams's play *The Glass Menagerie* elicited the greatest number of student responses (resultant from texts studied) at 26.7 per cent, followed by *Hamlet* (22.7 per cent). However, in total, the four Shakespearean plays listed on the reading list (also *Henry IV*, *Antony and Cleopatra* and *A Midsummer Night's Dream*) totalled 31.5 per cent of answers. Lawler's *Summer of the Seventeenth Doll* was the next most popular play. The most popular novel was John Fowles's *The Collector*, generating 16.7 per cent of student replies and thereafter, predictably, novels by Dickens, Brontë, Austen, Hardy, Lawrence and Twain influenced student answers. Despite the many more literary works listed on the syllabus, *Great Expectations*, *Wuthering Heights*, *The Mayor of Casterbridge*, *Pride and Prejudice*, *Huckleberry Finn* and *Heart of Darkness* continued to dominate what was being taught. Two Australians who drew significant numbers of student answers were Randolph Stow (8.8 per cent) and Patrick White (5.7 per cent).

What is clear from examining reading lists since 1945 is that even though some authors such as Shakespeare regularly appear on reading lists (prescribed or recommended), titles constantly changed over time. Additionally, there was a shift away from works by English writers from the mid-1970s towards writers with more diverse backgrounds, and an emerging dominance of Australian writers. Yet, a core literary canon, comprising Austen, Conrad, Eliot, Hardy, Shakespeare and the American Arthur Miller seemed to exist. The works of other writers appeared to revolve around this central pantheon.

More recent trends

Between 1991 and 2005, the most popular work at Year 12 level around the country was Miller's *The Crucible*, appearing on both English and Literature reading lists. The next most popular work was also a play, Shakespeare's *Hamlet*. The most regularly listed novel was Hardy's *Tess of the d'Urbervilles*, just ahead of Tim Winton's *Cloudstreet*, the highest-ranking Australian work. *Cloudstreet* appeared on both general English and Literature reading lists too, but, like *The Crucible*, was more recurrent on English rather than Literature syllabuses.

For Literature, the most frequently listed work was poetry by an Australian – Gwen Harwood's *Selected Poems*, appearing 37 times. Helen Gardner's collection *The Metaphysical Poets* then followed, with 31 listings. Chaucer appeared 20 times, but only on the New South Wales and Victorian syllabuses (where *The Prologue to the Canterbury Tales* was the work most commonly listed). Euripides's *The Bacchae* was also regularly programmed in Victoria, but nowhere else in Australia. Years earlier, the 1950 *English Examiners' Report for WA* noted that students better tackled *The Prologue* than they did *The Nun's Priest's Tale*. *Hamlet* was the most popular play tackled that year and the examiners wondered why *Romeo and Juliet* and *A Midsummer Night's Dream* had been "so neglected". Approximately 60 years after the war, the popularity of some selections, such as *Hamlet*, had not changed.

The most popular novel in Literature, Australia-wide, for 1991–2005 was *Heart of Darkness* by Joseph Conrad, then *Tess of the d'Urbervilles*, *Wuthering Heights* and *Emma*. Two Shakespearean plays dominated reading lists, *Hamlet* and *King Lear*. *The Tempest* and *Othello* were also popular. Mary Shelley's *Frankenstein* was a frequently listed novel. Newer novels such as Caryl Churchill's *Top Girls* and Margaret Atwood's *The Handmaid's Tale* joined *Huckleberry Finn* and *Great Expectations* as common works. Australian writers finally joined the pantheon in this period. *No Sugar* by Jack Davis appeared 23 times on the Literature reading lists, as did Patrick White's *A Fringe of Leaves*. Davis's play and White's novel were particularly popular in Western Australia and Victoria.

The other change identified earlier that continued during the 1991–2005 period was the decline in the popularity of poetry. Essays had all but disappeared from Literature syllabuses, while short stories as a common form of work plateaued at approximately 3 per cent of the type of readings recorded. Novels accounted for 37.5 per cent of the works listed for Literature, while poetry remained at 27.3 per cent. Drama was constant as a form of work available for study in Literature at approximately 27 per cent of the total number of reading options available.

Writer nationality also reflected the further acceptance of Australian literary work as being worthy of study and of the internationalisation of Australia. Australian authors were more frequently listed, at 29 per cent, but the continued dominance of writers and work from England in Literature remained evident with 136 works, or 31.2 per cent, being from England, compared with 125 or 28.7 per cent being Australian. Works by American and Irish writers were also prevalent. The diversity of nationalities appearing thereafter is striking. Compared with 1945, a major change had happened. Multiculturalism was reflected in Literature reading lists. Writers with national origins as diverse as India (Rasipuram Narayan) and Italy (Giuseppe Di Lampedusa) had work included on reading lists, something that would have been inconceivable just three decades earlier.

By the close of the period under review, the most frequently listed work for Literature was a collection of poems by the American Adrienne Rich. Harwood's poetry collection was the second most popular work. Two other Australian works appear near the top of the list for the year: Davis's *No Sugar*, and a poetry collection by Judith Wright. However, Conrad's *Heart of Darkness* remained the most commonly listed novel. Works by Malouf, Hardy, Austen, Heaney, Chekhov, Wilde and White were still listed, as were Ibsen and Stoppard, but gone, among others, were Brontë, Dickens, Eliot, Twain and Lawler. Some of the works that were common on past reading lists had to make way for newer entries: contemporary and Australian. The work of many more female writers was also available for study in 2005. For Literature, the percentage was 31 per cent, compared with 1945 when only three female writers (5.6 per cent) had work listed for possible study.

The 2005 *WA English Literature Examiners' Report* noted that the poetry of Gwen Harwood and Seamus Heaney dominated student answers, as did the novels *Heart of Darkness* and *The Handmaid's Tale*. *No Sugar* was the most popular play in Western Australia. *Cloudstreet* and *Remembering Babylon* were other novels regularly referred to by students in their answers. Plays such as *Medea*, *Othello*, *The Tempest* and *Caucasian Chalk Circle* were also popular with students. These listings demonstrate that even after 60 years, some works or at least writers remained popular. Australia-wide, Shakespeare was still the most frequently listed writer in 2005. Chaucer, Chekhov, Conrad and Euripides followed. The inclusion and reading of Australian works is the biggest change to have taken place since 1945.

Certainly there were many more forms of work and choices available in 2005 than at any earlier time. While the novel dominated reading lists around the country, the nationality of writers was much more diverse than ever before, although writers from England remained dominant. Shakespeare, Hardy, Chaucer and Conrad appeared on the 1945 listings and these writers were still present in 2005, though some of their works available for study had changed. Stevenson, Poe, Daviot, Golding, Shaw and Hemingway, among others, were some of those writers who disappeared from reading lists altogether. Only two works remained constant throughout the period of study, so as to still be listed in 2005: *King Lear* and the *General Prologue to the Canterbury Tales*. Anthologies of poems, essays and short stories also lost their popularity, but do appear occasionally on modern reading lists. Biographies, such as that by Curie, once common on syllabuses, had no currency in Literature courses in 2005.

Conclusion

From the various states' reading lists and syllabus documents examined with ALIAS, there is a discernible commonality in what has been regularly itemised over the years.[6] The changes to syllabuses, examinations and course structures, along with Australia's political and cultural evolution since 1945, altered much about the English Literature courses offered at Year 12 level around the country. So too, did changes in curriculum theory and pedagogical practices. Yet, despite the shifts and the state variations, it is clear that, notwithstanding the influence of changes in methodology and theory on selection processes and the instruction of the subject, a core group of writers remained popular across the six decades since the end of World War Two.

Baseline data information such as that collated and discussed above helps practitioners, curriculum writers, analysts and critics to recognise significant trends and patterns over time and across locations, showcasing commonalities and anomalies. The statistical evidence collated for ALIAS suggests that there were, and are, common works found in Year 12 English Literature courses around Australia, with many by Shakespeare still the central and dominant texts throughout the period studied.

---

[6] The list of works recorded across Australia in syllabus manuals and handbooks from 1945 until 2005 does not tell us how many of these texts an individual student may have read. Examiners' Reports from recent years help in this regard, but a more valid way to determine the existence and nature of any literary canon beyond texts appearing on syllabuses is to compile lists of what individual Year 12 students are reading in schools Australia-wide. Such a task would be difficult to perform for today's Year 12 students, and impossible to recreate for those students of 20, 40 or 60 years ago.

Table 2.1: Various publicly examined Year 12 English courses offered in five different Australian states, 1945–2005

NSW		SA		TAS		VIC		WA	
1945–1966	English	1945–1965	English Literature	1945–1946	English	1945–1956	English Literature	1945–1968	English
1967–1975	English Levels 1, 2 & 3	1966–1974	English Leaving	1947–1968	English Literature	1957–1971	English Literature	1969–2005	English Literature
1976–1989	2 Unit English, 2A General Unit English, 3 Unit English	1975–1985	English	1969–1991	English Literature Levels II & III (1969–1990)	1972–1992	English Literature	1969–2005	English
					English Studies Level III (1971–1991)		English Expression		
1990–2000	2 Unit English, 2A General Unit English, 3 Unit English	1986–1990	English (P)	1980–1982	English Lit Level III (Alt. syllabus)	1993–2003	Literature Part B		
							English		
1990–2000	Contemporary 2 Unit English	1991–2005	English Studies	1983–1987	English Studies Alt.	2004–2005	Literature		
							English		
2001–2005	English Stage 6 Advanced & Standard			1991–2003	English Literature				
					English (1992–2003)				
					World Literature (1993–2003)				
				2004–2005	English Studies Alt.				
					English Communication				

Works Cited

Analysis of Literature in Australian Schools Database (ALIAS). www.australiancommonreader.com/syllabus. Web. 1 July 2013.

Beavis, Catherine. "Changing constructions: Literature text and English teaching in Victoria". *Teaching the English Subjects: Essays on English curriculum history and Australian schooling*. Ed. Bruce Green & Catherine Beavis. Melbourne: Deakin University Press, 2002. Print.

Board of Studies NSW (2009). English: Stage 6 syllabus. www.boardofstudies.nsw.edu.au/syllabus_hsc/pdf_doc/english-syllabus-from2010.pdf. Web.

Brock, Paul. "Changes in the English syllabus in New South Wales, Australia: Can any American Eehoes be heard?" *English Journal*, 73 (1984): 52–58. www.jstor.org/stable/817220. Web.

———. *Who's Doing What?: The senior English curriculum in Australian schools*. Melbourne: AATE, 1987. Print.

Corby, R. *About Us: The first ten years*. Perth: English Teachers Association of WA, 2011. Print.

Cormack, Phil. *Tracking English as a Curriculum Field: Historical tensions in a school subject*. 2004. http://ura.unisa.edu.au/R/?func=dbin-jump-full&object_id=unisa37845. Web.

Docker, John. (1984). *In a Critical Condition: Reading Australian literature*. Ringwood: Penguin. Print.

Examiners' Reports for English and English Literature, Victorian and Western Australian (1950, 1986–2005). Melbourne and Perth: University of Melbourne, University of Western Australia, Board of Secondary Education, WA Curriculum Council. Print.

Groden, M., Kreiswirth, M. & Szeman, I. eds. *The Johns Hopkins Guide to Literary Theory and Criticism*. Baltimore: John Hopkins University Press, 2005. Print.

Guillory, John. *Cultural Capital: The problem of literary canon formation*. Chicago: University of Chicago Press, 1994. Print.

Laidlaw, R. *Australian History*. South Melbourne: Macmillan, 1991. Print.

Macintyre, Margaret. "English: The state of the art". *Interpretations*. Perth: English Teachers Association of WA, 2001. Print.

McLean Davies, Larissa. "What's the story? Australian literature in the secondary English curriculum". Refereed paper presented at *Stories, Space, Place: Literacy and identity*. National Conference for Teachers of English and Literacy, Adelaide, 6–9 July, 2008.

Nader van Straalen, D.R. "An historical overview of the emergence of English literature as a secondary subject in Western Australian Schools, 1969–1984". Unpublished MEd Thesis, University of Western Australia, Perth, 2000.

Patterson, Annette. "Teaching literature in Australia: Examining and reviewing senior English". *Changing English* 15.3 (2008): 311–322. Print.

———. "Teaching English: Some remarks on the emergence of the sympathetic teacher in the English classroom". *Teaching Australian Literature: From classroom conversations to national imaginings*. Ed. B. Doecke, L. McLean Davies and P. Mead. Kent Town, South Australia: Wakefield Press in association with the Australian Association for the Teaching of English. 319–332. Print.

Public Examinations Board (1969). *WA Syllabus Manual for English*. Perth: Public Examinations Board. Print.

Rickard, J. *Australia: A cultural history*. Singapore: Longmans, 1988. Print.

Rosser, G. "Examining HSC English – questions and answers". *Change: Transformations in education*, 5(2), 91–109. Sydney: University of Sydney Press, 2002. http://hdl.handle.net/2123/4485. Web.

School Curriculum and Standards Authority. Courses. 2012. www.scsa.wa.edu.au/internet/Senior_Secondary/Courses. Web.

Smart, H., Steinbrecker, T. (Producers) & Adams, P. (Interviewee). *A New World for Sure: Australia since 1945*. Melbourne, Australia: ABC Video Series, 1987.

Western Australian Policy Committee of the Public Examinations Board. Minutes of the Special Meeting of the 29 June 1961. Item 1960/0207, Cons 1497.

Western Australian Public Examination Board for English. Minutes for 7 July 1961. Item 1960/0207, Cons 1497.

Wiltshire, John. "On F.R. Leavis and Sam Goldberg". *Cambridge Quarterly*, 25(4) (1988): 415–20. Print.

Chapter Three

DISCIPLINE AND SUBJECT

Academic literary studies and school English in Australia since 1945

Tim Dolin, Jo Jones and Patricia Dowsett

Teachers and syllabus writers have always had to balance the requirement that students read and write well with the very different demands of engaging with literature and other cultural texts – demands for skills in critical thinking, formal or rhetorical analysis, and social, cultural and literary history. The aim of this chapter is to lay the groundwork for what follows by discussing some of the key interactions between the academic discipline of literary studies and senior-secondary subject English in Australia and elsewhere since 1945. The profound institutional investment in English as *the* subject for the ethical formation of individuals in Australia goes back at least to the middle decades of the twentieth century, when students were taught to apply techniques of close reading not only to literature but to popular culture and everyday life. This chapter thus ventures back into the dangerous waters of the canon debates and the classroom. We consider how questions of canonicity shape and respond to conditions experienced in schools. As John Guillory observes, "it is only by understanding the social function and institutional protocols of the school that we will understand how works are preserved, reproduced and disseminated over successive generations and centuries" (*Cultural* vii).

Part One: 1945–1965

In 2005, when one of the Higher School Certificate examinations in English in New South Wales "required its candidates to 'deconstruct' an

SMS message (instead of, say, a scene from *Hamlet*), the federal Education Minister commissioned an inquiry into final year English curricula across the country" (Turner, "Literacies" 105). This incident, Graeme Turner argues, was symptomatic of controversies that had plagued subject English since it was transformed by media and cultural studies in the 1980s, and again in the era of "critical literacy". Critical literacy is "a mode of discourse analysis developed by theorists from the discipline of Education and enthusiastically taken up by state education bureaucrats influenced by the branch of systemic linguistics identified with Sydney Professor M.A.K. Halliday" (Turner, "Literacies" 106). In the ten years since Turner's article was published, critical literacy has remained "at the centre of every senior English syllabus in the country" (Turner, "Literacies" 106), displacing "the previously dominant disciplinary formations – literary criticism, primarily, and, more recently, although to a lesser extent, media and cultural studies" (Turner, "Literacies" 106).

Unsurprisingly perhaps for a leading figure in cultural and media studies, Turner is no champion of the usurper (although in fairness he is also alarmed and disheartened by the decline of cultural-studies pedagogy, once politically vital, into formulas and obfuscations). He argues cogently against critical literacy's prescriptive routines, in which "the end point is always already known in advance" so that (in Terry Threadgold's words) students simply learn "to mimic the discourses of the master" (Threadgold, 1997: 365; Turner, "Literacies" 109). Nevertheless Turner does recognise critical literacy as a (reductive) offshoot of cultural studies, describing the move "from litcrit to critlit" in schools as a continuation of

> subject English's shift from teaching spelling, grammar, comprehension and literature towards the development of other kinds of "reading" skills as it fell increasingly under the influence of media and cultural studies approaches. (Turner, "Literacies" 107)

It only takes a glance at earlier final year English papers to realise that there are serious problems with this narrative. Subject English in Australia is a complex, heterogeneous and poorly understood historical disciplinary formation, and any history that can be summarised as "from litcrit to …" is deficient. Certainly many early papers are intensively focused on literature – of which more below – but consider the Victorian English first paper in 1945, which, included this question:

3. (c) Write brief critical comments on the following advertisement as "sales talk": –

FASCINATION FOOTWEAR

FOR ALL THE FAMILY

Fascination shoes, sandals, slippers have only one quality, THE BEST. During wartime our plant supplied only the services. Our products were found on every front. Tread the paths of peace in our footwear. The smartest style for every foot at prices that you can pay. [15 marks.]

(University of Melbourne 8)

At least some upper-school English students in Australia *were* therefore required to demonstrate "other kinds of 'reading' skills" long before the advent of media and cultural studies. This question invites something very like a "discursive analysis of the politics underlying … media and other textual forms" (Turner, "Literacies" 107). Such analysis may not be familiarly semiotic but many teachers would instantly recognise what students were being asked to do: demystify the (now not very mystified or mystifying) interchange of the commercial – quality, reliability and value – and the affective, appealing to military virtues, national character and postwar sentiment. There is no question here that a critical reading of this advertisement is aimed at uncovering social inequalities and injustices or framing readers as agents of social change. Yet other English papers from the same period, like those from Western Australia in the 1940s, show that English examinees had to demonstrate a form of critical literacy. Section One of the WA papers simply asked students to "write an essay" on one of several topics. Some topics were in the Anglo-American tradition of the familiar essay made famous by Walter Murdoch – "The benefits of judicious idleness" or "Why I like the human race" or "Do adolescents need parents?" – but others are more serious: "What is fascism?"; "The power of the Press"; "The scientific feeding of the people" (University of WA 189–90).[1]

---

1   Note, in this connection, a topic from the same paper, "The bore and my efforts to avoid him", which students were invited to answer in the form of either an essay or a short story: an early example of the valuing of creativity in pre-Dartmouth English. Topics in the 1945 Victorian Leaving English paper were: On travelling by train; The man on the land, The best things in life, Should sport be voluntary or compulsory in school?, What in your opinion makes a good companion?, "Great spirits never with their bodies die." (University of Melbourne 7)

What these few examples appear to indicate is that in some states at least, upper-school English began taking its present shape much earlier than the 1980s, and that this process accelerated with the profound social transformations taking place in postwar Australia. The nature and extent of these transformations are clearly evident in the pressure to modernise secondary education during this period. One of the most notable examples was the select committee formed in New South Wales under the chairmanship of Harold Wyndham, the Director-General of Education, to survey secondary education in that state. The report, presented to the Minister in 1957, led directly to the 1961 Education Act, which completely overhauled the system in New South Wales.[2] Wyndham's committee recognised first of all that there was "growing demand for young people to stay at school to the Leaving Certificate stage but who do not wish to go to university" (55). Yet the upper-school curriculum was not concerned "with the whole of the teenage population, [but only a] selected part of it" (9) – matriculants.[3] Only "7.5 per cent of a typical secondary school matriculate", the report noted, and "one-third of those who proceed to university fail in their first year" (55).

What did these teenage students need? The committee settled on eight basic requisites: health, mental skills and knowledge, capacity for critical thought, readiness for group membership, the arts of communication, vocation, leisure, and spiritual values. Several of these were relevant to English: mental skills and knowledge (skills of reading, writing and computation), the arts of communication, and a capacity for critical thought. Children were entitled to "the world of knowledge opened to them in Literature, History, Geography and Science", and while science "inculcates a mode of thought, ... literature affords opportunity for the cultivation of taste and critical perception" (58). Equally, the arts of communication were deemed so significant "that their cultivation must be cited as one of the aims of education" (59). Finally, the committee acknowledged the vital role of schooling in the development of a capacity for "self-reliant thinking ... reflected in personal standards of taste, in the exercise of discrimination and in a healthy

---

2   Its major recommendations were "the abolition of entry examinations for high schools; the extension of secondary schooling from five to six years; the establishment of the Secondary Schools Board; and the introduction of the Higher School Certificate and Leaving Certificate" (MGSE 1).

3   "It was in 1927 that, in England, the phrase 'the education of the adolescent' was first officially used to describe secondary education. In this view, secondary education must serve the needs not only of the few of scholastic inclination, but of all boys and girls in their teens" (33).

habit of scrutinizing new facts and judgements" (58), arguing that without critical thinking individuals cannot reach "a full measure of personal growth" and are "prey to the worst devices of 'mass communication'" (58).

There is a perceptible undertone of moral panic here over the encroachment of American popular culture, something we would be more likely now to associate with F.R. Leavis and the *Scrutiny* movement, or even some aspects of early left-Leavisite British cultural studies (parts of Hoggart's *The Uses of Literacy*, for instance). This is certainly not what critical thinking is meant to equip students to resist in the cultural studies-inflected Australian English curricula since the 1980s. Yet an unmistakable pre-cultural-studies emphasis on critical thinking is present, and it is instructive. It confirms that subject English continued to have a vital social mission in the new world of postwar secondary schooling, and that its mission involved much more than literary criticism.

Of course subject English developed unevenly throughout Australia between 1945 and 1965 – only recall the different roles and powers of external curriculum and examination boards, each led by university English departments that were governed by different critical assumptions and biases – and we cannot extrapolate from New South Wales to the rest of the country in sketching out a historical context. Nevertheless it is incontrovertible that the opening up of postwar secondary education to students with a range of abilities and social backgrounds (including migrants) created the conditions that would lead to the splitting of English into two in the mid-1960s. As we describe in the following section, by the end of the 1960s all states had divided English into a general subject that would provide young people with much-needed communication and critical skills, and a more advanced subject designed for those wishing to enter university, for whom a predominantly literary education would arm them with the knowledge required to undertake academic literary studies, and/or the cultural capital required to progress into the professional-managerial classes. Already in the 1940s there were significant differences in what constitutes literary studies in different states. These differences, evident in examination papers, are so striking, in fact, as to suggest that in upper-school English the study of literature was never a single discipline or practice, but had widely differing aims and approaches.

A brief comparison of some questions from Victorian and New South Wales English papers from 1945 and 1950 illustrates the point. In Victoria in 1945, pass-level or Leaving-level English students (those not destined for university) were required to answer questions like these:

> Tell the story of the part played by Macduff in the action of the play. (University of Melbourne 1946, 9)
>
> Of the four stories read [in *Conrad: Four Stories*], which one has made on you the most striking impression? Discuss the story selected, supporting your choice by reference to plot, character interest, and setting. (10)

No honours-level or matriculation-level Victorian paper for that year could be found, but the New South Wales honours paper shows just how different literary study was at the higher level:

> "All good poetry is at first modern." What is meant by this statement? Is it true?
>
> "Our interest in people in books is above all a moral interest." Do you agree? Discuss the matter.
>
> "Does it matter whether we can tell exactly what a particular passage of verse means?" (You might take an illustration from Shelley, say, or from Blake, or from Eliot.)
>
> "Subject-matter in literature is of no importance." Apply this to some works you know. (NSW BSSS 44)

The 1950 Victorian Honours paper is similar to the 1945 New South Wales paper except that it was divided into two parts. In the first part students were faced with two unseen and unidentified excerpts requiring critical appraisal: an excerpt from Milton's 1644 pamphlet in defence of a free press, *Areopagitica*, concerning the moral benefits of "books promiscuously read"; and a Hopkins-like poem, "Stormy Day" (1940), by the Irish poet and BBC scriptwriter W.R. Rodgers. The questions in Part II are even more challenging and provocative than those in the New South Wales paper above, and they show a deep engagement with complex and difficult critical and theoretical questions:

> "The artist ought to be in his work like God in creation, invisible and all-powerful; let him be felt everywhere but not seen." Discuss this idea.
>
> How do you feel about Oscar Wilde's statements that "no (literary) artist desires to prove anything" and that "all art is quite useless"?

> What is the function of the literary critic? (University of Melbourne 1951)

If there are echoes of some familiar Leavisite dicta scattered through ("our interest in people in books is above all a moral interest"), there is also plenty of evidence here for reassessing the common view that literary study in school English before the 1980s was dominated by a form of uncritical "literary appreciation". The importance of modernism should not be underestimated here (see also Chapter 14 below, "Modernism and modernist criticism in Australian upper-secondary English"), and the quotations from Flaubert and Wilde call up the prehistory of modernism in continental, anti-realist, aestheticist thought against which Leavis was reacting at Cambridge (his "great tradition" realigned modernism with an organic nineteenth-century realist tradition, leading to James and Lawrence, not to the linguistic and subjective experimentation of Joyce, Woolf, Pound and Eliot). In these questions we can also see the presence of a genuine critical self-consciousness, an openness to big theoretical questions about literature and criticism.

In summary, then, the 20-year period between 1945 and 1965 was not a pre-theoretical, uncritical desert of colonial deference, old-style aesthetic appreciation and litcrit. At one extreme, postwar subject English taught cultural critique and popular culture criticism, and at the other, highly sophisticated and theoretically self-aware approaches to literature and literary criticism.

Part Two: 1965–1982

The mid-sixties to early 1980s was a period of immense social and educational change that had a dramatic impact upon English and Literature teaching across Australia. With student retention rates increasing rapidly during the 1960s and most students not destined primarily for university, upper-school subject English had to cater for a new type of student with different educational needs. Simultaneously the burgeoning number of examination candidates led to various state boards of secondary studies being formed as "autonomous" bodies. It is a story intertwined with the decline of the subject professor's status, which significantly altered the role of the English don in shaping secondary English curricula, and was symptomatic of wider trends to challenge the relevance and authority of institutions and the decision-makers within them. What emerged from this era was an English subject no longer dominated by universities. English expanded to include a broader range of literatures and pedagogies that accommodated the expectations of a more diverse, formally educated populace.

The English split

During the 1960s and 1970s the upper-school English subjects in Australia were successively divided into two. Each state named the new subjects slightly differently, but in each case one was a version of what came to be called "English Expression" and the other a version of specialist literary study (although literature also remained as a smaller component of English Expression subjects). This division was backed up by vocational education and science advocates who perceived literature to be a specialist subject area without relevance to employers or non-Arts faculties of universities, and gave consensus support for a model of English that would produce secondary graduates that were sufficiently "literate" to gain employment or undertake tertiary study. Thus, English Expression, a compulsory subject, included an emphasis on writing skills and the "appreciation" of literature, while Literature, an optional specialist study, focused on the study of canonical texts in a more detailed way consistent with the Cultural Heritage model of English teaching that dominated classrooms at that time. Following Macken-Horarik, the term "cultural heritage" is used neutrally here to denote "a longer tradition, linked to induction of readers and writers into the great works of the literary canon":

> It calls for specialised ways of knowing and privileges immersion in and close study of poetry, novels and drama. [...] From a linguistic point of view, complex and highly crafted texts constitute the field of study. Students read and write their way into literate textuality. (Macken-Horarik 10)[4]

Predictably, the split created a hierarchy of English subjects (English Expression was subordinated to the more advanced specialist subject) and provoked new questions about the function and value of English, and of literature in English programs. What was English for? Whose interests did it serve? Was it valued because it was compulsory or compulsory because it was valued? And what place should literature have within English?

In Western Australia the English split was precipitated by the Petch Report (1964). Conducted by an Englishman, James A. Petch of the

---

[4] For an alternative view of literary study and cultural heritage see Chapter 17 of this volume.

Northern Universities' Joint Matriculation Board, the Petch committee reported that the curricular control of school English by external decision-makers had wide-reaching effects on the subject. We highlight this report because it relates closely to debates in other states over literature and instrumentalism, literature and culture, and literature and elitism – debates provoked by the ideological shifts taking place in literary studies during the 1960s and 70s:

> While it can be disputed that all educated men [sic] should be students of English Literature, it cannot be disputed that participation in an Anglo-Saxon culture involves of necessity some degree of competence in the writing and understanding of English as the means of communication within that culture. (Petch 10)

The emphasis here on cultural participation and communication reflects the emerging prominence of cultural analysis in the United Kingdom during this period. Raymond Williams's *The Long Revolution* (1961) developed a persuasive model for cultural analysis by examining the cultural revolution in democratic industrial Britain in terms of the rise of literacy and the popular press, and the institutional and technological changes that transformed culture and led to the growth of English.

Specialisation

The separation of English into Expression and Literature foregrounded English subject "specialisation", which was the framework through which educationalists were coming to view English. It was no longer a subject that just anyone could teach, but was recognised as fulfilling functions in society that were important enough to demand a specialist teacher. By 1969 all states had separated their English courses, "a momentous change to secondary English curricula" (Yiannakis 106), which significantly reduced students' exposure to canonical literary texts and the reading praxis that had characterised subject English until then. Many teachers were resistant to the split but gradually adapted to the challenges of the new curriculum and the increasingly student-centred school environment. The new pedagogy, with its emphasis on "pastoral guidance" (Hunter 140), assisted them in negotiating the needs of the new class demographic and the new areas of responsibility they brought to secondary English:

> To the traditional genre division of poetry, prose (or novel), and drama have been added Australian literature, modern literature, language

study, wider reading, mass media, clear thinking, written English, comprehension and comment. (Bennett and Hay, *Directions* 2)

These additions and others like them were being made to curricula nationwide, indeed worldwide, in the 1960s and 70s, and they foreshadow a tendency for English to keep taking on additional text types, areas of study and approaches. Where the autonomy of English had previously been restricted by its subordination to academic literary studies and the control of its professors, that autonomy now became vulnerable to even more demanding external needs. Hence the difficulty of pinning down the content and purpose of English in any historical moment without reference to complex institutional politics and the ever-increasing skillsets required to be a competent English teacher.

English teachers' associations

The momentous changes of this period could not have been successfully carried through without the cooperation of the state English teachers' associations, which formed during the 1960s. These associations provided a network of collegial support and exchange that was particularly timely in an era of subject change caused, in part, by emergent educational theory, including that of the "London School". The new "Growth" philosophy of teaching in language and literature was being worked out in Britain, America and Australia, and the English teachers' associations became effective forums for the dissemination of these ideas (Biggins 2). Significantly, the genesis of the English teachers' associations depended upon the involvement of university academics, and the fact that the first presidents were members of English departments at the universities or teachers' colleges reflects an interesting realignment of the relationship between tertiary and secondary English during the 1960s and 1970s, as universities slowly relinquished some of their curricular control but took key roles in these burgeoning professional associations. This is true at a national level where the first four presidents of the Australian Association for the Teaching of English were also professors. Three of the professors were professors of English (A.D. Hope, 1965–67, Leonie Kramer, 1968–70, and James McAuley, 1970–75], and one was a Professor of Language (R.D. Eagleson, 1976–80) (AATE website).

The "Growth" model of English

"The new philosophy" about language and literature to which Biggins refers is the "Growth model," also known as the "New English" or "personal growth pedagogy". Its origins were the 1966 conference held at Dartmouth College entitled "What is English?" The lasting legacy of the conference was a whole new model of English teaching that weaves through the curriculum a concern with students' personal growth. Under this model, literature became an experience and a way to empathise and share others' lives:

> The developmental view presented in [John Dixon's 1966 book] *Growth Through English* forced attention to the processes of interaction through which children acquire competence or expressiveness in language and strengthened conceptions of the teacher's obligation to guide and foster this development. (Dixon, *Growth Perspective of the Seventies* xv)

In addition, the Growth model opened up new learning opportunities with greater emphasis on "creativity in the English classroom" (xii). This was the direction taken by James Britton and Nancy Martin at the Institute of Education, University of London, who formed the "London School", which endorsed personal and democratic uses of literacy:

> Harold Rosen, Nancy Martin, James Britton and John Dixon made a parallel leap away from the reading of canonical texts by celebrating and encouraging student writing and tapping into what was seen as the authentic voice of working-class children. Instead of reading an imposed body of someone else's "great literature," it was argued, children should create their own. (Peel 96)

The Growth model privileged experiential, personal and creative responses to texts:

> Growth in English starts with an interest in students, their experiences and "ways of talking and writing" as a point of entry to classroom work on texts. In preparing students to read a text, for example, teachers prioritise the "here and now of you and me" in interacting with students. They are keen to ensure that all students can read a text with understanding and they want to explore their reactions to this. (Macken-Horarik 9–10)

To critics of the Growth model it polarised literature and literacy, and its claim to help students find their own path to enlightenment disadvantaged children from working-class families. The perceived lack of direct teaching meant that children had to find their own way, making working-class children much more vulnerable to being left behind:

> Those students well equipped by life experience and opportunity to intuit the desired skills are thus rewarded, while those unable to intuit these are denied an opportunity to learn. Neither the content to be mastered nor the criteria that apply for evaluation of students' efforts are made clear. (Christie and Horarik 162)

For genre theorists, moreover, the Growth model's lack of directive teaching meant these students were "denied an opportunity to learn. Neither the content to be mastered nor the criteria that apply for evaluation of students' efforts are made clear" (Christie and Horarik 162).

Australian literature

Australian literature had been studied in upper-secondary English before the 1960s, but during this period it received a significant boost from the foundation of new tertiary institutions that offered a greater range of courses and transmitted the value of Australian literature through the secondary English syllabus and examination committees. Universities were expanding and booming – "both in funding and in ideas" (Jordan 77). Bruce Bennett identifies the period 1960–75 as a third phase of the introduction of Australian literature courses into Australian universities, "a period during which undergraduate and graduate studies in Australian literature have increased and diversified, but with little public discussion of aims or intentions" ("Australian" 114).[5] Australian poets had been included on secondary syllabuses since the 1920s, and the ALIAS database shows that the late 1940s included *Flynn of the Inland* (Ion Idriess), *Robbery Under Arms* (Rolf Boldrewood), *The Wide Brown Land* (George Mackaness and Joan Mackaness), *Haxby's Circus* (Katharine Susannah Prichard), *The Timeless Land* (Eleanor Dark), *Five Radio Plays* (ed. Arthur Phillips) plus poetry in various anthologies. The status of the national literature on the secondary text lists reflects the slower growth of Australian literature despite the establishment of new Australian literary journals in the 1950s and 60s legitimating Australian literature and contributing to its acceptance as a serious area of scholarship. Two decades later, the text lists expanded from

---

5   Bennett identifies the first phase as "1940-9, the decade during which Commonwealth Literary Fund lectures commenced; the second 1950-9, the years of public debate about the role and value of Australian literary studies in universities" ("Australian" 114).

20 works to 66 works by Australian authors and the later lists included the plays *The One Day of the Year* (Alan Seymour) and *Summer of the Seventeenth Doll* (Ray Lawler), novels *For the Term of His Natural Life* (Marcus Clarke), *The Getting of Wisdom* (Henry Handel Richardson) and *Voss* (Patrick White), non-fiction works *Two Ways Meet: Stories of Migrants in Australia* (Louise Rorabacher) and *The Tyranny of Distance* (Geoffrey Blainey) as well as many Australian poets such as Kenneth Slessor, Judith Wright and those in *The Penguin Book of Modern Australian Verse*.

The Bullock Report

Britain's *Bullock Report* (1977) was a significant influence upon the understanding of English teaching in schools internationally, including Australian curriculum development in the 1970s. Chaired by Sir Alan Bullock, the Committee of Inquiry into Reading and the Use of English in Great Britain produced *A Language for Life*, which encouraged reading throughout the curriculum, the expansion of reading, and exposing students to "good" fiction. *A Language for Life* was included as a teacher reference book on one state syllabus (Western Australian English, 1977). It recommended that teachers "engineer" opportunities "to bring the right book to the right child at the right time" (128) and that schools should have the books both to create and meet the demand for a general increase in reading needs (129). In teaching literature, "the main emphasis should be on extending the range of the pupil's reading. True discernment can only come from a breadth of experience" (132). While educational trends coming out of the UK and USA were certainly influential, English teaching in Australia was not merely a case of overseas adoption. There have been many contextual factors shaping English curricula in Australia, including economic pressures, population growth, social change (such as multiculturalism and the search for a national identity) and the establishment of separate state-based education systems (Davis and Watson 152). In the 1960s and 70s these inevitably shaped, and indeed overcrowded, English into an amalgam of Personal Growth, Cultural Heritage and Skills models. It absorbed each new change as an "add-on" rather than a substitution, and was about to be shaped similarly by the inundation of educational and sociological theories.

Theory and cultural studies

Simultaneously during this period cultural studies began as an inter-disciplinary field, emerging from programs of cultural, communications or media studies in the (then) Colleges of Advanced Education, the new interdisciplinary universities (especially Griffith and Murdoch) and the Institutes (later, universities) of Technology that began appearing from the mid-1970s onwards. (Turner, "Canonical" 179)

These institutions were instrumental in introducing trainee schoolteachers to the radical ideas of the New Left in Britain, continental theory, and a range of literary, philosophical, educational, and social thought developed locally and overseas, including the thought of Saussure and Husserl, Derrida and de Man, Althusser and Macherey, Bakhtin and the Russian Formalists, Bourdieu, Vygotsky and Freire, Barthes and Halliday, Kristeva and Cixous, and Foucault and Deleuze. These various ways of examining power, social control and student learning produced new pedagogies and approaches to texts. Intertextuality, for example, was brought into prominence by the poststructuralist Julia Kristeva in the mid-1960s. She devised the term to identify the multiple ways in which the literary text comprises other texts and interacts with them "by means of its open or covert citations and allusions, its repetitions and transformations of the formal and substantive features of earlier texts" (Abrams 364).

The examination papers of this era suggest there had been a shift in ways of thinking about texts and their teaching, such as in Western Australia when a student-centred approach to text selection was recommended in the 1974 English syllabus:

> In choosing texts, teachers should consider the particular interests and needs of individual classes. It is recommended that wide reading be encouraged, and that students should not confine themselves to a selection of texts with a strong bias in one direction. Teachers should, however, choose texts with an eye to possible contrasts and comparisons of theme and form. (BSE 80–81)

Similarly, the syllabus advises:

> The recommended texts are to be studied as the means to an end, and not as ends in themselves. The aims of the reading course are to extend the interest of candidates; to interest candidates in techniques of writing; to promote an attitude of critical awareness in candidates when they read. (87)

These syllabuses provide insight into the aims of English and how the ways in which they were articulated expressed changing emphases and adaptations of theory and understandings about English. In the 1980s and beyond, critical literacy theories were to change English Studies, as were information technologies and the study of media.

Part Three: 1982–2005

The 1980s brought with them the most significant disciplinary challenges since the introduction of English into universities in the late nineteenth century. The publication of Terry Eagleton's *Literary Theory* in 1983 initiated a whole generation of students (and a wider audience) in the philosophical and theoretical debates that were tearing the discipline apart. Eagleton's book also itself made a major contribution to those debates, which had gained momentum in radical postwar spaces, including the Marxisms of cultural theorist Raymond Williams, historian E.P. Thompson and anthropologist Richard Hoggart, and the poststructuralist critiques levelled at modern institutions and linguistic and narrative systems by Derrida, Foucault, Deleuze and Lyotard. Eagleton's iconic work remains a powerful reminder of disciplinary crisis: it is testimony to the potency of the critique that arises from the ranks of English itself.

Significantly, Eagleton prefaced his accounts of phenomenology, structuralism and poststructuralism with a critical account of the history of English that framed it as an un-selfcritical discipline, dedicated at first to belletrism and lofty pronouncements about the ennobling power of a refined aesthetic response, and latterly as a subtle instrument in class regulation. Eagleton tackled head-on the then still-dominant legacy of F.R. Leavis – especially in Australia, where it was widely influential through the *Scrutiny* movement (see Hilliard). Leavis had to be exposed and overthrown if a materialist literary studies were to take root, for under Leavis literary study had become inextricably linked to class power and oppression. Literature was promoted as a civilising force and students of literature were promised upward mobility, thereby subduing working-class discontent and blocking real historical change. Eagleton writes of Matthew Arnold that "the pill of middle-class ideology was to be sweetened by the sugar of literature" (23). Arnold – Victorian poet, critic and Inspector of Schools – epitomised the notion of literature as a worthy substitute for religion in the battle to control a newly literate and newly organised proletariat (on Eagleton and Leavis, see also chapter 14).

As Eagleton showed (and before him Raymond Williams in *Culture and Society* [1958]), English had its origins in the nineteenth-century social criticism of British industrialism. Literature was the mainspring of "culture" narrowly conceived by Arnold as a few specially enlightened "moral and intellectual activities" separate from, and offering "a mitigating and rallying alternative" to, the discourses of industrialism such as utilitarianism, political economy, and progress (Williams 17). As Williams went on to observe, and over his lifetime to analyse, the problem with culture is "that we are continually forced to extend it" (Williams 249). This is more or less what happened in Australian universities and schools in the 1980s: English was forced to expand the domain of literary studies, first in what came to be known as the "canon wars". Jeanette Winterson, Toni Morrison, Gabriel Garcia Marquez, Salman Rushdie and many other non-white and/or non-male writers began appearing on undergraduate and upper-school syllabus lists (ALIAS). And second, English departments began offering different types of cultural texts under the banner of "literary studies", including popular texts such as music, advertising, television, comic books and film.

As in the 1960s reforms, the mid 1980s to early 1990s were a time of radical rethinking of the secondary schooling system generally, particularly as many more students remained in school until Year 12. Government inquiries into large and diverse student cohorts were the subject of the 1985 Blackburn Report and the 1991 Melbourne Declaration. Questions about the types of texts worthy of study were at the forefront of thinking, as were democratic and equitable forms of assessment. By the mid-1990s a number of states included film study as a key aspect of their syllabuses. Between 1990 and 1995 Roland Joffé's 1984 film *The Killing Fields* was the eighth most commonly listed text in Australian English syllabuses, with feature films *The Year of Living Dangerously* (Weir 1982), *Picnic at Hanging Rock* (Weir 1975), *Careful He Might Hear You* (Schultz 1984), *The Purple Rose of Cairo* (Allen 1985), *Sophie's Choice* (Pakula 1982) and BBC television's *Edge of Darkness* (1985) all featuring on the ALIAS database as prominent teaching texts within the same five-year period.

There is little doubt that the syllabus changes of this period were exciting and innovative. The availability of video technology and the study of media texts gave English teaching an advantage it had never before enjoyed. Teachers could open a door to students who found little enjoyment in traditional literature, inviting them into a subject through a combination of recent and popular texts, now re-framed as *au courant*, socially relevant, and (for English teachers anyway) undeniably "cool". In the English classroom, textual analysis of all and every type of text reveals unjust social and gender hierarchies and the newly visible shapes of race discrimination. Exposing the workings of textual power relations was and still is believed to make students effective critical thinkers while liberating them from the trammels of the old literature-centred English studies.

Teachers enjoyed the new shapes of their subject, and understandably so, but Bill Green, Phil Cormack and Jo-Ann Reid noted in 2000 an interesting phenomenon at work in the culture and history of secondary English teaching. An effect of the possibly self-congratulatory mood of the 1990s was something of a collective amnesia where, as the proponents of cultural studies reshaped English in the universities, many in the teaching community took up a simplified version of the cultural studies narrative about the old English ("Leavisite" tendencies, the canon and close reading) versus the new (myriad texts types and postmodern blending of high and low culture). What was lost here was any connection with the innovative content and analysis that, as the ALIAS data show, was so clearly part of Australian English teaching in the decades before. Not only did exam papers of the 1940s and 50s include questions that elicited advanced rhetorical skills in response to questions outside of the gambit of literature studies, as we have shown, but ALIAS also reflects the breadth of texts that were formally studied as part of school English from the earliest year of analysis. While canonical writers held a valued place in matriculation studies in the 1940s and 1950s so did essays and speeches. Non-traditional texts were often present in state syllabuses earlier than is generally expected, such as in David Attenborough's non-fiction volume *Zoo Quest in Paraguay* (South Australia, 1970–74) or Karl Marx's 1848 *The Communist Manifesto* (Victoria 1983). Australian popular plays such as *The One Day of the Year* (first listed in Victoria in 1963, and on many state syllabuses over the next two decades) have also enjoyed a long presence on this list, notwithstanding that Australian literary texts have had a steady presence for the full timeframe of the study.

There is no doubt that school English foreshadowed many of the developments of cultural studies decades before the changes of the 1980s and 1990s. With heightened pressures on teachers to account for levels of student literacy or "expression", and the basic teaching requirement of making content relevant, current and engaging, teachers have continually shaped and reshaped their curriculum and syllabus to reflect the learning and teaching requirements of changing social and demographic states. Somewhat ironically, the evangelical tendencies of Leavisite understandings about subject English – that good teaching of complex ideas and texts has potentially transformative effects on students of all backgrounds – had undoubtedly contributed, at least in part, to the unacknowledged sophistication, flexibility and success of the subject before the cultural studies reforms. It seems as if later cohorts of teachers can't acknowledge the versatility and ingenuity of their forebears, whose innovations pre-empted the cultural studies transformations of decades later.

It may be the case that the twists and turns of the subject history outlined here reflect a sort of Oedipal narrative. Exponents of cultural studies at universities "wrote back" to the conservative discipline formations of previous decades, where the conservative and imperial shapes of English studies required overhauling. To survive, university English departments admitted much greater diversity in the types of texts that warranted advanced formal study and also, and vitally, "interrogated" the hegemonic structures of literature and expanded the types of human experiences and subjectivities worthy of engagement. As the energy and excitement of the cultural studies turn made their way into school curricula, a complex set of conditions emerged. As in the tertiary arena, text lists expanded and new areas of content opened up. Even so, it is important to say here that in schools the transformation was never as great. Many non-traditional texts have populated lists and exam papers since at least the 1940s. To hitch secondary English to the revolutionary movement in the discipline in the 1980s is to forget the subject's own past. The transformative shape of cultural studies in schools was certainly linked, in a type of continuum, to both the self-fulfillment models of Dartmouth and the deeply interconnected ideas of Leavis. In an interesting paradox Leavis, by the 1980s, had become deeply unfashionable – an arch-"fogey" – even as the integration of cultural studies into secondary English become deeply enmeshed with pre-existing understandings and beliefs that actually stemmed from one of the "founding fathers" of subject English himself.

Yet, it is also important to note that by the early 1990s literary theorists had started to question the sweeping changes wrought by cultural studies in the 1980s. For instance, John Guillory notes in *Canon, Syllabus, List* (1991) that it is reductive and fallacious to argue that traditional literary canons reflect an active process of exclusion, and does not account for the conditions of either literary production or the educational institutions in which the texts are taught. While the canon reflects particular literary values at a particular time, to imagine that it can be changed by opening it up only makes the canon a more totalising entity. Many academic cultural studies theorists began questioning the tenets of the new discipline almost as soon as it was established, but because it was so compatible with subject English it was difficult to stop the juggernaut as it hurtled onward in a form that sublimated the complexities and subtleties of its own process.

By the 2000s the most commonly included texts across Australian state syllabuses were *Cloudstreet*, *Othello*, *A Doll's House*, *Blade Runner* and *Things Fall Apart* – a telling list. It suggests that by this time inclusions were made less to do with any inherent aesthetic, historical or cultural virtue, but rather because of the capacity that the texts offer to expound on the analytical frames of cultural studies – race/ethnicity, gender, social class – and interrogate concepts of Australian nationhood and the dimensions of new technologies. While the study of English has always been about ideas, the conceptual shapes offered by cultural studies are in evidence here. As Graeme Turner noted in 2007, by the 2000s cultural studies in school English is dominated by reductive and dogmatic adherence to certain political paradigms, and notions of "othering" have become a way of responding that is not only inauthentic but removes complex ideological dimensions of works and pays no regard to aesthetic qualities. To complete the Oedipal narrative, one might claim that the cultural studies turn implanted a distrust of literature as a cultural and artistic entity – killing its forbear – to the point that the study of literature has a much reduced presence within tertiary studies and is largely absent from formal secondary school studies. While the school subject remains "English" in name, the majority of the texts studied are popular texts, media texts, film/television and/or documentary texts. Literature in the form of prose, poetry and drama still exists within larger syllabuses, but is given far less attention. We would also claim that a close understanding of the formal conventions of literary texts and any developed sense of sophisticated readings and analysis is gone for the majority of students. While a subject devoted to literary study is offered in most states it is a comparatively small subject that declines in numbers at the years go on.

Works cited

Abrams, M.H. *A Glossary of Literary Terms*. 9th ed. Boston: Wadsworth Cengage Learning, 2009. Print.

Analysis of Literature in Australian Schools Database (ALIAS). www.australiancommonreader.com/syllabus. Web. 12 January 2016.

Australian Association for the Teaching of English (AATE). "Distinguished members". AATE, 2016. Web. 8 Jan. 2016.

Bennett, Bruce. "Australian literature and the universities". *Melbourne Studies in Education* 18.1 (1976): 106–55. Print.

——. Professing English Today: An inaugural professorial lecture presented at University College, University of New South Wales, Australian Defence Force Academy, Canberra, on 27 May 1993. Canberra: University College, University of New South Wales. 1993. Print.

——, and J.A Hay, eds. *Directions in Australian Secondary School English*. Camberwell, Vic: Longman Australia, 1971. Print.

Biggins, Bob. "Some current developments in English in Western Australian secondary schools". *English in Australia* 11 Oct (1969): 51–61. Print.

Blackburn Report. Victorian State Board of Education. Summary and analysis of Regional Board of Education responses to the Structural Recommendations of the Ministerial Review of Postcompulsory Schooling. Melbourne: State Board of Education, 1985. Print.

(BSE) Board of Secondary Education. *Leaving English*. Perth: n.p., 1974. Print.

Bullock, Alan. A Language for Life: Report of the committee of inquiry appointed by the Secretary of State for Education and Science under the chairmanship of Sir Alan Bullock (The Bullock Report). London: Department of Education and Science, 1975. Print.

Christie, Frances and Mary Macken-Horarik. "Building verticality in subject English". *Language, Knowledge and Pedagogy: Functional Linguistic and Sociological Perspectives*. Ed. Frances Christie and J.R. Martin. London: Continuum, 2007. 156–183. *EBSCOhost eBooks Academic Collection*. Web. 21 Dec. 2015.

Davis, Diana, and Ken Watson. "Teaching English in Australia: A personal view". *Teaching and Learning English Worldwide*. Ed. James Britton, Robert E. Shafer and Ken Watson. Clevedon: Multilingual Matters, 1990. 151–74. Print.

Dixon, John. *Growth through English*. New York: National Association for the Teaching of English, 1966. Print.

——. *Growth through English Set in the Perspective of the Seventies*. New York: National Association for the Teaching of English, 1975. Print.

Eagleton, Terry. *Literary Theory: An introduction*. Oxford: Blackwell, 1983. Print.

Green, Bill, Phil Cormack and Jo-Anne Reid. "Putting our past to work …" *English in Australia* 127–128 (2000): 111–117. Print.

Guillory, John. "Canon, syllabus, list: A note on the pedagogic imaginary", *Transition*, 52 (1991): 36–54. *JSTOR*. Web. 27 Jan. 2016.

——. *Cultural capital: The problem of literary canon formation*. University of Chicago Press, Chicago, 1993.

Hilliard, Christopher. *English as a Vocation: the Scrutiny movement*. Oxford University Press, Oxford, 2012. Print.

Hoggart, Richard. *The Uses of Literacy: Aspects of working life, with special reference to publications and entertainments*. Harmondsworth, Middlesex: Penguin Books in association with Chatto & Windus, 1958. Print.

Hunter, Ian. *Rethinking the School: Subjectivity, bureaucracy, criticism.* St Leonards, NSW: Allen and Unwin, 1984. Print.

Jordan, Kath. *Larrikin Angel: A biography of Veronica Brady.* South Fremantle: Round House, 2009. Print.

Kermode, Frank. *The Sense of an Ending: Studies in the theory of fiction: with a new epilogue.* New ed. Oxford; New York: Oxford University Press, 2000. Print.

Macken-Hoararik, Mary. "Making productive use of four models of school English: A case study revisited". *English in Australia* 49.3 (2014): 7–19. *Informit.* Web. 21 Dec. 2015.

MCEETYA. Melbourne Declaration on Educational Goals for Young Australians. December 2008. Web. 23 July 2014.

Melbourne Graduate School of Education (MGSE). Curriculum Policies Project. *Report of the committee appointed to survey secondary education in New South Wales (Wyndham Report).* Graduate School of Education, University of Melbourne. Web. 23 Jan 2016.

New South Wales Board of Secondary School Studies (NSW BSSS). *English Honours Paper.* Sydney: Government Printer. 1945. Print.

Peel, Robin. "'English' in England: Its history and transformations". *Questions of English: Ethics, aesthetics, rhetoric, and the formation of the subject in England, Australia and the United States.* Ed. Robin Peel, Annette Patterson, and Jeanne Gerlach. Routledge, 2000. 39–115. Print.

Petch, J.A. *A Report on the Public Examination System in Western Australia.* Nedlands: University of Western Australia, 1965. Print.

Turner, Graeme. "Cultural literacies, critical literacies and the English school curriculum in Australia." *International Journal of Cultural Studies* 10.1 (2007): 105–14. *Sage Journals.* Web. 11 Mar. 2015.

———. "Cultural Studies 101. Canonical, mystificatory and elitist?" *Cultural Studies Review* 15.1 Mar. (2009): 175–87. *Informit.* Web. 20 Mar. 2015.

University of Melbourne. School Leaving Examination – December 1945. English. First Paper. Melbourne: Melbourne University. 1946. Print.

———. School Leaving Examination – December 1950. English. Honours Paper. Melbourne: Melbourne University. 1951. Print.

University of WA. Leaving Certificate Paper 1945. Perth: Government Printer, 1946. Print.

Williams, Raymond. *The Long Revolution.* London: Chatto and Windus, 1961. Print.

Wyndham, Harold S. Report of the committee appointed to survey secondary education in New South Wales [under the chairmanship of H. S. Wyndham] (Wyndham report). Sydney, NSW: Government Printer, 1958. Print.

Yiannakis, John. "A possible literary canon in upper school English Literature in various Australian states, 1945–2005". *Issues in Educational Research* 24.1 (2014): 98–113. Web. 12 July 2014.

Part II

Histories

Chapter Four

FRAMING THE LITERATURE CURRICULUM

Ian Reid

Compilation of the ALIAS (Analysis of Literature in Australian Schools) database is a scholarly service for which educators will be grateful. In ways not previously possible it allows general impressions and opinionated assertions about curriculum change to be checked against an array of factual records. Its value can go further than that, for while it is most obviously useful in resolving some initial questions about syllabus content, this piece of research apparatus may also help to illuminate more complex issues. As those who put together the ALIAS list of lists are well aware, when we know only what reading has been prescribed for school students over a span of several decades we have not begun to discover how they interpreted it and what they learned in the process.

A booklist, then, does not in itself constitute a curriculum in literary studies, though it is a convenient starting point for considering what does. Its utility may depend on other information, often less salient and less readily available for analysis. This includes information about several circum-textual factors that frame the curriculum. "Circumtextual" (Reid, *Narrative Exchanges*; MacLachlan and Reid) signifies here anything that may serve as a tangible adjunct to listed texts: official and unofficial rubrics inscribed in classroom practice, resource materials designated for use in teaching and learning, or examination structures that tend to elicit some kinds of responses rather than others – such things can all contribute to the circum-textual framing of items set for study. Basil Bernstein was the first influential theorist to apply the metaphor of framing to educational situations. As he uses the term, it "refers to the degree of control teacher and pupil possess over the selection, organisation and pacing of the knowledge transmitted and received in the pedagogical relationship" (205–6). Subsequently others have developed framing analysis in relation to the English curriculum in particular (e.g. Reid, *The Making of Literature* 58; Hart; Doecke and Reid; Andrews).

This chapter will discuss some of the ways in which the curriculum for literary studies has been framed for and by senior secondary Australian classrooms. It will focus on the late 1980s for two reasons: curriculum developments during that period are relatively well documented, and it was a time of significant reform in the teaching of English and Literature. "Literature" in this context can refer both to the literary component in an "English" subject and to the more intensive study of English Literature as a separate subject; the two have normally sat side by side in the senior years of Australian secondary schooling across all states. Particular reference will be made here to the Literature Study Design and associated Course Development Support Material devised in the late 1980s for the innovative Victorian Certificate of Education (VCE). Subsequent modifications of the VCE are beyond the scope of this discussion.

* * *

Suppose a historian of education wishes to ascertain whether – and if so, how – the place of Australian literature in the senior secondary curriculum has changed since the mid-twentieth century. Up to a certain point, lists of set texts throughout that period provide interesting information; they may seem to show, for example, a steady growth in the number and range of Australian titles across most states during the decade from the mid-1960s to the mid-70s. But this observation would hardly take us more than a small first step forward, because such lists amount only to a *latent* curriculum, a potential repertoire from which teachers and students may or may not, in practice, have selected certain materials. Plainly no menu of texts can indicate individually their actual status – that is, which of them became objects of study in particular situations, let alone the precise nature and extent of their usage.

Some texts on a syllabus list may be required objects of study, while others are just optional selections within a possible range. Moreover, even a "core" prescription usually gives some latitude for choice: although it may be necessary for all Year 12 students in a certain course to study at least one or two plays, and one or two novels, and so on, these will probably be selected by a teacher for any given class from the items officially listed in each category, and a public examination paper will have a sufficiently flexible structure to cater for a diverse cohort of students whose preparation is based on different texts. Consequently the fact that a particular book title is set by a curriculum authority tells us nothing about the extent of its uptake in classrooms or – when it is chosen for study – about the purposes to which it may be put.

An unpublished report illuminating the practical importance of this point was presented to the Literature Board of the Australia Council in 1989. It contains the results of a commissioned investigation by the Centre for Studies in Literary Education (CSLE) at Deakin University into "The Use of Australian Literature in Schools". The research found that while, in general, Australian literature figured more substantially at that time in prescribed and recommended curricula around the nation than had been the case a few years earlier, the true situation was in some respects less satisfactory than this seemed to indicate. Many teachers and some syllabus committees tended in practice to depend narrowly on a few well-worn texts. Certain genres (e.g. short fiction and non-fiction) were thinly represented and analysis of public examination scripts suggested that in most cases the numbers studying the Australian texts were disproportionately small.

The report went on to amplify this last point by showing the distribution of student choice across answers to a range of Victorian HSC English and Literature examination questions on different texts. (These courses were being phased out at the time, soon to be replaced by the new VCE.) If a particular book appears in a certain proportion of exam answers, one can reasonably infer – even after allowing for other factors – that a roughly corresponding proportion of teachers had selected it for classroom study, equipping and motivating their students to discuss it in the exam. Figures cited in the CSLE report for the percentages of candidates who chose to write on each set text reveal that only a small handful of Australian books achieved much popularity. For instance the HSC (Victorian) Group 1 English Literature syllabuses for 1986 and 1988 included, in each year, one Australian text in a list of seven for the novel section; in 1988 this novel was Jessica Anderson's *Tirra Lirra by the River*, and a healthy 23 per cent of exam answers for the novel section discussed that book, but in 1986 the Australian novel was Patrick White's *The Eye of the Storm* and it attracted a mere 0.5 per cent of the answers. The "other literature" section of the syllabus contained eight texts in each of those same two years; in 1986 one of them was Australian, Ray Lawler's play *Summer of the Seventeenth Doll*, and 19 per cent of the students wrote about it in the exam, but in 1988 there were two Australian texts in that section, David Malouf's *Antipodes* and Beverley Farmer's *Home Time* (both volumes of short stories), which together mustered less than 2 per cent of the exam answers. Those examples suggest that genre may have influenced the uptake of available texts (e.g. plays tending to be more attractive for study purposes than short stories), and perhaps also that texts featuring relatively accessible themes or stylistic features have generally greater appeal (White's novel, on which only one student in every 200 chose to write, may well have seemed more "difficult" to study in a course dominated by anxiety about public examinations). There are other possible factors, such as the reliance on class sets that entrench "old favourites": being an expensive investment, class sets have a slow turnover, and teachers generally feel bound to use existing sets. (This was probably the case with the Lawler play, for instance, which had first appeared in Victorian text lists many years earlier.) School library collections are often similarly limited, with certain individual titles recurring predictably from school to school, though again the fact that a particular book is held says nothing about its actual usage.

However, there seems no doubt that a further, deeper consideration affected (consciously or not) the choice of some listed texts (whether Australian or not) rather than others: namely, how amenable in a teacher's or examiner's eyes a particular text was to certain predominant assumptions about reading at that time. Peggy Mares (10) characterises these assumptions as "personalist", and they are discernible in several circumtextual elements shaping literary studies at the senior secondary level. In an incisive analysis, Mares adduces statements in South Australian curriculum guides from the 1970s and early 80s to show that for English, and particularly English Literature, the official emphasis falls on developing students' self-knowledge and identity. This, she argues, is not a localised phenomenon; it is in keeping with the predominant educational thinking of that period, centred on notions about personal growth rather than on the development of discipline-specific concepts or skills. (On the international durability of "personal growth" approaches to English, see Reid, "The Persistent Pedagogy"; also Peel, Patterson and Gerlach.) Drawing further evidence from two kinds of material, recorded classroom lessons and examination papers, Mares considers certain pedagogical and assessment procedures that framed the literature curriculum. She discerns three strands of personalism:

a focus on characters in texts, regarded as virtual persons; an emphasis on students' individual responses to texts; and an assumption that reading should establish a direct communicative relationship with the author. Thus examiners, she remarks (13), "frame questions that make it difficult for candidates *not* to write all about characters" (for instance: *How does Hamlet cope with his problems?* or *The trouble with Hamlet was that he didn't know what he wanted. What do you think Hamlet wanted?*). Similarly, Mares provides transcribed passages of classroom interaction to demonstrate how a pervasive assumption "that the *personal* is what is important" has become "embedded in the everyday routine exchanges" between teachers and students (13). Other researchers have observed the same pattern in English classes elsewhere in Australia around this time; for instance Kelly-Byrne notes examples of a "focus on human relationships, individual dynamics and personal development" (88).

The normal procedure, Mares finds, is "to concentrate attention on an apparently uncritical and open-ended sharing of personal responses to authors and to the characters they have constructed" – so that "teaching literature, even at senior levels, is now less about texts than about the personal selves of the readers" (16). There is a further irony here, as Mares remarks. In this period, examiners often insist in their reports that they are looking for candid personal responses to texts and questions, as if students should remain or pretend to remain unaware of being assessed within a competitive system; yet in reality "one of the abilities being evaluated is the highly developed skill of constructing an answer so that it appears fresh and honest even though it is written at the end of a year of careful teaching for this very moment" (15). Mares's scrutiny of high-rated scripts indicated that successful candidates did not in fact challenge the terms of questions or produce unorthodox opinions. The questions posed in these examination papers gave them no "space for definition or disagreement" (16). She observes that it would hardly be possible, "if you were unlucky enough to be that unimaginable candidate who honestly disliked Shakespeare", to give a genuinely personal response to this 1986 question: *Imagine that some of your friends have annoyed you by declaring that Shakespeare's plays are "the dullest and most boring plays ever written." Write a defence of one or more of Shakespeare's plays, explaining what you have found to like and enjoy.*

Taking at face value the ostensible encouragement to write from one's heart could certainly have dire consequences for an examinee – a fact which Garth Boomer, one of Australia's most eminent educators in the English field at that time, demonstrated tellingly by a simple experiment. He gave seven essays on the same topic to 26 experienced teachers of Senior English at a conference in New South Wales with a request that each be graded on an A to E scale assuming all were produced by candidates for the HSC (matriculation) examination in that state. He also asked the teachers to provide a few comments on each essay to support their grading. What Boomer did not disclose until after completion of the marking was that only six of the essays were by matriculation-level students; Boomer had written the seventh himself, and it boldly challenged the terms of the question, which was this: *Discuss the view that Polonius is merely the portrait of a talkative, self-satisfied old minister of state*. Here is how Boomer's piece began:

> Polonius is not merely any of these things. He is not even a portrait. He is a character, written into a play by Shakespeare, who lives only when some actor in the latest production of *Hamlet* takes to the stage and interprets the lines into tones and mannerisms and foibles. According to the negotiation between the producer and the actor, Polonius may be actively evil or simply a bag of wind. He may be old and pitiful or old and detestable. He may be self-satisfied or ditheringly insecure. But what the actor makes Polonius is not the end of it. Polonius is also defined by the other actors and the action itself.
>
> I get sick of all this talking about characters in plays as if they actually exist. I mean, you can spend hours sitting around wondering whether Hamlet really wanted to get into his mother's bed, but why bother? (10)

And so on, in an increasingly colloquial vein. Three markers awarded this answer an A grade, four a B, five a C, four a D (meaning borderline) and ten an E (outright fail). Comments included "irrelevant" (several markers used this label for it), "flippant", "facile" and "evasive". In an article discussing his mischievous experiment, "The Day I Failed Matriculation English", Boomer summarises the matter in these words:

> I think you know why I failed. I failed because I began paragraph 2 with "I get sick of all this talking" and because I refused to play the game of matriculation essay writing on drama which involves judicious citing of instances (with apt quotation), ordered and specific reference to the question, and earnestness (i.e. respect for Shakespeare). I broke the ground rules by expressing myself and implying disregard for authority (the examiners). (12)

In short his response was too personal – "expressing myself" – or rather, paradoxically, it wasn't personal in the approved conventional manner. As Alan Sinfield (quoted by Mares) remarks in a chapter of the book *Political Shakespeare*, "questions which appear to invite a personal response are often all the more tyrannical; candidates are invited to interrogate their experience to discover a response which has in actuality been learnt" (132). The dishonesty of this solicited performance calls to mind a cynical aphorism variously attributed to Groucho Marx, Jean Giraudoux and George Burns: "The secret of success is sincerity. Once you can fake that, you've got it made."

To many educators in Australia it was increasingly evident by the mid-1980s that such disingenuous attempts to elicit from students of literature a pretence of personal engagement, masking an inculcated routine, were symptoms of a fundamental problem in contemporary English studies – the problem that Mares identifies as a pervasive personalism. The following passage summarises her findings:

> What I see in the current rhetoric of curriculum statements and in the daily practices of teaching and examining literature is that the emphasis has shifted away from teaching about texts and contexts – perhaps in flight from the aridity of older styles of teaching and examining framed by models of traditional literary criticism – to concentrate attention on an apparently uncritical and open-ended sharing of personal responses to authors and to the characters they have constructed. That is, teaching literature, even at senior levels, is now less about texts than about the personal selves of the readers. (16)

Mares goes on to mention a number of uncomfortable consequences of this personalist pedagogy. She suggests

> that readers who learn that what teachers and examiners value is the ability to submerge themselves in texts and to take the characters as "real" make the perfect audience for soap operas like *Dynasty* or *Dallas*; that students who leave school believing that when they read they are in direct personal communication with the mind of the writer are unlikely to have the skills to distance themselves from the manipulative power of advertisements and political manifestos; and finally, that to frame talk about people – whether they are real readers or characters given life outside their texts – as if they were autonomous and decontextualised individuals in control of their own

situations is to make it all the more difficult for students to "formulate an identity" in the face of the social pressures of the world in which they are growing up. (17)

* * *

In most parts of Australia by the late 1980s, critical interventions such as the one by Mares had generated a momentum towards substantial reform of the literature curriculum, particularly for the post-compulsory years of schooling. The book in which Mares's analysis appeared contained other essays, written by educators in different parts of Australia, that were convergent with hers in some of their implications and in taking the view that systemic change was overdue. Pam Gilbert questioned the emphasis of "writing as process" pedagogy on the personal experience of student writers and on its linkage with the notion that a literary text is "a natural, creative and unified expression from a gifted individual" rather than a "constructed artifact" (Hart 30–31). Bill Green's essay challenged the received view that literary appreciation must be at the heart of English studies, arguing instead for a more rhetorical conception of literature "in the service of critical-democratic schooling" (Hart 64). My own piece in the same book contended that narrow notions about appropriate genres were constricting syllabus lists, classroom practices and assessment regimens – not only the selection and grouping of set texts for senior students of Literature to read but also the routinised writing activities that they were licensed to undertake in response to that reading (Hart 77).

Those were among a considerable number of Australian voices calling for a redesigned curriculum in English and Literature at that time. By the second half of the decade the pressure for change had become most insistent in Victoria, though other states were contemplating similar reforms. Such stirrings emerged in the context of a more general movement for curriculum renewal in post-compulsory education, responding to a widespread recognition that secondary schooling systems were not well attuned to some of the social and economic realities of contemporary Australia and were not catering adequately for the increased number and diversity of students staying on into Year 12. The changing educational climate of the mid-80s is clearly visible in documents assembled for the Curriculum Policies Project conducted by the University of Melbourne's Graduate School of

Education (MGSE) and discussed by Yates, Collins and O'Connor. One of the many valuable outcomes of that project is an online repository of key official curriculum documents for each Australian state at mid-decade points from 1975 to 2005 (MGSE). In Victoria the process of educational reform gained considerable impetus from the 1985 Blackburn Report, the product of a wide-ranging ministerial review of post-compulsory schooling in that state. Among other things, the Blackburn Report recommended the introduction of a common two-year certificate, the Victorian Certificate of Education or VCE, marking the culmination of integrated secondary schooling for vocational and general courses alike; the development of a "broad, general curriculum relevant to all students"; and the establishment of a Victorian Curriculum and Assessment Board (VCAB) to implement it. Declaring its commitment to school-based decision-making within the new VCE framework, the Victorian Education Department formed consultative committees for each "field of study" to develop Study Designs that would provide comprehensive curricular structures and assessment principles while allowing ample room for schools to make choices suitable for their own students.

Overtly political decisions, then, constituted an important part of the framework for the new VCE English and Literature, though the Study Designs that then emerged in 1987–89 were also shaped more specifically by debates and critiques such as those mentioned above within the subject field itself, being seen as a corrective to particular problems inherent in the previous Victorian Higher School Certificate (HSC) public examination system. The new VCE subject field comprised two studies, English and Literature. The former was compulsory: all students had to undertake four English units during Years 11 and 12 (a "unit" required a semester of full-time work), completing at least three of them satisfactorily for the award of the VCE. Literature was an optional study, though literary material figured substantially in English as well. The distinctive emphases of these two studies were summarised simply at the beginning of the English Study Design: "English approaches language development through a variety of contexts in which it is used. Literature focuses primarily on the close study of texts" (1). Nevertheless the same document went on to explain that reading and the study of texts was a focal area for all four units of English (along with the craft of writing and the presentation of issues and argument), and the specified work requirements included "a collection of finished pieces of work which result from reading, interpreting and responding to a range of texts, in a variety of forms" (3). Those features of the study were further described as involving "a variety of printed, visual, aural and oral texts [... to] assist students to develop a critical comprehension and appreciation of their own culture, as well as the cultures of others, past and present" (9).

So while the main emphasis of VCE English was on proficiency in language development, those who developed its Study Design saw a need to ensure that students' reading would include diverse texts of a literary kind. For instance, among the work requirements for Units 3 and 4 (taken in the final school year), students had to read, study and write about four texts selected from a list published annually in the *VCAB Bulletin*, at least three of which were to be within a specified range of print genres: "novels, collections of short stories, collections of poetry and song, film scripts, plays, biographies, autobiographies and other non-fiction texts"; further, at least one of these selected texts would be "by an Australian or about Australians", and at least one a work of prose fiction (27–28).

The introduction to the Study Design for VCE Literature states that it "shares with English a general focus on the skilled use of the resources of language but has a particular and distinctive focus: literature comprises texts which are valued for their use of language to recreate and interpret experience imaginatively." An important acknowledgement follows: "What is considered as literature can alter with shifting attitudes, tastes and social conditions. Accordingly the study encompasses works which can vary in cultural origin, genre, medium and world view and includes classical and popular, traditional and modern literature" (1). That relativistic statement, a key part of the circumtextual apparatus providing an official frame around the curriculum for literary studies in the VCE, sends a clear message to teachers and students about the status of any list from which texts are selected. Literature is to be seen not as a fixed category but as something notional, conditional, that goes on being *made and remade* – not only by authors but also by readers, by the publishing industry, and by various institutions including educational bureaucracies. A simple database of set texts, detached from the context of guiding documentation and other authoritative adjuncts, could not in itself convey this concept, and would therefore fail to register a significant change in the nature of the curriculum. The real story about what persists and what gets reformed in literary education will often be found not so much in listed texts as in accompanying information about how those texts are to be read.

In summary, the VCE Study Designs for both English and Literature were attempting to reshape the subject field in three interrelated ways:

- to broaden students' reading beyond the triad of traditionally prestigious genres (poetry/drama/novel) by enlarging the span of admissible texts and specifying their curricular relationships
- to reframe approaches to literary study circumtextually through the nature and scope of accompanying reference material and recommended resources, thus making the intended principles and practices of learning more explicit for teachers, and through them for students
- to restructure and extend assessment tasks by requiring students to produce several different kinds of writing and to choose individually some non-prescribed texts for study.

It may be useful to comment further on each of those innovations, referring now to the Literature study in particular.

The generic range of texts listed for study in Victoria became significantly wider with the implementation of a VCE Study Design for Literature. That expansion is visible to some extent in the ALIAS database, which for 1992 (the new course's first fully operative year) shows notable departures from the English Literature syllabus structure and content that had remained almost unchanged in Victoria for more than 40 years. In 1960, for example, the set texts still conformed to exactly the same pattern as in 1950: a tale by Chaucer, a play by Shakespeare, an anthology of nineteenth-century British poetry, four plays to be chosen from a group that included more Shakespeare along with Sheridan, Shaw and other canonical dramatists, and four novels from a similarly traditional group such as works by Burney, Austen and Hardy. The 1950 syllabus permitted the possibility of studying just one Australian text (Dark's *The Timeless Land*); the 1960 syllabus permitted two (Stewart's play *Ned Kelly* and Richardson's novel *The Getting of Wisdom*). By 1970 the structure had been slightly modified but without affecting the generic range: again there were selections from Chaucer and another poet (Coleridge, Browning or Eliot), a Shakespeare play, four novels (one of which could be Australian) and four plays (one of which could be Australian) and in 1980 the prescriptive constraints were identical. In 1992 the picture became very different, though the ALIAS database reveals only part of it because text lists for the new VCE Literature study were actually presented in two stages, one of which remains below the ALIAS radar. What the database shows, accurately enough given its assumptions, is the prescribed list for Units 3 and 4 (corresponding to Year 12). What it does not show is the pair of lists for Units 1 and 2, which has a less formal status: in the words of the VCAB-published Course Development Support Material accompanying the Literature Study Design, it comprises "suggestions ... provided to assist in text selection" (101). However, the difference is only a matter of degree, because the "prescribed" list for Units 3 and 4 also leaves plenty of room for choice by individual schools. Without going into finicky detail here, one can characterise both suggested and prescribed lists for the new VCE Literature units as involving a greater diversity of text types: alongside novels, poetry and plays there are biographies and autobiographies, films and videos, historical studies, crime reports and collections of short stories, memoirs, letters and essays.

While emphasising the variety of genres available, the VCE Literature Study Design went further. Merely producing a list of recommended texts that covered a broader generic range than before would not have renovated the curriculum as thoroughly as its developers intended. The grouping of texts specified an obligatory distribution not only across genres but also across periods and national boundaries. For example, texts listed for Unit 1 are contemporary but those for Unit 2 are from earlier periods, a minimum of four Australian texts must be chosen for study during the four units, and for Units 3 and 4 the selection must include at least one novel, one performance text, ten poems, a collection of short stories, and two further texts chosen from a variety of specified genres. The Literature study, therefore, had much the same general purpose as English, through which (as noted above) students were intended "to develop a critical comprehension and appreciation of their own culture, as well as the cultures of others, past and present."

To understand the full import and extent of curriculum reforms embodied in VCE English and Literature, it is necessary to go beyond the lists of texts to some accompanying reference materials and recommended resources. (The ALIAS database does not capture them all, as they were published separately from the syllabus information itself.) These had the function of reframing approaches to the study of literature circumtextually, making the intended study principles more explicit for teachers and through them for students. A prominent example is the handful of publications recommended in the resources section of the Course Development Support Material bulletin issued by VCAB in 1990 to accompany the Literature Study Design. One of those items will illustrate the point. Proposing a detailed rationale for a broadened conception of literary education in schools, the booklet *Enlarging Literature: An Inclusive Role for Australian Writing* was jointly sponsored by the national Curriculum Development Centre and the Australian Bicentennial Authority and issued as a Commonwealth Government publication to every school in Australia through the Bicentennial Australian Studies Schools Project. This publication discussed several ways in which Australian literature should be given more ample scope at all levels of the curriculum, especially in the senior years of schooling. It provided numerous examples of different kinds of text "beyond the confines of belles-lettres" that could be studied with the aim of "demystifying 'literature' and making its educational value more accessible" (Reid, *Enlarging Literature* 19). These examples included collections of oral tales, short stories, speculative fiction, journalistic articles, song lyrics, autobiographical works, and the diaries and letters of explorers and settlers. Its argument had a semblance of authority not only because national government agencies (the Curriculum Development Centre and Bicentennial Authority) officially endorsed it but also because it evidently represented an emerging professional consensus: the booklet incorporates several "classroom reports" showing how this enlarged conception of literature was already being put into practice successfully in schools of various kinds, along with a supporting paper prepared by the Australian Association for the Teaching of English, which drew on the collective experience of numerous teachers from all corners of the country.

In addition to broadening the range of set texts and providing concomitant resources to guide teachers and students towards a particular view of literature, the third way in which VCE Study Designs attempted to alter the literature curriculum was by injecting more variety into assessment tasks. Students were required to produce, in response to their reading, several different kinds of writing other than the traditional essay form, and also to choose individually some non-prescribed texts for study.

To a large extent the assessment of students' work for the new VCE was school-based, but supervised by VCAB through "common assessment tasks" (known as CATs). The Study Designs and associated Course Development Support Material explained in detail the criteria and procedures for assessing levels of performance. No doubt the tight control exerted over teaching and learning by this means could be criticised, but at least its aims and methods were fairly clear. The work requirements and the common assessment tasks stemming from them covered an assortment of forms of writing, such as keeping a journal to note down impressions while reading, and developing a folio of finished responses (creative and analytical) to texts. One intention was to ensure that students were not confined to the somewhat artificial genre of the critical essay, a specialised academic routine quite different from more worldly modes of discourse such as the reviews that circulate through newspapers, magazines, radio and other media. Instead of following a standard formula in order to tell literary authorities what they already know about some text they have already declared to be worth knowing (as a critical essay does), a review usually serves to introduce, situate and appraise a recently produced text for a readership whose familiarity with it cannot be assumed. Accordingly there is more latitude in deciding on an appropriate tone, approach and frame of reference. In recognition of this, the VCE Literature Study Design based a whole set of work requirements on reviewing: in both Year 11 and Year 12, each student must discover independently a book that he or she thinks worthwhile, and evaluate it – first through an oral presentation to the class, with a written review following later. In Year 12 there must also be a study of some published reviews – a study that could for example involve formal group debates in class as to the critical assumptions and relative merits of a couple of appraisals of the same book. Ideally these activities would lead students towards a more thoughtful engagement with books and the book industry than is likely through traditional rites of appreciation.

It would be unduly romantic to view the VCE reforms as liberating the literature curriculum from the dead hand of tradition. Rather, the new Study Designs for English and Literature inevitably exchanged one kind of prescriptiveness for another, replacing a previous orthodoxy with what soon became a new orthodoxy, beneficial or not.

In Australian curriculum documents and classroom practices before the mid-1980s, "literature" was generally assumed to be a self-evident category, comprising written works of inherently superior artistry and lasting merit to which a reader should respond in ostensibly "personal" terms. Text choices might differ from year to year but the tacit basis for selection was seldom questioned. By about 1990 a substantial change had occurred, one that the foregoing discussion has illustrated with reference to the advent of VCE Study Designs – though similar developments were occurring simultaneously in most states. Since then, "literature" has continued in the senior school curriculum as a qualified concept with heuristic value *on the condition of acknowledging its status to be constructed and contestable.*

This modified status is not fully apparent from lists alone. The present chapter has argued that some shifts in the perceived scope and purpose of literary studies can best be seen in supplementary materials that frame those studies circumtextually. One further example is my 1984 book *The Making of Literature: Texts, Contexts and Classroom Practices*. What justifies its otherwise presumptuous mention here is that the uses made of it show plainly how the nature of required reading depends on more than set texts themselves. *The Making of Literature* has served to shape not only what Australian students read but also how they read it – a fact inconspicuous in the ALIAS database, which merely records this book as a recommended teaching resource for English in Western Australia from 1990 to 2003. Actually its influence has extended across other states and remained a reference point for professional discourse. Though such protracted attention may be undeserved, it does exemplify the effect of circumtextual framing. Welcomed at the time of its publication as a stimulus for syllabus committees to rethink "taken-for-granted assumptions about the literature curriculum" (Gill, review 7), it was subsequently endorsed in a Course Development Support Material bulletin issued in 1990 alongside the new VCE Literature Study Design. Still regularly invoked in subject association journals, this book has also figured in teacher education and in-service courses, with a flow-on into school classroom activities.

If *The Making of Literature* has indeed had "a decisive impact on English and Literature teaching" (Doecke, Framing Idiom 2), what is the nature of that impact? Apparently it has seemed "revolutionary" (Hayes; Gill, Introduction) because of its proffered "model for a contemporary literature classroom" (Bellis, Parr and Doecke, 166) – a model that, in the words of the Course Development Support Material for VCE Literature, is "characterised by collaborative and integrative approaches to literature and by treating questions about the production of literature as dynamic" (104). Its advocacy of a "Workshop" concept of active dialogic engagement with texts found favour "in contradistinction to more traditional understandings of the role of literature within the school curriculum – the 'Gallery'" (Bellis, Parr and Doecke 165). This "resonated with many secondary English teachers when the book was first published", according to Doecke, Davies and Mead, and "continues to appeal to later generations of teachers" (9). Much of its perceived usefulness, according to comments in the sources cited here, lies in its practical classroom-based insights into the material processes through which writing may become "literature".

Ongoing use of this book by reviewers, researchers, syllabus committees and classroom teachers illustrates some ways in which ancillary documents can frame the literature curriculum circumtextually, with a significant effect on how texts are chosen, how they are read, and how responses to them are assessed. Those three aspects – text selection, text interpretation and text response – correspond to what Bernstein's pioneering work on framing in education identifies as the basic triad of "message systems" (203): curriculum (that which counts as valid knowledge), pedagogy (that which counts as valid transmission of knowledge) and evaluation (that which counts as valid demonstration that the knowledge has been acquired). To a large extent, the construction of literary knowledge is an effect of framing.

Works Cited

Andrews, Richard. *Reframing Literacy: Teaching and learning in English and the language arts*. London: Routledge, 2010. Print.

Bellis, Natalie, Graham Parr and Brenton Doecke. "*The Making of Literature*: A Continuing Conversation". *Changing English* 16.2 (2009): 165–79. Print.

Bernstein, Basil. "On the classification and framing of educational knowledge". *Class, Codes and Control: Theoretical studies towards a sociology of language*. New York: Schocken, 1975. 202–36. Print.

"Blackburn Report" [report of the Ministerial Review of Post-Compulsory Schooling, chaired by Jean Blackburn]. 1985. Online summary at: http://web.education. unimelb.edu.au/curriculumpoliciesproject/Reports/download/Vic-1985-BlackburnReport1985.pdf. Web. 1 Aug. 2016.

Boomer, Garth. "The day I failed matriculation English". *Opinion [Journal of the South Australian English Teachers' Association]* 5.4 (1976): 10–12. Print.

Centre for Studies in Literary Education. The Use of Australian Literature in Schools: A report of a preliminary investigation conducted on behalf of the Literature Board of the Australia Council. Deakin University [commissioned report]. 1989. Print.

Doecke, Brenton. "Framing Idiom" [editorial]. *Idiom* 29.3 (1994): 2–4. Print.

——, Larissa McLean Davies and Philip Mead (eds). *Teaching Australian Literature: From classroom conversations to national imaginings*. Kent Town: Wakefield Press/ AATE, 2011. Print.

——, and Ian Reid. "Deconstructing classroom frames". *In Knowledge in the Making: Challenging the text in the classroom*. Ed. Bill Corcoran, Mike Hayhoe and Gordon M. Pradl. Portsmouth, NH: Boynton/Cook, 1994. 259–71. Print.

Dollimore, Jonathan, and Alan Sinfield (eds). *Political Shakespeare*. Manchester: Manchester University Press, 1985. Print.

Gilbert, Pam. "Authorship and creativity in the classroom: Re-reading the traditional frames". *Shifting Frames*. Ed. Kevin Hart, 1988. 24–39. Print.

[Gill, Margaret]. "M.G". "Review of *The Making of Literature*". *English in Australia* 73 (1985): 5–8. Print.

Gill, Margaret. [Introduction to reprinted articles]. *English in Australia* 49.2 (2014): 35. Print.

Green, Bill. "Literature as curriculum frame: A critical perspective". *Shifting Frames*. Ed. Kevin Hart, 1988. 46–71. Print.

Hart, Kevin (ed.). *Shifting Frames: English/Literature/Writing*. Geelong: Centre for Studies in Literary Education, Deakin University, 1988. Print.

Hayes, Terry. "*The Making of Literature* Revisited: A revolutionary text in its time, a text for these times". *Idiom* 50.2 (2014). Print.

Kelly-Byrne, Diana. *The Gendered Framing of English Teaching: A selective case study*. Geelong: Centre for Studies in Literary Education, Deakin University, 1991. Print.

MacLachlan, Gale, and Ian Reid. *Framing and Interpretation*. Melbourne: Melbourne University Press, 1994. Print.

Mares, Peggy. "'Personal Growth' as a frame for teaching literature". *Shifting Frames*. Ed. Kevin Hart. 6–18. Print.

Melbourne Graduate School of Education (MGSE). Curriculum Policies Project. http://web.education.unimelb.edu.au/curriculumpoliciesproject/Reports/. Retrieved 1 Aug. 2016.

Peel, Robin, Annette Patterson and Jeanne Gerlach. *Questions of English: Ethics, aesthetics, rhetoric and the formation of the subject in England, Australia and the United States*. London: Routledge, 2000. Print.

Reid, Ian. *The Making of Literature: Texts, contexts and classroom practices*. [Kent Town, South Australia]: Australian Association for the Teaching of English, 1984; reprinted 1988. Print.

——. "Genre as frame: Redesigning courses for English/Literature/Writing". *Shifting Frames*. Ed. Kevin Hart. 77–89. Print.

——. *Enlarging Literature: An inclusive role for Australian writing*. Canberra: Commonwealth Schools Commission, 1988. Print.

——. *Narrative Exchanges*. London and New York: Routledge, 1992; reprinted 2014. Print.

——. "The persistent pedagogy of growth". *English Teachers and Work: Narratives, counter narratives and arguments*. Ed. Brenton Doecke, David Homer and Helen Nixon. Kent Town, South Australia: Wakefield Press/AATE, 2003. 97–108. Print.

VCE English Study Design. Melbourne: Victorian Curriculum and Assessment Board, 1989. Print.

VCE English Course Development Support Material. Melbourne: Victorian Curriculum and Assessment Board, 1990. Print.

VCE Literature Study Design. Melbourne: Victorian Curriculum and Assessment Board, 1990. Print.

VCE Literature Course Development Support Material. Melbourne: Victorian Curriculum and Assessment Board, 1990. Print.

Yates, Lyn, Cherry Collins and Kate O'Connor. *Australia's Curriculum Dilemmas: State cultures and the big issues*. Carlton: Melbourne University Publishing, 2011. Print.

Chapter Five

INSCRIBING CULTURE

The history of prescribed text lists in senior secondary English in NSW, 1945–1964[1]

Jacqueline Manuel and Don Carter

"Everything is forever imprinted with what it once was."

(Winterson)

Introduction

Those who completed senior secondary English in New South Wales (NSW) during the twentieth century can likely recall the texts they were compelled to read. Equally likely is that most, if not all of these texts were drawn from a canon of predominantly English literature that included poetry, fiction and drama, including Shakespearean drama. Almost certainly there was limited, if any, provision for teachers and especially students to select these texts. Likewise, there was little if any sense of agency in determining the ways they were read, experienced and examined. Successive senior English syllabus documents in NSW have variously subscribed to "the special educating power of Literature in its effect in developing the mind, filling it with high ideals and in its influence on refining and ennobling character" (NSW Department of Public Instruction 18). Literary study in

---

1   This chapter explores the NSW senior secondary text lists up to 1964. It is intended to be read in conjunction with the following chapter, which explores the text lists from 1965 to 2005.

senior English may have inspired in some an ongoing commitment to the pleasures and affordances of reading, including reading imaginative literature. But for many students the singular purpose of literary study in senior secondary English was and continues to be a far more pragmatic and indeed prosaic one: to pass the final school examinations (Brock, *History*, "Telling the story"; Rosser).

Since 1911, text lists for senior secondary English in NSW, coupled with an external examination regime, have assumed an increasingly determinant role in shaping and defining the purpose and identity of the subject at the senior school level. Each secondary English syllabus from 1911 to 1945 and the final year of each senior secondary English syllabus from 1911 to the present has been accompanied by a list of mandatory texts and types of texts for study and examination. Historically, these lists have functioned as part of a unique amalgam of local, context-specific influences on the formation of senior English in NSW: the largest and most highly centralised and regulated educational jurisdiction in Australia, in which English remains the only compulsory subject in the curriculum from Kindergarten to Year 12, and the only compulsory subject required for matriculation.

The value of text lists for curriculum history

As historical curriculum documents, the lists can serve as prismatic sources of evidence. Most immediately, they substantiate the virtually continuous positioning of Western canonical literature and literary study at the heart of the subject at senior secondary level in NSW. The forms of fiction, poetry, drama, Shakespearean drama and non-fiction have enjoyed uncontested prominence in senior English from the first syllabus of 1911 to the present. Although "the curriculum subject of English is continually reviewed and revised ... the status of literature is rarely questioned" (Goodwyn 212). Goodwyn's case can be extended to the rarely questioned, much less problematised, orthodoxy of mandatory text lists. In NSW the lists do not merely recommend a range and quantity of literature for study. They 'prescribe' it. Such lists are known as "Prescribed Texts" or, as in more recent decades, "Prescriptions". The nomenclature alone is suggestive of the regulatory function of these documents, with system-wide compliance monitored and enforced through the external high-stakes examinations in the final year of schooling.

For the better part of a century, the decision-making processes involved in setting these text lists have been controlled and guarded by select groups with minimal, if any, democratic involvement of or consultation with the broader majority of English educators, and certainly not with students.[2] Contrary to Gallagher's claim, school syllabuses do not "begin the canonical process" (66). The process of determining what counts as literature; the extent and nature of its presence in senior secondary English; the uses to which it is put in the formation of the "well educated" (NSW Department of Public Instruction iv) person; and the ways it is experienced by students are encoded in syllabus versions of the subject and imposed upon teachers and students through the standardising apparatus of text lists and examinations.

While the prescribed text lists can illuminate the "what, where and when" of study in senior secondary English in any given year since 1911, far less transparent is the "how and why" of such study. A comparative analysis of texts lists yields quantitative data on the number, types and titles of texts set for study and the historical periods from which they are drawn. In turn, this mapping affords insight into patterns of privileging: the presence or absence of particular texts and types of texts on successive lists becomes emblematic of their perceived worth as vehicles for transmitting and perpetuating certain sets of values and beliefs about cultivating the ideal citizen.

Interpretations of the text lists alone, however, considered in isolation from the suite of associated historical curriculum documents and critical scholarship, are inevitably provisional. The lists offer only partial clues to understanding "the presence and influence of visible and submerged" (Beavis 288) institutional, cultural and disciplinary discourses, values and ideologies that have shaped their production and preserved their authoritative status. As mechanisms of control and social closure (Parkin; Rosser 18), the lists have operated in concert with syllabus documents, examinations and examiners' reports as a potent form of "disciplinary technology" (Hunter), inscribing and propagating the "disciplinary norms" (Reid, "Wordsworth") of the subject at senior secondary level.

The purpose of this chapter is to chart and interpret patterns, continuities and disjunctions in senior secondary English text lists in NSW, using the primary sources in the ALIAS database and relevant secondary sources from the corpus of research literature in the field. We are interested in the design and content of the lists, the factors and processes that have driven and influenced the selection of texts, and what these conceal and

---

2   See Brock, *A History of English Syllabuses in NSW*, "Telling the story"; Rosser.

reveal about the conceptualisation of the subject at key historical moments. Because a single chapter cannot account for the entire sweep of curriculum documents contained in the ALIAS collection, we have structured the discussion in two parts. This chapter focuses on key documents up to 1964. The following chapter takes up the story of senior secondary text lists from 1965 to 2005. Together, they constitute an inclusive mapping of almost a century of selected senior secondary English curriculum materials from NSW.

A rationale for the analysis of key text lists and syllabus documents in NSW

In the historical period encompassed by the ALIAS database, there have been two watershed moments of curriculum renewal in NSW senior secondary English: the Wyndham Scheme introduced in 1962 and examined for the first time in 1967, and the McGaw reforms endorsed in 1999 and examined for the first time in 2001. Less momentous, but nevertheless important in the complex narrative of the subject, were the changes to the syllabus text lists and examinations that occurred in 1945, 1953 and 1974. Sitting outside the parameters of the ALIAS database are other syllabus documents that warrant initial attention for the purposes of contextualising the history of senior English text lists in NSW. The most significant of these is the 1911 *Courses of Study for High Schools* (NSW Department of Public Instruction) that figures as a historical landmark in the narrative of secondary English in NSW. Since the ALIAS database is collated chronologically, the analysis of the NSW primary sources is undertaken chronologically. This approach affords considerable opportunities to apprehend certain continuities and discontinuities in the nature and role of text lists in NSW over the span of the twentieth century.

In undertaking the comparative inquiry reported in this chapter, we applied an analytical framework to text lists associated with the senior secondary English syllabus from 1911 through to the list in operation immediately prior to the commencement of the new senior secondary English courses (Higher School Certificate) in 1965. The analytical framework was based on the content and structure of the lists themselves and, where appropriate, information gleaned from syllabus and examination documents. Included in the analysis of text lists were types of texts (eg. fiction, poetry, drama, Shakespearean drama, non-fiction, film, media, multimedia) and differentiation in senior English courses; the number of texts in each category of types of texts; the range of choices within each category of types of texts; mandatory or prescribed texts; examinable texts; provision and scope for student selection of texts; status of texts (eg. classic/canonical; contemporary; popular); heritage of texts (eg. British, Australian, Indigenous, Asian and other international texts); stated, implied or recommended approach to textual study; and statistical data on course candidature in each year.

Methodologically, this analysis sits within a social constructivist tradition that attends to the need for "specificity and contingency" (Tyler and Johnson 4) in any account of the history of a particular field of learning and its manifestations in localised educational settings (Ball, "Competition and Conflict"; Ball and Lacey; Brock, *History*; Cormack, "Tracking local curriculum histories"; Goodson; Goodson and Medway; Sawyer, "Lost Opportunities", "Growth Model", *Simply Growth?*).

In interpreting the findings of the analysis, we have drawn on the comprehensive research and scholarship of Brock and Rosser: their historical curriculum work in the field provides rich insights into the "back stage" (Goffman 5) story of how and why particular senior secondary English syllabus documents, text lists and examinations came to be. In addition, we have brought to bear on this study our own knowledge and experience of curriculum and policy development processes, acquired over many years in our various past roles as Chief Examiner, NSW Higher School Certificate English Standard and Advanced courses, 2007–2011 (Manuel); Member, Board of Studies NSW (Manuel); Chair of English Board Curriculum Committees (Manuel); Board of Studies NSW[3] Board Inspector, English (Carter); and leadership and participation in Board of Studies NSW Syllabus and Prescriptions Advisory Committees, Panels and Working Groups (Carter and Manuel). Having occupied positions as insiders for a period of time, we bring to this present inquiry a blend of perspectives and understandings that would not otherwise be readily accessible to curriculum historians relying solely on primary and secondary documentary sources.

The origins of secondary English text lists in NSW

The historiography of subject English, in both local and international settings, records the enduring struggle for control over its purpose and substance and its susceptibility to being co-opted for a variety of cultural, political

---

3   Board of Studies NSW: since 2014 Board of Studies, Teaching and Education Standards (BOSTES).

and ideological agendas.[4] In NSW, as in other contexts, the formation and development of senior secondary English has been similarly marked by often robust debates. This struggle frequently materialised in public and academic arguments about the definition of literature and literary study, the range and types of literature students ought to experience and the relative emphasis given to teaching language skills such as writing, reading, grammar and spelling (Ball, "English since 1906", "Competition and Conflict"). In NSW, the text lists published over the course of a century represent the end-products of these enduring debates about the "what" of literary study in senior English.

Text lists have been a convention in NSW since 1911. It is therefore necessary to provide some background to the text list from the 1945 syllabus documents by first briefly exploring its predecessors. As the initial state-authorised version of secondary curriculum, Peter Board's *Courses of Study for High Schools* (NSW Department of Public Instruction)[5] has salience as a baseline primary source for "retrieving intellectual history" (Reid, "Persistent" 100), since it inaugurated a number of now normative discourses and practices. Of the four mandatory "common ground" subjects in the 1911 *Courses of Study for High Schools*, English is singled out as the subject which, through the study of literature, "the High School will exercise its highest influence upon the general training of the pupils" (NSW Department of Public Instruction 5).[6]

Prior to the 1911 curriculum, the dominant conceptualisation of English in education in Australia during the later part of the nineteenth century had been inherited from the British classical-liberal tradition which, at that time, focused on rote learning, memorisation and the grammatical analysis of texts. As Brock and also Rosser detail, the content of secondary English education prior to 1911, including prescribed text lists, was designed, controlled and examined by the University of Sydney. Students studied set works drawn from the accepted (and at that time uncontested) canon of predominantly English literature.

---

4   See Ball; Ball, Kenny and Gardiner; Ball and Lacey; Barcan; Brock, *A History of English Syllabuses*; Carter; Cormack, "Tracking local curriculum histories"; Goodson and Medway; Green and Beavis; Manuel; Manuel and Brock; Mathieson; Michaels; Reid, "Persistent pedagogy"; Rosser; Sawyer, "Simply growth"; Selleck; Shayer.

5   See Crane and Walker and Hughes and Brock for a more detailed coverage of the 1911 curriculum documents and the contexts in which they were produced.

6   See for example, Barcan; Green and Beavis.

The positioning of literature in the 1911 courses of study for high schools

In the early years of the twentieth century, however, this classical-liberal paradigm came under increasing scrutiny. To deliberately differentiate it from Classics, subject English was installed at the centre of the school curriculum in the belief that it would equip students with the necessary linguistic, cognitive, aesthetic, ethical, moral and critical capacities necessary for success across all other subjects and in the adult world (Cormack, "English/Literacy" 6). This aspiration would be realised as students were initiated and socialised into the dominant culture through reading its great works of English literature. That such literary experiences should also "arouse interest and create enjoyment" (NSW Department of Public Instruction 18) if they were to contribute to the holistic growth of the student is a belief that has since become normative in the rhetorical English curriculum.

This first secondary English syllabus in 1911 staked out the territory and defined the purpose of the subject by proclaiming the "moral, spiritual and intellectual value of reading literature" (NSW Department of Public Instruction 18). The evangelistic tenor of the early twentieth-century debates about the centrality of literature as a civilising force in the education of the young was equally captured in more public conversations, such as for example, in a piece by Professor Perkins published in the NSW *Education Gazette* in 1905. Perkins avowed that "in our literature we have the most sacred relics of our race ... the love of it idealises and humanises life ... in general, unless a taste for literature be acquired in early life, it but rarely lightens our ways in the after times" (NSW *Education Gazette* 137).

These lofty sentiments reprised the Arnoldian ideal of the ennobling power of literature as "the best that has been thought and said" (Arnold iii). Literature, as a "potent symbolic category" (Mellor, O'Neill and Patterson 41) was elevated as the medium for "heightening personal perception and refining sensibility; inculcating social propriety and enhancing public morality; and promoting social solidarity and national identity" (Pope 8). This moral and ideological investment in the affordances of literature in transmitting and reproducing a dominant culture was later galvanised in the 1921 Newbolt Report in Britain. Formulated and released against the backdrop of a post-Great War society, wrestling with the dual moods of grief and optimism, the Report spoke for its time in its aspirations for greater social justice and education of the masses, particularly the working classes. There was an especially robust insistence throughout on the engagement with literature as a "form of education in human relations" for "the development of human character" (Newbolt 20, 21). The report declared that "English is not merely the medium for our thought, it is the very stuff and process of it ... It connotes the discovery of the world by the first and most direct way open to us, and the discovery of ourselves in our native environment" (20).

This belief in (certain kinds) of literature as the storehouse of cultural capital and the wellspring of moral, ethical and aesthetic education became one of the enduring visible discourses of senior secondary English education in NSW. The Cultural Heritage (or Arnoldian) model of subject English figured prominently in the 1911 and most subsequent senior secondary English syllabuses in NSW, underscoring the extent to which the purpose of literature in a syllabus at any given time has been "a constitutive and inseparable part of history in the making" (Brannigan 304).

The development of the 1911 text lists for secondary English

The process of constructing the 1911 English syllabus, including the text list, was a centralised one led by the then Director-General of Education in NSW, Peter Board (Brock, *History*, "Telling the Story", "Some Aspects of Secondary English Education", "Processes involved in curriculum change", "The Struggle for Curriculum Development"; Campbell and Sherington; Hughes and Brock).[7] Board later chaired the Board of Examiners, Department of Public Instruction (established in 1913 and superseded in 1936 by the Board of Secondary School Studies). The required content for each year of the four-year program of study in secondary English was set out in two parts: "Literature" and "Language". The Literature sections for the first two years of secondary English comprised three sets of seven prescribed texts: set A, B and C. The intention was that the text list would be implemented in a three-year cycle, meaning that new text lists would not be published for at least three years after the release of the original list. In the first year of secondary English, the seven prescribed texts were a mix of fiction, poetry and non-fiction (essays, histories and biographies) (NSW Department of Public Instruction 15–17).

---

7   For detailed coverage of this historical period, see Campbell and Sherington, and Hughes and Brock.

In the second year, students again studied the seven texts prescribed, with a "more detailed study" expected for the Shakespearean play (*The Merchant of Venice, Henry V, Julius Caesar* in set A, B and C, respectively). In the third year of secondary English the quantity of texts listed increased to eight. Students were to study all eight texts including a Shakespearean drama. In the third year, the texts on the list requiring a "more detailed study" included Milton's "L'Allegro" and "Il Penseroso" and James Russell Lowell's poems, Wordsworth's shorter poems, and *Laureata* from Shakespeare to Byron, in sets A, B and C, respectively. In the fourth year of secondary English the sets of lists were reduced from eight to six texts. Students were to study all six of these texts, including a Shakespearean drama, and two texts in each set were identified for "more detailed study" (NSW Department of Public Instruction 15–17).

The text list for the final year of school English (Fourth Year[8]) included familiar canonical titles such as those by Chaucer, Shakespeare (*Julius Caesar, As You Like It, The Tempest, The Merchant of Venice, A Midsummer Night's Dream, Macbeth, Coriolanus, A Winter's Tale*), Dickens, Holmes, Ruskin, Carlyle, Austen, Eliot, Gaskell, Alcott, Emerson, Addison, Burke, Kingsley, Stevenson, Bacon, Gibbon, Milton, Lamb, Coleridge, Shelley, Byron, Wordsworth, Kipling, Longfellow, Scott, Tennyson, Arnold and Lowell. The list was transparent for its obeisance to the high literary culture of the time, with a predominance of male writers and British canonical texts. On the list for Second Year, one Australian writer's work was included: Amy Mack's *A Bush Calendar* (1909) (NSW Department of Public Instruction 16).

In contrast to the Literature component of the 1911 syllabus, the Language component was brief and general. It consisted of part "(a) Composition – Oral and written, and part (b) Grammar, Prosody, Word Composition. Practice in speaking and reading" (15). The syllabus discouraged the explicit teaching of grammar or decontextualised language skills, emphasising instead the aim of meaningful engagement with language through reading and writing:

> Formal instruction in the theory of expression will scarcely be needed. In any case, it is doubtful whether such instruction is effective in securing a good style of composition. The aim in this course is to

---

8   In 1918, an extra year was added to the secondary curriculum, meaning the Intermediate Certificate occurred after three years of study and the Leaving Certificate after a further two years of study (Hughes and Brock 26).

develop an intelligent interest in the mother tongue and *not to acquaint pupils with a body of details*. (NSW Department of Public Instruction 21, 22)

In terms of 'how' the study of literature was to be enacted in the classroom, the 1911 syllabus was, from the vantage point of history, in many respects a forward-looking manifesto of progressive educational philosophies. Its rationale for the place of English in the curriculum championed a child-centred approach to education: the teacher was positioned as a "sympathetic figure" (Green and Cormack 262) instantiating a Rousseau-inspired vision of "sentimental education", balancing authority with benevolent intentionality and attentive guidance through the "artifice and manipulation of 'well-regulated' liberty" (Green and Cormack 254). This belief in the importance of some scope for "liberty" in students' learning was evident in the curriculum structure, with "about one half of the school time" allocated to "the field for the *student's choice* according to his [sic] individual aptitudes or his [sic] prospects for a future career" (NSW Department of Public Instruction i). The syllabus recommended that teachers "leave scope for variations in detail of the programmes" (iv), which extended to the practice of encouraging students to choose their own reading materials, in addition to those prescribed, and to initiate their own topics for composition. Since 1911, the mandating of, and legislation for, minimum hours for each subject area in the curriculum has remained a feature of education in NSW to the present, although the allocation of half of the school timetable to individual students' pursuits was steadily eroded as the number of subjects in the curriculum grew substantially in the early decades of the twentieth century.

The "Notes and Suggestions" section of the 1911 document shed further light on the conceptualisation of English and the view of the student and teacher. They included extensive pedagogical advice to support the effective development of a student's "judgement", "habits of thought" and "self-government". Inherent in this advice, aimed at meeting the "subjectification and socialisation" purpose of education (Biesta), was an emphasis on cultivating the "well educated", increasingly independent young citizen:

[t]he library, the laboratory and the workshop are essential adjuncts of the school for secondary instruction. The part that each of these takes in the education of the pupil should be governed by the fact that *it is there that he [sic] has to do work on his own account, and is most dependent on his [sic] own personal effort. In each of them he [sic] is an investigator, an experimenter ... The art of independent study depends partly upon*

> *the power of the pupil to discern what he [sic] should record in the form of notes.* ... But at no time should notes be dictated to the pupil. (NSW Department of Public Instruction v; emphasis added)

Approaches that encouraged active engagement with learning with an eye to pupils' enjoyment anticipate later twentieth-century pedagogical models, particularly the "workshop" model that gained currency during the 1980s and 1990s (Reid, *Making*). Similarly, a foregrounding of the aesthetic and imaginative dimensions of literary experience foreshadows the reader-response literary theories that emerged in the 1980s.

In terms of the content of English that was examined, the Leaving Certificate (LC) examinations up to 1940 were inseparably bound to the text lists. In the school-based program of study in English, however, there was some latitude for teacher choice in reading materials in the junior secondary years.[9] The syllabus allowed for some student choice in the selection of wide reading material and composition that were not tied to examinations. Until 1945, the text lists for both the Intermediate Certificate (junior secondary) and the Leaving Certificate (senior secondary) were closely prescribed. Since 1953, however, prescribed text lists were confined to the syllabus for the final year of schooling. Ironically, the credibility of the discourses in successive rhetorical curriculum and educational policy documents, particularly at the senior secondary level (discourses of, for example, student choice, self-directed learning, creativity, growing independence and teacher flexibility in implementing the syllabus) has over the course of the twentieth century been gravely undermined by the regulatory and constraining power of the text lists and examinations in the final year of schooling.

Although the Notes and Suggestions accompanying the 1911 syllabus – written and signed by Board himself – were considerably abridged in the following revised editions, they continued to draw attention to the scope for individual teachers to vary and adapt the syllabus to suit the needs of their particular students. In 1913, for example, the Notes and Suggestions reminded teachers that

> it is not the object of the syllabus to tie all teachers down to a uniform treatment of the subject presented ... It is intended that the examination papers should embrace a wide range of questions so that pupils who

---

9   "While teachers are not required to select books from the appended list, they must, if they desire to use others, submit their choices for the approval of the Chief Inspector of Schools" (Board of Secondary School Studies 3).

have been taken through the course, but have had the various subjects handled in somewhat different ways by different teachers, may find within the scope of the examination paper a sufficient supply of questions to test the pupil's knowledge on the lines on which the course of instruction has been treated. (NSW Department of Public Instruction iv)

The strictures of the examinations, however, tended to nullify the syllabus rhetoric of liberty, choice and flexibility. Commenting on the advice to teachers set out in the 1913 revised edition of the curriculum, Crane and Walker wrote that

> in theory, teachers had always had this freedom [to vary the requirements of the syllabus depending on their students' needs], but in practice they had not been able to use it because the demands of the examination system discouraged any such variations ... It can be fairly claimed that, despite official denials to the contrary, the syllabus had become an "examination syllabus" which teachers were to "cover" if their students were to make any kind of showing in the Intermediate and Leaving Certificates ... A stranger picking up a New South Wales high school syllabus in the early 1920s would have assumed that the only aim of the school was to set a fixed amount of work to be studied by every boy and girl so that they could pass in certain examinations. (119)

Even in its infancy, the senior secondary program of study was perceived to be at the service of a centrally administered and controlled examination system that, for English, was based in large part on the authority of the text list. What's more, the practice of publishing an examiner's report each year, detailing the examiner's views of the strengths and weaknesses in the candidates' examination performance, added a further layer of control, by proxy, to an already highly regulated examination system. In its reporting of student achievement, the reports served to further shape and standardise reading and writing practices in senior secondary English. In effect, the amalgam of text lists, examinations and examiners' reports came to function as the de facto syllabus in the final year of secondary schooling. The substance, texture and scope of the program of learning in classrooms were sharply demarcated and steered by the expectations and agendas of the external examination (Brock, *History*, "Telling the Story", "Some Aspects", "Processes", "Struggle"; Rosser).

The role of the university sector in shaping senior secondary English text lists in NSW

One of the "submerged" discourses in the history of senior English in NSW pertains to the role of the university sector, particularly the University of Sydney, in the construction and reproduction of the subject's identity. The text list in 1911, for instance, mirrored the reading set out for undergraduate English at the University of Sydney. It consisted of adult literature in traditional canonical forms and favoured genres. To this day, it is the exception to find popular literature or the now distinct category of Young Adult Literature among the list of texts prescribed for senior secondary study. Both Brock and Rosser detail the powerful and complex "top-down" influence of the University of Sydney on the "what and how" of English in schools in NSW during the early to mid twentieth century. Through its academics occupying the key role of chair and other positions on senior secondary English syllabus committees, and as Chief Examiners for the final English examinations, the university exerted extensive and sustained control as arbiters and custodians of the content of senior secondary English.

The University operated as the "gatekeeper" (Rosser 6), determining matriculation requirements and thereby governing access to tertiary education through institutionalised processes of elite social closure. Rosser has argued that "the powerful bias towards the academic preferencing of the English of Sydney University" in the construction of text lists and the nature of examinations functioned as "the framing 'disciplinary technology', reinforcing values and reading regimes developed elsewhere in the curriculum, and serving as a filter for higher learning" (Rosser 6).

The limited scope of the present discussion precludes a more thorough coverage of this pivotal dynamic. The key point to be made for the purposes of the present argument is that the text list of 1911 and the subsequent text lists for another 63 years were heavily influenced by the prevailing sets of values, beliefs and ideologies of individual and groups of academics, principally from the University of Sydney.

Institutionalising senior secondary English text lists

The structure and much of the substance of secondary English as set out in the 1911 syllabus remained relatively constant through 15 editions (issued with only minor amendments) until 1943. There was turnover in the titles appearing in the text lists for each year, but the required types of texts for study in each year remained unchanged. This continuity applied to the examinations until 1940, when another section was added to the Leaving Certificate examination: Section D (NSW Department of Education).

While the social, cultural, educational, economic and other material conditions within which senior secondary schooling operated certainly shifted significantly after 1911, other features of this early conceptualisation of the subject did not. What endured from 1911 to 1943 (and indeed to the present) in the form of vestiges or direct inheritances can be summarised as follows:

- A valuing and inscribed ideology of literature as a civilising, moralising and nation-building force and as a potential source of pleasure and personal edification.
- Prescribed text lists as a powerful regulatory apparatus, married to final examinations.
- External examinations in the final year of secondary schooling with results in English tied to university entrance.
- The yearly publication of an Examiner's Report.
- Government-legislated mandatory hours for subject English (and other core curriculum subjects).
- A centralised process of governmental control and regulation of syllabus documents, text lists and examinations.
- A predominance of British canonical literature and the Cultural Heritage model of English.
- Mandated types of texts and quantities of texts.
- A privileging of written forms of students' literary responses.

The 1945 secondary English Syllabus

In 1944, however, a range of changes to the structure and content of the secondary English syllabus occurred, representing the first major revision of the 1911 document. In August of that year, a "Special Edition" of the *Courses for Study for High Schools* for implementation in 1945 was issued. It flagged a transition to a revised means of distributing syllabuses in the following years. The 1945 syllabus document appends a Note: "[t]his Syllabus replaces that published in the 15th edition of the *Courses of Study for Secondary School*. For the convenience of teachers and students, each new subject syllabus will in future be published separately" (NSW Department of Education 6). From this point on, all secondary syllabuses in NSW were published as discrete documents, a practice which endures to the present day. The decision to publish subject syllabuses separately was partly a consequence of the burgeoning of subjects in the curriculum since 1911. It also paved the way for the formal treatment of secondary curriculum subjects as distinct domains, each accruing its own particular content, pedagogy, research base and discourses as "internally differentiated epistemological communities" (Ball, "Competition and Conflict" 1). The syllabus for each subject was also henceforth the responsibility of appointed Syllabus Committees operating under the auspices of the Board of Secondary School Studies and its later iterations. These committees designed, and then put forward for Ministerial approval, revised syllabus documents, including text lists.

The 1945 senior secondary English syllabus was notable for its apparent recalibration of the emphases in secondary English, principally through its heavy focus on the Language component of the syllabus. So much so that for the first time, the Language study requirements preceded, and in terms of content, predominated, in the hitherto more balanced Literature and Language structure of secondary courses. The Language and Literature components comprised the following sub-sections:

Language

   Grammar;

   Spelling;

   Composition – comprising sub-sections: technical skills, sentence construction, paragraph structure, words and vocabulary, phrases and idioms, direct and indirect speech, corrections of errors, simple paraphrasing, note-taking, summarising, letter and telegram writing, and punctuation. (Composition for "more advanced classes" should be encouraged in original and creative writing ... to give expression to their thoughts and feelings);

History of Language;

   Speech Training – comprising sub-sections: voice-training exercises, ear-training exercises, articulation exercises, and simple intonation exercises.

Literature

> introduce the pupil to a selection of suitable literature ... leading to a finer appreciation of its merits;
>
> foster a love of good books and the desire to read not only widely, but wisely;
>
> students should be encouraged to talk and write of books simply and sincerely;
>
> some knowledge of poetic technique and the patterns of verse should be progressively acquired;
>
> while no course in the History of English Literature is prescribed, it is expected that by the end of the fifth year pupils will have some orderly chronological conception of the leading writers and a slight acquaintance with them. (NSW Department of Education 3)

A number of reference books and secondary English text books were listed to assist in teaching the Language component of the syllabus, in clear contradistinction to the forthright advice in the 1911 syllabus to avoid the use of text books. However, the section in the 1945 syllabus on composition, "Original and Creative Writing", stated that:

> Pupils should be trained and encouraged to give graphic expression to their own thoughts and feelings on topics within the range of their own experience. Such efforts, in the earlier years, should include exercises in narrative, descriptive and imaginative composition. Classes more advanced in the course might be encouraged to attempt essays of a reflective, critical, argumentative and biographical character with the emphasis on grace and style in addition to lucidity. (4)

These recommendations convey something of the spirit of English evident in the 1911 syllabus in their nod to a student-centred pedagogy, the experiential and affective, and to creative and imaginative writing. The final examinations, however, continued to occlude the opportunity for students to demonstrate creative and imaginative writing. The questions maintained an emphasis on the discursive essay and lower-order descriptive responses to questions that focused on, for example, grammar, literary terminology and punctuation.

One important change in the 1945 syllabus occurred in the structure of the course of study. For the first time, the syllabus in English did not differentiate content for each year of secondary schooling, as had been the case from 1911 to 1944. Instead, it presented the mandatory content generically, with all students in each year studying the same prescribed subsections of the Language component. The Literature component encouraged wide reading of literature with the aim of fostering "a love of good books and the desire to read not only widely, but also wisely" (NSW Department of Education 5). No specific texts were prescribed for the Literature component in each year, except for the final year in preparation for the LC. Importantly, this change to the prescriptive nature of the text lists, whereby only the texts required for study and examination in the final year of secondary English were prescribed, has remained policy and practice in NSW to the present.

In terms of the rhetorical curriculum, the absence of a prescribed text list for each year of secondary English apart from the final year, and the very general requirements for the Literature component may have offered teachers (and possibly students) more scope and liberty in the selection of texts and their treatment in the junior secondary classroom. The syllabus included the recommendation that

> examples of prose, poetry, and drama, appropriate to the interests and powers of pupils at each stage, should find a place in the literature course of the five years. Adequate representation should be given to Australian literature, both prose and verse. (NSW Department of Education 6)

Advocating the reading of Australian literature in each year of secondary English has likewise become normative, with the current junior English syllabus requiring the study of Australian literature and the Year 12 text list incorporating a range of Australian titles in the Standard, Advanced, English as a Second Language and Extension 1 courses (Board of Studies NSW).

Despite the unshackling of junior secondary English from the sovereignty of prescribed texts lists, the emphasis in the 1945 syllabus and in those that followed through to 1952 placed more stress on grammar, spelling, micro-language skills and the study of and about language than did the 1911 English syllabus (Brock, *History* 53). The heavy emphasis on the Language component of the course in each year and in the final external examinations, reduced the position of the previously more dominant Literature component during this mid-century period.

Senior secondary text lists from 1945-1952

From 1945 to 1952, the secondary English syllabus and examination requirements remained virtually unchanged, apart from some revisions to the text lists. The "Prescribed Books" for 1945 consisted of Shakespeare's *Macbeth* and Cairncross's edited volume, *Eight Essayists*. An additional three texts were listed for "general reading": *English Verse, Old and New* (Mead and Clift, Eds.) Dickens's *David Copperfield* and an anthology, *Short Stories of To-day* (Marriott, Ed.) (NSW Department of Education 24). There was no stated provision for students' own wide reading or selection of texts for study and examination in the LC year.

The examination paper (for the LC Pass course of 1945) included six questions, divided across four sections: A, B, C and D. Sections A and B required students to, for example, paraphrase an unseen passage; rewrite a paragraph inserting punctuation and correcting grammar; compose a Letter to the Editor using five words from a given list; and define literary terms such as personification, allegory and metaphor and provide an example of each. Sections C and D of the papers included an essay on *Macbeth* and essays on the Essays set for study, and essays on the verse, or short stories set for study, or *David Copperfield*.

The Examiner's Report for the 1945 Pass Paper (published in the NSW *Education Gazette*, 1946) reveals the pre-occupation with the functional literacy of students in their responses (spelling, grammar and vocabulary), including in their responses to the literary texts they had studied. The Report bemoaned the generally poor knowledge and understanding of literary terminology. Commenting on the performance of students in rewriting a passage to correct its faulty grammar, the Report noted: "The frequency with which the elementary grammatical blunders in this passage were missed was surprising and disturbing" (201). The "common errors" in spelling were listed at the end of the Report. In the same vein, the Examiner's Report on the 1946 LC examination lamented that: "It is disappointing to find that students imagine they can pass a Leaving Certificate (LC) Examination without being able to write a sentence."[10]

Again, in reporting on the 1948 LC examination, Professor Waldock (then Chief Examiner from the University of Sydney) remarked that "[i]t seems that many pupils are conversant with the correct *theory* of good usage, but from lack of practice or attention continue to commit the old

---

10   See A.J. Waldock. "Leaving Certificate Examination, Examiner's Report, English – Pass Paper 1946" (*NSW Education Gazette* 129).

mistakes ... candidates are still very weak in fundamentals – far too many, for example, do not know what a noun is, let alone an abstract noun."[11] Typically, the Examiner's Reports from this period reported in the main on students' lower-order skills, with meagre commentary on the quality of the students' sustained responses to questions about the prescribed texts.

The English syllabus and senior secondary text lists from 1953–1964

As is evident in the tenor and substance of the Examiners' Reports during the second half of the 1940s there was growing concern about the state of senior English (from 1944 onwards):

> [i]t had become generally accepted by those in positions of authority that by 1952 a crisis had arisen in the way in which the subject was being taught and learned, and that the 1944 syllabus needed to be replaced. A study of the Minutes of the English Syllabus committee, the Minutes of the Board of Secondary Schools and the Chief Examiners' Reports of the Leaving and Intermediate Certificate examinations reveals a general picture of serious dissatisfaction with the standards of English in N.S.W. secondary schools in the period leading up to 1953 and especially from 1948. (Brock, *History* 19)

There had only been one notable revision to the 1911 secondary English syllabus published up to this point: that of 1944, implemented in 1945. The perceived "crisis" in senior English was driven by alarm at the apparent decline in student achievement (which was later proven by Wyndham to be a result of statistical errors, rather than a decline in actual LC results) (Brock, *History*, "Telling the Story", *Who's Doing What?* "The possibilities", "Changes"). Brock's and Wyndham's (1957) comprehensive coverage of this period of reform exposes the intricate back-stage processes and personalities that instigated and directed the development and release of the 1953 senior secondary English syllabus.

In a break with the tradition of English Syllabus Committees developing syllabuses for secondary English, the 1953 syllabus was developed by the

---

11 See A.J. Waldock. "Leaving Certificate Examination, Examiner's Report, English – Pass Paper, 1948", unpaginated, Private Papers of D.B. Bowra stored in the library of the then Sydney Teachers' College, later known as Sydney College of Advanced Education – Institute of Education, and now incorporated within the Faculty of Education and Social Work, The University of Sydney.

English Teachers' Group (ETG). The ETG was the only professional association for English teachers in NSW at that time and was an invitation-only group of males (Brock, *History* 20): "several in the movement had taught in Britain under the influence of the Newbolt Report. The Group consciously pursued a kind of British club tradition" (54). The syllabus produced by the ETG was approved by the Board of Secondary School Studies after it was endorsed with only minor amendments by the English Syllabus Committee (20).

Thus, in noticeable contrast to its immediate predecessors, the refashioned syllabus of 1953 "reflected the Newbolt Committee's conception of what English should be" (54). The Newbolt Report was suffused with a belief in the transformative and democratising powers of ("great") literature, asserting that "English is inseparable from the development of thought" (54). Although the Newbolt Report had been published in 1921, its informing philosophies and its discourses of nation-building found rich expression more than three decades later in the 1953 English syllabus in NSW:

> [i]n its importance to the individual and to society ... the study of English goes far beyond the acquisition of mere skills in the subject. For the pupil, no other form of knowledge can take precedence over a knowledge of English. *In an English speaking community it must always be the central subject of the curriculum*, for it is basic to comprehension and progress is all studies; *it is, moreover, an important influence in the shaping of personality* ... Competence in English is equally important to the community as a whole, for the complex activity of human relationships depends upon co-operation, which is attainable only through language communication. *Civilisation is based on people's awareness of human qualities, problems and values; and there is no better way of gaining this knowledge than through the reading of literature.* (NSW Department of Education 1) (Emphasis added)

In its intention and directives for teaching and learning in English, the content of the 1953 syllabus chimed most audibly with the syllabus of 1911, rather than with that of 1945. This syllabus re-instated literature to a central position, and encoded the familiar features of the Cultural Heritage model. But, as Homer observed, it would be reductionist and simplistic to categorise syllabus documents as being wholly defined by any one model, and the 1953 English syllabus lends weight to this argument. Although the syllabus was clearly inscribing a Cultural Heritage model of English, it also advocated principles of progressive education and what later became known as the Growth model. It encouraged the integration of content and process, reading and writing, thought and feeling, and the imaginative and the cognitive. It consistently stressed the need to ensure all learning and activities in English should be "integrated" rather than fragmented:

> [t]he intention of this Syllabus is to give pupils an experience of their language as a means of transmitting thought. Thought – its expression and its comprehension – is, therefore, the foundation of the Syllabus. This insistence on thought may do little to prevent isolation of the several parts of the Syllabus, and to prevent the teaching of any one part as an end in itself. (NSW Department of Education 1)

The recommendations for pedagogy set out in the extensive "Commentary" in the syllabus were replete with the language and discourses associated with the New Education:

- "All composition should arise from the needs of the pupil, i.e., from the kind of thought the he [sic] needs to express. Much of the pupil's work demands the capacity to expound ideas" (12).
- "Opportunities should be found for personal writing … It must always be remembered that the subjects for all this work (composition) should be drawn from the pupil's own experience" (12).
- "No teaching of Literature can be held to be successful if it has not encouraged the pupil to read for himself [sic]; and if the pupil has been persuaded to take up a book of his [sic] own and read it for pleasure, something has been achieved" (21).
- In selecting books, "the tastes and interests of the pupils must be of considerable influence" (22).
- "Free use should be made of the radio and films" (23).
- "The first aim must be to encourage reading for the pleasure and satisfaction that can be derived from books" (24).
- "The teaching of literature should be directed to an understanding of the work as a whole" (24).
- "Most of the time allotted (to poetry) should be spent in giving the children an enjoyable experience of poetry" (27).
- "Oral discussion should predominate in the treatment of prose" (29).

Of note is the endorsement and inclusion of non-print types of texts in English (radio and films) and pervasive allusions to students' enjoyment and pleasure as a primary aim of the courses. There is no research, however, on the extent to which non-print and non-canonical types of texts or attention to students' enjoyment and pleasure were in fact included in classroom teaching and learning. Although the syllabus recommended (rather than prescribed) the inclusion of a wider range of types of texts, the examinations did not provide any opportunity for responding to these.

The Newbolt conceptualisation of the subject found expression not only in the philosophical orientation of the 1953 syllabus, but also in its revised structure, comprising "A. Expression of Thought; B. The Comprehension of Thought; and C. Literature" (NSW Department of Education 8). The quest to integrate the language and literature components of English was evident in the attempt to harness sections A and B (the development of literacy skills) to the broader study of literary genres, styles, conventions and historical periods. In this regard, the syllabus implied a positioning of the student – in terms of what was later developed by Britton – as "spectator and participant" (209).

Importantly, the 1953 syllabus was accompanied by a major change in the LC examination format. Prior to 1953, the LC examination consisted of one three-hour paper, consisting of Sections A, B, C and, since 1940, D. From 1953, however, there were to be two, two-hour papers: Paper A – Expression and Paper B – Literature. "Sections C and D of the 1945 syllabus in English have been deleted" (NSW Department of Education 3). Paper A – Expression – was created to appease the concerns about the apparent declining standards in English literacy. The revived Literature component of the new syllabus was visibly rendered in the deliberate restructuring of the final examination. Given the pronouncements in the syllabus about the need for an integrated approach to the study of language and literature, the separation of these components for examination exposed a contradictory set of principles at work: the pedagogical advice advocating an integrated approach to teaching and learning appeared to conflict with the structure and focus of the two examination papers. The new format of two, two-hour English papers introduced in 1953 has remained unchanged to the present.

Interestingly, the content of the 1953 text list for the LC English course did not shift dramatically from those of previous years. Students were to study two Shakespearean plays (*Macbeth* and *As You Like It*); a novel (either *Silas Marner* or *The Mill on the Floss* or *Pride and Prejudice* or *All That Swagger*); *Essays of Today* (Pritchard, Ed.); the poetry of Tennyson, Arnold, and

Browning contained in the anthology *Representative English Poems* (Coombs, Ed.); and the poetry of Lawson. Noticeably, the 1953 prescribed text list included the works of two Australian writers: Henry Lawson and Miles Franklin.

In the years from 1953 to 1964, the text lists were periodically revised, with a recycling of titles and included, for example, works by Bunyan, Spenser, Marlowe, Milton, Jonson, Donne, Boswell, Sheridan, Blake, Wordsworth, Coleridge, Keats, Shelley, Byron, Tennyson, Scott, Robert Browning, Dickens, Thackeray, Hopkins, Yeats, Conrad, Shaw and Eliot. As was the case since 1945, texts were not prescribed for junior secondary English. Recommendations were made for suitable types of texts during the junior years, but teachers were encouraged to select materials on the basis of their suitability for their specific cohort of students. The practice of providing recommendations rather than prescribing texts for study in junior secondary English persists to the present in NSW, affording teachers and students a potentially less heavily regulated and standardised experience of the subject in the enacted curriculum.

Conclusion

In the preceding discussion we have sought to explore the "what, where and when" of literary study in senior secondary English in New South Wales up to 1964. From the outset we proposed that the text lists, treated in isolation from the composite of mandatory curriculum documents and relevant historical research, can function only as two-dimensional characters in the broader narrative of the subject's history. Having collated evidence from the ALIAS database about the categories and titles of texts set for senior secondary study, we have been equally interested in pursuing the question of *why* selected texts, discourses and beliefs were consistently valued and endorsed in the localised setting of NSW.

From the comparative analysis presented in this chapter, a number of conclusions can be drawn about the authoritative status of text lists in the history of senior secondary English in NSW. The most conspicuous of these is the tightly prescribed nature of the lists. They offered teachers and students almost no leeway in selecting what would be studied, when and how it would be studied, or how it would be examined. As powerful mechanisms for control, the lists operated in tandem with external examination programs that, like the syllabus documents and the lists themselves, were centrally developed and carefully regulated through systems that privileged a particular set of assumptions, ideologies and hegemonic discourses about what would count as literature, literary study and the "well educated" citizen (NSW Department of Public Instruction iv). These proved remarkably durable throughout the first six decades of the twentieth century. Freighted as it was with a cultural, ideological and emotional economy, subject English became a site for staging a broader project of nation-building and for the pursuit of a vision of a common culture, common language and common literacy practices.

Just as visible as the prescriptive nature of the lists and their regulatory function was the persistence of British canonical literature in the titles mandated for study. Teachers and students played little if any role in "the process of canon formation" (Guillory 45): the syllabus, text lists and examinations represented a predominantly cultural heritage model of the subject, with the text lists reproducing the canon that was flourishing in university undergraduate English courses both locally, nationally and internationally. Likewise, the questions for the Leaving Certificate examination (which operated as a powerful arbiter of university entrance and elite social closure) reflected the prevailing literary critical models of university English departments. The influence of tertiary versions of subject English was also apparent in the structure of the English syllabus at senior secondary level, organised as it was in terms of the study of Literature and Language. Although the rhetorical curriculum typically expressed the aim of integrating these two, often competing, dimensions the examination structure and questions generally militated against this aim.

Ironically, the senior secondary text lists and examinations from this period compelled students to respond to and appreciate the artistic, imaginative work of past poets, authors, dramatists and other writers, but simultaneously rendered invisible (and therefore of minimal status and little official value) the student's own artistic and imaginative life. For students and teachers, the experience of subject English at senior secondary level in NSW could be characterised as one of deference to a version of the cultural past as it was inscribed in the canonical literature of the time. In making this observation, we are not disputing the validity of that cultural past as worthy of study – then or now. Rather, the analysis of the text lists from this historical period has underlined the extent to which the lists and examinations were instrumental in imprinting and advancing the interests of some more powerful social groups at the expense of others. In partnership at the centre of this educational and cultural mission were two formidable protagonists: the prescribed text list and the compulsory examination.

Works Cited

Analysis of Literature in Australian Schools Database (ALIAS). www.australiancommonreader.com/syllabus. Web. 20 November 2014.

Arnold, Matthew. *Culture and Anarchy: An essay in political and social criticism*. 1869. Oxford: Project Gutenberg. Web. 15 June 2013.

Ball, Stephen J. "Competition and conflict in the teaching of English: A socio-historical analysis". *Journal of Curriculum Studies* 14 (1982): 1–28. Print.

———. "English since 1906". *Social Histories of the Secondary Curriculum: Subjects for study*. Ed. Ivor F. Goodson. Lewes, United Kingdom: The Falmer Press, 1985. 53–88. Print.

———, Alex Kenny, and David Gardiner. "Literacy, politics and the teaching of English". *Bringing English to Order: The history and politics of a school subject*. Ed. Ivor F. Goodson, and Peter Medway. London: The Falmer Press, 1990. 47–86. Print.

———, and Colin Lacey. "Revisiting subject disciplines as the opportunity for group action: A measured critique of subject subcultures". *The Subjects in Question*. Ed. L.S. Siskin and J.W. Little. New York: Teachers College Press, 1995. 95–122. Print.

Barcan, Alan. *Two Centuries of Education in New South Wales*. Sydney: NSW University Press, 1988. Print.

Beavis, Catherine. "Twenty first century literature: Opportunities, changes and challenges". *The International Handbook of English, Language and Literacy Teaching*. Ed. Dominic Wyse, Richard Andrews and James Hoffman. London: Routledge/Taylor and Francis, 2010. 33–44. Print.

Biesta, Gert. "Becoming world-wise: An educational perspective on the rhetorical curriculum". *Journal of Curriculum Studies* 44.6 (2012): 815–826. Print.

Board of Senior School Studies NSW English. *(Syllabus and Commentary) Forms V and VI: First, Second and Third Levels*. Sydney: NSW Government Printer, 1965. Print.

Board of Studies NSW. *English Stage 6 Syllabus*. Sydney: Board of Studies NSW, 1999. Print.

Brannigan, John. *New Historicism and Cultural Materialism*. London: Palgrave Macmillan, 1998. Print.

Britton, James. "What's the use? A schematic account of language functions". *Educational Review* 23.3 (1971): 205–19. Print.

Brock, Paul. "Changes in the English syllabus in N.S.W. Australia: Can any American voices be heard?" *English Journal* 73.3 (1984b): 53–58. Print.

———. A History of the Development of English Syllabuses in New South Wales Secondary Education, 1953–1976: A 'continuum' or a 'series of new beginnings'? Unpublished PhD thesis. Armidale: University of New England, 1984. Print.

———. "The possibilities of Kuhnian paradigmatic shift in curriculum change: A case study – Higher School Certificate English in NSW". *Curriculum Perspectives* 2.1 (1985): 31–36. Print.

———. "Processes involved in curriculum change: A case study of New South Wales, Australia". Ed. Roslyn Arnold. *Timely Voices: English teaching in the eighties*. Melbourne: Oxford University Press, 1983. 174–186. Print.

———. "The struggle for curriculum development in English Studies with special reference to New South Wales". *Australian and New Zealand History of Education Society (ANZHES) Journal* II.1 (1982): 18–33. Print.

———. "Some aspects of secondary English education in Australia". *Working Papers in Australian Studies*. 3. London: Institute of Commonwealth Studies, University of London, 1986. Print.

———. "Telling the story of the NSW secondary English curriculum: 1950–1965". *Teaching the English Subjects: Essays on English curriculum and history in Australian schooling*. Ed. Bill Green and Catherine Beavis. Geelong: Deakin University Press, 1996. 40–70. Print.

———. Who's Doing What? The senior English curriculum in Australian schools. Norwood: AATE, 1987. Print.

Campbell, Craig and Geoffrey Sherington. *The Comprehensive Public High School: Historical perspectives*. New York: Palgrave Macmillan, 2013. Print.

Carter, Don. The Influence of Romanticism on the NSW Stage 6 English Syllabus: Interwoven storylines and the search for a unifying narrative. Unpublished PhD thesis. Sydney: The University of Sydney, 2012. Print.

Cormack, Phil. "English/literacy and anxiety about the future: A case-study from the turn of the 20th century". Paper presented at the *Biennial Meeting of the International Federation for the Teaching of English* (2003). Melbourne, Australia, July 5–8.

———. "Tracking local curriculum histories: The plural forms of subject English. *Changing English* 15.3 (2008): 275–291. Print.

Crane, Allan Robert and William George Walker. *Peter Board: His contribution to the development of education in New South Wales*. Melbourne: ACER, 1957. Print.

Gallagher, S. V. "Contingencies and intersections: The formation of pedagogical canons". *Pedagogy* 1 (2001): 53–67. Print.

Goffman, Erving. *The Presentation of Self in Everyday Life*. New York: Doubleday, 1959. Print.

Goodson, Ivor F. "Towards curriculum history". *Social Histories of the Secondary Curriculum: Subjects for study*. Ed. Ivor F. Goodson. London: The Falmer Press, 1985. Print.

———, and Peter Medway. *Bringing English to Order: The history and politics of a school subject*. United Kingdom: Routledge, 1990. Print.

Goodwyn, Andrew. "The status of literature: English teaching and the condition of literature teaching in schools". *English in Education* 46.3 (2012): 212–227. Print.

Green, Bill and Catherine Beavis, eds. *Teaching the English Subjects: Essays on English curriculum history and Australian schooling*. Geelong, VIC: Deakin University Press, 1996. Print.

———, and Phil Cormack. "Curriculum history, 'English' and the New Education; or, installing the Empire of English?" *Pedagogy, Culture and Society* 16.3 (2008): 253–67. Print.

Guillory, John. "Canon, syllabus, list: A note on the pedagogic imaginary". *Transition* 52 (1991): 36–54. Print.

Homer, David. Fifty Years of Purpose and Precept in English Teaching 1921–1971: An overview with special reference to the teaching of poetry in the early secondary years. University of Melbourne: Unpublished Master of Education thesis. 1973. Print.

Hughes, John and Paul Brock. *Reform and Resistance in NSW Public Education: Six attempts at major reform, 1905–1995*. Sydney: State of New South Wales (Department of Education and Training), 2008. Print.

Hunter, Ian. "Culture, education and English: Building the principal scene of the real life of children". *Economy and Society* 16.4 (1987): 568–588. Print.

Manuel, Jacqueline. "Making its debut: What teachers think of the new Higher School Certificate English syllabus in New South Wales – report of a survey of reachers of English in NSW government secondary schools". *English in Australia* 134 (2002): 67–77. Print.

———, and Paul Brock. "W(h)ither the place of literature?: Two momentous reforms in the NSW senior secondary English curriculum". *English in Australia* 136 (2003): 1–18. Print.

Mathieson, Margaret. *The Preachers of Culture: A study of English and its teachers*. London: George Allen and Unwin, 1975. Print.

Mellor, Bronwyn, Marnie O'Neill, and Annette Patterson. "Re-reading Literature teaching". Ed. Jack Thomson. *Reconstructing Literature Teaching: New essays on the teaching of Literature*. Norwood: AATE, 1992. 40–55. Print.

Michaels, Wendy. The Constitution of the Subject English in New South Wales Senior English Syllabus Documents 1953–1994. Unpublished PhD Thesis. Sydney: Macquarie University, 2001. Print.

Newbolt, Harold. The Teaching of English in England: Being the report of the Departmental Committee appointed by the President of the Board of Education to inquire into the position of English in the educational system of England. London: HMSO, 1921. Print.

New South Wales Department of Education. *Courses of Study for High Schools*. Sydney: NSW Department of Education, 1940, Print.

———. *Courses of Study for High Schools*. Sydney: NSW Department of Education, 1945. Print.

———. *Courses of Study for High Schools*. Sydney: NSW Department of Education, 1939. Print.

———. *Syllabus in English*. Sydney: NSW Department of Education, 1953. Print.

New South Wales Department of Public Instruction. *Courses of Study for High Schools*. Sydney: NSW Department of Public Instruction, 1911. Print.

New South Wales *Education Gazette*. Sydney: Government Printer, 1905. Print.

Parkin, Frank. *Marxism and Class Theory: A bourgeois critique*. London: Tavistock, 1979. Print.

Pope, Rob. *The English Studies Book: An introduction to language, literature and culture*. 2nd ed. London: Routledge, 2002. Print.

Reid, Ian. "The persistent pedagogy of 'growth'". *English Teachers at Work: Narratives, counter-narratives and arguments*. Eds. Brenton Doecke, David Homer and Helen Nixon. Kent Town: AATE/Wakefield Press, 2003. 97–108. Print.

———. *The Making of Literature: Texts, contexts and classroom practices*. Norwood: AATE., 1984. Print.

———. "Wordsworth institutionalised: The shaping of an educational ideology". *History of Education, Journal of the History of Education Society* 31.1 (2002): 15–37. Print.

Rosser, Gary. Disciplining Literature: Higher School Certificate prescribed texts for English: 1965–1995. Unpublished PhD thesis. University of Wollongong, 2000. Print.

Sawyer, Wayne. "Language, literature and lost opportunities: 'Growth' as a defining episode in the history of English". *Re-Visioning English Education: Imagination, innovation, creativity*. Eds. Jacqueline Manuel et al. Putney: Phoenix Education, 2009a. Print.

———. "The Growth model of English". Susanne Gannon, Mark Howie and Wayne Sawyer. *Charged with Meaning: Reviewing English*. 3rd ed. 2009b. Putney: Phoenix Education. 19–30. Print.

———. Simply Growth?: A study of selected episodes in the history of Years 7–10 English in New South Wales. Unpublished PhD Thesis. University of Western Sydney, 2002. Print.

Selleck, Richard J. W. *The New Education: The English background 1870–1914*. Melbourne: Pitman, 1968. Print.
Shayer, David. *The Teaching of English in Schools 1900–1970*. London and Boston: Routledge and Kegan Paul, 1972. Print.
Tyler, D. and L. Johnson. "Helpful histories". *History of Education Review* 20.2 (1991): 1–8. Print.
Waldock, A.J. Leaving Certificate Examination, Examiner's report, English – Pass Paper 1946, *NSW Education Gazette*, 1 April, 129, 1947. Print.
Wyndham, Harold. S. (Sir). Report of the Committee Appointed to Survey Secondary Education in New South Wales. Sydney: Government Printer, 1957. Print.
Winterson, Jeanette. Opening address at the Sydney Writers' Festival. Sydney: Sydney Opera House. May 20, 2008.

Chapter Six

PROVENANCE AND TRANSFORMATION

The history of prescribed text lists in senior secondary English in NSW, 1965–2005[1]

Jacqueline Manuel and Don Carter

> History is the analysis and interpretation of the human past that enables us to study continuity and change over time ... It is an act of both investigation and imagination ... a means to understand the past and present ... Historical knowledge is a pre-requisite for understanding the world in which we live. History is *magister vitae*, "teacher of life". (Siena College)

Introduction

In the previous chapter, we explored the senior secondary text lists from 1911 to 1964, drawing on the curriculum materials contained in the Analysis of Literature in Australian Schools (ALIAS) database, along with secondary sources relevant to this field of inquiry.[2] As identified in that

---

[1] This chapter extends the discussion presented in the previous chapter. For a more detailed explication of the methodology and critical approach to the analysis of texts in both chapters, refer to the previous chapter.

[2] See Ball; Ball, Kenny and Gardiner; Ball and Lacey; Barcan; Brock; Carter; Cormack 2008; Goodson and Medway; Green and Beavis; Manuel; Manuel and Brock; Mathieson; Michaels; Reid, "Wordsworth Institutionalised"; Rosser; Sawyer; Selleck; Shayer.

discussion, there has been a small handful of pivotal moments of reform in a century of senior secondary English curriculum in NSW. These occurred in 1945, 1953, 1965, 1974 and 1999.[3] Prior to 1965, the senior secondary English syllabus culminated in the qualification of the Leaving Certificate (LC) after five years of secondary schooling. With the introduction of the Wyndham Scheme (beginning with Form I in 1962 and examined for the first time in 1967), the LC was replaced by the Higher School Certificate (HSC). Secondary schooling was extended by one year, with this new HSC qualification awarded to students who successfully completed six years of secondary schooling. This structure of four years of junior secondary schooling followed by two years of senior secondary schooling is the model that continues to the present day. For this reason, our discussion here concentrates on the senior secondary English text lists and associated primary sources for the HSC from its formal endorsement in 1965 to 2005 (the last set of documents contained in the ALIAS database).

In this chapter we are interested in charting the patterns of "continuity and change" (Siena College) in the NSW text lists and interpreting the extent to which these lists have both perpetuated and challenged the orthodoxies of senior secondary English – orthodoxies that had their origins in the early twentieth-century versions of the subject in NSW.

Senior secondary English text lists up to 1964

Based on evidence in the ALIAS database, it may be the case that senior English text lists from other Australian states and territories "never amount to predictably representative subsets of any recognisable literary canon at any given historical moment" (see Chapter One of this collection). From the analysis of the senior secondary text lists in the previous chapter, however, it is apparent that in this state, the lists disclose an enduring orientation to a Cultural Heritage model of English which was as transparent as it was consistent during the first half of the twentieth century. From 1911, the prescribed lists not only preferenced British canonical literature – they also inscribed a conceptualisation of the subject that was bound up with ideologies of the "well educated" (NSW Department of Public Instruction iv) citizen, nation-building and the role of literary study in this broader cultural project (Cormack). The text lists, yoked as they were from the outset to high-stakes external examinations and matriculation, became

---

3   See Brock, *A History of English Syllabuses*; Rosser.

increasingly determinant in shaping and reproducing certain "epistemic assumptions" (Reid, "Romantic Ideologies" 32) and "constitutive preoccupations" (24). Principal among these was an Arnoldian and Newbolt-inspired belief in the centrality of literature and literary study as a "form of education in human relations" which would contribute to "the development of human character" (Newbolt 20, 21).

By the 1960s the text lists for senior secondary English in NSW had become institutionalised in terms of both their contents and their status. They closely prescribed the "what and when" of teaching and learning in senior English by mandating the study of specific texts within the categories of fiction, drama, Shakespearean drama, non-fiction and poetry. The mandatory requirements were enforced through the external examination system which, like the texts lists themselves, was controlled by small groups of university academics or individual academics chiefly from the English Department at the University of Sydney (Brock, *History*).

Typically, English syllabus documents in the first decades of the twentieth century included recommendations for pedagogy and advice to teachers about the need to ensure students' experience of English was personally meaningful and enjoyable. The 1945 syllabus, for example, directed teachers to:

> introduce the pupil to a selection of suitable literature ... leading to a finer appreciation of its merits;
>
> foster a love of good books and the desire to read not only widely, but wisely;
>
> students should be encouraged to talk and write of books simply and sincerely.
>
> (NSW Department of Education, Courses)

In practice, however, the stringent examination requirements left little room to realise the aims laid down in the rhetorical curriculum. During this historical period the prescribed text lists and the examinations afforded almost no latitude for teachers to choose the texts they would teach in the final year of English, nor to experiment with alternative pedagogies. There were even fewer opportunities for students to exercise any degree of personal choice in what they were to read and how they were to read it.

Although the revised syllabus of 1953 embraced the discourses and philosophies of Progressive education that had been represented so fervently in the 1921 Newbolt Report, the attempts to re-imagine subject English in the senior years in NSW were ultimately stifled by normative practices at the service of a seemingly impermeable examination regime. Through their powerful regulatory functions, the text lists and the final examinations determined the purpose of subject English in senior secondary classrooms throughout the early decades of the twentieth century.

Despite the mid-century reforms to the senior English syllabus there was subsequent and intensifying concern about the suitability of the tertiary-derived senior English courses for the full range of students entering the senior years, at least a percentage of whom did not intend to matriculate to university. Hence, during the 1950s the wheels of reform to secondary education and curriculum in NSW were once again set in motion and would culminate with the introduction of what is now referred to as the Wyndham Scheme. Substantial reform of the secondary curriculum took place under the stewardship of Harold Wyndham, who was appointed as Director-General of Education in 1952. Of this period, Hughes and Brock note that "[i]n the 1950s the pressures of a burgeoning student population, increased retention, concerns about student 'wastage' ... and the emergence of a more prosperous economic climate, combined to enable the realisation of proposals that had previously not been enacted" (59). A confluence of forces was the catalyst for the 1957 Wyndham Report, the final recommendations of which were eventually approved with the *Education Act* of 1961.[4]

The first HSC senior secondary English courses

In 1962, the new English syllabus for Form I came into effect with syllabuses for Forms II, III and IV following in successive years. The senior secondary syllabus for Forms V and VI, along with the text lists for Form VI, were published in 1965 and implemented in 1966. The inaugural Higher School Certificate (HSC) examinations occurred in 1967, maintaining the post-1953 structure of two, two-hour English papers (Paper A: Expression and Paper B: Literature) (NSW Department of Education).

By 1966, when the first cohort of students was undertaking Form V under the Wyndham Scheme, the senior secondary English syllabus had moved from a single course for the Leaving Certificate to a Higher School Certificate English subject with three courses to "cater for the range of

---

4   For a more detailed coverage of the 1950s and 1960s reforms see, for example, Brock, and Hughes and Brock.

ability among students" (Wilkes 8). The new HSC English curriculum was organised into three tiered courses, each with its own syllabus, text list and examination requirements. The Third Level, Second Level and First Level English courses were designed to cater for a far more differentiated cohort of students. The Third Level course was intended for the student "whose main interests and abilities may lie in other subjects" and who "should be able to express themselves effectively in English and comprehend it in its spoken and written forms" (NSW Department of Education 1965 9). The syllabus for this course, undertaken by a majority of students entering the senior years, was "an integrated course in the reading, writing and speaking of English" (1). Its objectives were "to develop students' ability to understand and respond to good literature within the range of their competence and interests, and to improve their skills in comprehension and in oral and written expression" (1). Second Level catered to the student who had "attained a good knowledge and content" with "some ability in this subject" (10). The greater emphasis on the study of literature in this course was underscored by a distinctly Leavisite set of epistemic assumptions about the purpose of and approach to literary study:

> The English syllabus at Second Level is a syllabus in language and literature. Although the requirements of each part are set out separately, there is no rigid division between them, and every opportunity should be taken of making one illuminate the other. While no allocation of time to the different parts of the syllabus is prescribed, it is envisaged that the literature work might occupy 75% of the course, and the language work 25%.
>
> The aims of the course are to:
>
> develop and refine individual response to literature;
>
> develop ability to recognise, describe and assess qualities of thought and feeling expressed in various forms of literature; and
>
> develop an understanding of literature of other ages.
>
> (NSW Department of Education 5)

Even though the Second Level course – as well as the First Level – was organised into literature and language sections, with a stress on the need for an integrated treatment of both in the classroom, the recommended allocation of 75 per cent of class time to literary study revealed the implicit values at work in this syllabus. The dominance of literary study for the more able students of English was substantiated through direct appropriations of the discourses of the Cambridge School (Brock, *History*). Even more forcefully, the First Level course elevated the role of literary study such that it was distinguished from the other two courses in two ways: "by the larger area traversed, and by the depth and complexity of the treatment envisaged" (NSW Department of Education 13). This was the course reserved the gifted student who had "attained a good knowledge and content" at an advanced level (13).

In its structuring of senior English into Language and Literature sections, the new HSC Second and First Level courses preserved a key aspect of the tradition established by its predecessors. It departed from that tradition, however, through a number of key amendments. The two higher-level courses ramped up the attention to canonical literary study with a more pronounced endorsement of the then ascendant Leavisite literary critical orientation to reading and response. Further, there was a marked increase in the *quantity* of texts required for study in the Literature component of both courses. This was especially so in the First Level, Form VI course in which students were to study: four novels; four poets; two plays; two Shakespearean plays; and four language topics (NSW Department of Education 15).

Formulating senior secondary English text lists for the new HSC

At no other point in the history of senior secondary English in NSW had the text requirements been so rigorous as they were in 1965: 12 texts to be studied and examined in the First Level course in the HSC year; nine in Second Level; and five in Third Level. In addition to literary study, each course included a language study component. The three categories of literature for mandatory study in the Literature section of each course were drama, fiction and poetry. First Level and Second Level also mandated the study of Shakespearean drama, and Third Level required the study of nonfiction (essays) in addition to the core mandatory genres. The compulsory study of Shakespearean drama has been a feature of the more demanding senior English courses from 1965 to the present. In Third Level, the study of a Shakespearean drama was optional and continued to be optional in all later equivalent senior English courses (such as, for example, HSC Standard English in 1999).

The decision to mandate the study of Shakespeare in only the higher-level courses encoded a particular set of assumptions and biases about what kinds of literature were deemed appropriate for only the more gifted students of English. Similarly, the decision to remove the study of essays from the prescribed lists for Second and First Levels (whilst retaining this category for Third Level) revealed the Syllabus Committee's preconceptions about the type of student fit for each course and the type of literature that would be most suitable for different "classes" of student based on assumptions about the their vocational pathways. The role of literature as a core defining element of subject English permeated each of the three courses, with the points of differentiation occurring in the quantity, type and titles of texts prescribed and the recommended portion of class time to be spent on literary study.

One of the more significant changes in senior English was the compulsory study of poetry as a core type of text for all courses. Prior to 1965, poetry could be avoided due to a loophole in the structure of the LC examinations (Brock, *History*). From 1965 to the present, the study of prescribed poetry has remained compulsory for all English courses, as has the privileging of drama and fiction. Likewise, the legacy of listing a range of titles in each literary category, from which the teacher had to select the required number of texts for study, became a feature of all successive prescribed text lists in NSW up to and beyond 2005.

In the rhetorical curriculum the quantity of texts in each category may have appeared, at first glance, to have offered teachers some degree of professional freedom in selecting and teaching texts for their particular classes. Although there was a range of titles within the mandatory categories of poetry, fiction and drama, the Shakespearean drama was set for all students, reflecting the "top-down" influence of the university sector in determining what would count as worthy of study in secondary English.

The influence of the University of Sydney on the 1965 senior secondary English syllabus and text lists

During the period of development of the 1965 senior secondary English syllabus, Professor G.A. Wilkes (who held the Chair in Australian Literature at the University of Sydney), was appointed Chair of the HSC English Syllabus Committee. Wilkes informed his departmental academic colleagues at the University that the new HSC syllabus, bibliography and texts lists "meant that much of what had usually been covered in the English I course at the University would now be handed over to schools" (Brock, *History* 165). In addition, virtually all of the 45 books cited in a bibliography designed to assist students in the language component of the syllabus were used in undergraduate courses at the University.

The literature and the approach to literary study recommended in each of the three HSC English courses was driven by the influence of Professor Sam Goldberg (Challis Chair and Head of the University of Sydney's Department of English). Goldberg was a committed though not an uncritical Leavisite (Brock, *History*). Goldberg had objected to what he saw to be the "prevailing emphasis in the Leaving Certificate examinations in English upon acquiring mere *knowledge about* literature and literary genres" (19). He was reacting against what he believed was the "straight-jacketing and rather stultifying application of the Cultural Heritage model of English, as it had become formularised in the Leaving Certificate examination" (23). Goldberg's influence meant that the new HSC English syllabus was underpinned by the Cambridge English paradigm. As a result there was a stated emphasis on the development of the student's honest personal response to the text through sensitive and discriminating reading. This was also in tune with the concept of English that was then flourishing amongst the English staff at Sydney Teachers' College (18). The syllabus cautioned against formulaic pedagogy that focused on isolated features such as plot, character and setting at the expense of understanding how the interrelationships between these and other factors contributed to the total meaning of the work, or its "organic unity".

The syllabus retained a substantial section on the study of the English language that the Leavisite advocates on the English Syllabus Committee were unable to jettison. Indeed, from the 1911 English syllabus through to the 1965 English syllabus the conceptualisation of English preserved, with varying degrees of emphasis, this bipartite structure of English as the study of literature and language. In 1976, however, the Language section of the syllabus was removed completely when the then English Syllabus Committee argued that "the separate Literature and Language components forced students to separate two aspects of English artificially. Literature and language, it was decided, should be integrated, not separated" (Brock, *History* 57) thus reinforcing a stated but not structurally manifested aim of both the 1953 and 1965 English syllabuses.

It is important to note that during this period, the NSW Board of Secondary School Studies (established in 1932) was dissolved in 1961. In its place, two separate boards were established: the Secondary Schools Board (1961–1987) and the Board of Senior School Studies (1961–1987). One of the consequences of this separation of responsibility for junior secondary and senior secondary curriculum, policy and examinations was the steady differentiation in conceptualisations of junior secondary English and senior secondary English. While junior secondary English was far more responsive to progressive definitions of the subject (post-Dartmouth), the senior secondary English syllabus remained remarkably immune to the stream of theoretical, pedagogical and research-based advances occurring during the second half of the twentieth century (Brock, *History*; "Telling the Story", "Changes in the English Syllabus"; Sawyer).

As evidence of the relative impermeability of senior English to the shifts in the field, both locally and internationally, there was little scope in the HSC for students' creative and imaginative writing. The more demanding First and Second Level courses and examinations almost exclusively demanded sustained analytical and interpretive writing and response to literature, with students' own imaginative writing neither encouraged nor legitimised. Despite the overtures encouraging students' honest personal response, the conceptualisation of English continued to be characterised by a "gallery" approach of literary study (Reid, *Making*). Given the weight of content in these courses (with, for example, the requirement for First Level students to study 12 texts and four language topics in a single year), students' imaginative and other non-examinable writing could be allocated modest, if any, attention in the classroom.

The content of the 1965 senior secondary English text lists

Each of the three senior English courses had its own text list and recommendations for pedagogical approaches. The text lists for each course constituted predominantly British canonical literature, with a sprinkling of Australian and North American titles throughout each course, such as, for example, White's *Voss*, Judith Wright's poetry, Twain's *Huckleberry Finn*, Miller's *The Crucible* and *Death of a Salesman*, Salinger's *Catcher in the Rye*, Horne's *The Lucky Country*, and Seymour's *The One Day of the Year* (NSW Department of Education 1–6).

As alluded to earlier, the vast majority of texts set for study in each of the three 1965 HSC were on reading lists in the first, second and third years of the undergraduate English program at the University of Sydney. The bulk of the texts had their origin in the Cambridge 'Tripos': the 'canon' of texts authorised by *The Great Tradition*, *The Common Pursuit*, and the many articles published over the years in *Scrutiny* (1932–1953). Prominent among these favoured writers were:

> Poetry: Chaucer, Donne, Milton, Pope, Hopkins, T. S. Eliot
>
> Fiction: *Joseph Andrews, Emma, Wuthering Heights, Tess of the d'Urbervilles, Sons and Lovers, Lord of the Flies*
>
> Drama: *Oedipus Rex, Saint Joan, Murder in the Cathedral, Waiting for Godot*
>
> Shakespearean drama: *Othello* and *King Lear*.

It is reasonable to conclude that the candidates for the newly instituted HSC, like those who went before them, experienced a predominantly Cultural Heritage conceptualisation of the subject, fortified by the Arnoldian, Newbolt and Cambridge English vision of mainly British canonical literature as the reservoir of moral, ethical, spiritual, intellectual and social capital. The prescribed text lists did not include any popular texts, media or film of the time, although the syllabus encouraged the use of film and media in the classroom. Again, as in the 1953 syllabus, the recommendations for broadening the types of texts to be experienced in the classroom were not formally sanctioned since these types of texts were not included in the prescribed lists or examinations: the study of poetry, fiction and drama was the centre of gravity of the subject.

The first HSC English examinations

In 1967 the first cohort of "Wyndham" Form VI students sat for the HSC examinations. First, Second and Third Level courses were examined separately; there was no common component, thus retaining the principle in operation since 1911. While the syllabus itself invited the honest personal response of students to the prescribed texts, the examination questions reproduced the dominant Leavisite critical paradigm. The disjunction between the discourses of the syllabus and the assumptions embedded in the examinations revealed what Sinfield described as an inherent contradiction between the rhetorical and enacted curriculum: "questions which appear to invite a personal response are often all the more tyrannical; candidates are invited to interrogate their experience to discover a response which has in actuality been learnt" (Sinfield 132).

Although the 1965 syllabus, and those that followed it, promoted the values of individual engagement with and responses to texts in personally meaningful ways, for the examination students were expected to "produce, under pressure of time and circumstance, the contrived effect of sensitive, thoughtful spontaneity" (Mares qtd. in Mellor, O'Neill and Patterson 41). The syllabus intention to liberate literary study from the formulaic, derivative approaches that ultimately inhibited any genuine personal response to a text was palpably undermined by the demands of the examination and the examination questions. As Mellor, O'Neill and Patterson observed, literary study and reading continued to be "constructed as a private and personal matter" which encouraged "students to regard their responses as personal and individual – yet paradoxically universal – and ideologically neutral" (41).

Historically, the Wyndham Scheme constituted a watershed moment in curriculum reform in NSW secondary education. The signature innovations in curriculum design, the vision of a more inclusive curriculum to meet the needs of an expanded and expanding student population, and the concerted attempts democratise the processes of curriculum formation were features of this period of reform. In terms of the conceptualisation of senior English, however, the ghosts of the previous four decades hovered – in the text lists, the examinations and the consequent imperatives of classroom practice and literary study. Both the text lists and the examinations acquired an even more authoritative status through their contrapuntal orchestration of the "what, when, where and how" of senior secondary English.

HSC English syllabuses and text lists from the 1970s to 1990s

From the first HSC examinations in 1967 through to the early 1970s, there were minor amendments to the senior English curriculum. In 1974, the HSC English courses, along with courses in all other subjects, were rebadged: Third Level became 2 Unit A (renamed 2 Unit General in 1979); Second Level became 2 Unit; and First Level became 2 Unit/3 Unit Related. This change occurred in order to streamline the matriculation process, with all students required to complete a minimum of 10 units of study, two of which had to be English. Apart from the change in nomenclature, the three senior English courses deviated little from the model of English set out in the First, Second and Third Level courses of the original HSC in 1965. Differentiation between the courses once again occurred through the relative emphasis on the study of literary texts and the depth and nature of critical inquiry.

As was the case in the 1965 syllabus, the development of the critical capacity of students was seen to be more appropriate for those undertaking the higher level courses: 2 Unit Related and 3 Unit. The 2 Unit General course, designed for the majority of students, promoted "enjoyment" and "understanding" of texts, with the teacher encouraging students to read widely for pleasure and insight, rather than developing the capacity for critical analysis. The hierarchical structure of the senior English courses revealed the continuation of the conceptualisation of the subject at this "general" (formerly Third) level course. The move to broaden the theoretical and pedagogical approach to senior English in the lower-level "general" course, whilst continuing to preserve the Cultural Heritage and Leavisite emphases in the higher-level courses, encoded assumptions about the nature of students and the purpose of the subject. It was assumed that more able students were to be trained in the art of discernment and literary analysis, whereas the less able students were encouraged to enjoy their studies and extend the use of their imagination. The implication here was that the imaginative dimensions of education were synonymous with lower-order learning or junior secondary English and were therefore regarded as somewhat frivolous and not appropriate within the more serious academic realm of literary appreciation and criticism in the senior years.

In their focus on fostering an appreciation for literature, the higher-level courses positioned the student primarily as a "spectator" (Britton). The 2 Unit General course provided the most radical departure from this traditional model. In addition to the study of fiction, poetry and drama was a new component called the "Topic Area" that allowed for a more thematic approach to texts. This course also encouraged approaches to writing, reading and response that were by now mainstream in the 7–10 English syllabus, such as, for example, "imaginative recreation" (Adams). However, the higher-level courses – 2 Unit and 3 Unit – remained anchored in a Leavisite model of literary study.

There was no provision in these senior courses for students to select texts for study in their final year. Students undertaking the 2 Unit/3 Unit course were required to study a total of seven prescribed texts: two poets (from a list of ten) two novels (from a list of 12) one Shakespearean drama and two additional plays (selected from a list of eight). Indicative of the sustained, century-long influence of the Cultural Heritage model in the senior years, the higher-level courses stipulated that for both poetry and fiction: "Either ONE may be chosen from the pre-twentieth century and

ONE from the twentieth century; OR TWO may be chosen from the pre-twentieth century" (Board of Studies NSW 1999 50). Thus, despite the increase in titles listed in the text lists since 1965, the options for text selection continued to be circumscribed by these kinds of increasingly restrictive regulations.

The text lists from 1965 to the 1980s continued to draw on staples from the British canon but also showed a steady increase in the representation of Australian writing from, for example, Rosemary Dobson, Lee Cataldi, Robert Gray, John Tranter, Jack Davis, Bruce Dawe, Tim Winton, Dorothy Hewett, David Malouf, Louis Nowra, David Williamson, and Peter Goldsworthy.

HSC English in the late 1980s and the 1990s

According to Meiers and Sawyer, English in the 1980s appeared to be unified by a kind of grand theory or grand narrative, underpinned and nourished by the ubiquity of the Personal Growth model in the junior secondary English syllabus. However, the relative stability of that decade gave way to robust "theory debates" emanating from the academy that continued into the 1990s. These debates spilled over into the secondary school English curriculum. Characteristic of this period was a heightened interest in the identity of English (at both the tertiary and secondary school levels) with competing critical theories, literary theories and, significantly, the increasing authority of constructivist models of teaching and learning vying for ascendancy. The semblance of a unifying narrative of the subject was arguably no longer evident (Meiers and Sawyer).

During the late 1980s and the early 1990s a number of contextual forces – such as, for instance, Australia's changing social and economic circumstances, a more diversified student population resulting from immigration, alongside high youth unemployment – rendered the Wyndham Scheme senior English courses "insufficient for, and ill-suited to the needs, interest and capacities of a significant proportion of their candidature in the 1990s" (Manuel 67–68). In addition, by the early 1990s there had been a marked decline in enrolments in the more academically rigorous HSC courses, including the HSC English courses.[5] This decline was apparent not only

---

5   Between 1991 and 1996, for example, there had been a dramatic decline in enrolments in 3 Unit and 2 Unit Related courses: the candidature in these two English courses declined by nearly 50 per cent. During these years, the 2 Unit Related course enrolments dropped from 15,031 to 7,750 students. The 3 Unit

in enrolments in the higher-level courses as students elected less demanding courses in order to fulfil the requirement of a compulsory two units of English.[6] There was also a striking pattern of variation in achievement levels of particular cohorts of students. Male students in rural areas and parts of South-Western Sydney, for example, were performing at 0.7 of the state average, while females in more economically privileged locations in the metropolitan area were achieving at 1.3 of the state average (McGaw 6). The HSC appeared to be contributing to, rather than redressing, issues of social and educational disadvantage.

The evidence pertaining to student enrolments, achievement levels and "standards", together with the other contextual factors, was the catalyst for the McGaw Review of the HSC that constituted the "first systematic review of the Higher School Certificate since its inception" (McGaw 5–6). These reforms eventually encompassed the entire senior secondary curriculum, but were initially triggered in the mid-1990s by a "long, loud and anguished cry from the English teaching community" to re-evaluate "the longer term approach to the curriculum structure and examining of the Higher School Certificate courses" (Board of Studies NSW Senior English Review Committee 193).

By the time of the McGaw Review, the then Board of Studies NSW had adopted a more transparent approach to syllabus and text list development. In contrast to previous curriculum development processes, the formation of the 1999 English syllabus was more inclusive of the English teaching profession. Syllabus, Prescriptions (text lists) and Advisory Committees were no longer controlled and dominated by representatives of the university sector. Although the curriculum reform agenda continued to be centrally managed by the Board of Studies and its committees, sub-committees and advisory groups, the consultation processes with the profession and broader community were arguably more democratic than had been the case for most of the twentieth century.

---

    course experienced a dramatic drop in candidature from 3,592 in 1991 to 1,730 in 1996 and decreased further by 1999, with a mere 1,490 students enrolled in the 3 Unit course (BOSTES NSW. Web. 4 June. 2-15).

6   2 Unit Contemporary English was introduced as an additional course in the HSC in 1988 and was based on a more thematic conceptualisation of the subject that reflected the innovations that had occurred in the 7–10 English syllabus from the 1970s.

Transformations to senior secondary English in NSW

By 1999 the new HSC (Stage 6) English syllabus was endorsed by the Board of Studies NSW and officially replaced the 1965 Wyndham Scheme HSC when it was implemented in classrooms in 2000 and examined for the first time in 2001. Included in the new suite of senior English courses was a 2 Unit English as a Second Language course, which was recognised as fulfilling the requirement for all students to include at least two units of English in their HSC. The broader range of English courses was intended to provide an incentive for capable students to undertake advanced studies, address the needs, interests and capacities of a widely diverse cohort of students, and enhance the "rigour" of courses.[7] It is worth noting that the candidature for the final year English examinations had grown from a mere 1,428 in 1925 to more than 61,000 by 1996 (BOSTES NSW, HSC Statistics). Although many of these students did not intend matriculating to university they were nevertheless required to complete two units of English to be awarded the HSC. Like its 1976 predecessor, the remodelled 1999 syllabus was endeavouring to cater to the larger and more heterogeneous student population and the greater range of post-school pathways they might pursue. If the imperative for all students to study English in the senior years remained, it was necessary to remake the English syllabus for the spectrum of students now entering the HSC.

In the redesigned syllabus, as summarised in the excerpt below, all students were required to undertake one of three 2 Unit English courses: Standard, Advanced and ESL. Students undertaking the Advanced course could elect to enrol in a further one or two units of English: English Extension 1 and English Extension 2.[8]

---

[7] In the final version of the senior English syllabus, students undertaking English (Advanced) could undertake English Extension 1 (resulting in 3 units of English), and students who undertook and completed EE1 in the Preliminary year (Year 11) could undertake the additional English Extension 2 course in the HSC year (Year 12), resulting in 4 units of English. This significant innovation provided scope for the first time in the history of the HSC to open the way for students to study four units of English: a pathway previously only available for students studying mathematics and the sciences. The English teaching profession had maintained for decades that English was as demanding and intellectually challenging as mathematics and the sciences, and it was therefore reasonable that opportunities for gifted students to complete four units of English be provided, rather than maintain the maximum of three units (which has been the case since the Wyndham reforms of the 1960s).

[8] The Stage 6 English syllabus was differentiated into the preliminary year (Year 11) and the HSC year (Year 12), thus replicating earlier syllabuses in which the final year of secondary schooling was regulated by the final examination.

Overview of the 1999 English Stage 6 Courses

To fulfil the requirements for the Higher School Certificate, students in NSW must complete one Preliminary (Year 11) course and one HSC course from: English (Standard); English (Advanced); and English as a Second Language (ESL). Students undertaking English (Advanced) may choose, in addition, to study English (Extension 1). Students undertaking English Extension 1 may choose to undertake English Extension 2 in Year 12 (Board of Studies NSW, *English Stage 6 Syllabus* 13).

The internal organisation of the majority of previous senior English syllabuses in terms of Language and Literature sections (with the Literature section arranged according to the categories of fiction, poetry, drama and non-fiction) gave way to a modular structure that reflected a responsiveness to later twentieth-century critical, linguistic and literary theories and pedagogies. Because senior English syllabuses prior to the 1999 reforms (with the exception of the 2 Unit General and 2 Unit Contemporary English courses) were organised according to traditional literary categories, the texts themselves were positioned at the hub of the subject. The new syllabus, however, shifted the prevailing paradigm by repositioning texts within a range of conceptual frameworks: that is, a common Area of Study and Modules (with Electives contained within these Modules).

Consequently, the text as a hermeneutic entity was no longer the initial entry point of study. Instead, the text was to be read through the prism of the conceptual framework of the Module and the selected Elective within the Module. Modules, such as, for example, "Texts and Society" (Standard Module C) included a choice of three Electives: "The Institution and Personal Experience"; "Exploration and Travel"; and "Consumerism" (Board of Studies NSW, "Prescriptions 2001–2003" 15–16). Students were required to study one Elective within this Module using the prescribed text as an exemplar of the particular conceptual or thematic focus of the Module and Elective. For example, in Elective 2, "Exploration and Travel", students would "respond to and compose a range of texts whose purpose is to document aspects of exploration and travel and consider how personal views and interests shape documented experience" (Board of Studies NSW, "Prescriptions 2001–2003" 16).

The modular design of the syllabus meant that all students (apart from students in the ESL course) would, for the first time in senior secondary English in, study a common component for 40 per cent of the course: the Area of Study. The remaining 60 per cent of each course was divided between Modules: three Modules in Standard and Advanced and two Modules in ESL. The following table provides an overview of the structure and content of the Advanced English course. The Standard and ESL courses were similarly structured, but with variations in the conceptual focus of the Modules and the allocation of time to the Area of Study.

Table 6.1, HSC English (Advanced) course overview

HSC English (Advanced) course (120 indicative hours)				
In the HSC English (Advanced) course, students analyse and evaluate texts, and the ways they are valued in their contexts. The course requires the study of at least FIVE types of texts, one drawn from each of the following categories: Shakespearean drama; prose fiction; poetry; drama or film; nonfiction or media or multimedia.				
Content common to the Standard and Advanced courses — **AREA OF STUDY** Provides students with the opportunity to explore, analyse and experiment with: • meaning conveyed, shaped, interpreted and reflected in and through texts • ways texts are responded to and composed • ways perspectives may affect meaning and interpretation • connections between and among texts • how texts are influenced by other texts and contexts.				45 indicative hours
MODULES Students choose 1 elective from each of the 3 modules.				
Module A: Comparative Study of Texts and Context	**Module B: Critical Study of Texts**		**Module C: Representation and Text**	
The comparative study of texts in relation to historical or cultural contexts.	A single text study – the evaluation of ideas and expression.		The study of how textual forms, choice of language and perspectives represent information, processes and ideas.	75 indicative hours
Texts, the Area of Study and Module electives ARE prescribed for the HSC.				

(Board of Studies NSW, "Prescriptions 2001–2003" 15)

Because the text functioned as an exemplar for the representation of a given concept or perspective, the approach to textual study was therefore shaped by the Module rubric and in turn, the Elective rubric. Similarly, the Area of Study ("Change" from 2001–2003, and "Journeys" from 2004–2008) instructed students to "explore the ways in which the notion of change [or journeys] is considered and expressed through texts" (Board of Studies NSW, "Prescriptions 2001–2003" 9). The concept determined the ways in which a particular text would be approached and interpreted.

Of the four components of the new syllabus (Area of Study; Module A; Module B; and Module C) only one of these – Module B – maintained a distinctively Leavisite orientation to the study of texts, albeit in a hybridised fashion. That is, students were required to undertake a "Critical Study of Texts" in Advanced English or a "Close Study of Texts" in Standard English. Students would engage in close textual analysis, interpreting and evaluating the text's ideas, language forms and features and arrive at judgements about "textual integrity" (an adaptation of the Cambridge English concept of "organic unity"). The rubric for this Module called for students' informed personal response to a single text, echoing the directives of the 1965 First and Second Level courses that were steeped in the ideas and discourses of Cambridge English. For Advanced students, this personal response was to be tested against the views of others. Importantly, the Advanced Module B required a consideration of the context in which the text had been produced, received and valued over time (Board of Studies NSW, "Prescriptions 2001–2003" 18), thereby extending the parameters of the historically embedded Leavisite literary critical model.

Reactions to the new senior secondary English syllabus

The conspicuous transformation of the senior English syllabus attracted considerable criticism in the public arena. For some conservative commentators, it constituted state-sanctioned postmodernism, while for others, it emitted the odour of cultural relativism. Former Prime Minister John Howard, while commenting on syllabuses in general across Australia, labelled them "incomprehensible sludge" (*The Age*). In a similar vein, Christopher Koch's Foreword in *Education and the Ideal* (Smith) declared the "deep concern" of many citizens about the existing state of education. Koch asserted that education was languishing in a state of "cultural crisis" and lauded the book's contributors for being "engaged in a courageous and timely undertaking" (Smith viii). According to Koch, the contributors to his book had "expose[d] a situation which should give serious concern to anyone who cares for the survival of a civilised society: that is, one where objective truth is believed to be worth pursuing, and where basic common values and freedom of thought are taken for granted" (Smith viii). Fomented by adverse reactions to the English curriculum in particular, these alarming claims of "cultural crisis", moral decline and threats to a "civilised society" were as familiar and predictable to the historian of secondary English education as they were contestable (Carter).

In part, this "panic" was generated by the redefined concept of literature and literary study in the 1999 senior English syllabus. The term "texts" was adopted to enable the inclusion of a broader range of materials for study, including multimedia, multimodal and digital texts. In fact, oral forms such as a speech were considered a "text". This represented a historic departure from the definition of literature assumed in senior English in NSW from 1911. The syllabus did not presume that all texts were of equal value to the individual or to broader society. It did, however, embrace the theoretical tenets of, for example, "cultural studies", "reader-response" and "critical literacy" models, thereby opening up the potential for teachers and students to explore a wider range of types of texts drawn from canonical, contemporary and popular categories. It also foregrounded the active role of the student in "discerning how meaning is made, sustained, valued, and contested, situating [them] as active creators of meaning through language ... as well as critical interpreters of others' language" (Manuel 68). The reactionary responses of some critics concealed their disquiet at the apparent challenge to the hegemony of a particular version of subject English in schools – one chiefly informed by the Cultural Heritage model.

While some critics may have condemned the new senior secondary English syllabus on the grounds that it had apparently rewritten the hitherto dominant narrative of the subject, closer scrutiny of the prescribed text lists and later, the examinations, would have revealed the extent of the continuities with, rather than the disruptions to, the pre-1999 versions of senior English in NSW.

Senior secondary English text lists from 1999

Almost a century on from the 1911 English syllabus, the orthodoxy of centrally developed and controlled prescribed text lists and external examinations remained unchallenged. While the content of the lists and the examinations may have shifted, the architecture of the final year of secondary schooling bore the same stamp of tight regulation and constraining specifications for study that had been the hallmarks of all previous senior secondary English syllabuses in NSW.

In developing the prescribed text lists for the senior English courses, the Board of Studies' guidelines stipulated that there would be no greater than a 15 per cent turnover of new texts in any given set of new Prescriptions.

This limitation applied to print texts and not to film, media and multimedia texts. The rationale for this regulation was in the main a pragmatic one. A higher turnover of new texts could place significant cost pressures on schools and impose a greater burden on teachers in preparing for and resourcing new texts each time the Prescriptions list was revised.[9] Importantly, this 15 per cent limit on new texts at any given time did not include texts that had been prescribed for study since 1965. That is, if a text had been prescribed in any previous HSC, it did not "count" as a new text. There was, as a result, a healthy pool of potential texts to draw upon without infringing the 15 per cent rule. That pool was predominantly canonical and it is worth remembering that the lists from 1965 onwards often included titles from writers who had regularly (and in some cases, continuously) appeared on lists between 1911 and 1964: for example, Chaucer, Shakespeare, Donne, Dickens, Austen, Hopkins, Wordsworth, Coleridge, Byron, Browning, Yeats, Eliot and Wright. In effect, the patterns of preferencing in the text lists from 1911 to 1999 disclosed the longevity of the "constitutive preoccupations" (Reid, "Romantic Ideologies" 24) of the subject at senior secondary level in NSW.

Included in the Board's guidelines for developing the prescribed text lists for the 1999 English courses was a set of criteria to be utilised by the Prescriptions Advisory Committee in its decision-making process. The inclusion of any text was to be based on judgements about the text's "merit and cultural significance; suitability for the needs and interests of students; and opportunities for challenging teaching and learning" (Board of Studies NSW, "Report" 4). Decisions about the merit, cultural significance, suitability and affordances of texts prescribed for study were no less driven by sets of values, ideologies, assumptions, censorship practices and vested interests than they were in previous times. The greater representation of the English teaching profession and community representatives in the decision-making processes served to some extent to redistribute the power and control that until the 1980s had consistently resided with a small group from the university sector.[10] The confidential back stage negotiations within

---

9   Revisions to the prescribed text lists have occurred each 4–6 years between 1999 and 2015.

10 Notwithstanding the more inclusive processes of text list production, the role of Chief Examiner of most of the HSC English courses continued to be held by university academics: this filament of tradition served to maintain the top-down influence on the nature and emphases of the subject at senior secondary level. There was a tacit assumption that academics in the tertiary English discipline would bring a level of expertise, research knowledge and scholarly insight that would bolster the "rigour" of the HSC examinations.

the more representative advisory committees about what would remain on, be added to or removed from the text list were robust, however, and at times polarised the membership of these committees. At other times, the censorship practices were staged in the public arena. Individuals and interest groups worked through the political system and the media to censor and eventually eliminate certain texts from the published lists, based on ideological or moral objections.[11]

The sustained authority of the texts lists

The first Prescriptions accompanying the new HSC English Syllabus (Board of Studies NSW, "Prescriptions 2001–2003") set out the text requirements for each course. Standard English entailed the study of at "least four types of prescribed text, one drawn from EACH of the following categories: prose fiction; drama; poetry; nonfiction or film or media or multimedia texts" (Board of Studies NSW, "Prescriptions 2001–2003" 6). For Advanced English, students would study "at least five types of prescribed text, one drawn from EACH of the following categories: Shakespearean drama; prose fiction; drama or film; poetry; nonfiction or media or multimedia texts" (Board of Studies NSW, "Prescriptions 2001–2003" 7). In addition, both Standard and Advanced students would study "a wide range of additional related texts and textual forms" and a "prescribed stimulus booklet" associated with the Area of Study (Board of Studies NSW, "Prescriptions 2001–2003" 6).[12]

A brief snapshot of the quantity of texts listed from 1911 to 1999 illuminates the extent to which the lists had expanded, although the regulatory requirement for a minimum number of types of texts to be studied in each course remained intact. The 1911 syllabus, for instance, listed 18 titles for the final year of English (to be implemented over a three-year cycle), with a minimum requirement of six texts to be studied, plus the History of Literature and History of Language components. By 1965, the list for First Level included 19 titles, with a minimum requirement of 12 texts to be studied. In 1999, the list for the Advanced course contained 15 titles in

---

11 See Nick Enright. 'What Should Our Children Read? *English in Australia* 121 (1998).
12 HSC English (ESL) Course Text Requirements: "the close study of AT LEAST THREE TYPES OF PRESCRIBED TEXTS drawn from prose fiction; drama; poetry; nonfiction; film or media or multimedia texts; a wide range of additional related texts and textual form a prescribed stimulus booklet." The Area of Study focus in the first Prescriptions was "Perspectives" (Board of Studies NSW 24).

the Area of Study (from which one text was to be selected) and 34 titles distributed across the three Modules A, B and C. From these titles, four were to be selected for study.

Texts appearing in the 1999–2005 text lists that had also appeared on text lists since 1911 included: *Hamlet, Julius Caesar, King Lear, Richard III* and *The Tempest*; selections from *The Canterbury Tales*; Donne's poetry; Wordsworth's poetry; *Wuthering Heights*; *Emma, Northanger Abbey* and *Pride and Prejudice*; *Tess of the d'Urbervilles*; *Huckleberry Finn*; T. S. Eliot's poetry; and Lawson's short stories.

Although the 1999 text lists contained a greater quantity of texts than in previous versions, the layered nature of the regulations about the number of prescribed types of texts, coupled with the modular structure, imposed considerable restrictions on choice. For example, if poetry was selected for study in Module A, it could not be selected for study in any other Module or in the Area of Study. The result was a more complex and arguably more restrictive process of text selection than that required for previous lists, which were organised according to the literary categories of fiction, poetry, drama and non-fiction. Having selected, for instance, fiction and poetry in Advanced Module A (which required the selection of two texts), Shakespearean drama in Module B and non-fiction in the Area of Study, the remaining prescribed text – drama or film – had to be selected from Module C. In 2001 (the first set of Prescriptions for the 1999 syllabus), the choices available for drama or film in Advanced Module C were Sophocles's *Antigone* or Benigni's *Life is Beautiful*. Thus, the potential for more diverse choices, implied by the quantity of texts on the lists did not always translate into practice due to the need for strict compliance with the syllabus directives. The increased quantity of titles on the text lists did not equate with increased freedom for teachers and students.

In comparison with the equivalent course in the previous syllabus, the text requirements for Advanced English fell from seven prescribed texts to five. Shakespearean drama remained compulsory, as did poetry and fiction, other drama *or* film, and nonfiction *or* media *or* multimedia texts. Approximately 40 per cent of the texts listed in the Advanced Modules and Electives were canonical. For example: Sophocles's *Antigone*; Chaucer's "The Pardoner's Tale"; Donne's poetry; *Hamlet, The Tempest, King Lear*, and *Julius Caesar*; *Emma*; Wordsworth's poetry; and *Jane Eyre*. A further 30 per cent of the Advanced Module Prescriptions were contemporary texts such as Winton's *Cloudstreet*, Ondaatje's *In the Skin of a Lion*, Malouf's *An*

Imaginary Life, Hughes's *Birthday Letters* and Plath's poetry. The remaining third of the list was made up of contemporary texts, including a number of films, websites and media (Board of Studies NSW, "Prescriptions 2001–2003" 18–23).

In contrast, the list of 29 texts for the Standard course Modules included only three canonical texts: *Macbeth*, Lawson's short stories, and Owen's poetry. The majority of texts on this list were drawn from contemporary and popular categories (Board of Studies NSW, "Prescriptions 2001–2003" 12–17). Given the range of options of texts within each Module, it was entirely possible to complete the HSC without having studied any canonical texts in the Year 12 Standard and ESL courses.

As was the case in earlier versions of senior English, the Cultural Heritage model maintained its foothold through the text lists for the higher-level courses. Most obviously, this was evident in the continued mandating of Shakespearean drama for Advanced students and in the range of prescribed texts and approaches to their study, especially in Module B, which most closely reproduced the Leavisite critical method.

Because the text lists developed for the 1999 senior syllabus were organised in the first instance in terms of conceptual frames rather than literary categories, the lists could be more accurately labelled as prescribed concepts for study, each with its own emphases and expectations for reading and responding. Although the intent of the syllabus was to integrate the study of English around the pivot of students' "composing and responding", the division of the subject into an Area of Study and Modules was arguably as problematic as the earlier versions' bipartite structure of Language and Literature, or according to literary categories. From an analysis of the rhetorical curriculum of 1999, a strong case could be made for the philosophical, theoretical and pedagogical continuities between the Area of Study and the Modules. In practice, however, the Area of Study and Modules tended to be treated as self-contained components because they were examined as self-contained components. Ironically, the nexus between the syllabus and the examinations' structure militated against the kind of holistic conceptualisation of the subject that the syllabus, on paper, implied.

Text lists and the "popularity" of recurring titles

The unique interdependence of the NSW senior secondary English text lists and external examinations has meant that there is no simple or transparent correlation between what had appeared on the lists and what had in fact been studied in classrooms in any given year. The presence or absence of a certain text on the list was not commensurate with its popularity. Take for example the recurring presence of Patrick White's prose fiction over the past half a century. One of his novels was set in Advanced Module A as an option to be studied in conjunction with the poetry of Rosemary Dobson. Within Module A, there was a range of texts from which two texts were to be chosen for study. Because White's novel remained on the text list for six successive years, it is possible to conclude that White's fiction was popular – but popular with those who created the text list, not necessarily teachers (and students). In the six years of White's novel being on the text list, there were potentially more than 360,000 students who could have studied it. In reality, the actual take-up of this text in the classroom was miniscule: fewer than 0.003 per cent of students during this six-year period studied White's novel for their HSC.[13]

Similarly, conclusions about the popularity of Australian texts – based on their appearance on successive lists – need to be informed with data about the take-up of those texts in practice. While each section of the HSC, in each of the courses, had typically included at least one Australian title, the only title in the entire list that was and continues to be unavoidable is Shakespearean drama in the Advanced course. Given the demographic of experienced senior English teachers and the emphases in their own literary education the patterns of text selection between 1999 and 2005 can be seen to reflect the enduring popularity (signifying take-up) of familiar British canonical texts, particularly in the Advanced course.

Related texts of students' own choosing

A significant innovation of the 1999 syllabus, intended to strengthen student engagement and learning, was the addition of "related texts" of students' own choosing as a requirement in the Area of Study (for Standard and Advanced), Modules A and C for Standard, and Module C for Advanced. However, it can be argued that this innovation merely compounded an already complex and constricted set of requirements for the study of senior English and added an additional layer of regulation, often leading to confusion for teachers and students.

---

13   BOSTES statistical data pertaining to numbers of students responding to examination questions on each prescribed text.

Since the examination necessitated reference to these related texts, students were compelled to incorporate these as part of their study of the prescribed text within the Area of Study and Modules specified above. The inclusion of students' own selections of related texts was intended to validate the principles of student choice, agency, engagement and increasing autonomy in the study of English. While philosophically and theoretically laudable in intent, the requirement constituted another stratum of complexity as students were not only required to study their prescribed text within the context of the Module and Elective rubric: they were also now "obliged to choose" additional texts, independently selected and studied, but nevertheless chosen in accordance with the defined Prescriptions rubrics.

The related texts of students' own choosing had ramifications for the teaching of the senior English courses and for the examinations. With scant advice offered in the syllabus, teachers and students were unclear as to how many related texts to study in association with each prescribed text. They were unclear about the types of related texts to be studied: for example, if the prescribed text was a prose fiction text, could a related text also be a prose fiction text? Or should it be a different type of text? With regard to the examinations, both teachers and students were, in the absence of clear directions from the syllabus or the examination specifications, unaware from year to year about how many related texts candidates would be required to include in the examination questions, and the degree of emphasis to be placed on the related text/s in the candidate's discussion of the prescribed text.

Incorporating related texts was generally perceived by students as an added imposition, rather than as an opportunity for exercising personal agency. The status of students' own related texts in examinations became increasingly fraught, with value judgements about the appropriateness and quality of those texts applied at the examination marking centres. Texts that were drawn from popular culture or frequently cited were often considered by markers to be less intellectually or aesthetically weighty and from this, inferences were made about the capacities of the candidate. Debates about the quality, length, type of text and its perceived worth became commonplace in the examination marking centres. These debates revealed the old fault-lines between those who saw themselves as upholding the status and integrity of the traditionally defined subject by resisting the inclusion of texts from popular culture, including from the digital realm, and those who endorsed the value of such texts and saw the benefits of cultural studies principles co-existing alongside the study of traditional canonical texts.

Furthermore, anecdotal evidence highlighted that the task of selecting and studying related texts had become another part of the HSC "game", accruing its own set of strategies adopted by students to satisfy this requirement. With the growth of social media during the early part of the twenty-first century, students began to share their tactical ideas for dealing with the issue of related texts: a related text could be "invented", and if incorporated deftly into the essay, the marker would not know if it was authentic or not. For example, one student's essay response included reference to a related text that was an "unnamed painting, by an unknown painter, at an unknown point in history".[14] Yet, this "related text" was incorporated into the essay response thereby registering compliance with the need to refer to a related text. There were virtually no guidelines in place for markers to address these forms of creative fabrication in the examination.

Text lists and the restructured examinations

The long-established convention of two, two-hour English examination papers was internally reconfigured for the first examination of the 1999 syllabus in 2001 (for Standard and Advanced). Paper 1 examined the Area of Study, common to both the Standard and Advanced courses. Repeating earlier practice, Paper 1 included unseen texts, in this case germane to the Area of Study focus, with a series of short-answer questions. Sections II and III of the paper required a sustained creative response and a sustained essay on the prescribed and related texts explored in the Area of Study, respectively. Paper 2 for Advanced and Paper 2 for Standard each required three sustained essay responses to the prescribed and related texts in each of the three Modules. Students' performance in the examinations constituted 50 per cent of their final HSC result. School-based assessment made up the other 50 per cent of the HSC result.

Once again, the rhetorical curriculum promised a far greater range of ways for students to demonstrate their learning in addition to the production of the traditional literary critical essay under examination conditions. It specified that students would "respond to and compose texts critically and imaginatively, in order to extend experience, gain access to and evaluate ideas and information, and synthesise the knowledge gained from a range of sources to fulfil a variety of purposes" (Board of Studies NSW, "Prescriptions 2009–2014" 36). In practice, however, the school-based assessment became

---

14   A student script read at the marking centre by the co-author (Manuel) who was Chief Examiner of HSC Standard and Advanced English, 2007–2011.

heavily geared towards preparation for the high-stakes examinations, with "pen and paper" written tasks predominating in the internal assessment program and obligatory in the examinations. The omnipresence of the final external examinations continued to govern classroom pedagogy and assessment and fuelled an ever-burgeoning commercial "industry" built around the HSC examination.

Conclusion

This discussion has investigated the features of NSW senior secondary English text lists at two pivotal moments of reform: 1965 and 1999. Although the Wyndham Scheme of 1965 ushered in major structural and other changes in the school curriculum, it also reproduced a host of inherited "epistemic assumptions" (Reid, "Romantic Ideologies" 32) and "constitutive preoccupations" (24) that had driven senior secondary English in this state since 1911. Foremost among these were the assumptions about the role of the subject in the cultivation of the "well educated" citizen (NSW Department of Public Instruction iv) equipped with certain ethical, moral, aesthetic and intellectual qualities deemed appropriate for their democratic participation in society and for the conduct and character of their personal lives. To this end, the "constitutive preoccupations" of senior English throughout the better part of a century have been evident in the inherited practice of continuously privileging certain kinds of literature and approaches to literary study. Even with the expanded parameters of the subject in the 1999 syllabus through the inclusion of a wider range of texts and the requirement of students' related texts of their own choosing, the processes of authorising and enforcing compliance with a compulsory syllabus, text lists and examinations have been as robust from 1999 onwards as they were in the preceding decades, despite the considerable shifts in the socio-cultural, material and economic contexts in which senior secondary education has occurred. The prescribed text lists and the examinations have continued to function as powerful gatekeeping and sorting mechanisms for entry to higher education. Teachers and students have been compelled to work within a tightly regulated, highly prescriptive and standardising system; a system notoriously resistant and even impervious to the diverse needs of heterogeneous communities across the state.

On this point, there has been a noticeable lack of research evidence pertaining to students' and teachers' experiences and perceptions of HSC English (or senior English prior to 1965). The NSW Board of Studies,

Teaching and Educational Standards once conducted student exit surveys. The data from these surveys, however, were generally unreliable in that the sample of respondents was consistently small and therefore unrepresentative. While the analysis of written curriculum documents such as the syllabus, text lists and examinations can offer valuable insights into the lineage of senior English and the extent to which these have served to maintain indices of disadvantage and inequity, there is a pressing need to gather and foreground the views of those who enact and receive the curriculum in classrooms.

The historical study of texts lists and the circumstances of their production reveal at best the consistent marginalisation of teachers and students from the decision-making processes that have ultimately directed and determined the quality of their experience of senior English. There is more than a sliver of irony in this observation, given the provenance of current curriculum documents and the argument put forward in this chapter: that is, the continuities in the senior secondary English curriculum from 1911 to 2005 are considerably more striking and pronounced than the handful of attempted transformations over the course of the twentieth century. Since 1911, official curriculum documents have perpetuated the discourses of nurturing individual autonomy, selfhood, participatory ways of being, freedom, choice and the personal satisfactions and affordances that can flow from encounters with literature. Yet, as the analysis here and in the previous chapter underscores, such discourses have remained largely rhetorical against the uninterrupted authority of prescribed texts lists and compulsory, high-stakes examinations.

Works Cited

Adams, Peter. "Dependent authorship: Writing from the inside out". *Reconstructing Literature Teaching: New essays on the teaching of literature*. Ed. Jack Thomson. Norwood: AATE, 1992. 149–167. Print.

Analysis of Literature in Australian Schools Database (ALIAS). www.australiancommonreader.com/syllabus. Web. 20 November 2014.

Ball, Stephen J. "English since 1906". *Social Histories of the Secondary Curriculum: Subjects for study*. Ed. Ivor F. Goodson. Lewes, United Kingdom: The Falmer Press, 1985. 53–88. Print.

——, Alex Kenny, and David Gardiner. "Literacy, politics and the teaching of English". Ed. Ivor F. Goodson, and Peter Medway. *Bringing English to Order: The history and politics of a school subject*. London: The Falmer Press, 1990. 47–86. Print.

——, and Colin Lacey. "Revisiting subject disciplines as the opportunity for group action: A measured critique of subject subcultures". *The Subjects in Question*. Ed. L.S. Siskin and J.W. Little. New York: Teachers College Press, 1995. 95–122. Print.

Barcan, Alan. *Two Centuries of Education in New South Wales*. Sydney: NSW University Press, 1988. Print.

Board of Senior School Studies NSW. "English (Syllabus and Commentary) Forms V and VI: First, Second and Third Levels". Sydney: NSW Government Printer, 1965. Print.

Board of Studies NSW. Report on the Draft English Stage 6 Syllabus consultation / Senior English Review Committee. Sydney: Board of Studies NSW, 1997. Print.

Board of Studies NSW. "English Stage 6 Syllabus". Sydney: Board of Studies NSW, 1999. Print.

——. "English Stage 6 Prescriptions: Area of Study Electives and Texts Higher School Certificate 2001–2003". Sydney: Board of Studies NSW, 1999b. Print.

——. "English Stage 6 Prescriptions: Area of Study Electives and Texts Higher School Certificate 2009–2014". Sydney: Board of Studies NSW, 2008. Print.

[BOSTES NSW] Board of Studies, Teaching and Education Standards. "Annotations of prescribed texts". Web. 15 January 2015.

——. "HSC Statistics Archive". Web. 23 March 2015.

Britton, James. *Language and Learning*. Harmondsworth: Penguin, 1978. Print.

Brock, Paul. "Telling the story of the NSW Secondary English curriculum: 1950–1965". *Teaching the English Subjects: Essays on English curriculum and history in Australian schooling*. Ed. Bill Green and Catherine Beavis. Geelong: Deakin University Press, 1996. 40–70. Print.

——. "Changes in the English syllabus in N.S.W. Australia: Can any American coices be heard?" *English Journal* 73.3 (1984b): 53–58. Print.

——. A History of the Development of English Syllabuses in New South Wales Secondary Education, 1953–1976: A 'continuum' or a 'series of new beginnings'? Unpublished PhD Thesis. Armidale: University of New England, 1984a. Print.

Carter, Don. The Influence of Romanticism on the NSW Stage 6 English Syllabus: Interwoven storylines and the search for a unifying narrative. Unpublished PhD thesis. Sydney: The University of Sydney, 2012. Print.

Cormack, Phil. "Tracking local curriculum histories: The plural forms of subject English". *Changing English* 15.3 (2008): 275–291. Print.

Enright, Nick. "What should our children read?" *English in Australia* 121 (1998): 23–28. Print.

Goffman, Erving. *The Presentation of Self in Everyday Life*. New York: Doubleday, 1959. Print.

Goodson, Ivor F. and Peter Medway. *Bringing English to Order: The history and politics of a school subject*. United Kingdom: Routledge, 1990. Print.
Green, Bill and Catherine Beavis, eds. *Teaching the English Subjects: Essays on English curriculum history and Australian schooling*. Geelong, VIC: Deakin University Press, 1996. Print.
Hughes, John and Paul Brock. *Reform and Resistance in NSW Public Education: Six attempts at major reform, 1905–1995*. Sydney: State of New South Wales (Department of Education and Training), 2008. Print.
McGaw, Barry. *Their Future: Options for reform of the Higher School Certificate*. NSW: Department of Education and Training Co-ordination, 1996. Print.
Manuel, Jacqueline. "Making its debut: What teachers think of the new Higher School Certificate English syllabus in New South Wales – Report of a survey of teachers of English in NSW government secondary schools". *English in Australia* 134 (2002): 67–77. Print.
———, and Paul Brock. "W(h)ither the place of literature?: Two momentous reforms in the NSW senior secondary English curriculum". *English in Australia* 136 (2003): 1–18. Print.
Mathieson, Margaret. *The Preachers of Culture: A study of English and its teachers*. London: George Allen and Unwin, 1975. Print.
Meiers, Marion and Wayne Sawyer. "Essential Learning Prep to Year 10 English Curriculum Area": A discussion paper prepared in July 2004 for the Victorian Curriculum and Assessment Authority as theoretical background for development of the Victorian Essential Learning Standards, 2004. Print.
Mellor, Bronwyn, Marnie O'Neill, and Annette Patterson. "Re-reading literature teaching". *Reconstructing Literature Teaching: New essays on the teaching of literature*. Ed. Jack Thomson. Norwood: AATE. 1992. 40–55. Print.
Michaels, Wendy. The Constitution of the Subject English in New South Wales Senior English Syllabus Documents 1953–1994. Unpublished PhD thesis. Sydney: Macquarie University, 2001. Print.
Newbolt, Harold. The Teaching of English in England. Being the report of the departmental committee appointed by the President of the Board of Education to inquire into the position of English in the educational system of England. London: HMSO, 1921. Print.
New South Wales Department of Education. *Courses of Study for High Schools*. Sydney: NSW Department of Education, 1945. Print.
———. *Syllabus in English*. Sydney: NSW Department of Education, 1953. Print.
———. *Syllabus in English*. Sydney: NSW Department of Education, 1965. Print.
New South Wales Department of Public Instruction. *Courses of Study for High Schools*. Sydney: NSW Department of Public Instruction, 1911. Print.
Reid, Ian. *The Making of Literature: Texts, contexts and classroom practices*. Norwood: AATE, 1984. Print.
———. "Romantic ideologies, educational practices, and institutional formations of English". *Journal of Educational Administration and History* 28.1 (1996): 22–41. Print.
———. "Wordsworth institutionalised: The shaping of an educational ideology". *History of Education, Journal of the History of Education Society* 31.1 (2002): 15–37. Print.
Rosser, Gary. Disciplining Literature: Higher School Certificate prescribed texts for English: 1965–1995. Unpublished PhD thesis. University of Wollongong, 2000. Print.

Sawyer, Wayne. "Seminal books on English teaching". *Reviewing English in the 21st Century*. Ed. Wayne Sawyer and Eva Gold. Sydney: Phoenix Education, 2004. 23–35. Print.

Selleck, Richard J.W. *The New Education: The English background 1870–1914*. Melbourne: Pitman, 1968. Print.

Shayer, David. *The Teaching of English in Schools 1900–1970*. London and Boston: Routledge and Kegan Paul, 1972. Print.

Siena College. "What is history and why study it?" Web. 7 April. 2012.

Sinfield, Alan. "Give an account of Shakespeare and Education, showing why you think they are effective and what you have appreciated about them. Support your comments with precise references". *Political Shakespeare: New essays in cultural materialism*. Ed. Jonathan Dollimore and Andrew Sinfield. Manchester: Manchester University Press, 1985. Print.

Smith, N., ed. *Education and the Ideal*. Sydney: New Frontier Publishing, 2004. Print.

The Age (2008). "Rudd to scrap Howard's history". Web. 14 March. 2009.

Wilkes, Gerry. A. "The English syllabus as a whole". *The Teaching of English* 7 (1965): 6–21. Print.

Chapter Seven

LITERATURE AT SCHOOL IN NSW

Some recent history

Wayne Sawyer

Introduction

In this chapter I would like to examine what may be called the culture of school literature in a period of recent history in New South Wales (NSW), Australia – centred particularly on the 1980s and early 1990s. The intention is to place some of the literature in the ALIAS (Analysis of Literature in Australian Schools) database into a specific historical, geographical and pedagogical context. The 1980s in NSW are interesting since they were years of transition from one set of English syllabuses to another in both the junior (Years 7–10) and senior (Years 11–12) secondary years. Often through investigating changes brought about during such transitions, highlighting the characteristic "cultures" of historical moments becomes more possible.

Examining syllabuses gives one picture of the culture of school literature as seen through institutional imperatives. However, I would also like to approach this discussion through accounts of practice in Higher School Certificate (HSC—i.e. years 11–12) classrooms by focusing on selected literary texts in specifically selected years. The classroom practices will be my own pedagogical practices as recorded in my lesson notes made as an English teacher in the years selected. As most teachers would recognise, the production of subject English in the classroom can provide useful insight into the ways in which centralised curricula can play out, especially in the context of syllabuses which are externally examined.[1] In focusing on records of my own past teaching, I am picking up, in a very small way, recent historical work by Medway et al. (2014) in telling the story of three London schools from 1945 to 1965, partly using such documents as class teaching programs and student workbooks. Detailing my own classroom teaching is not meant to represent anything that is typical in any overall sense, much less anything exemplary. However, I believe that characteristics of my teaching practice in these years would be recognised by teachers from that era (and, indeed, would still be recognisable in the NSW context today). Discussing my teaching in this way allows me to anchor the discussion of the period by focusing on a small selection of texts (one from each of the chosen years that also, overall, represent a range of HSC English courses) and some classroom practices used in teaching these texts within the institutional imperatives of syllabuses and examinations. While it is true that "a curriculum made only of teachers' intentions (can) be an insubstantial thing" (Barnes 14), it is also true that the teacher "is the main medium ... through which the combined forces of 'the curriculum', 'the critics', 'the cultural heritage' ... are channelled ... the teacher still stands at the junction where students' sense of *their* cultural contexts is encountering the strongly institutionalised 'subject' to be studied" (Reid 43). Characteristics of my own teaching practice may provide some insight into the ways in which the texts from the ALIAS database could have been read, produced and enacted in NSW at these times. In any case, I will be attempting to broaden the classroom practice discussion by examining articles from the journals of the NSW English Teachers' Association that dealt with these same texts either in the particular years I am discussing or from one or two years either side of them.

The junior (Years 7–10) syllabuses of the time carry their own versions of the culture of literature teaching. Those that straddle this period were published in 1971 and 1987. In each case, literature was a central context on which the subject focused:

> No apology is made for the special prominence given to literature, as drawing together the threads and concerns of English in a particularly fruitful way. (NSWSSB *Notes: General Bibliography* 7)

---

[1] While the HSC includes a significant percentage of marks which are internally awarded, and while in-school assessment changed in its value and nature in the transition from one set of syllabuses to another, the general characterisation of New South Wales HSC English as "externally examined" holds true.

> Of all the 'contexts' of English, none is more important than literature. (NSWSSB *Notes: Literature* 1)
>
> Literature provides a unique context for language growth through expansion of the student's individual world. (BSE 1987 45)

The dominant theme in each case was the importance of the range and quality of student engagement with literature (NSWSSB *Syllabus* 12; BSE 1987 45). In each case, the emphasis was on *experience* and *response* (NSWSSB *Syllabus* 13; BSE 1987 45). Each junior syllabus advocated quite specific practices. In 1971 these were: *interpretative expression* (e.g. reading aloud, dramatisation); *critical expression*; *critical appraisal of others'* responses; and students' own *creative expression* (including using the forms of fiction, poetry and drama). Writing was not to be confined to literary criticism, but was to value the "pupil's own response" (NSWSSB *Notes: Literature* 2).

In 1987, particularly singled out were "imaginative re-creation" practices, which had been popularised by Stratta, Dixon and Wilkinson in *Patterns of Language*, itself published in the period between the two syllabuses. Examples of these in the 1987 junior syllabus included: rewriting scenes from a different point of view; scripting episodes from a novel for radio or television; or writing an alternative ending to a novel, play or short story (BSE 1987 48). The 1971 document focused more explicitly on literature as linguistic artefact, having, as one objective, the ability to respond to "the form of a work, its structure and style; its parts and their relations to one another and the whole ... its narrative and descriptive methods ... its management of dialogue, imagery, humour, irony, its control of pace, tone and rhythm" (NSWSSB *Syllabus* 13). While valuing the "pupil's own response", the syllabus encouraged close reading and urged teachers to emphasise "the contribution of (language) to total meaning and value" (NSWSSB *Syllabus* 13).

Teaching the NSW Higher School Certificate courses

In turning now to my own HSC teaching, I will deal with one text from each of four years: 1980, 1988, 1992 and 1993. The years are chosen to throw light in each case on a different English course, in order to cover a range of the syllabuses and courses in which these texts sat. Particular texts are chosen over others because most were also the subject of a publication – usually a journal article – issuing from the NSW English Teachers' Association (ETA) in close proximity to the years in which I taught the texts. Such publications could be a unit of work, a study guide, critical analysis, commentary and so on. Given the role of the ETA in supporting school English pedagogy in NSW, such publications open a broader window into practice than the work of an individual teacher. Taken together, discussion of these texts, and the work around them, attempts to give a sense of the range of possibilities for practice made available by the relevant syllabuses, the examinations and the publications of the local professional journals at the time.

1980: 2UA

I taught my first Year 12 class in 1980 in a course then known as 2 Unit A. The "A" in 2 Unit A meant in practice that students who chose this course were generally regarded, or saw themselves, as, weaker at English than the 2 Unit[2] group. Though these were the days when only a minority of students stayed at school beyond Year 10, my 2 Unit A class ranged widely in ability at, and interest in, English.

Unlike other states, there were no separate courses in English and English Literature in NSW. All English courses in the HSC were focused primarily on reading literature. Requirements laid down by the Senior Secondary Schools Board in that year required the study of an anthology of poetry (any anthology, with a small list of six listed as suggestions only), two novels and two plays (or one play and a 'General Prose' [non-fiction] text). The novels we studied were Muriel Spark's *The Prime of Miss Jean Brodie* and Thomas Keneally's *The Chant of Jimmie Blacksmith*. Drama texts were Ray Lawler's *Summer of the Seventeenth Doll* and Alan Seymour's *The One Day of the Year*.

The text I will discuss here is *Summer of the Seventeenth Doll*. The school in which I was teaching was in Sydney's outer western suburbs, and about half the students were the children of first or second generation migrants from Central and Southern Europe and South America. What they made of the Australia represented in this text I probably never asked or even thought about. According to my lesson notes, emphasised during our reading were key tensions in the play, such as between suburbia (regular hours, low wages, conformity, boredom) and the bush (traditional masculinity, challenge, independence, mateship), age and youth, past and present, dream and reality, and marriage and the layoff. These tensions were treated as

---

2 The term "unit" strictly speaking refers to the amount of time spent in English per week. One unit was equivalent to 3x40 minute periods per week. Hence, 2 Unit courses were the equivalent of six such periods or four hours per week. Students in the 3 Unit course studied English for the equivalent of 9x40 mins – or six hours – per week.

driving such themes as change, the passing of time and the shattering of illusions. Students had a study guide to be answered each night following that day's class reading and discussion. It focused on events, the presentation of characters, settings and the language of specific dialogue. In class we were reading the play, discussing the development of the characters and the particular issues, themes and ideas that were being raised. We discussed the symbolism of birds, butterflies and the dolls. We discussed the movement from anticipation and excitement to disillusion and bitterness. We discussed Lawler's questioning of the myth of the Outback – its values and loyalties – in 1950s (or 1970s) urban Australia. This was a particularly fertile area for discussion – if the play was reflecting the confusion of a society still trying to cling to old myths and illusions, had Lawler overlooked a capacity for adaptation in these characters or this country? However, a play is a play and, while time constraints meant we could not spend too many lessons on performance, we did discuss at strategic points, directorial possibilities: "How would you portray ... ?" "How would this exit be carried out?" "How could we capture the atmosphere of exhausted heat?" "What is the effect of the scenery here?"

NSW ETA *Newsletter*[s] in 1978 and 1980 carried units on the play. The emphasis of the first of these was on close reading scene-by-scene, characterised by "Why?" and "How?" questions. It also focused on larger discussions around mateship, the play's symbolism, aspects of language and the development of particular characters. It also, interestingly, asked students to consider the degree to which the play in the late 1970s was already dated (Yeo). The approach to *The Doll* in the 1980 *Newsletter* was entirely through dramatic work. Aimed at HSC classes, it particularly emphasised improvisation through "imaginative re-creation". This included improvising scenes from earlier, happier layoffs, or scenes such as Roo applying for a job at Lyman's paint factory, or characters' interior monologues as the clock strikes twelve to usher in the New Year (Farrar).

The 1976 2UA syllabus under which this text was studied aimed at developing "the ability to understand and respond to good literature within a range of competence and interests". Literature was to represent "the contemporary and the local, as well as ... the literature of other times and places". Chosen texts were to "have a ready appeal, and ... at the same time offer sufficient maturity of thought, feeling and expression to justify study and to provide an introduction to intelligent, adult reading" (BSSS *Syllabus* 1976 10). A theory of reading underpinned the course, captured in the notion of personal response: in the treatment of texts, the main emphasis should be upon the individual's response to books read attentively. Such responses should above all be honest, and be soundly supported by reference to what the text actually says and to the impact and pattern of the work as a whole. The treatment envisaged is thus one of careful reading and thoughtful general interpretation and evaluation, rather than of exhaustive detailed analysis (BSSS *Syllabus* 1976 10).

There was even a suggested pedagogy: private reading, followed (especially in the case of poetry and drama) by whole-class reading, then "free discussion" to clarify views, testing these against the evidence of the text – and then:

> When it became apparent that those taking the course had failed to perceive something important about the work, the presentation of views other than their own might be introduced, but there would be no call to impose any such views, or to shape reactions into some supposedly orthodox pattern. All that is required is that personal responses should be honest and thoughtful, and backed by knowledge of the text. (BSSS *Syllabus* 1976 10)

The specific Drama section of the syllabus stated that "(d)etailed textual study is not envisaged", putting an emphasis on the play "as a script for acting as well as a literary work" and on dramatic structures such as parallels, contrasts, sub-plots, mood and tempo. The relevant examination question in 1980 was: "Explore some of the conflicts dramatised in *Summer of the Seventeenth Doll*". The openness of "explore" reflects one side of the philosophy of the syllabus, but sound knowledge of "what the text actually says" about key conflicts is obviously also centrally important. I was probably glad we focused on those tensions throughout the play. However, one would hope that students also realised these conflicts partly through discussing the play as a script for performance.

1988: 2U (Related)

My next relevant Year 12 class was in 1988. Under a newer syllabus, I was then teaching a 2 Unit (Related)[3] / 3 Unit class. I was in a different school – a newer western Sydney, outer suburban comprehensive, very Anglo-monocultural. The 2 Unit course, on which I will focus here, was defined in the syllabus by the nature of student interest, being designed "for those with

---

3   The 3 Unit course was the most "demanding" level of English available. The term "Related" referred to the fact that the 3 Unit course officially "include(d)" the 2 Unit course.

a particular interest in English, who wish to study plays such as *King Lear*, or the poetry of Donne, or the novels of Jane Austen or Patrick White". Its objectives repeated the aims of the previous syllabus, viz.: to "improve the ability to understand and appreciate spoken and written English, and to speak and write English well" and to "develop and refine individual response to literature in English, both past and present" (BSSS *Syllabus: 2/3 Unit* 1982b, 2 Unit section 1). "Close reading" and "close attention to ... detail" were the key strategies. Nevertheless, the syllabus began its discussion of textual study with the notion that "Any sophisticated concept of 'literary criticism' is ... unhelpful" and then went on to outline a preferred pedagogy as "discussing and exchanging opinions as well as ... writing about their own ... taking part in 'workshop' productions of scenes from a play, and ... reading poetry aloud" (BSSS *Syllabus: 2/3 Unit* 1982b, 2 Unit section 2).

In the 2 Unit (Related) course, two poets were to be studied, to include either Donne or Slessor. Two fictional works were to be studied, to include either *Pride and Prejudice* or selected stories of Henry Lawson. Two plays were to be studied, in addition to a compulsory Shakespeare (*Othello*).[4] None of the sections Poetry, Fiction or Drama could draw only from the twentieth century. My chosen 2 Unit (Related) course texts were Coleridge, Donne (specific set poems for each), *Pride and Prejudice*, *Tirra Lirra by the River*, *Othello*, *Who's Afraid of Virginia Woolf?* and *Equus*.

I have chosen *Othello* from the 2 Unit (Related) course for discussion. The syllabus's overriding emphasis in drama was on treating plays as performance, such as in adopting "the standpoint of directors and actors to consider how a particular role should be developed, and what features of a given scene a good performance should bring out" (BSSS *Syllabus: 2/3 Unit* 1982b, 2 Unit section 7). Again, *any* interpretation would not suffice. "Close study" is required – one might focus, for example, on how imagery could define a character (BSSS *Syllabus: 2/3 Unit* 1982b, 2 Unit section 7–8).

Our study of *Othello* began with the distribution of a study guide which students were to answer independently outside of class, bringing any problems it raised to class for discussion. Under the examination structure of

---

4   In each year of the 2 Unit Related course, there was a compulsory Shakespeare play, which all students in this course were required to study and which would be a compulsory part of the exam. In addition, until 1993, Poetry and Fiction nominated two poets/texts, one (and only one) of which had to be studied, e.g. in 1988, students were required to study either Donne or Slessor for Poetry and either *Pride and Prejudice* or selected Henry Lawson short stories for Fiction. In that sense, either Donne or Slessor / *Pride and Prejudice* or Lawson is "compulsory".

two exam papers – *Resources and Uses of English and Shakespeare* and *Poetry, Fiction, Drama* – *Othello* had more marks allotted to it than any other text on which the students were to be examined. We devoted a week to simply (re-)reading the play in class, with students keeping running notes on issues discussed, such as imagery, character development (and the relation between these things) and so forth. In then returning to early Acts for deeper consideration, we considered the position of Othello, including his clear public view of himself, alongside Iago's ascending villainy. Shakespeare's characteristic portrayal of immorality through style, eloquence and intelligence was a focus. Iago's language was a particular consideration and led to discussions of the different manifestations of "proof" in the play. We then focused on the major speeches in Acts IV and V. After all of this close reading, we turned to performance considerations. In one exercise, for example, students were to prepare a set of director's notes on selected speeches that included written justification of their directorial decisions. Alongside this work, students had already been set other small writing exercises to complete at various points – for example, "What do you think of Othello at this point in the play?" – as well as particular studies of Desdemona, Emilia and Bianca. In detail, students were to consider very precisely how Iago was a foil (or not) for other major characters in the play. Similarly, Othello as tragic hero was the subject of extended discussion. The unit culminated in group-assigned tasks that focused on close reading of extracts and covered, for example: key Othello/Desdemona scenes; the sequence of events leading to Othello's death; Iago's soliloquies; the Emilia–Desdemona relationship; and particular sets of polarities in the play (black/white; deceit/truth; illusion/reality; love/hate).

The unit made strong use of one of the ETA publications for that year, which was very detailed and targeted at quite specific scenes, lines and aspects of language from the play, all in the context of seeing it through performance decisions (Michaels). The unit covered areas such as improvisations of specific lines; and contrasts between public and private scenes, and between duologues, soliloquies and asides – each with an eye to performance. Theatrical and visual imagery was considered from the point of view of designers, lighting technicians, stage-managers. Language was dealt with in detail through focusing on areas such as antithetical imagery, blank verse and rhyming couplets, pauses and silences, contrasts between longer speeches and short exchanges, and ironic subtext in Iago's speeches. In the following year, the ETA published a unit on *Othello* which began with two lessons on parallel improvisations ("Imagine you are the father of …").

Following lessons covered the labelling of scenes ("The anger of Othello", "Desdemona appeals" etc.), character analyses through developing character portfolios, viewing a television production, finding textual references for particular themes aspects of performance, and an essay based on an extract (McPherson).

The relevant examination question in 1988 began with a quote from Othello himself:

> My parts, my title, and my perfect soul
> Shall manifest me rightly. (Challis *Othello*, I ii 30–31)

Students were asked to argue a point of view on: "How does Shakespeare establish Othello's nobility for us? Do you see this nobility as consistent or inconsistent with Othello's later passion?"

1992: 3U

By 1992, I was at a different school again – once more in outer suburban western Sydney, but very diverse, with students from Middle Eastern, Central European and African backgrounds, though most were Australian-born. I was teaching the 2 Unit (Related) / 3 Unit course from the same 1982 syllabus.[5] It is the 3 Unit course on which I will elaborate here. "(M)ore demanding work" was the course's rationale (BSSS *Syllabus: 2/3 Unit* 1982b, 3 Unit section 1). Nevertheless, the syllabus repeated the 2 Unit (Related) syllabus's strictures against "(a)ny sophisticated concept of 'literary criticism'", as well as repeating the 2 Unit (Related) preferred pedagogy of discussion, exchanging opinions, taking part in "workshop" productions of scenes from plays and "reading poetry aloud" (BSSS *Syllabus: 2/3 Unit* 1982b, 3 Unit section 2). The 3 Unit syllabus also repeated the objectives of the 2 Unit (Related) course with the additional objective of providing "for deeper and more extensive study of particular authors and topics" (BSSS *Syllabus: 2/3 Unit* 1982b, 3 Unit section 1). The chosen 3 Unit courses in my class were *Special Study of William Wordsworth* and *Further Study of Modern Poetry*, which dealt with Plath and Levertov. I will be dealing with this latter course here.

Poetry was claimed in both the 3 Unit and 2 Unit (Related) syllabuses to be "the most demanding part of the English Syllabus … (and) also potentially the most rewarding" (BSSS *Syllabus: 2/3 Unit* 1982b, 2 Unit section 5; 3 Unit section 4). This level of challenge was said to come about

---

5   The syllabus was published in 1982 and first implemented in 1983.

through language that was denser and more highly wrought, more remote from everyday idiom and often using older literary conventions (BSSS *Syllabus: 2/3 Unit* 1982b, 2 Unit section 5; 3 Unit section 5). Honest personal response was valued over knowledge of periods, genres, language conventions – even literary criticism. Close reading of the language was the key pedagogy, leading ultimately to seeing the connection of form to meaning (BSSS *Syllabus: 2/3 Unit* 1982b, 2 Unit section 6; 3 Unit section 6).

Having already studied Wordsworth, our work on this elective began with an outline of the period between the Romantics and the Moderns. We then read all of the Plath poems to discuss initial reactions to the selected poems ("The Applicant", "Lady Lazarus", "Nick and the Candlestick", "Daddy", "You're", "Kindness", and "Ariel") as a corpus. I introduced the students to Plath's biography, stressing the point that personal experience is transformed through art and that the poems should not be read from the life alone. We proceeded then by discussing the poems in turn, focusing closely on the language, with a small piece of writing to do for each, some of which invited overall commentary, some of which focused closely on a particular image or aspect of language. The work on Plath moved towards larger discussion of the world of the *Ariel* collection.

As with Plath, we began the study of Levertov with a reading of all of the poems ("Ways of Conquest", "The Woman," "Don't You Hear That Whistle Blowin'", "In Thai Binh [Peace] Province", "The Poem Rising By Its Own Weight") as a group. Levertov's biography was introduced with the same strictures as Plath's . Students were given a poem-by-poem study guide to be completed in advance of the study of each poem. Again, we proceeded by discussing the poems in turn, focusing closely on the language, with a small piece of writing to do for each, most of which this time focused closely on a particular image or aspect of language.

After working on the individual poets, time was spent on discussing how the two poets represented ideas and forms and how these might help define "modern poetry". As the students were familiar with Lowell from the 2 Unit (Related) section of their course, we discussed Plath as a confessional poet, while asking whether Levertov could / could not also be given this label. A Levertov study guide that we used had been published by the ETA in 1986 (Manion) – not recent certainly, but its questions allowed students to build notes on basic issues about the poems while class discussion focused on close reading. In 1992, the ETA published an article on the *Modern Poetry* elective that picked up issues in both sets of poems, such as both poets' relationships with men as presented in the poems. In the article, Levertov's and Plath's lives were discussed in relation to the writing of poetry itself and this was followed by a discussion of confessional poetry. The article presented a useful table for students to use in further note-building around individual poems (Gardner and Gonzalvez). We also read and discussed in some depth a number of academic articles on the poets.

The examination question that year was appropriately challenging. Students were to focus on both "Ways of Conquest" (Levertov) and "Nick and the Candlestick" (Plath) – which were printed on the exam paper – to address the ways in which the two poems expressed the relationship between the inner self and the outer world. There was a stimulus to introduce the question, consisting of a quote from Plath and a statement on the ways poets bridge the space between the inner self and the outer world by exploring a personal response to an object, event or feeling.

1993: 2U General

The last class I wish to consider – because it gives a perspective on a quite different approach to text – is my 2 Unit General class in 1993. Among the 1982 syllabuses, 2 Unit General was regarded as the course "which the majority of candidates (were) expected to take" (BSSS, *Syllabus: 2U General* 1982a: 1). Picking up the theme of the 2 Unit (Related) syllabus in defining the course by exemplar texts, it began with the argument that while it was "allowing for such possibilities as the study of Shakespeare, (it was) especially concerned to provide access to contemporary culture, and to equip students to take an informed interest in literature and in language in a variety of contexts" (BSSS *Syllabus: 2U General* 1982a 1).

Its objectives were:

> To improve the ability to understand and appreciate spoken and written English, and to speak and write English well.
>
> To encourage students to read a wide range of books with pleasure and understanding, to develop individual response to literature, and to promote thoughtful and articulate responses to the language of other media. (BSSS *Syllabus: 2U General* 1982a 1)

The syllabus claimed to hold in "balance" different models of English as well as balancing literature and non-literary material. It emphasised "careful reading and interpretation and challenged [students] to extend their experience through reading, writing and talking about literature of substance and complexity and through appreciating the content and form of other media employing language". Imaginative writing was encouraged (BSSS *Syllabus: 2U General* 1982a 2). Across Years 11 and 12, texts were to include poetry, novels, short stories and general prose, from different periods and places, and could include English translations. "Access" to the language and the concerns of literature was felt to be a potential problem for these students and the approach to textual study was "to widen a student's range of response, and to show the interest and enjoyment that become possible once ... barriers are overcome". The first approach to be followed was "to put the students in possession of a world – in a poem or play or novel – that may otherwise have remained closed to them". The next step was to "place more emphasis on what students make of their reading". Class and group discussion were encouraged in order to "formulate various reactions, [compare] divergent responses and [go] back to the text to defend or modify them". In addition, the teacher was to develop in students "a growing awareness that while first thoughts and assertions of opinion may have their value, they can sometimes be shown to have missed the point, and that further, more thoughtful reading is generally more rewarding" (BSSS *Syllabus: 2U General* 1982a 2). "Response" was again the key theme – the word or a close variant of it occurred nine times in the six-page syllabus under the headings *Objectives* (twice), *The Study of Texts* (twice), *The Study of Non-Literary Material* (once), *Year 11* (twice), and *Year 12/Poetry* (twice). The syllabus explicitly rejected the use of literary works to "illustrate" general themes because "this tends to subordinate the works themselves, or to encourage only a partial reading of them" (BSSS *Syllabus: 2U General* 1982a 5). The problem with this was that the syllabus also argued that in Year 12 "students should be able to pursue particular interests in topic areas" (BSSS *Syllabus: 2U General* 1982a 4). It was this statement that brought into the 2 Unit General HSC course the notion of a Topic Area, which could mean that the study of literature in that particular context came very close to using literature to "'illustrate' general themes". Students were required to study two poets, two fiction texts and two plays. In addition, they were to study a text that sat within a designated Topic Area. In 1993, my class studied Peter Skrzynecki, Wilfred Owen, Criena Rohan's *The Delinquents*, Peter Goldsworthy's *Maestro*, Michael Gow's *Away* and David Williamson's *The Removalists*. Topic Areas for 1993 were *The Family* and *Working Lives*. We studied *Working Lives* and our chosen text was an "Act" from Robert Caswell's television mini-series script, *Scales of Justice*, which concerned police corruption. The relevant Act was *The Job*, which focused on the dilemma of a young probationary constable who witnesses a theft by a senior officer. Topic Area study was meant to include supplementary material as well as the central text, so the introduction to the Topic Area for my students was setting up a scrapbook in which they could include other material (ads, cartoons, articles, lyrics, film summaries) that could be analysed and discussed alongside *The Job* in the exam. We read the script, analysed the relevant television episode and set about discussing the various aspects of "working lives" that the text covered. These became such Working Lives sub-topics as: the job as forming one's identity, job pressures, training, and gender roles. Students became experts in groups on these sub-topics, led class discussion on them and supplied detailed notes on their area of expertise. We discussed some supplementary material in common (the television series *Hill Street Blues* and *The Bill*, along with song lyrics and newspaper articles), as well as material students had chosen themselves – and of course we discussed how all of this was to be managed and how to make strategic selection from this material for exam purposes. A young female police officer came to school to address the students; by picking up sub-topics I had sent her, her talk itself became a piece of supplementary material – a text. She highlighted key issues for probationers in the police force, what it meant to be part of a team, the role of female officers, the police as a family, and how personal lives can be affected by the job.

Scales of Justice did not have an ETA unit published near the time of teaching. The exam question that year was "What impressions did you form of your chosen topic from your set text?" and "How did the supplementary material you have gathered affect your understanding of the topic?" It could hardly have been more open-ended and raised, I think, the problematic issue of using texts to "'illustrate' general themes".

Discussion

In reviewing this period, a key concept highlighted in all syllabuses is *response*, and response with close attention to the text. One might say that what is repeatedly envisaged is response disciplined by the words on the page. That 1976 syllabus, which enjoined teachers of 2UA texts such as *Summer of the Seventeenth Doll* to forego "exhaustive detailed analysis" and to aim for responses which are "honest and thoughtful, and backed by knowledge of the text" but not to "impose … views, or to shape reactions into some supposedly orthodox pattern" (BSSS *syllabus* 1976 10), was asking teachers to walk a fine line. There is, of course, no necessary contradiction between response and close reading. One only has to read the critical work of a theorist such as Stanley Fish (e.g. *Self-Consuming Artefacts*) to see that. Nevertheless, teachers have to walk the line between, on the one hand, "individual response" which is "honest and thoughtful" and captured in "free discussion" and "general interpretation and evaluation" without views or orthodoxies being "imposed"; and, on the other, having "detailed" enough analyses for exam purposes, particularly when students "had failed to perceive something important about the work." Although this is not an impossible walk, it can be difficult, which is why the examination sometimes becomes the de facto syllabus. The teacher can feel that any potential areas raised by an examination do need to be covered, and "exhaustive detailed analysis" easily becomes a driver.

Response disciplined by text is also repeatedly evident in the professional literature of the time. When in 1977 the NSW English Teachers Association published *English in Secondary Schools: Today and Tomorrow* (Watson and Eagleson), its discussions of teaching literature, combined with the other material coming out of the NSW ETA in that same year, suggests a set of characteristic practices in classroom teaching of literature that included class and group discussion, improvisation and dramatic re-enactment, and the validating of personal response, especially through writing. All of this, however, was in the context of a strong focus on teaching literature as an exercise in how language works (e.g. Carroll et al, Christie, Johnson, Tucker, Ward, Williams). The kind of literature study that is explicitly advocated in the professional literature of 1977 overwhelmingly concerns study of the literary uses of language (see also Boardman, Case, Eagleson, Harkin and Carleberg, Homer, Kramer).

In 1982, the Australian Association for the Teaching of English published *New Essays in the Teaching of Literature* (Mallick, Moss and Hansen) – a collection of papers from the Literature Commission of the Third International Conference on the Teaching of English held in Sydney in 1980. Reader-response theory was one of two central theoretical underpinnings of the collection (the other was the need to contextualise reading and texts and to broaden the object of study to include products of the culture beyond high art). These essays argue the need to value individual response, but are nuanced in different ways: "a critical evaluative response" is desired, but ought not to be forced "too soon", pushing out the student's personal response (Woolley 29); "close attention to the words on the page is a very fine thing … (but) pupils should first encounter the text … and *nothing else*" (Summerfield 115); "(t)eachers [ought not to] see their role as one of giving information about literature or one of imposing literary judgements on students", but they can work toward responses that are "more informed" (Mallick 191–192); "(l)iterary texts should be ... handled in such a way as to invite a genuine response to or engagement with the text by the student. There must be far more concern with the language of literature and its form" (Moss and Higgins 215). Jack Thomson in *Understanding Teenagers' Reading* from 1987 is very explicit about reader-response theory as a key driver of his model of the reading development of adolescents, with his particular interest being the work of Wolfgang Iser.

Implicit in the syllabuses that drove the work on *The Doll*, *Othello*, Plath and Levertov, and *Scales of Justice* are the social and relational aspects of the literature classroom. "[R]eading issu[ing] naturally into discussion" (BSSS *Syllabus* 1976 10) is a theme repeated throughout the various syllabuses, which are underpinned by a conscious concern for the social processes that define an English classroom. This may be entirely expected in a junior classroom with a junior syllabus as a driver, but is not necessarily so in a system driven by high-stakes public examination. Yet the central importance of discussion dominates all of the syllabuses, many of the ETA resources, and is a bedrock activity in teaching the texts. Response, therefore, is not positioned by institutional entities that drive the HSC teaching of literature, such as syllabuses or work published by professional associations, as an activity undertaken in isolation, but, rather, as an activity within an "interpretive community" (Fish *Naturally*) of the classroom. In fact, given the exam-driven context, the degree of concern in senior syllabuses for the quality of the literary experience in a classroom is noteworthy:

> The range of the course is designed to appeal to a wide variety of interests, and texts should be chosen and combined in ways that will capture enthusiasm and repay closer study. Students should be encouraged to engage with the issues that emerge from the imaginative and non-imaginative works which they read (BSSS *Syllabus:2U General* 1982a 4).

Even the examination questions, with their direct second-person address to the student ("Do you see this nobility as consistent ... ?"; "What impressions did you form?") convey the culture of response and (perhaps by stretching a point given the examination context) of community. Part of Peel's research on student readers highlights "the productive and socially interactive reading practices of higher education English student readers", who prioritise "the social motivation for reading" (Peel 166, 169). Importantly, Reid's preferred "workshop" model of English, in which the reading and the writing of texts operate each on the other, occurs most fundamentally through dialogic exchange. I would argue that the culture of literature teaching in this period sees the practice, the resources, the examination of *The Doll, Othello,* Plath and Levertov, and *Scales of Justice,* as making and performing a version of "literary sociability" (Kirkpatrick and Dixon). Reid, in fact, argues that "intensive collaboration between students ... needs to be fostered as part of a comprehensive development of exchange relationships in literary education" (36).

Did the pedagogy – as recommended in syllabuses, in important reading from the time and in my version of practice – link to more general trends of the time? Certainly pedagogy was far more within what Barnes at the time called an "Interpretation" as opposed to a "Transmission" paradigm. I do not want to make this argument on any grounds to do with the Progressive or the Romantic, but rather in quite different terms, viz. that in the classroom, social relationships are tied to intellectual work. Barnes' research into teachers' attitudes to writing showed that it was "precisely those teachers who value[d] social relationships who also value[d] intellectual exchange" (Barnes 145). This is an important issue about the intellectual work of the literature classroom. It is not that dialogism or relationality are an add-on. I would argue about secondary literature teaching that dialogue is actually fundamental to that process of walking the line between individual response and close attention to the text. Refinement of an intellectual position on a text needs the "sociable" work of discussion.

A word needs to be added about the place of Australian literature in my selections. The reader may have noted that my 1980 2 Unit A selections and 1993 2 Unit General texts were almost all Australian. Across what were regarded as the more challenging courses – 2 Unit (Related) in 1988 and 3 Unit in 1992 – only one Australian text was chosen: Jessica Anderson's *Tirra Lirra by the River.* Did my personal selection reflect the choices actually on offer in those years by the relevant curriculum Board? While there was a reasonable coverage overall of Australian texts, in this period it is certainly true that at the 2 Unit level they occupied a much greater proportion of the "less" demanding 2 Unit A and 2 Unit General courses. This position was exacerbated by the very high proportion of Australian texts in a new (1989) course: 2 Unit Contemporary, in which "[t]he focus for literature study [was] reading for understanding, enjoyment and exploration of issues, rather than close literary or textual study" (BSE *Syllabus: Contemporary English* 1988 1). In this course, in both 1992 and 1993, 28 texts were on offer and in each year, 20 of these were Australian. This was at a time when the national literature was at something of a high point in its critical history. In the contemporaneous second edition of the *Oxford Companion to Australian Literature*, Heseltine marks the period through the 1980s and 1990s as one of "increasing professionalism" and particularly high energy in regard to critical work in Australian literature (Heseltine 205–206). In 1981, *The Oxford History of Australian Literature* appeared, in 1988, the *Penguin New Literary History of Australia*, and between these, John Docker's well-known (1984) critique of the Australian literary critical establishment, *In a Critical Condition*.

So, was the relative prevalence of Australian texts in the 2 Unit A/ General/Contemporary courses a cause for particular comment? To a large extent the 2 Unit (Related) lists very much reflect what Yiannakis identifies as a nationwide "core literary canon comprised of Austen, Conrad, Eliot, Hardy, Shakespeare and ... Arthur Miller (as a) central pantheon" (107). There was a canon and it was largely British-centric in the 2 Unit (Related) courses. More interesting, however, was the place of Australian literature in the most demanding course of all – 3 Unit – which made the issue of the place of Australian literature in this NSW context somewhat more complex. In 1988, seven courses were available as 3 Unit electives. Two of these were entirely Australian and, additionally, Australian writers made up half of the Special Study of Modern Poetry (Harwood) and Modern Fiction (Winton and Astley) electives. This was reduced somewhat in 1992 and 1993, though both years had an Australian elective and, additionally, it would have been possible in 1993 to study only Australian plays in the Modern Drama elective. Finally, it is worth keeping in mind that the 2 Unit General course was the course "which the majority of candidates (were) expected to take" (BSSS, *Syllabus: 2U General*, 1982a 1). This could have resulted, then, in most HSC students reading mostly Australian literature.

In fact, the process of text selection deserves some brief comment. Teachers will more often than not begin their thinking about text selection based on the texts they love themselves. If Peel's research findings are reflected in Australia, English teachers become English teachers because they love reading (Peel 175ff). Something like "literary quality", then, is probably a first consideration. However, teachers – and systems leaders, such as text selection committees – need to take into account a number of factors in choosing texts. The balance between these can be tricky. One issue is appeal – this is not just about pandering to popular taste, but a genuine concern that the role of the course and, indeed, the text, is to go beyond the exam and help create lifelong readers: "[t]o encourage students to read a wide range of books with pleasure and understanding, to develop individual response to literature" (BSSS *Syllabus:2U General* 1982a 1). A teacher's experience of what "works well" in classrooms, particularly around that anxiously desired process of discussion, is a closely related factor.

Text selection committees may seek the more local and more contemporary texts when thinking about students who will need extra support in the subject. Nevertheless, even the notion of relevance is tricky – it isn't just found in the immediate context and can be manifest in a wide variety of texts from many times and for different reasons. Note how the 1976 syllabus tries to balance these concerns: literature is to represent "the contemporary and the local, as well as ... the literature of other times and places". Chosen texts were to "have a ready appeal, and ... at the same time offer sufficient maturity of thought, feeling and expression to justify study and to provide an introduction to intelligent, adult reading" (BSSS *Syllabus* 1976 10). Note, too, that the 2 Unit General syllabus aims not only for reading "with pleasure and understanding" and providing access to contemporary culture, but doing so with "literature of substance and complexity" (BSSS *Syllabus: 2UGeneral* 1982a 1–2). In recent years, as new texts have come onto HSC Prescribed Texts lists in NSW, the Board of Studies has provided annotations to new texts. The headings for these are interesting, presumably capturing a set of criteria for that text being chosen. They are:

- Merit and cultural significance
- Needs and interests of students
- Opportunities for challenging teaching and learning (BOS).

Finally, in terms of literary theory, while, as I hope I have shown, there was a recognisable reader-response pedagogy in the collective institutional culture of HSC literature study, I think practice was probably more eclectic and strategic in reality. I'm not sure that in conducting close reading I wasn't as likely to be committing New Criticism as echoing the reading practices of Stanley Fish. Certainly, the written literary criticism which my students were given to read and discuss often included the big names of New Criticism, as exemplifying what close attention to the text can produce. My main caveat would be that, in attempting to implement the spirit of each senior syllabus, students were expected to engage with the plurality of responses in a classroom and to test these against the text. English teachers at the time – as they always do when they are collectively "inside" the institutions formed by syllabuses, examinations, professional publications and practice – formed a version of "epistemic communality" (Ball 1) within the contingencies of that institutional context. I hope I have here explained a version of that communality.

I would like to thank Jane Fitzpatrick of the New South Wales Board of Studies, Teaching and Educational Standards, and Patricia Dowsett of the University of Western Australia for their great assistance in finding and supplying many of the documents discussed here.

Works cited

Ball, Stephen J. "Competition and conflict in the teaching of English: A socio-historical analysis". *Journal of Curriculum Studies* 14.1 (1982): 1–28. Print.
Barnes, Douglas. *From Communication to Curriculum*. Harmondsworth: Penguin, 1976.
Board of Secondary Education (BSE) NSW. *Syllabus Years 7–10 English*. North Sydney: Board of Secondary Education. 1987. Print.
——. *Syllabus: 2 Unit Contemporary English*. North Sydney: NSW Department of Education. 1988. Print.
Board of Senior School Studies (BSSS) NSW. *English Syllabus, Year 11 and Year 12: 3 Unit, 2 Unit and 2 Unit A Courses*. Sydney: New South Wales Department of Education. 1976. Print.
——. *English Syllabus, Years 11 and 12: 2 Unit (General) Course*. North Sydney: Board of Senior School Studies. 1982a. Print.
——. *English Syllabus, Year 11 and Year 12: 2/3 Unit (Related) Course*. North Sydney: Board of Senior School Studies. 1982b. Print.
Board of Studies (BOS) NSW. *English Stage 6 Annotations of Selected Texts Prescribed for the Higher School Certificate 2015–20*. Sydney: NSW Board of Studies, 2013. Web. 31 December 2015. <www.boardofstudies.nsw.edu.au/syllabus_hsc/pdf_doc/english-annotations-2015-20.pdf/>
Boardman, Graham. "The teaching of language: Years 7–10". *English in Secondary Schools: Today and tomorrow*. Ed. Kenneth D. Watson and Robert D. Eagleson. Ashfield: English Teachers' Association of New South Wales, 1997. 361–376. Print.
Carroll, Chris, et al. "Teaching English: Comments on everyday issues". *ETA (NSW) Newsletter* (1977, November): 3–16. Print.
Case, Gilbert. "Poetry". *English in Secondary Schools: Today and tomorrow*. Ed. Kenneth D. Watson and Robert D. Eagleson. Ashfield: English Teachers' Association of New South Wales, 1977. 412–415. Print.
Christie, Frances. "Les Murray's poetry – and Year 11". *ETA (NSW) Newsletter* (1977, September): 15–18. Print.
Eagleson, Robert D. "Variation in language". *English in Secondary Schools: Today and tomorrow*. Ed. Kenneth D. Watson and Robert D. Eagleson. Ashfield: English Teachers' Association of New South Wales, 1977.63–77. Print.
Farrar, Pat. "Doing something different with *The Doll*". *ETA (NSW) Newsletter* 5.80 (1980, September): 1–5. Print.
Fish, Stanley. *Self-Consuming Artefacts: The experience of seventeenth century literature*. Berkeley: University of California Press, 1972. Print.
——. *Doing What Comes Naturally: Change, rhetoric and the practice of theory in literary and legal studies*. Durham and London: Duke University Press, 1989. Print.

Gardner, Elizabeth and Daphne Gonzalvez. "Modern poetry option– Sylvia Plath, Denise Levertov: Some general comments", *The Teaching of English* 2.92 (1992, July): 48–50. Print.

Harkin, Jim and Carleberg, Marjorie. "Ideas for integration of Language and Literature". *English in Secondary Schools: Today and tomorrow.* Ed. Kenneth D. Watson and Robert D. Eagleson. Ashfield: English Teachers' Association of New South Wales, 1977. 387–391. Print.

Heseltine, H.P. "Criticism". *The Oxford Companion to Australian Literature*. Ed. William H. Wilde, Joy Hooton and Barry Andrews, 1994. 200–207. Print.

Homer, David. "The teaching of literature". *English in Secondary Schools: Today and tomorrow.* Ed. Kenneth D. Watson and Robert D. Eagleson. Ashfield: English Teachers' Association of New South Wales, 1977. 342–360. Print.

Johnson, Ron. "Teaching poetry: One approach". *ETA (NSW) Newsletter* (1977, November): 21–22. Print.

Kirkpatrick, Peter and Robert Dixon, eds. *Republics of Letters: Literary communities in Australia,* Sydney: Sydney University Press, 2012. Print.

Kramer, Leonie. "Integration of Language and Literature". *English in Secondary Schools: Today and tomorrow.* Ed. Kenneth D. Watson and Robert D. Eagleson. Ashfield: English Teachers' Association of New South Wales, 1977. 379–386. Print.

Mallick, David. "Text and reader". *New Essays in the Teaching of Literature.* Eds. David Mallick, Peter Moss and Ian Hansen. Norwood: AATE, 1982. 191–213. Print.

Mallick, David, Peter Moss, and Ian Hansen, eds. *New Essays in the Teaching of Literature.* Norwood: AATE, 1982. Print.

Manion, Shirley. "The poetry of Denise Levertov". *English Teachers' Association of NSW Newsletter* 2.86 (1986, April):41. Print.

McPherson, Deborah. "*Othello*". *English Teachers' Association of NSW Newsletter* 2.89 (1989, April):15. Print.

Medway, Peter, et al. *English Teachers in a Postwar Democracy: Emerging choice in London schools, 1945–1965.* New York: Palgrave Macmillan, 2014. Print.

Michaels, Wendy. "*Othello, the Moor of Venice*". *English Teachers' Association of NSW Newsletter* 1. 88 (1988, February): 6–9. Print.

Moss, Peter and Christine Higgins. "Afterword and way ahead". *New Essays in the Teaching of Literature.* Eds. David Mallick, Peter Moss and Ian Hansen. Norwood: AATE, 1982: 214–216.

NSW Secondary Schools Board (NSWSSB). *Syllabus in English for Forms I–IV*. Sydney: NSW Department of Education, 1971. Print.

——. "General bibliography and commentary". *Notes on the Syllabus in English, 1.* Sydney: NSW Secondary Schools Board, n.d. Print.

——. "Literature". *Notes on the Syllabus in English Years 7–10, 3:* Sydney: NSW Department of Education, n.d. Print.

Peel, Robin. "Beliefs about English in England". *Questions of English: Ethics, aesthetics, rhetoric and the formation of the subject in England, Australia and the United States.* Eds. Robin Peel, Annette Patterson and Jeanne Gerlach. London and New York: Routledge Falmer. 2000. Print.

Reid, Ian. *The Making of Literature: Texts, contexts and classroom practices.* Norwood, S.A.: Australian Association for the Teaching of English. 1984. Print.

Stratta, Leslie, John Dixon, and Andrew Wilkinson. *Patterns of Language: Explorations in the teaching of English*, London: Heinemann. 1973. Print.

Summerfield, Geoffrey. "Literature teaching and some of our responsibilities". *New Essays in the Teaching of Literature.* Eds. David Mallick, Peter Moss and Ian Hansen. Norwood: AATE, 1982: 112–123.

Thomson, Jack. *Understanding Teenagers' Reading: Reading processes and the teaching of literature*. New York: Nichols Publishing; London: Croom Helm; Melbourne: Methuen. 1987. Print.

Tucker, Ernie. "Imaginative re-creation of literature". *English in Secondary Schools: Today and tomorrow*. Ed. Kenneth D. Watson and Robert D. Eagleson. Ashfield: English Teachers' Association of New South Wales, 1977. 398–399. Print.

Ward, John. "Involvement with literature". *English in Secondary Schools: Today and Tomorrow*. Ed. Kenneth D. Watson and Robert D. Eagleson. Ashfield: English Teachers' Association of New South Wales, 1977. 392–397 Print.

Watson, Kenneth D. and Robert D. Eagleson, eds. *English in Secondary Schools: Today and tomorrow*, Ashfield: English Teachers' Association of New South Wales, 1977. Print.

Williams, Geoff. "Exploratory talk", *English in Secondary Schools: Today and tomorrow*. Ed. Kenneth D. Watson and Robert D. Eagleson. Ashfield: English Teachers' Association of New South Wales, 1977. 202–208. Print.

Wooley, Jan. "The expressive response". *New Essays in the Teaching of Literature*. Eds. David Mallick, Peter Moss and Ian Hansen. Norwood: AATE, 1982. 18–30. Print.

Yeo, Philip. "*Summer of the Seventeenth Doll* – Ray Lawler". *ETA (NSW) Newsletter* 5.78 (1978, September): 26–28. Print.

Yiannakis, John. "A possible literary canon in upper school English literature in various Australian states, 1945–2005" *Issues in Educational Research*, 24 (1) (2014): 98–113. Print.

Chapter Eight

TURNING AROUND ENGLISH

Distant reading and rapid subject change from 1980 to 1995

Jo Jones

Any teacher worth their salt will tell you that textual intimacy is at the heart of good English teaching. Days, weeks, years and decades are built around the patterns worn by the modular blocks of class periods, term weeks and academic years. But within this regulated space, teachers of secondary English see patterns of learning take place, as students come to know the journey of a plot as it unfolds or perceive the way a simple character can represent a convergence of complex ideas. When we teach texts we are fortunate enough sometimes to witness new intellectual understandings, sensibilities taking shape, and authentic personal connections and resonances. There are moments in an English class studying novels, plays, poems or films when teacher and students alike share the power of narrative events. The swish of Julia's skirt in George Orwell's *1984* indicates to Winston Smith that she might in some way represent a forbidden type of freedom. Replicant Roy Batty in Ridley Scott's *Blade Runner* mourns the nihilistic state of the universe, knowing memories of his life's events will vanish with his impending death, all gone "like tears in the rain". In Tim Winton's *Cloudstreet* a lost and disaffected Quick Lamb, badly injured while roo-shooing, looks up to see his brother, Fish, rowing their dinghy impossibly through a wheat-field and wordlessly internalises the strange paradox that divinity works through the ordinary. The eponymous Breaker Morant (Weir 1979) challenges the Highland Guards' firing squad to "shoot straight ya bastards; don't make a mess of it" and dies before the purple light of a spectacular dawn in a kind of glorious unexplained sacrifice. Part of the teacher–student connection is the intensity of being so "close up" to powerful human experiences, whether through close reading of a text or in the analysis of the specificity of *mise-en-scène* in particular films. Much of what is both required and rewarding in teaching is to do with closeness: shared experience and interpretation and how the intimacy of close reading – syntax, diction, quirks of phrasing, subtleties of rhythm – reveals myriad voices and special stories. With many of the key narratives that we study, literature is a matter of interiority and immersion: we know them and feel them, and we encourage students to do the same.

For English teachers in both secondary or tertiary contexts, the process of Franco Moretti's *distant reading*, on initial contact, is deeply foreign – a specifically empirical approach of initiating massive data collection and analyses across large swathes of time. Attuned to Moretti's methods and approach, the Analysis of Literature in Australian Schools (ALIAS) database illuminates our subject from a different, more remote, viewpoint. The conclusions reached through distant reading are necessarily "second hand: a patchwork of other people's research *without a single direct textual reading*" (Moretti 2). This study seeks patterns observed from a distance, where connections are discernible through similarities in genre and form, language and style, plot and theme. The digital form of ALIAS yields information not only on the authors and texts most included on state syllabuses but also the way the syllabus makers of certain periods are inclined to favour certain text types over others. Patterns of text inclusion over a substantial span of years and decades – waves of advance and retreat – evidence both the complexity and necessity of distant reading in this field. The patterns themselves are both familiar and surprising as one works chronologically through lists, as texts move up and downward on a hierarchical list: so many journeys of ascent and descent.

English and English Literature have been separate subjects since the 1960s. English is commonly supposed to be the more energised and dynamic of the two, an assumption that always struck me as strange when I was in the classroom, particularly as Literature typically attracts more motivated and "able" students, students who often read for pleasure not to fulfil humanities/literacy requirements for tertiary entrance. The patterns that emerged from analysis of text inclusions in the ALIAS database, however, do indeed reflect the common assumption about the English/Literature divide. English *is* more dynamic and volatile, which, if you consider it from another angle, is quite logical, since educators work harder to make connections and meaning for students who might not see any direct benefit from textual studies. By contrast ALIAS data shows us the "steadiness" of Literature. Text lists change much less, and maintain a much closer connection to longer cultural patterns, the traditional British literary canon and historical and cultural continuities. (Among the most commonly listed authors during the last two decades of the twentieth century were Joseph Conrad, Emily Brontë, Jane Austen, the Metaphysical Poets and Shakespeare.) It is important to note that this does not mean that the varied iterations of Literature courses have withstood changing disciplinary demands and changing educative expectations. It is true, however, at least for the period under analysis here, that English has been the more radical and responsive subject. As this essay will discuss, the textual inclusions in senior secondary general English courses are deeply affected by the current socio-historical conditions of their writing and rewriting, but in ways that are often unexpectedly complex and not always straightforwardly "progressive". In fact, texts selected for syllabuses over the decades of this study reflect deep and enduring cultural contradictions and ambiguities. What this particular study shows is how rapidly change occurred in subject English when massive changes in social and educative systems coincided with unprecedented disciplinary upheaval. As cultural studies paradigms transformed university English departments, school English also "turned" to many of its tenets: "turned" to popular fiction texts, "turned" to film, "turned" to politicised modes of analysis. The changes wrought during this time still affect the shapes of subject English in Australia to this day.

This chapter identifies trends in the most included texts on Australian state syllabus lists across three five-year spans: 1980–85, 1985–90 and 1990–95. It considers the particularities of each five-year period observed from a distance. The accompanying three tables have been generated from the ALIAS database for each period. They include the 30 highest ranked texts in each group[1] and include data gleaned from each Australian state during the specified time. Texts that rank highly, therefore, may do so both because of their relative longevity on the list (that is, having been included for a number of years), or their inclusion across a number of individual state syllabuses simultaneously, or these combined factors. As all informed "distant reading" analysts are ready to admit, this method has its limits and this

---

1 The three tables at the end of this essay contain the top listed texts over three specific periods – my aim was to include the top 30 texts, but as so many texts are listed in equal places, it is impossible to include the same number. Therefore, Table 8.1 lists 29, Table 8.2 lists 30 and Table 8.3 lists 25.

type of study does not explain the complex and intricate process of how either individual texts or syllabuses unfold in individual times or locations, but reveal large-scale complexities more vast in scale and scope; they give us insights into subject English in the large, more abstract space of the nation – how, as Benedict Anderson famously termed it, it is an "imagined community" held together across time and space.

Adopting Moretti's predilection for metaphor in thinking about distant reading, I will explore the *fabric* of English text selection visible in ALIAS data from afar. The tight vertical "warp" threads form the foundation on which the cloth is woven. They are the strong foundational principles on which texts are selected and included for study on state English syllabuses. For some decades now the emphasis has been on: 1) direct cultural, textual and aesthetic familiarity and relatability; 2) currency – texts must reflect or contain a kind of immediate relevance to national social/cultural contexts; and 3) general "teachability" or a simple and useful unity of form and theme that make them useful texts for students when they have to respond to texts in formal ways, such as under examination. The "weft" of the threads is altogether more varied and changeable, with certain colours and textures coming through to the surface of the fabric at certain historic/cultural moments and being woven under at others. As in a piece of fabric, the weft brings colour, texture and variance to the cloth. Among these colours are notable strains and strands, dominant colours, textures and patterns. From an analysis of the most included texts on Australian state syllabuses from 1985 to 1995 there a number of threads, including the following strongest narrative and thematic threads: 1) war, particularly Australians at war; 2) East and South-East Asian conflict; 3) Indigenous experience; and 4) cautionary narratives and questions of "progress". While there are specific historical and cultural indicators for the prominence of these categories, some of them are both surprising and telling in their continued presence on syllabus lists throughout the decades, even when immediate cultural relevance may seem long past.

As English is the course that tends to change in order to remain immediate and relevant, there are satisfying patterns of inclusion that reflect historical and social preoccupations and indeed reinforce the courses status as *au courant*. It also inflected by the kind of rich and intimate teaching knowledge gained through cycles of classroom teaching that are, as I have already mentioned, so reliant on close reading. As Jonathan Freedman observes, "the paradoxical effect of Moretti's polemic for distant reading is then to remind us of the continuing importance of its double, twin and dialectic companion, close reading" (Freedman). Through this paradoxical process, the new angles revealed through the long-focus ALIAS database are enriched by close-focus insights that classroom familiarities can bring. Looking through the many entries on the ALIAS reports is like looking through a list of old friends, with many inclusions one would expect; even so, there are surprises that make a familiar list suddenly strange and puzzling. Seeing our discipline and subject from a different vantage point is a creative and productive exercise.

1980–1985

Compared to the lists that come after it, the 1980–1985 text list (Table 8.1) is vitally important to this study as it indicates the predominantly *literary* qualities of English before significant changes to both school subject and academic discipline were brought to bear on the construction of syllabus material. The inclusion of titles from the Australian literature canon is both significant and, perhaps to more recently qualified teachers, surprising. Those characteristically "general English" features of selected texts – the warp of accessibility, relevance, currency – is garnered from the category of the well-recognised and popular Australian literary "middlebrow". While later lists reflect different assumptions (accessible texts means shorter, often popular and often YA texts, short stories, non-fiction or expository works, and many more visual texts such as feature films), accessibility and relevance in 1980–85 were still strongly anchored to the literary. The lists are evidence to that, within the literary field itself, there are so many wider cultural insights to be gained, including the kind of examination of the self and society present in so many iterations of subject English.

George Johnston's *My Brother Jack* (1964), Katharine Prichard's *Coonardoo* (1928) and Randolph Stow's *The Merry-Go-Round in the Sea* (1965), the first three novels listed in Table 8.1, stage in-depth considerations of ethical and social questions in complex narratives that span lengthy periods of time. In varying degrees the stories of the key male characters in these novels belong in the tradition of the Bildungsroman. While they might not be strictly novels of formal education, they are certainly novels of learning, formation and maturation. These three novels also express the very Australian cultural preoccupations with history, culture and the nation as explicated by Russel Ward's iconic *The Australian Legend* (1962) and, later, Graeme Turner's *National Fictions* (1986). These include the vexed relationship between Australia and Britain, the ambivalences of colonial history, Australian strains of masculinity that are uneasy with emotion or interiority, Australia's relationships to war and sacrifice, divided allegiances to the city and the bush, and the valorisation of the worker as a national type.

A list defined by so much Australian content, which also includes important novels such as Henry Handel Richardson's *The Getting of Wisdom* (1910), Thomas Keneally's *The Chant of Jimmie Blacksmith* (1972), Ruth Park's *The Harp in the South* (1948), and Dymphna Cusack's *Caddie* (1953) reflects, like Ward's text, the kind of celebratory nationalism familiar from the cinematic revival of the 1970s and the approaching Bicentenary. They are distinctively Australian (rather than British) stories. The list is headed by the respected figures of an Australian literary canon, in the days when even the existence of world-class Australian literature, let alone the idea of an Australian canon, was still highly contentious. Many of these Australian texts, and often the lives of their authors, connect closely to the complex celebration of nation through the markedly left-wing figure of the Australian worker. Indeed the prominence of these texts recalls the left-wing origins of so much Australian artistic activity at this time, whether through connections to people associated in the 1950s and 1960s with the Australian Communist party (Katharine Prichard), or those who openly declared their working-class pedigree and left-wing affiliations, such as George Johnston. There is little doubt that, notwithstanding the complex and varied reasons behind text selection, an allegiance to forms of radical nationalism is expressed in these syllabuses. In 1980 the Whitlam Labor government's dynamic, youthful nationalism was still in the air. Australia's unique cultural identity, and its self-conscious rejection of the Anglo-Australianism of earlier decades (for excellent discussions see S.J. Ward and Pender), was not only celebrated but supported by funding bodies formed to promote Australian artistic and cultural endeavours, including the Australia Council (*Australia Council Act 1975*) and the Australian Film Commission (1975). One does not have to look far to find public statements that encapsulate the energy of this time. In 1972, for instance, Whitlam stated in an election speech that the purpose of more effective and fair arts funding was to "establish and express an Australian identity through the arts and to promote an awareness of Australian culture abroad" (cited in Whitlam Institute). Perhaps, even more iconically, in 1969 Phillip Adams wrote that Australians need to "see our own landscapes, hear our own voices, dream our own dreams" (Adams).

The other group of texts that have natural narrative and thematic connections is the large group I have designated "cautionary narratives and questions of progress". The dominance of dystopian narratives, it is often recognised among teachers, is to do with the weft of English: shorter prose narratives, often novellas, with dramatic fast-moving plots and characters that embody a spirit of individual defiance, social dissent, anti-establishment thinking and the rejection of totalitarianism in all its forms. The most obvious texts are well-known dystopian novels such as Aldous Huxley's *Brave New World* (1931), George Orwell's *1984* (1949) and Joseph Heller's *Catch-22* (1961). Yet novels and plays such as Graham Greene's *The Power and the Glory* (1940), Muriel Spark's *The Prime of Miss Jean Brodie* (1961), Arthur Miller's *The Crucible* (1953) and Chinua Achebe's *A Man of the People* (1966) also warn of abuses of power (often by an oppressive government) and the law. (It is worth considering the possibility that the dominance of this type of narrative reflects the ongoing influence of the Cold War, which was still the defining global threat at this point in time.) Put alongside the important Australian middlebrow texts that championed thinking individuals who deviate from the established order, we can begin to see how English came to be considered by many as the progressive subject among the secondary humanities subjects: a subject about independent-minded, politicised individuals intended to contribute to the making of such people.

Of the 29 texts that make the 1980–85 list, 20 are novels, or more specifically realist novels. As Moretti observes, the link between realist novels and nations is strong in the European tradition, where novels became a forum for enacting and debating the complexities of nationhood. Novels bring seriousness and status to questions of formation and belonging, but interestingly, are formally impossible for nations of non-European nations to construct due to cultural differences in shapes and expectations of narrative. Yet Moretti offers no explanation for the paradoxically European yet non-European status of the settler-colonial state.[2] Therefore, one could argue that the form of the novel is dominant in Australian English courses because it exerts the seriousness and status of English in the Australian curriculum but also because it is capable of tracing the complex interactions between literature and the emerging nation. The very Eurocentrism of the realist novel – linear narratives and cumulative cause/effect patterns of character development – reinforces and questions our relationship to our Britishness, the inherited culture that we negotiate in a different land, with its conflicted associations of landscape and home. There is little doubt that school syllabuses are a central cultural space for playing out these tensions.

---

2   He discusses Japanese, Indian and Brazilian novels (among others) as examples of the many (or perhaps most) non-European cultural narratives cannot be contained in the realist "cause and effect" narrative of the Western novel and that, indeed they inevitably change and break the form the work with.

1985-1990

The period 1985–1990 is certainly the most unsettled and chaotic period for secondary English of all the periods under discussion here. There are three reasons for this. Firstly, technological changes made it possible to include films and television texts as part of the English teaching experience. Not only could texts be played at school through the new cheap video cassette technology but teachers could also videotape programs/films directly from the television and bring them into the classroom for teaching purposes. Secondly, and related to this, syllabuses expanded to include a much greater range of non-novel texts, including autobiography and biography, feature film, and full-length non-fiction (often social commentary). The third most dramatic change is the rapidly diminished presence of Australian texts, and the virtual disappearance of Australian novels.

In terms of the "weft" of subject English, change naturally came about quickly once these visual technologies became available and the form of texts (visual and non-visual) opened up across state syllabuses. The most significant casualty was the novel, the backbone of subject English, soon supplanted by visual and/or shorter texts that for practical reasons suited educators' purposes just as well. Film versions of written narratives, including novels, playtexts, and biographies, made texts accessible and easier to interpret; and of course it was possible for students to respond to assessment tasks about written texts even if they had not read the original version. In fact all major texts listed have film versions, some of which are highly awarded "classic" films in their own right: *The Grapes of Wrath* (Steinbeck 1939, Ford (dir.) 1940), *A Streetcar Named Desire* (Williams 1947, Kazan (dir.) 1951) and *One Flew over the Cuckoo's Nest* (Kesey 1952, Forman (dir.) 1975) among others.[3] Few teachers (then and now) would not make use of a good adaptation in the classroom to enhance understanding, particularly in English (as opposed to Literature) courses when so much emphasis is placed on accessibility. In 1985–90, the popular dystopian novels remain on the list (most with film versions) in addition to a significant rise in the number of popular stage plays.

As a number of contributors to this volume have observed (most particularly Manuel and Carter, Doecke and Davies), the second half of the 1980s was a time of great change in English and in senior schooling generally, with more students staying at school, especially those who previously would have entered the workforce at 15 (a shift affected by material factors such as youth

---

3   Interestingly, the turn to film adaptations coincides with the rise in North American texts.

unemployment, but also social forces that led to the recognition of the rights of working-class and disadvantaged groups to a longer and richer education). Coinciding with a shift in the discipline of English both overseas and in Australian tertiary English departments, the demise in the status and use of literary texts in the secondary classroom seemed inevitable. Marxist cultural thought, led by Raymond Williams, Richard Hoggart, and others, valorised the study of non-literary texts, particularly popular forms and works, and Marxist theory, led by Terry Eagleton, questioned the class underpinnings of the cultural status of literature. Taking these factors into account it is little wonder that longer literary novels disappeared from the list, although dystopian fiction remained central, as it was suited to cultural materialist critique, and assisted the perception of English as a radical and democratic course.

The only text listed 10 times on state syllabuses during this five-year period is A.B. Facey's autobiography *A Fortunate Life*. Like so many other text on the 1985–1990 list, Facey's work had the advantage of a television/film adaptation that closely followed the written version. *A Fortunate Life* is also such a significant inclusion at this time because of its chronological structure, first person narration, and straightforward conversational style, and because it is an autobiographical account of a then and still iconic white-Australian experience of rural poverty, working-class hardship and the experience of war (in this case Gallipoli, 1915). In the increasing absence of Australian fiction on syllabuses, it fills many of the technical and ideological "spaces" left by the departure of the Great Australian Novel: it deals with typically (male) Australian experience with a likable, stoic and enduring narrator. Also, the autobiographical frame of the text is very "novelistic" with its cause and effect sequence: an impoverished boy with a life marked by adversity is ultimately rewarded with a long and settled "fortunate" life. The "true story" status, in many contexts, would be an advantage, perhaps adding to its relevance and appeal. This is not just the esoteric product of a privileged and culturally remote elite but contains the blood, sweat and toil of a real man. Remembering that this was the period of Australia's Bicentenary, the nationalistic zeal for dinkum working Australians, described by Turner in *National Fictions* as dependent on "the assumption of a connection between egalitarianism, democracy, and individualism" (82–83), is never far from the classroom, despite the decline in the study of Australian novels.

When David Stratton described the high-quality, original and markedly Australian films of the 1970s as *The Last New Wave* in his iconic 1980 publication of the same name, he may not have had any idea how long this wave would take to roll into shore, the canonical national cinema of this time still having a presence in Australian classrooms today. While the major films of this period, including *Breaker Morant*, *The Chant of Jimmie Blacksmith*, and *The Getting of Wisdom* were produced in the 1970s, they did not arrive on school syllabuses until the mid-late 1980s. But their powerful presence is of central importance to the many changes within subject English at this time. The only films listed in the top 30 places during this time are Australian films and, just as importantly, some of the key texts are filmed versions of written texts (*Blacksmith*, *Wisdom*). The power of this relatively new and exciting space in cultural production came to the classroom in such a way that it automatically assumed the status and authority that *My Brother Jack*, *Coonardoo*, and *The Merry-Go-Round in the Sea* had held a decade earlier. To many people Australian stories were, and are, so often film stories.

The energy of change in this period is still perceptible in the list – the verve of radicalising and "freeing up" a subject for a new student audience. There is a "new" English linked to the excitement of a newly established and world-renowned film industry telling "our" stories, the new weapons in the teachers' arsenal of short, dramatic, exciting and popular texts that potentially engaged students more immediately and, possibly, to a whole new degree. Yet it is impossible to consider this period without also recognising what was lost. This includes the connection subject English had with radical Leftist figures within the Australian literary scene, who also wrote "for the people" and who perhaps now seem ancient relics in comparison to the excitement of so much that is new. Also, the decline of Australian novels set limits on the cultural self-examination that earlier texts invited. A case in point is Bruce Beresford's *Breaker Morant*, which is a Boer War film based on Kenneth G. Ross's 1978 play of the real-life trial of poet and bushman Harry ("Breaker") Morant. The story features a conventional courtroom structure, the audience follows the court marshal and immediate execution of Morant and his fellow officer and accomplice Lieutenant Peter Handcock. The narrative appears to span three or so weeks, with flashbacks to the conflicts with the Boer groups that inspired the Australians' revenge killings of prisoners of war and a German missionary. Here, Australian characters are rebellious, driven by national allegiances and mateship, and satisfyingly insubordinate to the British – a rendition of national character that is still striking in its Romanticism. The courtroom case poses the ethical dilemmas attached to the types of acts necessary and/or morally defensible in situations of war. It encourages the view that the Australian did "the necessary" in war even through it was not palatable to British sensibilities. They were then persecuted for it in a terrible and hypocritical betrayal of the parent nation to its unrefined but honest offspring. The two officers are shot before an arresting and affecting background of a vast highland scene and a purple dawn. While there is little doubt at how effective this film would be in plunging the class into a gripping story, one cannot help but compare the depiction of male characters changed by war in the syllabus novels of the previous five years, most pertinently *My Brother Jack* and *The Merry-Go-Round in the Sea*. In longer narratives, where characters are often developed over longer expanses of time, the more complex effects of war on the traumatised and haunted self unfold. Coping mechanisms are essential after the end of war and heroism remains a fraught notion. Privileging feature films to the exclusion of Australian novels arguably signifies a greater loss than gain.

1990-1995 and beyond

During this final period, the choice of text inclusions seems to settle somewhat after the excitement of so much that was new and different in the previous half decade. After the explosion of new textual forms, more varied and culturally diverse texts appear on lists. The Australian novel returns but the era of the lengthier literary middlebrow novel is unequivocally over. Likewise, dystopian fiction does not have the dominance it once enjoyed. Popular plays remain in widespread use, often in tandem with the film adaptations. Australian texts from Indigenous writers appear for the first time (Colin Johnson's *Wild Cat Falling* [1965], Sally Morgan's *My Place* [1987], and Borg and Hyllus's *Women of the Sun* [1981]), and female and immigrant stories assume a higher position (Gillian Bouras's *A Foreign Wife* [1986], Anita Desai's *Village By the Sea* [1982]), as do working-class tales featuring protagonists that are not sympathetic Australian males (Willy Russell's *Educating Rita* [1983], David Williamson's *The Removalists* [1971]). Fascinatingly, novels and feature films that rank highly on the ALIAS list deal with stories of war and upheaval in East Asia (Ballard's *Empire of the Sun* [1984] and Joffé's *The Killing Fields* [1984][4]), perhaps taking the lead from the success of the previously listed and internationally awarded film (based on Christopher Koch's novel), *The Year of Living Dangerously* (Weir 1982).

Although it had been some decades since general English broke away from the literary canon, the canon debates about representing minority

---

4   Interestingly, it is not until at least a decade later that Australian English course started to deal with any version of the Australian genocide and related acts of mass killings. It is not until the prominence of Kate Grenville's novel on syllabus lists after the 2006 publication of *The Secret River* that these topics were meaningfully integrated into the curriculum.

and disempowered groups in university reading lists clearly had a significant effect on syllabus and text list construction by the early 1990s. In the historical moment of the Mabo judgement (1992), Keating's Redfern Park speech (1992), Keating and the Labor Party's establishment of Asia-Pacific Economic Cooperation (APEC) forum, and the related public discussion about Australia's shift away from traditional European alliances, it seems strongly apparent that subject English had much to be proud of in bringing current and dynamic texts to students.

In terms of the warp and weft of subject English, the warp (practical reasons for choosing texts) has not substantially changed since this time. Texts still must be engaging and relevant. The weft, however, remains changeable; we see the move away from the nationalistic (possibly parochial) Australian literature of earlier times, even though there are so many unacknowledged losses in terms of more complex literary stories. The fabric itself remains recognisable but changing, responsive to the always shifting needs and demands of the course, meaningfully reshaping itself as subject and society move and settle. Having said this, I do not intend to end this essay on any straightforward note of triumph. We must remember that in the next decade many aspects of English would be the target of journalists and cultural commentators, politicians and even prime ministers, mostly due to the politicised nature of text selections and the centrality of a politically and aesthetically informed analytical process. There is much more work to be done with the ALIAS database as it shows in the 1995–2000 and 2000–2005 periods the return of texts that arguably had their most useful and relevant moments in previous decades, such as *Breaker Morant*, or perhaps outstayed their usefulness, such as *Wild Cat Falling* and *Educating Rita*, even as new texts emerged and the subject continued to change and morph.

I do not mean to suggest that the story of "English" resolves nicely into its most enlightened and informed shape by 1995, demonstrating how we "progressed" from a flawed and antiquated course to a unifying progressive one. Rather what it does show is how sensitively responsive English can be: it can have moments where it elegantly and adeptly meets the needs of our students through an informed engagement with the world around us, whether through elegant literary journeys of the 1980s, or the Zeitgeist effect of the text selections of the early 1990s. While we, as English teachers, are necessarily and permanently "up close" to English, stepping back to observe from a distance reinforces to us our own vital and paradoxical position as both conduits and critics of the cultural conditions in with we are constantly immersed.

Table 8.1: All State 1980 to 1985
Subject: English
The most popular work by title report

TITLE	AUTHOR'S NAME	FORM	TOTAL
My Brother Jack	Johnston George		12
Coonardoo	Prichard Katharine	Prose/Novel	10
Merry-Go-Round in the Sea, The	Stow Randolph	Prose/Novel	10
Twelve Poets (1950–1970)	Craig Alexander	Poetry	10
Separate Peace, A	Knowles John	Prose/Novel	9
Spectrum Two	Bennett Bruce, Cowan Peter, Hay Johns	Short Story	9
1984	Orwell George	Prose/Novel	8
Brave New World	Huxley Aldous	Prose/Novel	8
Break into Day	Small K	Poetry	8
Getting of Wisdom, The	Richardson Henry Handel	Prose/Novel	8
Loved One, The	Waugh Evelyn	Prose/Novel	8
Catch-22	Heller Joseph	Prose/Novel	7
Chant of Jimmie Blacksmith, The	Keneally Thomas	Prose/Novel	7
Macbeth	Shakespeare William	Drama	7
Power and the Glory, The	Greene Graham	Prose/Novel	7
Adventures of Huckleberry Finn, The	Twain Mark	Prose/Novel	6
All Quiet on the Western Front	Remarque Erich	Prose/Novel	6
Chosen, The	Potok Chaim	Prose/Novel	6
Classic Australian Short Stories	Murray-Smith Stephen, Waten Judah	Short Story	6
Crucible, The	Miller Arthur	Drama	6
Harp in the South, The	Park Ruth	Prose/Novel	6
Leopard, The	Di Lampedusa Giuseppe	Prose/Novel	6
Mainly Modern	Colmer Dorothy, Colmer John	Poetry	6
Outsider, The	Camus Albert	Prose/Novel	6
Plays of the Sixties	Charlton J, Lessing Doris, Rattigan Terence, Shaffer Peter, Waterhouse Keith	Drama	6
Prime of Miss Jean Brodie, The	Spark Muriel	Prose/Novel	6
Room of One's Own, A	Woolf Virginia	Essays	6
Winter Sparrows, The	Liverani Mary Rose	Biography	6

Table 8.2: All State 1985 to 1990
Subject: English
The most popular work by title report

TITLE	AUTHOR'S NAME	FORM	TOTAL
Fortunate Life, A	Facey Albert	Biography	10
1984	Orwell George	Prose/Novel	9
Brave New World	Huxley Aldous	Prose/Novel	9
Death of a Salesman	Miller Arthur	Drama	9
Scales of Justice	Caswell Robert	Drama	9
Chosen, The	Potok Chaim	Prose/Novel	8
Equus	Shaffer Peter	Drama	8
My Name is Asher Lev	Potok Chaim	Prose/Novel	8
Breaker Morant	Beresford Bruce	NonPrint Media Film TV DVD etc	7
Catcher in the Rye	Salinger J.D.	Prose/Novel	7
Chant of Jimmie Blacksmith, The	Schepisi Fred	NonPrint Media Film TV DVD etc	7
International Forum: Contemporary Essays	Elder Bruce	Essays	7
One Flew Over the Cuckoo's Nest	Kesey Ken	Prose/Novel	7
Romeo and Juliet	Shakespeare William	Drama	7
Spectrum Two	Bennett Bruce, Cowan Peter, Hay John	Short Story	7
Stories from Suburban Road	Hungerford Tom	Biography	7
Streetcar Named Desire, A	Williams Tennessee	Drama	7
Bell Jar, The	Plath Sylvia	Prose/Novel	6
Educating Rita	Russell Willy	Drama	6
Getting of Wisdom, The	Beresford Bruce	NonPrint Media Film TV DVD etc	6
Grapes of Wrath, The	Steinbeck John	Prose/Novel	6
Harp in the South, The	Park Ruth	Prose/Novel	6
Man for All Seasons, A	Bolt Robert	Drama	6
Micro Invaders	Reinecke Ian	Non-Fiction	6
Sleepers Wake	Jones Barry	Non-Fiction	6
Strength of Tradition, The	Holt Ronald	Essays	6
Tyranny of Distance, The	Blainey Geoffrey	Non-Fiction	6
Unreliable Memoirs	James Clive	Biography	6
Whose Life is it Anyway?	Clark Brian	Drama	6
Year of Living Dangerously, The	Weir Peter	NonPrint Media Film TV DVD etc	6

Table 8.3: All State 1990 to 1995
Subject: English
The most popular work by title report

TITLE	AUTHOR'S NAME	FORM	TOTAL
Educating Rita	Russell Willy	Drama	17
Wild Cat Falling	Johnson Colin	Prose/Novel	17
My Place	Morgan Sally	Biography	13
Hard God, A	Kenna Peter	Drama	12
Brave New World	Huxley Aldous	Prose/Novel	11
Empire of the Sun	Ballard J G	Prose/Novel	11
Foreign Wife, A	Bouras Gillian	Biography	11
Killing Fields, The	Joffe Roland	NonPrint Media Film TV DVD etc	11
Removalists, The	Williamson David	Drama	10
Things Fall Apart	Achebe Chinua	Prose/Novel	10
Women of the Sun	Borg Soria, Maris Hyllus	Drama	10
After the First Death	Cormier Robert	Prose/Novel	9
Bell Jar, The	Plath Sylvia	Prose/Novel	9
Crucible, The	Miller Arthur	Drama	9
Death of a Salesman	Miller Arthur	Drama	9
Delinquents, The	Rohan Criena	Prose/Novel	8
Fixer, The	Malamud Bernard	Prose/Novel	8
In Duty Bound	Elisha Ron	Prose/Novel	8
My Brother Jack	Johnston George		8
My Name is Asher Lev	Potok Chaim	Prose/Novel	8
No Sugar	Davis Jack	Drama	8
One Flew Over the Cuckoo's Nest	Kesey Ken	Prose/Novel	8
Stories from Suburban Road	Hungerford Tom	Biography	8
Tyranny of Distance, The	Blainey Geoffrey	Non-Fiction	8
Village by the Sea, The	Desai Anita	Prose/Novel	8

Works Cited

Adams, Phillip. "Our film industry". *Speaking of Us: Voices from twentieth-century Australia*. Ed. York, B. Canberra: National Library of Australia, 1999. 83–86.

Analysis of Literature in Australian Schools Database (ALIAS). www.australiancommonreader.com/syllabus. Web. 13 June 2016.

Anderson, Benedict. *Imagined Communities: Reflections on the Origin and Spread of Nationalism*. London: Verso, 2006. Print.

Freedman, Jonathan. "After close reading: A review of Franco Moretti's *Distant Reading*". *The New Rambler*. Web. Aug 1 2016. <http://newramblerreview.com/images/files/Freedman-review-of-Moretti.pdf>

Guillory, John. *Cultural Capital: The problem of literary canon formation*. Chicago: University of Chicago Press, 1993. Print.

Moretti, Franco. "Conjectures of world literature". *New Left Review*, 1 Jan–Feb (2000): 54–68. Print.

Pender, A. "The mythical Australian: Barry Humphries, Gough Whitlam and 'New Nationalism". *Australian Journal of Politics & History*, 51 (2005): 67–78. Print.

Stratton, David. *The Last New Wave: The Australian film revival*. Angus & Robertson, 1980. Print.

Teese, R., and J. Polesel. *Undemocratic Schooling: Equity and quality in mass secondary education in Australia*. Melbourne: Melbourne University Press, 2003. Print.

Turner, Graeme. *National Fictions*. Sydney: Allen & Unwin, 1986. Print.

Ward, Russel. *The Australian Legend*. Sydney: Oxford University Press, 1962. Print.

Ward, S.J. "The 'new nationalism' in Australia, Canada and New Zealand: Civic culture in the wake of the British world". *Britishness Abroad: Transnational movements and imperial culture*. K. Darian-Smith, P. Grimshaw & S. Macintyre. Eds. Melbourne: Melbourne University Publishing, 2007. 231–263. Print.

Whitlam Institute. "Environment, culture, heritage". Web. 20 June 2016. <www.whitlam.org/gough_whitlam/achievements/environmentcultureheritage>

Chapter Nine

CHANGING THE SUBJECT

Text selection and curriculum development in VCE English 1990

Larissa McLean Davies and Brenton Doecke
with Prue Gill and Terry Hayes

Introduction

Schooling is about who "you" are. As Althusser famously remarks, schooling "hails" or "interpellates" individuals as "concrete subjects" (47), instilling in them a sense of who they are and where they belong in society. This is not to deny that a school education involves learning knowledge and skills, but crucially bound up with this learning is the inculcation of certain patterns of behaviour and dispositions that produce "submission to the rules of the established order" (6) and an acceptance of the place assigned to you in society.

Although Althusser was writing nearly half a century ago, his understanding of the way schooling hails or interpellates individuals still strikes us as an apt way to characterise what typically happens with educational reform. This can be illustrated by *The Melbourne Declaration on Educational Goals for Young Australians* (2008), a bi-partisan document designed to produce the kind of citizenry required by a twenty-first-century economy, involving what has become familiar rhetoric about the need for students to acquire "the essential skills of literacy and numeracy", and for data to be made available relating to the performance of students and schools that would guarantee accountability (MCEETYA).

The Melbourne Declaration is one of a series of policy statements at a federal level, stretching back to *Australia's Language: The Australian Language and Literacy Policy* (DEET), a white paper published by the Hawke Labor Government in 1991, whereby Australian Federal Governments of both political persuasions have successively implemented a neoliberal policy agenda involving so-called standards-based reforms (Parr, 2010). This agenda has progressively diminished concern for social justice and recognition of how communities are served differently by a school system weighted heavily towards those who have the cultural capital to succeed (cf. Doecke, "Kookaburras"). Young people from socially disadvantaged communities are classified as failing by a system that is actually failing them, ensuring their marginalisation, even when it is ostensibly concerned about lifting their performance. Indeed, the very concept of "performance" is culturally loaded, embodying standards of judgement that are blind to the diversity of languages and cultures that comprise Australian society (cf. Breen; Doecke and Breen).

High-stakes testing, particularly in the post-compulsory years of schooling, serves to reinforce this discrimination (Teese). In Victoria, the study of an English subject is compulsory,[1] and must be counted among the "top four" of five subjects studied when a student's tertiary entrance ranking is determined. English, including the texts that are selected for study, is clearly an important mechanism for bringing about this kind of differentiation within a standards-driven system (Teese). Yet this was not the original intention of the VCE, or how VCE English was imagined by those who worked to bring about this reform. The VCE as it was originally conceived was a brave and imaginative attempt to develop an English curriculum that might challenge the bleak scenario entertained by Althusser and others for whom schooling inevitably privileges the interests of social elites.

This intention reflected the tenor of educational policy under the Cain Government (1982–1992), perhaps the last progressive Victorian Labor Government prior to the ascendancy of standards-based reforms, as reflected in a significant policy document, *Ministerial Paper Number 6* (Minister of Education, 1984). The language of this document differs quite markedly from policy rhetoric today:

---

[1] In the current Victorian Certificate of Education (VCE), three English subjects are offered at Year 12 (final year), what we will call mainstream English, which includes a study of texts (with a strong focus on literary texts) and language; a specialist Literature subject; and a specialist English Language subject. While the specialist subjects attract relatively low numbers (less than 5,000 students), about 45,000 students sit the mainstream English exam each year.

9.1 The Government intends that all students have access to educational experiences that are challenging, purposeful and comprehensive and that result in all students improving their educational achievement.

9.2 Formal access is not enough. Although all young people are entitled to a full secondary schooling many are discouraged or diverted from taking full advantage of those opportunities. While some students may leave school prematurely because of factors beyond the control of the schooling system, others may leave because of unsatisfactory schooling experiences. The practices and processes that schools adopt greatly affect the way young people respond to the educational opportunities formally available to them. Real access requires that programs take account of differences in social and cultural background and that teaching methods provide for differences in pace and style of learning.

This significant Ministerial paper was followed a year later by a *Ministerial Review of Compulsory Schooling* led by Jean Blackburn in 1985. This two-volume report recommended radical changes to post-compulsory schooling in Victoria, contending the existing curriculum needed a complete overhaul to accommodate greater school retention and increasingly diverse student cohorts (Blackburn). Key recommendations of the Blackburn Report were to design a curriculum that encompassed vocational and more traditional academic subjects, and to provide access to education for all (Blackburn).

As is often the case, English was central to realising these curriculum goals. VCE English, developed in the late 1980s, was consequently conceived as "a common study", a meeting ground where students from "different social and cultural backgrounds" could come together, and where they would find their diversity valued through participating in a curriculum that was designed to "foster self-esteem in all students by enabling them to use the English language confidently" (VCAB, *VCE* 1). The aim of English as a "common study" was to equip students with a capacity to use the English language for "effective participation in Australian society", involving "an ability to understand the various uses of the English language and to employ them effectively for a range of purposes" – participation that was to be realised through providing "active learning situations in which students take increasing responsibility for their language development" (1).

A key initiative for achieving "real access", as far as VCE English was concerned, was to provide a comprehensive text list for study that might cater for a diverse range of interests. This chapter draws on the text lists for English in the Analysis of Literature in Australian Schools (ALIAS) database, as well as associated examination papers, curriculum documents and other publications at the time (most notably *Idiom*, the journal of the Victorian Association for the Teaching of English [VATE]) to investigate how literature was deployed for the purposes of a democratic and equitable curriculum for all, and the challenges faced by those attempting to achieve this aim. We are treating the ALIAS archive as a working document that can be read alongside other archival material from the time. That past is not something that can be rendered as an "objective" account of what really happened. We are offering one interpretation of the development and implementation of VCE English that is obviously open to contention and further interpretation. To this end, we have invited two colleagues who were actively involved in VCE English to engage with our account of what happened, and to offer insights into the experience of teaching literary texts during the 1980s and 1990s, thus enriching our own archival readings and investigations.

The road to the VCE

Before turning our attention to the VCE in 1990, we shall consider some of the key ideas that led to this curriculum reform. Specific aspects of the course, such as text selection, cannot be understood outside the overriding purpose that shaped it.

In an essay published in the third issue of *English in Australia*, the journal of the Australian Association for the Teaching of English (AATE), Tony Delves conveys a sense of the impulse that culminated in this reform. Delves asserts that as English teachers "we" – the use of the first person plural is telling – "must be concerned with our students as vital, spontaneous, social beings who are being educated in a culture-destroying and soul-destroying community" (Delves, "English" 34). English, he claims, "has as much to do with the growth of the whole person" as with instilling literacy. It is, he opines, "by means of language that we extend our range of experiences, delving into the unmeasurable limits of man's thought, feelings and beliefs" (Delves, "English" 34).

In his account of his professional practice at Prahran Technical School, Delves envisages an English curriculum that is no longer reliant on text books, that has moved beyond the aridity of "grammatical, structural, vocabulary, punctuation and other exercises, all in their little boxes and columns" (Delves, "English" 37) and that has freed itself from the "stifling" effect of "university dominated" examinations (39). The sentence in his essay that is perhaps most symptomatic of a shift in thinking about English curriculum and pedagogy at the time is this one: "To the English teacher, what the child says or writes, as well as what he reads, ought to be literature" (36). Delves concedes that this is a "wider use of the term than is common in the designation of Literature with a capital 'L'", and that "it may not be good literature – it may even be incredibly poor" (36). He is nonetheless advocating the "tremendous importance" of "small 'l' literature", a situation where "the student reads literature, writes literature, thinks and acts literature" (37)

That Delves was Head of the English and Social Studies Department at Prahran Technical School at the time of writing this essay is significant, for it points to the way the postwar expansion of secondary education prompted teachers like him to question the suitability of the existing curriculum to cater for their students' needs. The students in their classes came from migrant and working-class backgrounds, and they did not possess the kind of cultural capital of pupils in elite private and selective state high schools for whom the Higher School Certification (HSC) examination in English constituted a suitable vehicle for demonstrating their capacity for university study (cf. Teese 23–37). That curriculum, as Teese observes, was inspired by "the ideal of the liberal intellectual", an individual who was capable of writing essays under exam conditions that demonstrated a style and sophistication that was "remote from the life-styles of many children" (Teese 35–36).

The circumstances reflected in Delves's essay were similar to those experienced by educators like Harold Rosen and John Dixon in England in the 1950s and 1960s as they likewise sought to develop English curriculum that children from working-class backgrounds would find meaningful (see Medway et al.). In teachers like Tony Delves and Gerry Tickell Australia produced its own advocates of an inclusive pedagogy informed by a larger vision of English's purposes than the competitive academic curriculum that served the interests of social elites who sent their children to private schools. The resources they produced, most notably the *Themes and Responses* series (Delves and Tickell), in some ways replicate work done in England by Clements, Dixon and Stratta in *Reflections: An English Course for students aged 14–18*. Both resources were inspired by a belief that students (to borrow the language of *Reflections*) might "develop sensitivity to life and a critical awareness of our common experiences" by engaging with a spectrum of writing, including a wide selection of literary writing, that grappled with themes that "were central to pupils' lives" and formed "part of a cultural heritage we all share" (Clements, Dixon and Stratta, "Teacher's Book" 3).

We shall not dwell on parallels that might be drawn between the work of Clements, Dixon and Stratta – exemplifying what came to be known as "Growth" pedagogy (Dixon; cf. Medway et al.; Doecke, "Time Travel") – and curriculum development in state schools in Victoria by teachers like Delves and Tickell, not to mention other educators who wrote resource books at this time (see e.g. Hannan and Breen; Carozzi) and made lively contributions to journals like *English in Australia* and *Idiom*. Delves – who had become Principal of Huntingdale Technical School – produced a book that offered an extended rationale for a reappraisal of English curriculum and pedagogy, making explicit links with the work of writers like John Dixon and James Britton (see Delves vii). A productive dialogue with educators in the UK who were advocating a more inclusive version of English was occurring, as a perusal of guest speakers at conferences shows. *John Dixon in Australia*, a publication produced by the Curriculum and Research Branch of the Education Department of Victoria, which included John Dixon's opening address to the 1973 VATE Conference (VATE), reveals that this dialogue had departmental support (Education Department of Victoria). All this work reflected a democratic impulse, which, by virtue of that very fact, sets it apart from educational policy today: a belief in a common curriculum and the possibility that all children, whatever their backgrounds, could participate meaningfully in that curriculum, building on the diverse cultures and experiences they brought to school and thus actively contributing in turn to a common culture in which all people could share.

Using the ALIAS database, an analysis of HSC English texts lists, syllabus and examination documents from the mid-1970s reveals both the influence of the innovative curricula and resources that we have been discussing, and an expansion of texts that are deemed worthy of study. It also shows tensions between these democratising forces and the high-stakes imperatives of final English examinations, most notably the need to distinguish between students for the purpose of university entrance. The move away from a conception of literature as an elite pursuit is perhaps evident in the 1976 direction to teachers of HSC English:

> The first object in studying these books should be to grasp as fully as possible, and to assess, whatever each book or group of books adds to our understanding – or our capacity to understand – ourselves and

the world. No doubt literary questions about how each book does so will arise in the course of reading and discussion; nevertheless, these questions should be subordinate. (VUSEB 187)

This focus on students responding to the universal themes in texts was facilitated by the organisation of the text list into seven groups of four. Themes were not "set" in this particular year for each group, although they had been previously, and would be subsequently (Teese). Instead, in 1976, teachers and students were encouraged to consider the connections between texts and the world as it was emerging. Teese writes of the 1970s: "There was now greater freedom for students to read and develop their interests and more unpredictability, which the syllabus writers insisted on to prompt authentic learning rather than exam preparation" (Teese 26).

There were clearly gains achieved during this period with respect to making HSC more accessible by providing an expanded text list, including Australian authors (Boyd's *Outbreak of Love*, Cook's *Wake in Fright*, Dawe's *Condolences of the Season* and an anthology of Australian poetry entitled *Twelve Poets 1950–1970*). The structure of the examination, however, served to ensure social distinctions were maintained, limiting efforts to move towards a democratic curriculum and a version of English that was open and relevant to all. While the syllabus purports to facilitate and honour the connections between students and the world in which they lived, the examination questions required them, among other tasks, to write an essay response to one of the texts listed, where they were meant to use their knowledge of the text to expatiate on universal themes, requiring a facility in handling a certain type of discourse which Teese argues privileges socially elite institutions and their students (Teese 30).

However, as youth unemployment skyrocketed and school retention rates increased during the 1980s (see Teese 39–40), the curriculum development associated with the names of educators like Delves and Tickell assumed even greater urgency. The competitive academic curriculum enshrined in the HSC, despite reforms in the late 1960s and 70s, was proving woefully inadequate to address the needs of the increasingly diverse cohort of students who were staying on at school with the collapse of the youth labour market, and an increasing number of state schools (e.g. St Albans High School, Brunswick High School, Footscray High School, Caulfield High School) as well as some Catholic schools (e.g. Nagle College in Bairnsdale) were implementing alternative programs (McRae, *Information*). Significantly, so were TAFE colleges, where many young adults returning to study found themselves – often students who'd made their way with difficulty through secondary school, and who had left as soon as they turned 15. This situation produced a proliferation of alternative courses to the HSC, providing options for study and pathways for young people who were not necessarily wishing to compete for university entrance. McRae's *English B* (VISE, 1982), originally developed by him in collaboration with his teacher education students at Melbourne State College under the title *Senior English: A Course of Study* (McRae, *Senior English*), was one of these courses, and it conveys a powerful sense of the impetus that would eventually lead to VCE English. We shall outline some of its chief characteristics briefly.

The section of *English B* entitled Literature Units is paradoxically more similar to the kinds of reading lists provided by university English departments than the reading list traditionally set for HSC (cf. Beavis, "Changing"). The units in English B include: Australian Literature (texts by Baynton, Franklin, Lawson, Hibberd, Williamson, Dawe, Wright), an Author study (Fitzgerald, Franklin, Hemingway, Orwell), Contemporary Prose (Paley, Vonnegut, Atwood, Brautigan, Doctorow), as well as suggested texts belonging to certain genres, such as Science Fiction and Romance. As an alternative course, it is as though its originators were upping the ante vis-à-vis the traditional HSC course by providing a diverse list of texts that were intellectually demanding and reflected the interests of young people on the verge of maturity and participation in a democratic society. A crucial difference with the HSC was that, for the purposes of assessment, students were to engage in a "sustained analysis" of the texts that could be "spoken or written or both". Teachers were told that the assessment should "not contain any elements of the teacher judging an analysis to be right or wrong by comparison with the teacher's or with standard critical analyses". The point was to seek from the student "detailed knowledge of texts and the capacity to draw from the text issues which the student sees as significant" (VISE 29).

HSC English text lists, syllabuses and examinations in the early 1980s reflect the need to address the growing numbers of diverse students undertaking the HSC, and the influence of courses such as English B. By 1981, two text lists were in operation. List A, consisting of substantive texts such as novels, plays and anthologies of poetry, offered texts that were set for individual close study. In 1983, the Part A text list consisted of the following texts:

Table 9.1: Part A text list HSC English 1983

Lawrence – *Sons and Lovers* (1913*)
Lessing – *Five* (1953)
Euripides – "The Women of Troy" in *The Bacchae and other Plays* (405 BC original performance)
Vonnegut – *Player Piano* (1952)
Park – *Harp in the South* (1948)
Camus – *The Outsider* (1942)
White – *A Fringe of Leaves* (1976)
Bolt – *A Man for all Seasons* (1954)
Anderson – *Tirra Lirra by the River* (1978)
Wallace-Crabbe – *The Golden Apples of the Sun* (1980)

*dates = first publication or production

While the Part A list was used for a more traditional essay response in the examination, the Part B list indicated that texts were to be used a resources to discuss themes and ideas. Further to this aim, the Part B list was accompanied by a rich list of supplementary reading that could also be drawn on in the examination. Consequently, by 1983, the English HSC list had dramatically expanded to 68 works.

This list reflected diversity akin to the sentiment evident in McRae's English B syllabus. Although texts by men still dominated the combined lists – only 15 of the 70 texts were by women – the number of Australian texts increased (21 of the 70). By comparison, 19 texts from English authors were set and the USA representation dropped to 13 texts. Texts by authors of other nations also increased, with four texts by German writers, two from Indian authors, and one from each of authors from New Zealand, Italy, Ireland, Greece, Trinidad, Turkey, France, Sweden and Argentina. While works of fiction (18), non-fiction (15) and biography (9) accounted for over half the list, newer text types and genres were also included in the text list for Part B. It must be said, though, that the generically innovative texts such as screen plays tended to be listed as supplementary reading for the eight Part B core texts which could be solidly classified as "fiction" or "non-fiction" print texts. The 1983 list included an ABC documentary on Australian involvement in Papua New Guinea and Raymond Briggs's graphic novel *When the Wind Blows*.

VCE – literary reform and a common study: opportunities and challenges

Following on from these changes in the 1980s, and inspired by the English B syllabus and the Technical Year 12 (T12) and Tertiary orientation program (TOP) offered as an alternative to HSC, the original VCE English included an extensive list of titles that students could read for the "Text Response" component of the course. The new curriculum reflected a supposition that the text list should convey a sense of the social and ethnic diversity of Australian society. This also reflects the view that the provision of texts that speak (say) to the experiences of young adults in different parts of Victoria might enable those students to gain access to the curriculum as a whole. In this particular year, as in 1983, 70 works were set for study, with Australian texts making up the largest number (26 out of 70), almost the sum total of works by English authors (13) and American authors (14) combined. Further, the VCE syllabus continued to build on the gender diversity of texts offered in the 1983 list. In 1990, 25 of the 72 authors listed on the whole syllabus were women, with six of the ten writers listed for Part A, requiring the close analysis of a single text, being women.

As can be seen from Table 9.2, the Part A list includes a range of contemporary and classic texts representing different cultural contexts, and offering different perspectives on Australia and Australians, including those of Aboriginal Australian poet Bobbi Sykes. While the 1983 Part A list spanned Ancient Greek to contemporary times, the VCE 1990 list is much more firmly located in the present, with half the texts being published in the previous decade, and each of these exploring, in different ways, challenges to notions of family (Masters, Robinson, Russell), twentieth-century prejudice and discrimination (Sykes, Mason), and the way individuals are "called into being" by the institutions of which they are a part. Teese et al note that texts set for study that represent an earlier (British) historical period are often viewed as having greater cultural capital than contemporary texts, and are thus taken up by those students in "fortified sites" (i.e. private schools), who are rewarded more handsomely by examiners in high-stakes environments. With this in mind, the 1990 Part A list can be read as actively resisting and re-imagining what literature is important for close study at the end of the twentieth century, and thus challenging the privileging of those texts deemed to be the property of social elites. The "oldest" texts on the list are by Lawson and Di Lampedusa, rather than works of canonical British or American fiction. In what can be interpreted as a deliberate effort to reconceive English and move away from an emphasis on traditional, canonical texts, Shakespeare's *Merchant of Venice* was placed on the supplementary list for Part B.

Table 9.2: Texts set for Part A 1990 VCE English Exam (Victoria)

Di Lampedusa – *The Leopard* (1958)
Friel – *Freedom of the City* (1973)
Jhabvala – *A Backward Place* (1965)
Johnston – *How Many Miles to Babylon?* (1974)
Lawson – *The Bush Undertaker and Other Stories* (story first published 1892 collection published in 1982)
Mason – *In Country* (1985)
Master – *Amy's Children* (1987)
Robinson – *Housekeeping* (1980)
Russell – *Educating Rita* (1980)
Sykes – *Love Poems and Other Revolutionary Actions* (1988)

While novels still formed the majority of those texts offered (24 works), and constituted 8 of the 10 texts on offer for Part A, there is a clear shift in the kinds of novels listed between 1983 and 1990. Non-print media and film (fiction and non-fiction) amount to 17 titles, 7 works are plays and 16 texts are non-fiction print. The organisation of the Part B list in 1990 further serves to facilitate the agenda of a "common study" and "English for all". The themes set for study are quite different in nature to those listed previously. Where the 1983 list focused on "Bonds and Relationships", the "World of Tomorrow", "Between Cultures" and the more abstract "Creativity" (VISE 97–98), the 1990 themes, "Justice", "Change, "The Family", and "Commitment", are broader. They can likewise be understood as attempting to provide opportunities for all students to engage with a range of texts by drawing on their experiences, thus facilitating acceptance of diversity and a critique of societal prejudices and hierarchies.

The dominant note struck in the articles and reports relating to the implementation of the VCE celebrates the changes of the curriculum and the new possibilities for engaging with texts. The Victorian English Teacher's Journal *Idiom* No.3, 1990, comprises a range of papers that were presumably presented at its annual conference earlier that year, one of them being Janet Hartrup's evocative account of teaching English at Debney Park High School, formerly Flemington Girls' School, where she taught English in the "old Home Eco. Room", "a great high ceilinged barn of a place", probably "one of the largest Home Eco rooms in the Southern hemisphere", built at a time when the expectation was that "the 'Flemington Girls' were destined to become domestic workers and housewives" (Hartrup 23–24). The students with whom Hartrup was working were ESL students, for whom "the very richness and diversity of the language ... generates apprehension" (24). Even her non-ESL students were "often fearful of launching into wider, deeper language" (24). Yet she also signals hope that there has been a change, that the VCE course provides "a shift in perspective" that opens up "opportunities for experimenting, for moving into less familiar modes of speaking and writing" (25).

An idea of the research into the teaching of literature out of which VCE English emerged can be gained from reading the contributions by Jack Thomson and Ray Misson to this particular issue of *Idiom*, both of whom cite Ian Reid's distinction between the "gallery" and the "workshop" in the opening chapter of *The Making of Literature* (Reid, 1984/1988), in order to advocate the value of more playful, but critical engagement with a wide range of texts beyond those that figure in traditional school syllabuses (Thomson, 1990 5; Misson 27). Thomson draws on the extensive body of research for which he had become known, where he had explored how teenagers variously reported their experiences of reading, including the links they were making between the texts they were currently reading and their previous reading. In *Understanding Teenagers' Reading*, he had organised the teenagers' responses into what he called "a Developmental Model", charting a pathway from "unreflective interest in action", through "empathizing" and "analogising", through to a capacity to judge the "significance" of the work as a "whole" and to cultivate a meta-critical awareness that recognised its status as a constructed artifact (Thomson, 1987 360–361).

In his contribution to this issue of *Idiom* – deriving from the keynote he had delivered to the VATE annual conference – Thomson again advocated the value of students "becoming conscious of their own constructive reading strategies" (Thomson, 1990 6), something that he was able to demonstrate through reporting his conversations with both struggling readers and more accomplished readers. The assumption is that "meaning is made by readers in interaction with the text" (4), requiring the possibility of a more diverse range of responses than channelling students' interpretations into the form of the literary essay. He then illustrates a variety of strategies – including reading journals and the playful rewriting of literary texts – that support this meaning-making process and appropriation of texts. Many of these practices were enthusiastically embraced by English teachers as part of their students' school-assessed course work.

VCE – present voices, past stories

To this point, we have been mapping the years leading to the introduction of VCE, and the reception and possibilities of the new course as we have reconstructed it through the archive – the ALIAS database and associated syllabuses, governmental documents and articles from professional journals. Here we ask our colleagues Terry Hayes and Prue Gill, who were teaching during this period, to respond to our archival account of the VCE English course and offer their own reflections and insights. In offering their responses, both Terry and Prue draw attention to the radical ways in which subject English changed during this period, but also the forces that ultimately limited and circumscribed this reform.

Terry's reflections

> My most vivid memories of those heady days of VCE curriculum reform are of two controversies involving text selection: the demonisation of the choice of When the Wind Blows, and the "battle of the prompt". The first was a very public media debate, the second, a fierce argument behind closed doors among progressive educationists who, until then, had been united in their support of the English Study Design.
>
> Raymond Briggs's graphic novel was one of 60 texts set on a prescribed list from which students were required to write on one in a two-hour external examination. The list went some way to matching the diversity of the student cohort (and their reading/viewing interests and habits) now required to do a common study. The Briggs text was a tentative step into the burgeoning world of hybrid multimodal texts. Instead, it became the "hook" for a concerted campaign by the gutter press, aided by conservative academics and commentators, on, as they saw it, the "dumbing down" of the English curriculum. An uncontroversial choice for a prescribed text list from 10 years earlier now, conveniently, became the catalyst for a defence of cultural literacy and civilisation as we knew it. A "comic book" on the same text list as Othello! The attack sufficiently traumatised an increasingly embattled curriculum authority into withdrawing When the Wind Blows from the list. Fawlty Towers was another victim. The trauma still resonates: it has taken VCAA over 20 years to prescribe another graphic novel (Spiegelman's Maus). Strategically, the Victorian Curriculum and Assessment Authority commissioned Professor Catherine Beavis

to write a scholarly rationale – "The literary and artistic merit of the graphic text as new textual genre and hybrid literary/artistic form", with the introduction of Maus *in an attempt to deflect potential criticism of this choice (Beavis nd).*

For teachers, like myself, who had taught in one of the alternative English courses, the VCE Study Design promised to deliver on many of the educational principles of those courses: school-based assessment with some form of moderation/verification, a writing portfolio, the valuing of oral work and, especially, the literacy in purposeful "real life" context dimensions of a communications/production task. The external assessment component, the text response, we realised would be the sticking point for students for whom exam-based assessment had proved unproductive in the past. The prompt sought to address that concern.

As a form of exam "question", the prompt challenged the hegemony of the analytical/critical essay as the preferred way of demonstrating an understanding of a text. Basically, the analytical question provided students with an interpretation to unpack and "evidence" from the text through varying degrees of agreement or disagreement with its proposition. The history of text response assessment suggested that the provided interpretation often caught many students unawares, unable to answer the proposed question. The prompt allowed for more varied interpretations of texts – what the wide cohort of students had been thinking about in working with a text – and not necessarily the one that a panel of assessors had in mind. To reiterate Ian Reid's distinction in The Making of Literature, *the analytical essay embodied the "gallery" approach to text study; the prompt encouraged the "workshop" approach, enabling students to not only critique and analyse, but to demonstrate their understanding by "playing" and experimenting with a text (Reid, 1984). To do so in an external exam context was a challenging yet not insurmountable objective, requiring responsive professional learning about both teaching and assessing such an approach. Instead, it produced often irrational obsessions about assessment reliability and question predictability (the "prepared" answer), resignations from committees and recriminations within the profession.*

Prue's reflections

As a teacher of the Tertiary Orientation program (TOP) in a TAFE College working with students who were using this course as a "second chance" after a not-so-easy secondary school experience, I was pretty nervous about the idea of bringing the disparate Year 12 courses under one umbrella. At our college, we decided that the best thing to do was to become involved in the development of the VCE, and we made contributions across several studies. Initially, we were won over by the brief to design new courses that were both intellectually challenging and accessible for all. These were optimistic times as teachers came together across systems (government, Catholic, private, TAFE, community providers) to talk about good teaching and learning. It was my first sense of being a member of a professional group of English teachers, and led to my introduction to the Victorian Association for the Teaching of English (VATE) membership.

Our early experiences with VCE were exciting ones. Piloting the new English study we had great support from the English Field of Study Committee (FOSC) and the Education Department English team. It was a time of ongoing professional development, and we were pleased with the work our students were producing in a course which valued a wide range of student skills and knowledge. The panel overseeing the regional and state moderation process was advised that "two equally expert assessors will differ in their assessment of a piece of work" (the words of Dr Viv Eyres, who was brought to Victoria from South Australia to help us develop the early VCE assessment systems) and we participated in discussions across the systems about the qualities that we wanted to recognise in student analysis of text. Those of us from alternative systems were listened to and respected when we argued for the acknowledgement of creative thought, engagement and voice in student work, as well as analytical thinking and the display of language skills. The large text list, the opportunity to draft work and the prompt approach to writing about text gave students plenty of scope to excel in a range of ways.

With the narrowing of the text list and examination format came an increasing emphasis on the form of the text essay – aided and abetted by the industry developing crib notes and sample essays for students. Marking the VCE English exam from the beginning of the VCE for many years, I witnessed a shift in student writing towards a standard structure (introduction, three key points, each teased out, illustrated by example and then linked, and rounded neatly with a conclusion). The formula is stifling, the essays predictable, the variety scarce, the imaginative thought hard to identify, the marking *experience pretty unexciting. Unfortunately teachers are becoming skilled at getting students from a range of backgrounds to "conform" to expectation, but it is too often an exercise in mimicry.*

Along with the narrowing that accompanies a standards-based testing regime, and the narrowing of the size and scope of the text list, is the narrowing of what it is considered suitable for students to read. Some texts that we have been teaching for years are considered out of bounds today. In a society that pledges itself to raising awareness about mental health, English teachers now are advised to be wary of the appearance of suicide, of homosexuality, of depression, of drug taking, of child abuse, of rape in the texts they choose.

VCE: curriculum of possibility and systemic failure

Despite the fact that the VCE was grounded in sound research into English curriculum and pedagogy, as is evident in Terry's and Prue's narratives, the original VCE English Study Design was mired in controversy from the moment of its inception – you could say that it became the stuff of a postmodern novel, with multiple points of view and conflicting perspectives that complicate any attempt to gain a perspective on those events. Margaret Gill gives an account of the way the mass media caricatured aspects of the new curriculum, completely ignoring the importance of the social challenge of developing "a comprehensive post-secondary program for all, and, in the case of English, offering a potentially inclusive curriculum capable of providing 'real learning to all young people'" (Gill 97–98). Instead, a range of press commentators lampooned the new course as a "Mickey Mouse" or "Monty Python" curriculum that fell woefully short of accepted intellectual standards and the cultural values of the wider public (103). When, as Terry Hayes notes, a so-called "comic book", namely *When the Wind Blows*, was set, this was taken to be a further sign of a deterioration of standards (even though this text had previously been listed in the 1983 HSC, albeit as a Part B text). As Helen Howells remarks, among those who opposed the new Study Design, there were members of the English teaching community "who wanted more 'rigour' in the Design, more direction about the materials to be studied, more emphasis on the basics of English language learning", who did not feel that the Design did "justice to supporting our cultural heritage", and who continued to be strong advocates of "the old exam system" (Howells 37). An example of such critique is

Kevin Donnelly's article, "In Praise of Literature", published in the VATE journal, *Idiom*.

Howells explores the difficult pathway that the Field of Studies Committee who had carriage of the development of the new Study Design had to negotiate vis-à-vis stakeholders who were unsympathetic to the democratic impulse behind their work and the ideal of a "common study". She tells a "cautionary tale" (Howells 37), showing how the proper responsibility of English teachers was to develop a curriculum that recognised the diverse needs of the new cohorts of students now staying on in school. This innovative approach to curriculum and assessment was radically undermined when the Victorian Curriculum and Assessment Board (VCAB) effectively reinstated a public examination system along traditional lines, usurping the plans for a school rather than external exam-based assessment practice. Although the development of school-based assessment had been conceived as an appropriate way of realising the richness of the language and learning envisaged by the Study Design, English assessment was quickly returned to a high-stakes end-of-year exam and comprised a test CAT (Common Assessment Task), which, along traditional lines, related to the "Reading and the Study of Texts".

Maintaining a high-stakes examination meant that "the reforms of the English curriculum led to no discernible improvement in relative social outcomes" (Teese 55). The richness of the original curriculum (which involved not only an extended text list, but innovative practices relating to writing and oral work and engagement with issues in the media, among other things) was steadily eroded almost from the very moment that it was implemented, turning into a competitive academic curriculum that now performs much the same kind of role as the HSC curriculum that it displaced. While the curriculum was designed to enable a diverse range of students to be engaged in English, and to empower teachers to genuinely meet the needs of their diverse cohorts, this flexibility was ultimately seen as a risk to "standards" and "quality", and also something that could not be sustained by the systems these students and teachers were part of. Indeed, Teese is at pains to emphasise that the failure of the original VCE did not reflect on its "educational and pedagogical merits". The key issue, rather, was that its proponents were pursuing "major curriculum change in the absence of structural reform" to the school system (Teese 55). His summary supports Howells's argument about the ways in which vested interests undermined the reform:

> From one side, the new integrated curriculum brought all students together. From the other side, in the schools they attended, they were drawn apart. Taught in settings that divided them on socio-economic, cultural and academic lines, they were made to meet in the same programme and exposed to the same set of learning demands. If an argument for commonality of civic culture seemed to justify bringing all students together, the values expressed through the common assessment tasks would tend to reinterpret "civic" as "academic". (Teese 55)

Teese's comments do not take into account the quality of the work that students in schools were producing through their engagement in continuous assessment as it was originally envisaged as part of VCE English. Tony McDonald, who was then coordinator of the Disadvantaged Schools Program at South Oakleigh Secondary College (formerly Huntingdale Technical School), observed in 1995 that the VCE was "doing nothing to improve the opportunities for the disadvantaged" (McDonald 18), while showcasing the work that his students were nonetheless able to accomplish when they could write for real purposes and audiences (16; see also Sorenson 27–33). Val Kent, a teacher at the same school, was able to show how her students engaged in formal experimentation through writing poetry (Kent), when they were able to make meaning out of their own experiences by engaging with selected literary texts, ranging from Tennyson's "Lady of Shallot" to Angela Carter's "The Company of Wolves" (Kent 36). These articles both indicate, however, that, after its introduction, the promise of the VCE had been lost, with the VCE becoming, as McDonald put it, nothing more than "a ratings game" (18).

Conclusion: back to the future

Althusser's account of the way schools "hail" or "interpellate" individuals only tells part of the story about the ideological role that schools perform in capitalist society. For it is always possible for someone not to reply, to refuse to accept how he or she is being "hailed". To hail "you" involves the presumption that "I" know who "you" are, and it is always conceivable – indeed, it is an ineluctable condition of our social relationships as they are mediated by the use of language – that there are dimensions that escape such an ascription, thus opening the possibility of resistance, of thinking "differently". Althusser acknowledges this in his essay by referring to the "heroism" of teachers who nonetheless try to teach "against" the dominant mores of the school, who resist "the system and the practices in which they are trapped" and try to open up other possibilities for their students beyond the constraints imposed by the system (Althusser 31).

As Prue and Terry's reflections show, VCE sought to legitimise a social space where teachers and students could come together and draw on the diversity of their experiences, exploring both the differences that separated them and the values that might unite them. This is how we understand the meaning of English as a "common study", something that was reflected in the openness of the curriculum with respect to both the writing that students were able to produce and the books and other cultural resources with which they were able to engage. The original Study Design might be said to have conceptualised English as a form of "literary sociability" (McLean Davies, Doecke and Mead), involving reading and responding to a diverse range of texts, thus transcending the narrow purposes of a competitive academic curriculum.

The failure of the VCE English Study Design might be characterised as the defeat of a vision of people from diverse social and cultural backgrounds coming together to engage in conversation with one another. Such a vision, as it was entertained by the various educators who were active in the development and implementation of a "common study", was at odds with the "real" conditions that would decisively shape its implementation, transforming it back into the very thing that it sought to displace. This was, as Howells, Gill and Teese show, a consequence of larger forces that were outside teachers' control, which completely undermined their autonomy and the responsibility they felt to develop a genuinely inclusive and participatory curriculum for the benefit of their students and the future of Australia as a genuine democracy.

This is not the only lesson to be drawn from the VCE story. Writing out of the US policy context, John Guillory has problematised the assumption that by providing a diverse range of texts for study, including texts that represent the experiences of minority groups, educators can effectively address the way those groups are discriminated against by the school system (Guillory). His point is exactly the same as that made by Teese, when he argues the need for structural reform that might address the inequalities that are created by the system, including – crucially – the capacity of different social classes to engage with the educational provision available to them. Guillory also argues, in connection with the emphasis on diversity, that educators sidestep the question of the representational status of texts, of the ways that texts actually relate to the conditions out of which they emerge. He points to the work of apparently progressive literary educators who focus on content, implying the message of the text is simply contained within it, rather than being the product of the context in which it is read and appropriated (Guillory). This tendency is evident in the presentations by Thomson and Misson that we have just referred to – both refer to the "ideology" of the text, suggesting reading consists in alerting students to the designs that texts might have on them. As we see through this analysis of the VCE and the period leading to its implementation, texts do not function in isolation and cannot be separated from the institutional and curricular ideologies which constrain them.

Yet for all these shortcomings in how the VCE English Study Design was implemented, the imagination initially invested in it makes it one of the most significant curriculum reforms in Victoria's, if not Australia's history. We wish to affirm the social ideal that it envisaged, as something from which English teachers as a profession might still find inspiration within the context of an increasingly regulated accountability culture.

Works Cited

Althusser, Louis. *On Ideology*. 1971. London: Verso. 2008. Print.
Beavis, Catherine. "Changing constructions: Literature, 'text' and English teaching in Victoria". *Teaching the English Subjects*. Ed. Bill Green and Catherine Beavis. Geelong: Deakin University Press, 1996. 15–39. Print.
——. "The literary and artistic merit of the graphic text as new textual genre and hybrid literary/artistic form". Victorian Curriculum and Assessment Authority, n.d. Web. 1 Aug 2016. <www.vcaa.vic.edu.au/documents/vce/english/graphic%20texts.doc>
Blackburn Report. Victorian State Board of Education. Summary and analysis of Regional Board of Education responses to the Structural Recommendations of the Ministerial Review of Postcompulsory Schooling. Melbourne: State Board of Education, 1985. Print.
Breen, L. Teacher Professional Practice and an Ethic of Care: An everyday problematic. Unpublished PhD thesis, Deakin University, 2014. Print.
Clements, S., John Dixon, and L. Stratta. *Reflections: An English course for students aged 14–18*. London: Oxford University Press, 1963/64. Print.
——. *Reflections: Teacher's book*, London: Oxford UP, 1963/1968. Print.
Carozzi, B. *Patchwork One*, North Melbourne: Cassell Australia, 1970. Print.
Delves, A.R. and W.G Tickell. *A Penny for the Old Guy: Themes and responses five*. Melbourne: Cassell Australia, 1972. Print.
Delves, T. "English as she is not taught". *English in Australia* 3 Nov (1966): 33–40. Print.
——. *Issues in English Teaching*, Carlton: Melbourne University Press, 1972. Print.
Department of Employment, Education and Training. *Australia's Language: The Australian language and literacy policy*. Canberra: Australian Government Publishing Service, 1991. Print.

Dixon, John. *Growth through English: A report based on the Dartmouth Seminar, 1966*, 2nd Edition. London: Published for the National Association for the teaching of English by the Oxford University Press, 1969. Print.

Doecke, Brenton. "Time travel (knowing our history as English teachers)". *English in Australia* 49. 3 (2014): 96–105. Print.

——. "Kookaburras, blue gums, and ideological state apparatuses". *English in Australia* 103 Mar (2013): 14–24. Print.

——, and L. Breen. "Beginning again: A response to Rosen and Christie". *Changing English: Studies in culture and education*. (20.3.2013): 202–305. Print.

Donnelly, Kevin. "In praise of literature". *Idiom* 3 (1992): 23–28.

Education Department of Victoria, *John Dixon in Australia, Exchange 16*, prepared on behalf of the Standing Committee for English in Technical Schools by the Curriculum and Research Branch, Carlton, Victoria, n.d.

Gill, M. "Who framed English? A case study of the media's role in curriculum change". *Melbourne Studies in Education* 35:1 (1994): 96–113. Print.

Guillory, John. *Cultural Capital: The problem of literary canon formation*. Chicago: University of Chicago Press, 1993. Print.

Hannan, L.K. and B.A. Breen. *Poetry is What: A book of poems*. F.W. Melbourne: Cheshire, 1970. Print.

Hartrup, J. "Debney Park High School". *Idiom* XXV. 3 Oct (1990): 23–25.

Howells, H. "Teacher professionalism and curriculum power: A cautionary tale". *English in Australia* 136 Autumn (2003): 27–39. Print.

Kent, V. "I want you to write me a poem … and I don't want it to rhyme". *Responding to Students' Writing: Continuing conversations*. Ed. Brenton Doecke. Norwood: AATE, 1999. 131–52. Print.

McDonald, T. "Why VCE fails the disadvantaged". *Idiom* [Journal of the Victorian Association for the Teaching of English] XXIX. 2 Aug. (1995): 11–19. Print.

McLean Davies, Larissa, Brenton Doecke and Phillip Mead. "Reading the local and global: Teaching literature in secondary schools in Australia". *Changing English: Studies in culture and education*, 20 (2013): 224–240. Print.

McRae, D. et al. *Senior English: A course of study*, Carlton: Melbourne State College, 1980. Print.

——. "Information about English B: A VISE Group 2 Subject, notes prepared by McRae for workshop on English B." Melbourne: Melbourne State College, n.d. Print.

Medway, Peter et al. *English Teachers in a Postwar Democracy: Emerging choice in London schools, 1945–1965*, New York: Palgrave MacMillan, 2014. Print.

Minister of Education. Curriculum Development and Planning in Victoria: Ministerial paper number 6. 1984. Print.

Ministerial Council on Education, Employment, Training and Youth Affairs (MCEETYA). *Melbourne Declaration on Educational Goals for Young Australians*, 2008. Web. 1 Aug 2016. <www.curriculum.edu.au/verve/_resources/National_Declaration_on_the_Educational_Goals_for_Young_Australians.pdf >

Misson, Ray. "Textual literacy". *Idiom* XXV. 3 (1990): 25–27. Print.

Parr, G. *Inquiry-Based Professional Learning: Speaking back to standards-based reforms*. Teneriffe, Qld: Post Pressed, 2010. Print.

Reid, Ian. *The Making of Literature: Texts, contexts and classroom practices*. Norwood: Australian Association for the Teaching of English, 1984/1988. Print.

Sorenson, A., et al. "In touch". *Idiom* [the Journal of the Victorian Association for the Teaching of English] XXIX. 2 Aug. (1995): 27–33. Print.

Teese, R. *Academic Success and Social Power: Examinations and inequality*. North Melbourne: Australian Scholarly Publishing, 2013. Print.

——, S. Lamb, and S. Helme. "Hierarchies of culture and hierarchies of context in Australian secondary education". *Cultures of Education: Proceedings for the 21st Congress of the German Society for Educational Research (DGfE)*. Ed. Melzer, W. and R. Tipplet. 71–92. Opladen and Farmington Hills: Verlag Barbara Budrich, 2009. Print.

Thomson, Jack. *Understanding Teenagers' Reading: Reading processes and the teaching of literature*. Norwood: Australian Association for the Teaching of Literature, 1987. Print.

——. "Helping students to develop textual power: Reading, writing and responding to literature". *Idiom* XXV (3 Oct 1990): 3–21. Print.

Victorian Curriculum and Assessment Board (VCAB). *VCE English Study Design*, Carlton: VCAB, 1990. Print.

Victorian Institute of Secondary Education (VISE). *Course B English*, Group 2, Melbourne: VISE, 1982. Print.

Victorian Institute of Secondary Education (VISE). *Handbook: English*, Group 1. Melbourne: VISE, 1983. Print.

Victorian Universities and Schools Examinations Board (VUSEB). *Handbook of Directions and Prescriptions for 1976*. Melbourne: VUSEB, 1975. Print.

Chapter Ten

CARNIVALESQUE CANONS

"Professors" and text selection in secondary English syllabuses in Western Australia, 1945–1975

Patricia Dowsett

In Australia during the 1940s and 1950s, Professors of English shaped the direction of their disciplines and subjects, in part through the prescription of their own textbooks on tertiary and secondary syllabus lists. This enabled them to disseminate the ideas contained within their textbooks as well as their personal literary interests. The conspicuous inclusion of professors' books over the three decades since 1945 highlights the intimacy and intricacy of many curriculum decisions made in the teaching of English at both the tertiary and secondary levels of education. In this chapter I tell a story of English in Western Australia, 1945–75, using the ALIAS database to examine common perceptions about professorial authority for the purpose of more closely scrutinising curricular control in senior secondary English.

As public intellectuals and figures of authority in growing Australian cities, professors guided the form and content of their subject by nature of their authority over the examinations and syllabuses. This situation was exacerbated in the case of the Professor of English who was in charge of a subject with wide ramifications in secondary schools because it was studied by all candidates for the public examinations. In Western Australia between 1945 and 1975, William Allan Edwards, known as Allan Edwards, was Professor of English at the University of Western Australia (UWA). During this period, UWA was the state's only university, thus authorising Edwards's professorial role and asserting his position as public intellectual and Chief Examiner for over three decades. For this reason, I discuss the history of English in Western Australia in terms of biography because Edwards, like Walter Murdoch before him, was appointed as the sole director of English syllabuses and examinations in the state and it follows that it was his educational and cultural experiences that shaped the version of English that developed during this period.

Leavisism and Allan Edwards

During the 1930s and 40s, the study of English was flourishing globally, with changes and shifts in literary theory aiding the discipline's status and credibility. In the United Kingdom, F.R. Leavis and T.S. Eliot were emerging as leading cultural and literary influences. Leavis was an author and literary critic who taught at Cambridge and founded *Scrutiny* magazine. First published in May 1932, *Scrutiny* sought to promulgate moral ideas about literature, to champion elite culture and to counter "the deadening effects of industrial society and a vulgar mass media" (Ryan and Ryan). Allan Edwards was largely considered a Leavisite, having studied at Cambridge during the 1930s and having had reviews published in *Scrutiny* in December 1932, June 1933 and June 1934. As recently as 1984, Edwards recalled the influence of *Scrutiny* on English Department staff at UWA, saying,

> Well I was one of the original contributors and certainly our copies of 'Scrutiny' were worn out very rapidly in Western Australia. We have a set now [1984] which looks as though it's been battered to death. He [Leavis] is certainly very important to me [...]. (Edwards, *Interview* 4)

But what appeared to be a stock standard Leavisite fraternity from the outside was actually a carnivalesque troop of educators teaching and celebrating the Arts on the inside. Beneath a surface of conventional Cultural Heritage canonicity, staff members at the university engaged with literary study in a distinctively contemporary way. Along these lines, Edwards's practices of appointing staff members on the grounds of their theatrical engagement with texts and modelling of creative practice, were practices unexpected of the Leavisite Edwards had been characterised as (Dale, *English Men*; Dale, *Enchantment*).

In 1941 when Edwards commenced at the University of Western Australia he brought the number of staff to three, alongside Associate Professor Henry Sherman (H.S.) Thompson and lecturer Alec King. The Professor's role in secondary English was not stipulated at his appointment, except where it was a requirement of the university to sit on the Public Examinations Board. Edwards's application for the professorship was supported by five letters of recommendation from across the globe, including one each from F.R. Leavis, then a Lecturer in English at Emmanuel College, and I.A. Richards, Fellow of Magdalene College, Cambridge (UWA Archives, staff file P202). In January 1941, following Edwards's appointment to the Chair in Western Australia, Vice-Chancellor George Currie wrote to him, describing secondary English in less than favourable terms: "English in this State, I think, is not taught to a frightfully high standard at school, so, just as I told you, there is plenty of room for teaching it" (UWA Archives, staff file P202).

During Edwards's tenure the university implemented new theories and modes of instruction but transposing them into the senior secondary curriculum was a much slower process:

> A study of curriculum documents, examination papers and classroom practices of the 1940s and early 1950s in Western Australia indicates that they were still significantly influenced by ideas and practices introduced in the 1912–15 period. Given this span of time, it is easy to see why such practices were accepted as "natural" or "normal" by many teachers and students. (Willis 116)

When Walter Murdoch and the Public Examinations Board were making decisions about the English syllabus and examinations, they affected approximately 30 schools and colleges. By 1942, however, the Committee of the Teachers and Examiners of English had formed, comprising representatives from the university and from schools. The meeting minutes of this committee reveal a greater number of UWA staff members participating in the duties of chairing and decision-making than just one professor, including staff members Alec King, Leonard (Len) Burrows and George Seddon.

In this way, Allan Edwards was not as solitary in curricular decision-making as Murdoch had been, though Edwards's emphases remain conspicuous in the restructure of the university courses and secondary text lists:

> His syllabuses were restructured on genre lines – poetry, drama, the novel.
>
> At the same time, he felt a study of powerful contemporary linguistic strategies – persuasive, scientific and poetic – might better be made to serve the interests of a postwar generation than traditional Old and Middle English. (Bradley 15)

This tribute to Edwards's relevant and modern approach to teaching literature is significant in the light of the criticism that Murdoch had faced for privileging Literature over Language (Dale, *English Men* 36). In spite of their ostensible differences Murdoch and Edwards had a lot more in common than commentators previously recognised. This mutual interest also included their adoption of the "New Education" Fellowship approach to child rearing and schooling. Alongside the "linguistic strategies" that David Bradley identifies, Edwards imported Cambridge principles, thus retaining an emphasis on teaching literature (the "classics") and on close reading. Edwards's broad involvement in cultural pursuits, his staffing appointments and his attitudes to literature teaching, however, appear more carnivalesque than classifications of Cambridge and Leavisite typically accommodate.

Despite being loyal to the English canon, as Murdoch was, Edwards was considered a breath of fresh air by many at the university because he brought energy for change. A member of the English Department between 1948 and 1960, David Bradley reflects that "to the Oxford-oriented department that Edwards inherited from Murdoch, whose syllabuses had scarcely changed in general character for 30 years, Edwards brought a fresh Cambridge vision and some original solutions" (15). Bradley highlights Edwards's emphasis on reading, by explaining that Edwards's response to the needs of Australian students, "was to throw out chronology and the historical canon and to entice students to read strenuously, with attention and intelligence: to confront their own lives with the experiences of books" (15). Part of this literary experience was captured by Edwards through drama, and through poetry for his colleague, Alec King, whose influence on the Western Australian text lists I will explore after examining Edwards's emphases.

Teaching drama and theatre

Edwards promoted literature and theatre to students at the University and to wider Perth society. Collin O'Brien, who worked with Edwards for more than two decades, is complimentary of the way that

> Edwards broadened the base of the English department by employing staff on the basis of their talents rather than their academic qualifications. As a result the department included actors, directors and music and theatre specialists who enlivened the place with their practical experience. ("Death closes literary era")

Edwards's employment practices resisted trends of the times that reflected the "anxiety about being recognised as a member of the cultural and intellectual elite" and shaped what was "valued in personality and training when selecting staff" (Dale *Enchantment* 14). Some of the staff members employed by Edwards included drama specialists Jeana Tweedie (Jeana Bradley), Neville Teede, Philip Parsons, and David Bradley, appointments representing evidence of liberal cultural engagement that appears inconsistent with Leavisite tendencies. The influence of these staff members upon the orientation of drama teaching in the state is recognised by foundation editor of *Westerly* journal, Robert (Bob) Smith:

> The inspirational teaching of David Bradley and Jeana Tweedie [...] was based on the tacit understanding that plays (especially those of Shakespeare) were composed as performance scripts, not for publication as light fiction, and even less as pedagogic exercises for the torment of high-school students. (10)

This engagement of student interest was made possible by the relatively small size of the University and the opportunities provided by its staff.

Writer Dorothy Hewett, who attended UWA as a student in 1940 and 1941, acknowledged that the university was somewhat provincial between the wars; but it was the small size that enabled close relationships to form between teachers, students, and local artists.[1] This opened up the study of English to a freer version, characterised by independent and liberal thinking about literature and the world, aided by Edwards's pedagogical approach, which privileged "appreciation" and the aesthetical appeal of English. For example, Edwards was of the view "that English ought to be fun and the lecturer ought to be a good performer, a good actor" (Edwards, *Interview* 5). Edwards recalled that this element of "performance" was uncharacteristic of university teaching at that time and he reminisced about the arrival of English Department staff member Len Burrows at UWA in 1949: "At first, not surprisingly, he was stunned by our circus cavortings, our ballad singing, our poetry readings, our play readings, our readiness to dash off lecture notes at a moment's warning – all most unacademic" (*Interview* 14). Thus, under Edwards's guidance, English was developing with progressive, artistic and emancipatory roots, a contrast to the discipline's

---

1   Hewett recalled that the Professor of English held play readings every month in his home for his students (89).

more conservative foundations where English was central to the curriculum for the purpose of civil formation and social control.

Contrasting the secondary text lists of 1945 and 1955 shows the growth in drama teaching and diversification of the national literatures as Edwards's tenure progressed. This growth mirrored what was happening at the tertiary level and at the time was considered "eccentric" by his English Department colleague, Bruce Bennett, an indication perhaps of his own position as much as Edwards's.[2] When Walter Murdoch presided over tertiary and secondary English between 1913 and 1939 the drama texts studied were all Shakespearean. In 1939, for example, they were *As You Like It*, *Richard II*, *Twelfth Night* or *Coriolanus*. By 1945, when Edwards had been Professor for five years, "Chaucer" and "Shakespeare" are listed alongside "Novels" and "Poetry" as though they were their own genres and Drama on the secondary curriculum remained as Shakespeare: *Much Ado about Nothing*, *Henry IV – Part I*, *Coriolanus* and *King Lear* (ALIAS).

In addition to the choice of texts, the specific interests of the Professor of English directed subject English in Western Australia. Edwards's preference for drama was shaping the curriculum but Edwards was most critical of candidates' apparent lack of understanding of the genre and aspects of the theatre. By 1950, the syllabus had moved away from appearing just as a text list and Edwards inserted a syllabus note to the Drama section advising that

> Candidates will be expected to have studied Shakespeare as a man of the theatre, as well as a great artist, and to have some knowledge of stage conditions, both Elizabethan and contemporary. In addition they will be expected to have discussed the differences between drama designed for radio production, and drama designed for the stage. (UWA, *1950 Manual* 89)

Moreover, Edwards's 1950 examiner's report is critical of teachers not stressing sufficiently "the acting and theatrical merits of a Shakespeare text" (88). Instead he assessed that candidates failed to recognise "that a blind man at a performance of Hamlet would undoubtedly miss a great deal, [such was Shakespeare's] great use of costume, pageantry, grouping, movement, and ballet" (Edwards, "Examiners" 88). This emphasis is indicative of the

---

[2] Bruce Bennett recalled that "Edwards expressed his eccentricity by admitting a little American literature into his genre-based close-reading courses of predominantly English novels, poems and plays" (*Professing* 19).

value Edwards placed on the *performance* of drama in English: "He believed the best way to study a play was to see a good performance, or, better still, to take part in a production" ("Curtain Up" 24).

Drama and the 1950s text lists

Edwards stressed the advantages of verse in the theatre, particularly radio plays. In his 1950 Leaving English examiner's report, for example, he recommended that more attention

> be given in class to the way verse may be used to control and emphasise pace, stress, and rhythm, and to the way in which verse allows and encourages heightened speech, vivid and daring imagery, and effective symbolism. ("Examiners" 88)

The attention to the performance of poetry in his pedagogy reflects the way in which Edwards made tutorials spontaneous and varied, often mounting play readings followed by lively tutorials ("Curtain Up"). This jovial method of teaching, disguised by the conventional Cultural Heritage text lists of the era, contributes to the story of how canons took on different forms in English classrooms according to local settings and staff members. As another example, 1950 was the first year that A.A. Phillips's *Five Radio Plays* appeared as a "Radio-Drama", a more contemporary genre and approach to drama, and one filling a cultural gap at a time when the "professional stage" was in decline (Griffen-Foley 223).[3] Moreover, its inclusion in the Leaving syllabus reflects the close relationship between the university and the community because university staff frequently appeared on radio: Walter Murdoch and Alec King regularly participated in public broadcasts and Murdoch's daughter Catherine King (wife of Alec), hosted her own daily radio program for women. Len Burrows also presented on this program (Burrows).

One avenue through which the plays were taught to secondary students was via the ABC Schools Broadcasts, with Alec King being a member of the ABC Education Broadcasting Committee, which produced relevant

---

3 A.A.Phillips, *Five Radio Plays* comprises *Fall of the City* by Archibald MacLeish, *Untitled* by Norman Corwin, *Dark Tower* by Louis MacNeice and *Fire on the Snow* by Douglas Stewart. Significantly, while it was included in Western Australian syllabuses, 1950–53, the only other states to prescribe it were Victoria (1949 English Literature) and Tasmania (1951 English Literature), for only one year on each occasion (ALIAS).

information sessions for Western Australian Leaving students.[4] The weekly Schools Broadcasts covered topics that were relevant to the Leaving English syllabus:

> The Education Section of the ABC arranged broadcasts for schools, and many staff were involved. I always gave a talk once a year before the examinations. I did a couple of unscripted discussions with students – the first one was excellent in rehearsal and not so good in the broadcast because the students tightened up; so for the second we secretly taped the rehearsal, and used that! One year we did a TV series on drama, which I presented, with Neville Teede (actor and tutor in English) and Jeana Bradley (nee Tweedie) taking part. (Barnes)

Lectures such as these were product of the networks and exchanges facilitated by a relatively small Western Australian population and the authority gained by being the state's sole university. It is evidence of how tertiary educators directly shaped secondary education via supportive lectures, a gesture that was true to the foundations of UWA tertiary and secondary English in Western Australia and which has since dissipated.

Australian literature

The university's *Arts Faculty Handbooks* of the 1950s show that the English curriculum was still "grounded in the British canon that Edwards knew from his studies at Cambridge in the 1930s with I.A. Richards and a young F.R. Leavis" (Brown 34). This British canon was retained and local writers were critical of the hesitancy with which the university began teaching Australian literature. In 1952, Alec King represented UWA's Department of English on the Public Examinations Board when at the meeting of Teachers and Examiners of English, a motion was passed "that as a matter

---

[4] The "Secondary Schools Radio and Television ABC Broadcasts" programmes had accompanying teaching notes that contained follow-up activities and further reading. For example, in Term One 1970, broadcasts for Leaving English alternated weekly with broadcasts for Leaving English Literature on Tuesday afternoons. Programmes included "Introduction to the English Literature Course" by Mr R. Forsyth (UWA), "The Leaving English Syllabus" by Mr J. Hay (UWA), and three weeks on Drama. Peter Cowan (UWA) presented on short stories and Mrs D. Lilley (Hewett) of UWA presented on "Styles of Writing" including F. Scott Fitzgerald, Hemingway and D.H. Lawrence. Colin Kenworthy (Graylands Teachers College) presented on *The Progress of Poetry* before Len Burrows (UWA) presented on Chaucer (EDWA).

of course some Australian prose and poetry be included in the Junior and Leaving syllabus as a whole each year" (UWA Archives, cons 394, 4 April 1952). This is the first explicit directive for the inclusion of Australian writers on the Western Australian secondary English syllabus.[5] It was likely to have been motivated by a public debate in the *West Australian* newspaper's "letters to the editor" section one month prior, and it followed national conversations about the teaching of Australian literature at the tertiary level. In 1951, Melbourne historian Geoffrey Serle submitted to *Meanjin* an outline of the Australian literary content taught in Australian universities. In response to Serle's article and published in the winter 1952 edition of *Meanjin*, Edwards wrote an article in favour of the growing interest in the study of Australian literature, detailing its range in the curriculum at the University of Western Australia. Edwards extends it to secondary schools: "Furthermore, we have some influence on the choice of texts for the Junior and Leaving examinations and have seen to it that Australian poetry and fiction are normally included in the secondary school curriculum" ("Australian" 175). According to John K. Ewers, however, the reluctance of the university's English Department to increase the study of Australian literature was to the students' detriment.

In a public conflict in March 1952, Ewers and members of the university's English Department exchanged letters to the editor of the *West Australian* newspaper. Ewers condemned "the comparative indifference of the English department of the University to the significance of Australian literature" and claimed that at the meeting of Teachers and Examiners of English, "a majority of teachers and examiners present disapproved of the attitude of the English department" ("Exam"). These claims ignited an equally curt response from Chief Examiner Alec King, who rejected Ewers's accusations as an "amusing fantasy" ("Exam"). King countered that the university's English Department staff "were among those who unanimously carried the motion that some aspects of Australian poetry and prose should be included in the Junior and Leaving syllabuses" ("Exam"). In addition, King critiqued the inclusion of literature for its own sake, rather than because it "makes known the best that has been thought and said in the world". He asserted

---

5   By contrast, in other states, Rolf Boldrewood's *Robbery Under Arms* was studied at Leaving level in English Literature in South Australia in 1946. and Mackaness and Mackaness's *The Wide Brown Land* poetry anthology was included in 1949 in New South Wales. In Tasmania, Katharine Susannah Prichard's *Haxby's Circus* was set in 1948, in Victoria *Five Radio Plays* was included in 1949 and in Western Australia Ion Idriess' *Flynn of the Inland* and Mackanesses' *The Wide Brown Land* were set in 1945 (ALIAS).

that "the English department does not discourage an interest in Australian literature: it tries, however, to serve the universality which a university stands for" ("Exam"). In response Ewers clarifies in yet another letter, that all the best literature in the world is not "exclusively thought and said by English writers" and that "a judicious combination of the best in English and Australian writing in University study courses might enrich us all" ("Study Courses"). Such a public debate is evidence of "the way in which essays, examinations and the secondary school curricula could be positively influenced by proponents of Australian literature" (Dale, *English Men* 155) and signifies a public expression of the tension in teaching English and Australian literatures within institutions and communities.

Teaching the national literature remained outside traditional scholarly practices but its profile lifted in English teaching in Western Australia with Edwards and King's involvement in the Commonwealth Literary Fund Lectures.[6] Edwards and King did not espouse much Australian literature to be worthy of academic attention so an anomaly then is the inclusion of Eleanor Dark's *The Timeless Land* in 1954 and 1955 text lists, and Walter Murdoch and Henrietta Drake-Brockman's *Australian Short Stories* in 1955 and 1956. These inclusions reflect the growing influence of the Fellowship of Australian Writers in Western Australia (FAWWA). The FAWWA were well aware of the plethora of talented writers in Australian literature, and had been lobbying the university to include it since 1969 (Kotai-Ewers 285). Bennett identifies the period 1960–75 as a third phase of the introduction of Australian literature courses into Australian universities, "a period during which undergraduate and graduate studies in Australian literature have increased and diversified, but with little public discussion of aims or intentions" ("Australian" 114). During this later "phase", members of the English Department at the University of Western Australia planned a new course in Australian Literature, which was "then a controversial move" (Haskell, "News" 7).

The course was "blocked for a time" (Bennett, "Australian" 106). For despite the establishment of new Australian literary journals in the 1950s

---

6   The Commonwealth Literary Fund lectures began in 1940, an initiative of the Commonwealth Government to establish a course of lectures on Australian literature as an integral part of university English courses. In Western Australia the first lecturers were Norman Bartlett, John K. Ewers, Paul Hasluck and William Hatfield, all members of the Western Australian branch of the Fellowship of Australian Writers. University staff members participated when King lectured on Australian poetry in 1947 and Edwards lectured on Australian short stories in 1952 (Edwards, "Australian" 175).

and 60s legitimating Australian literature and contributing to its acceptance as a serious area of scholarship, the university's Professorial Board was reluctant to introduce it as a course of study. In 1969 John Barnes sought the Board's permission to establish a course in Australian literature; this was approved but subject to delay as a result of the Board's fiscal stringency (UWA Archives, Minutes – Professorial Board). As it happens, Barnes was also a committee member of the FAWWA, as was writer and fellow lecturer at the university (1966–73), Dorothy Hewett. When fellow FAWWA committee member Bert Vickers learned that the Board was reconsidering its decision, he proposed "that an appeal from the FAWWA might help convince the academics" (Kotai-Ewers 286). Alongside these events, Allan Edwards spent his study leave in 1971 giving lectures on Australian literature at several Indian universities. His lecture topics included the writing of Judith Wright, A.D. Hope and Henry Handel Richardson (UWA Archives, staff file P202). Furthermore, upon Edwards's return from this leave, he reported to Deputy Vice-Chancellor Professor C.J.B. Clews that he had "brought back from Townsville detailed syllabuses of Australian Literature courses (undergraduate and postgraduate) which could prove useful to us in our own forward planning" (UWA Archives, staff file P202). The university's first course in Australian Literature (English 35) was introduced in 1973, an optional third-year unit. It was also during Edwards's tenure that American literature entered the Leaving syllabus: Robert Frost's poetry and Mark Twain's *Huckleberry Finn* were introduced in 1955 and from then onwards the range steadily increased. The 1965 syllabus, for example, prescribed non-British poets such as Judith Wright and Robert Frost, along with Arthur Miller's *Death of a Salesman*, Nigel Samuel's *Plays for Radio and Television*, Henry Handel Richardson's *The Getting of Wisdom*, Peter Cowan's *Short Story Landscape* and Vance Palmer's *The Rainbow Bird* (ALIAS).

Edwards viewed literature as representing life, and as a source of aesthetic and moral values. Accordingly, the criteria for evaluating texts were their content and the moral position of the author, evident in the process of close reading.

> The term 'close reading' refers not only to an activity with regard to texts but also to a type of text itself: a technically informed, fine-grained analysis of some piece of writing, usually in connection with some broader question of interest. The practice has multiple ancestors, including classical rhetorical description, theological exegesis and legal

interpretation, and also some cousins, such as iconology and psycho-analysis. All of these would have been familiar to the small group of accomplished British dons and poets whose efforts to reform literary study in the 1920s and 30s came to be called 'the New Criticism' and whose critical essays served as models for the practices that came to be called 'close reading.' (Herrnstein Smith 2)

This "close study" of texts teaches a clear process to purposeful reading. Edwards advocated this reading strategy, which recognises the intrinsic value of the text, because its own characteristics are the sole components of meaning rather than contextual factors. Leigh Dale cites former UWA English student Jim Wieland, who went on to become Professor and Head of the Department of English at the University of Wollongong. Wieland's criticism of this approach was that it was "naïve, text-centred, and a-historical. Any text we read had an autonomous, autotelic existence in which we were to find a universal and authoritative meaning" (Dale, *English Men* 116).

Tim Dolin argues, however, that "there are significant differences between American New Criticism and what is better known (and more often vilified) in Australia as Leavisism" (Chapter 14 of this volume). Dolin contends

> Both were associated with close reading, called "practical criticism" in Britain, but American New Criticism's signature disregard for context (the main reason for its portability) was completely at odds with Leavisite cultural criticism, which was effectively an engaged critique of the here and now, and fed into cultural materialism, on the one hand, and British cultural studies on the other (the Birmingham School was started by left-Leavisites). (286)

This argument suggests Edwards's experiences and practices are less Leavisite than first thought, for while Edwards introduced and maintained close reading in secondary and tertiary studies of English and literature he engaged with the "here and now, and fed into cultural materialism" to some extent through his emphasis on poetry readings, performance, contemporary drama and radio plays. Practical criticism transferred easily into the secondary context and for Edwards it averted the reproduction of received responses: "The essential thing was that they had not been primed up with the right answers, they had to find the answers themselves and they were judged on their ability to find and present intelligibly reasonably persuasive answers" (*Interview* 8). A product of Edwards's endorsing such an approach meant that frequently during his tenure, examination papers at both the university and Leaving Certificate levels began with an unseen passage, a practice which continues today.[7]

F.R. Leavis and the New Criticism in Western Australia

Edwards acknowledged that Leavis and Richards led him in Cambridge "to pay a good deal of attention to Practical Criticism" (UWA Archives, staff file P202). In fact, Edwards was "probably one of the very first academic people to put Richards's and Leavis's ideas into practice" (Edwards, *Interview* 11). Dale argues that Edwards was the only Chair of English at an Australian university "who had encountered the younger and then institutionally marginalised Leavis" (*English Men* 114). Terry Collits extends this claim by crediting Edwards with the importation and dissemination of Leavisism in Australia:

> Naturally enough, migrating Leavisism first touched these shores at Perth, with the professional appointment of a veritable "Scrutineer", Allan Edwards. The word was brought across to Melbourne by Jock Tomlinson in the early 1950s, and Leavis was more or less the sign under which the brilliant younger brigade of the department (Goldberg himself, Maggie Tomlinson, David Moody and Vincent Buckley) set about revamping its pedagogy. (25)

In the way that Collits describes, and as Dale argues, "Perth became a conduit of Leavisism" (*Enchantment* 193):

> Allan Edwards brought with him first hand involvement in the *Scrutiny* movement and related debates, and might have transformed the discipline had he not remained isolated at Western Australia. There, he built a department that reflected his views but did not transmit them beyond Perth until a movement of academic staff from UWA to Melbourne began in the 1960s. (*Enchantment* 287)

---

[7] In the 1952 second Leaving paper, students were asked to compare and contrast two unseen poems: "Song of the Galley Slaves" and "Thief". In the Reading Section of the 2012 WACE English Stage 3 paper, candidates could choose between two texts: a 2011 Anzac Day speech by Chaplain Mark Willis and an extract from a short story by Nigerian author Chimamanda Adichie, published in 2009. There are two compulsory questions in this section. Question 1 is "Discuss how either Text 1 or Text 2 constructs ideas about identity" and Question 2 is "With reference to at least one written text you have studied, explain how an understanding of context influenced your response to the text's ideas" (SCSA 3).

David Bradley suggests that Edwards "was not a Leavisite as that word came to be understood in Australia, except in so far as he would have agreed that, in the master's words, 'literary criticism is an appeal for agreement'" (15). In this way, Edwards has been wrongly characterised by Dale to some extent (*English Men*; *Enchantment*). Edwards was in favour of radio broadcasts and plays, a respect for media texts that is contrary to Leavis, who viewed mass media as inferior and product of a "culture crisis" (Leavis 5). Edwards's philosophy is evident in the Leaving English syllabuses in Western Australia. In addition to A.A. Phillips's *Five Radio Plays*, Nigel Samuel's *Plays for Radio and Television* was included in Western Australia 1961–65, but only elsewhere in New South Wales in 1962 (ALIAS), again highlighting the influence of university staff's interests (such as radio plays) upon the Leaving text lists in Western Australia, which was not similarly exerted in other states.[8]

Alec King

Another UWA staff member who came to influence the secondary English curriculum is Alec King. An Englishman, King met Catherine Murdoch, daughter of Walter Murdoch, at the London Day Training College in 1928, and returned with her to Western Australia where they married in 1929. King was "an Oxford man" but significantly, had trained as a teacher at the London Institute where he "had come under the influence of Mr. Gurrey,

---

[8] On the Western Australian syllabuses, teacher-reference books were recommended for teachers by examiners (UWA, *1948 Manual* 48) and in later years were intended for consideration as "additional text-books" (UWA, *1950 Manual* 91). E.G. Biaggini, a teacher and extension lecturer in Adelaide, published a number of books on literature and education, four of which were reviewed in *Scrutiny*, including one by Allan Edwards (Dale, *Enchantment* 194). Between 1965 and 1968, teacher-reference books in Western Australia included E.G. Biaggini's *The Reading and Writing of English* and *Sound and Sense in English*. Biaggini argues for mass education in literature and "writes as a moralist from a deep sense of social responsibility" (194), and his book *The Reading and Writing of English*, which was included on the Western Australian Leaving Syllabus as a teacher-reference book between 1950 and 1959 and then 1965 to 68, is prefaced by F.R. Leavis. The preface acknowledges that there is an increasing hostility to culture (xix) and explains that the book attempts "to bridge the widening gulf between those who know what a literary value is and the larger number who do not" (xiii). Biaggini encouraged students to make their own judgements in the Richards' tradition (Hilliard 131), a view passed down to Western Australian school students via Edwards. It was consistent with the perspectives of *Scrutiny* writers who had argued "the oppressive effects of external examinations on teaching" (125). Christopher Hilliard asserts that the postwar expansions of secondary education and the textbook industry further entrenched the authority of external examinations, which validated the status of the university and its Professor of English (125).

an enthusiastic admirer of Leavis" (Edwards, *Interview*, Additional notes 1).[9] King was appointed part-time Assistant Lecturer to the Department of English at the University of Western Australia in 1933.[10] His principal professional interest was poetry, particularly the modernist poets, and he was of the group of contemporaries who appealed to university students between the wars. Reflecting upon his student years at UWA, Norman Bartlett recalls that during the 1930s "Alec King kept us right up to the minute on the latest 'movements' in England and Europe" (61). During King's time at Oxford University he had been a member of a poetry group that included Cecil Day Lewis, Rex Warner and W.H. Auden ("Chair of English" 2).[11] King's interest in T.S. Eliot and in contemporary literature is evident in his choice of productions for St George's College and the University Dramatic Society, which he co-directed with historian, poet and politician, Paul Hasluck in 1936 – T.S. Eliot's *Murder in the Cathedral* – "just a year after the play's premiere in Canterbury" (Dunstone and Pope 292). His preference for Wordsworth is remembered by Dorothy Hewett, a student of King, who recalls that she was the only student to follow his suggestion when he told them that to understand Wordsworth's relationship to nature they should "'go out of the lecture theatre,' remove their shoes, 'and feel the grass springing under the soles' of their bare feet" (Hewett 87). This says as much about the joy of poetry for King as for Hewett.[12]

King and Edwards's differing literary preferences inevitably shaped text selection in the senior secondary English curriculum. Edwards was critical of some text selections but accepted them as part of a consultative process

---

9   King is the first of many notable teachers of English in Western Australia who was trained at the London Institute of Education, including Bruce Bennett and Eric Carlin. Furthermore, Percy Gurrey's *The Appreciation of Poetry* was listed on the English Literature syllabus for 16 years, 1965–1980, and signifies the influence of the Institute of Education, University of London ("the London School") upon the teaching of English in Western Australia.

10   He went on to be made Lecturer (1941), Senior Lecturer (1946) and Reader (1952) (Hay, "King").

11   The group was called the Poetry Writing Club. Day Lewis became King's brother-in-law (briefly) when Day Lewis married King's sister, Mary (La Nauze 82). This explains why the Alec King Collection, acquired by the University of Western Australia library in 2009, contains "a number of valuable first editions of Auden, Eliot, Joyce and C. Day Lewis, including some signed copies" (UWA, "Donations" 6). It also contains numerous volumes of *Scrutiny* magazine.

12   Dorothy Hewett's poetry was set for the secondary English curriculum in Victoria 1983, New South Wales 1985–86, 1993–95 and Tasmania 1993–94. Her play *The Man from Mukinupin* was set for various English courses in New South Wales 1994–98 and English in WA 1990–93 (ALIAS).

with teachers of English in the Committee of the Teachers and Examiners of English. For example, in Western Australia Chaucer was studied nearly every year between 1945 and 2001 despite examiners repeatedly recommending abolition of the Chaucer question:

> [...] because although he was friendly, human and humorous, he was difficult to read. Very few schoolchildren ever got to the point of reading him with ease and merely underwent drudgery – as did the examiners marking their answers. However, the teachers had insisted on the study of Chaucer. (Edwards qtd in "Leaving English Papers")

In this example, the syllabus lists provide us with insight not only into the many different ways in which value was attached to forms of writing and modes of reading in senior school classrooms, but also by whom.

There was a clear difference in the philosophies of Edwards and King, though they worked together for 25 years between 1941 and 1965:

> Edwards's enthusiasms for Freud were matched by King's more Jungian notions; the Leavisite's idea of the self-sufficiency of the literary text was counterpointed by King's reluctance to embrace ideology or theory. He preferred to deal with seamless linkings of poetry, the visual arts and music. (Hay, "King")[13]

There is no reason why disputing ideologies, such as those between Edwards and King, should limit the success or quality of teaching in an institution. Harry Heseltine remembers King and Edwards as "an unlikely duo [that] complemented rather than contradicted each other" (19). Dale notes that although the co-existence of King's "alternative discourse" seems incompatible with Edwards's view, it is evidence of how two apparently different approaches to literature could operate with one another "at the level of pedagogical practice" (*English Men* 116). It is a poignant acknowledgement when Edwards says about King:

> From the start he was an enthusiastic collaborator. Without his talented support I should have got nowhere. I was extremely lucky and I'm very grateful to him for his unfailing support and for his friendship. I missed him sadly when he left us. (*Interview*, Additional notes 2)

---

13 Hay also notes the Kings' contribution to Perth's cultural life, where Catherine and Alec turned their home into a vital and crowded meeting place for visiting and local artists, performers and community leaders, "a fusion of literature, life and creative imagination which informed his teaching" ("King").

The Professors' books

Alec King influenced secondary and tertiary English teaching through his books, particularly, *The Control of Language*, published in 1939, which he co-authored with Martin Ketley. Around this time, the conditions of war made textbooks difficult to source and first year English students at the university relied upon I.A. Richards's *Practical Criticism* and King and Ketley's *The Control of Language* to teach fundamental reading and writing skills. King and Ketley's text was also recommended as a reference book for use by teachers of Leaving English in the 1949 syllabus (UWA Archives, cons 394, 11 June 1948). It remained on the Leaving English syllabus until 1964. Despite criticism, significantly from C.S. Lewis, *The Control of Language* was notable for its chapter on poetry which was mostly non-academic, non-chronological and reflected the authors' great love of the form.[14] At the University of Western Australia it was Allan Edwards who lectured on *The Control of Language*. His 1942 lecture notes, held in the UWA library's Special Collections, are very detailed and specific.[15] They cover the Short Story, Idiom and Slang, Argument and Propaganda, Propaganda – Advertising, and Referential Writing. Edwards describes King's book as "wholly admirable" (Edwards, *Interview*, Additional notes 2), and Dale identifies its likely conspicuousness as "an indication of a congruity in approach that King and Martin Ketley's *The Control of Language* was favourably reviewed in *Scrutiny* prior to Edwards taking up his appointment in Perth" (*Enchantment* 190f).

According to David Bradley, *The Control of Language* "became the hallmark of the university's English department in the 1950s and was widely used in sixth-form English in the eastern states as an introduction to poetry" (15). This testament, however, is not substantiated by the ALIAS

---

14 C.S. Lewis is scathing in his attack on *The Control of Language* to which he gives the title *The Green Book* by the pseudonymous Gaius and Titius. He condemns it for promoting scepticism about values "on the surface" but instead promulgating their own set of values "which they believe to be immune from the debunking process" (Lewis 15).

15 As a point of interest, during the same year (1942), King lectured on "Milton, Dryden to Wordsworth" including lectures on Milton, Tennyson, Yeats, Auden and T.S. Eliot for which King recommends Leavis's *New Bearings*, stating it "is worth reading, and contains annotations on the 'Waste Land'" (King, "Lecture notes"). Continuing on from these, King lectures on Hardy's poetry, Hopkins, *The Faber Book of Modern Verse*, Hemingway's "The Killers", Donne and the Metaphysical Poets and Chekhov short stories. They confirm "a perspective that was generally humanistic rather than specifically" Leavisite as Leigh Dale deduces from King's other work (*English Men* 116).

database, which shows it to be on the Western Australian syllabus only for most years between 1949 and 1965. King also influenced the teaching of poetry on the secondary curriculum by offering greater diversity in the poetry on the text lists and in advising how it should be taught: "The young should be allowed to hear much poetry, skilfully and movingly spoken, undistracted by examination-anxiety or the need to be tested" (173). He also argues that not every teacher is "poetical" so teachers ought "to be selected and trained accordingly" (174).

King also shaped the development of Leaving English through the inclusion of his book *Writing* (1955), which was on the syllabus as a reference book in Western Australia between 1956 and 1964. It recognises the utilitarian purposes of writing. In *Writing* King identifies four main uses of language and argues that there is a close relationship between writing and living (preface vii). These four main uses are: to express ourselves; to give, receive, and ask for directions and instructions; to think out and record knowledge; to bring home to ourselves the meaning and value of experience (1). These disclose a range of functions of English for King, from utilitarian and fundamental communication purposes to more aesthetic and moral purposes such as character formation and "the humanising effect of literature" (Peel 53). King discusses language and writing, including analyses of expressive language, creative writing, fable writing and occasional writing. He argues that a clear mind creates clear writing, just as Edwards argued that "good thinking is an expression of good writing" (UWA Archives, cons 268, 16 Mar 1957). Although King's *Writing* was a reference book, that is, one recommended for teachers to use as support, it may or may not actually have been readily used by teachers. Nevertheless its inclusion does position the book as an authority on writing. Significantly, King took up the Chair of English at Monash University in 1966, the first year that both books were absent from the secondary syllabus since 1949.

The Rainbow Bird

Similarly, the influence of the Professor of English is evident in the inclusion of Vance Palmer's *The Rainbow Bird* (1957) as a short story option in the Leaving English syllabus in 1958. The book included an introduction by Edwards – "an illuminating preface" (Brissenden 98) – and was Edwards's own selection of Palmer's stories, those Edwards considered to be "the best thirteen" (Ross 733). Palmer's collection received many favourable reviews for its evocative symbolism and the quality of the writing, the story construction, and for its settings in different regions of Australia (sees Ross, Levis and Geering respectively). Dorothy Hewett recalled the time that, as a student, Palmer "turns up" in one of Edwards's tutorials (89). *The Rainbow Bird and Other Stories* by Vance Palmer, selected by Allan Edwards, was included on the Western Australian Leaving syllabus – and no other Australian senior secondary syllabus – for 15 years: 1958–59, 1964–65 and 1969–75 (ALIAS). It suggests that the way in which professors relate to English is passed on to secondary English, subject to the material requirements of universities and schools. Edwards's apparently conservative and stock-standard Cultural Heritage text list emerged from a diverse institution with a milieu of performance and creative writers. While Edwards is distinctly Leavisite in many of his approaches to literature, he cannot be characterised as a Leavisite totally and absolutely, such are his attitudes to teaching and involvement in cultural pursuits.

Another conspicuous inclusion on the Western Australian senior secondary text lists is the anthology *Charitable Malice: A Choice of Augustan Satirical Poetry* by lecturers in the university's Department of English, David Bradley (at UWA between 1948 and 1957) and Leonard Burrows (at UWA between 1949 and 1986).[16] *Charitable Malice* was prescribed for Leaving English in Western Australia, for the years 1956–57 and 1960–61, but in no other states. The format of this collection of eighteenth-century satire was reviewed by T.B. Tomlinson as "pleasing in a way that is distressingly unusual in school and university textbooks" (310). This positive review articulates the extent of the relations and networks in Perth literary circles, with Tomlinson having been a colleague of Bradley and Burrows when employed as a temporary lecturer at UWA between 1949 and 1953. Tomlinson returned to Perth following two years at Cambridge between 1950 and 1951, a similar path to Bradley, who attended Cambridge during 1951 and 1952.[17] They are further evidence of the extent of the Cambridge influence upon the teaching of English at the secondary and tertiary levels in Western Australia. Bradley and Burrows's *Charitable Malice* was taught and examined with a focus on form – specifically, the heroic couplet. The 1960 English examination paper, for instance, asks: "Choose TWO poems

---

16 Significantly, Burrows came to be appointed to UWA having studied at Sheffield University under Professor Knights, who was a Cambridge graduate, a co-editor of *Scrutiny* magazine and knew Edwards from Cambridge: "Harry Thompson had died and Prof Edwards wrote to various people including Professor Knights requesting applicants for the job" (Burrows).

17 John Barnes was another UWA staff member who attended Cambridge (1961–62).

from *Charitable Malice* to illustrate two markedly different uses of the heroic couplet" (UWA, *1960 Manual* 3). The heroic couplet was made famous by Chaucer, notably in *The Canterbury Tales*, and reflects the close attention paid in the curriculum to form and genre, poetic devices and performances, consistent with the philosophies of their Cambridge proponents.

Peter Cowan

Having been a student at the University of Western Australia in the late 1930s, Peter Cowan helped establish a new direction for the teaching of English in Western Australia as a tutor in the late 1940s. He is a crucial figure in the link between the teaching of English at the tertiary and secondary levels in WA during this time. For most of his 15 years teaching at Scotch College, Perth, between 1948 and 1962, he was also teaching at the university, usually part-time in the evenings. Cowan valued the relative freedom in selecting texts for study in the classroom: "It was left to your own good sense and to the good sense of other masters as to what you used. Very wide reading became possible [...] The whole thing was invigorating" (Cowan 45).[18] Cowan motivated the boys at Scotch College by using shock tactics to expose them to "worldly" ideas, such as essays on suicide and on mass extermination.[19] He exposed them to a broader range of literature and encouraged them to write about what they knew (Gregory 252). While a separate literary society allowed Cowan to expose students to a range of writers such as T.S. Eliot, Arthur Miller and even Patrick White, Australian writers were not Cowan's preference (254). Cowan once observed that Hemingway "was a man looking at life around him and seeing it with some clarity, and without the hopeless evasions of so much Australian writing" (qtd in Moran). Cowan's ideas of teaching English were clearly gendered and his literary influences were all male, including Ernest Hemingway, John Dos Passos, Thomas Hardy, Anton Chekhov

---

18   Cowan specifies Hemingway as one example of the "modern stuff" he could bring into the classroom: "In the sense that you could integrate contemporary work into the, say the Leaving English classes, that was good, and I did do that by bringing people like Hemingway's work into the classes. Of course, you immediately realised what a response was there if you were able to do this kind of thing. But some schools wouldn't have considered Hemingway should be brought anywhere near a school, and this sort of thing was still something that was being thrashed out. Nowadays it's obviously different" (Cowan 45).

19   The essays mentioned include C.J. Brackenridge's "The White Carnation" on suicide, Shelley Barker's "The Ordeal" about mass extermination and "The Mongrel Dog" by F. Owen about the death of a stockman (Gregory 252).

and Samuel Beckett (Moran). Significantly, many of these writers were included on the secondary and tertiary English syllabuses during Cowan's tenure as a Senior Lecturer at UWA between 1964 and 1979. This includes T.S. Eliot on the secondary syllabuses between 1968 and 1970 inclusive, Arthur Miller between 1962 and 1980, Patrick White in 1979 and 1980, Ernest Hemingway between 1973 and 1980, Hardy in 1967 and 1968 before 1971–80, Chekhov 1968–80 and Beckett 1971–80 (ALIAS).

Cowan resigned from Scotch College in 1962, having become more involved in his writing and having received a Commonwealth Literary Fellowship. He stayed on there until 1979 writing stories, producing several practical textbooks and editing *Westerly*. Through several of these texts, Cowan made direct contributions to the senior secondary syllabuses, with *Perspectives Two*, *Spectrum One*, *Spectrum Two* and *Short Story Landscape* appearing on at least one Western Australian syllabus between 1971 and 2005.[20] Along with Randolph Stow, who taught at the university in 1963 and 1964, Dorothy Hewett who taught there between 1966 and 1973 and later Fay Zwicky who taught there between 1972 and 1987, Peter Cowan represents the addition of creative writers to the department staff as another example of the expansion of the department and the studies of English under Allan Edwards (Burrows). It suggests a close relationship between creative practice and literary study at UWA. The creative writer-teacher figure such as Peter Cowan became a significant part of the story of the tertiary education tradition in Western Australia, a small part of which was through the inclusion of their books in the Western Australian English syllabuses. Cowan's *Short Story Landscape* as well as *Spectrum One*, *Spectrum Two* and *Perspectives Two* (edited with John Hay and Bruce Bennett) were long-term text list inclusions. In addition, Walter Murdoch, the Professor with whom the writer-teacher figure tradition began, had *Australian Short Stories* included in Western Australian English syllabuses in 1955 and 1956. This anthology he had co-edited with Henrietta Drake-Brockman.[21]

---

20   *Perspectives Two*, *Spectrum One* and *Spectrum Two* are short story anthologies edited by Bruce Bennett, Peter Cowan and John Hay. *Short Story Landscape* is Cowan's edited collection of short stories and was also on the Western Australian English syllabus 1965–67 (ALIAS).

21   Another writer-teacher figure, Randolph Stow, had his novel *The Merry Go Round in the Sea* included in English in Western Australia English between 1974 and 1984, and English Literature between 1981 and 1995. It was also set in all other states at various times. Similarly, Stow's *To the Islands* was set in English in Western Australia between 1990 and 2005 and in all other states. Fay Zwicky's *Collected Poems* was

Conclusion

Syllabus inclusions demonstrate the influence of the local university and its "professors" upon English teaching in Western Australia between 1945 and 1975. Specifically, Allan Edwards, the Professor of English at the University of Western Australia, was in a position to exercise extensive curricular control by nature of UWA's status as the sole university. During the 1940s and 1950s, subject English in Western Australia retained much of its emphasis on British canonical writers but broadened to include Australian literature and contemporary texts. Allan Edwards imported a version of "Cambridge English" marked by literary study, practical criticism and the Leavisism which was to influence English across Australia in the 1960s. Yet beneath this surface of traditional canonicity there was a distinctive way in which university staff engaged with literary study. Edwards emphasised literature and drama in English courses and introduced the reading practice of practical criticism to nurture students' independent thinking ahead of rote-learned "respectable" opinions. Unquestionably, the secondary English curriculum was shaped by the staff of an expanded Department of English involved at various times in the Teaching and Examiners of English committees, including Edwards, Alec King, H.S. Thompson, David Bradley, Jeana (Tweedie) Bradley, Len Burrows and Peter Cowan. The number of government secondary schools rose considerably during the 1950s and early 1960s, which saw the responsibility for decision-making drift away from the monopoly of the professor and there was greater diversity instituted in secondary syllabuses, including the "professors' books". While the conspicuous inclusions of professors' books over the three decades since 1945 highlight the complexity and intricacy of many curriculum decisions made in the teaching of English at both the tertiary and secondary levels of education in Western Australia, the creative practice, theatrical engagement and "carnivalesque" approach to texts suggest the significance of institutions and personnel at a local level: "not just a set of individual texts or authors but rather a set of institutions and institutional practices which regulate the making and transmission of (literary) meanings in a given society" (Carter 18).

---

set in English Literature in Western Australia between 1996 and 2001 (ALIAS). Significantly, poet Zwicky's appointment was to a lectureship in American and Comparative Literature ("Fay Zwicky").

I would like to thank Tony Hughes D'Aeth from the University of Western Australia, for providing constructive feedback on an early draft of this chapter. I also acknowledge the generous support of the APA and University scholarships that funded this research.

Works cited

Analysis of Literature in Australian Schools Database (ALIAS). www.australiancommonreader.com/syllabus. Web. 29 November 2015.

Barnes, John. "Re: English Teachers' Association of WA". Message to the author. 26 Aug. 2013. Email.

Bartlett, Norman. "Perth in the turbulent thirties". *Westerly* 22.4. (Dec. 1977): 61–69. *Westerly Digital Archive*. Web. 24 Aug. 2014.

Bennett, Bruce. "Australian literature and the universities". *Melbourne Studies in Education* 18.1 (1976): 106–55. Print.

———. "Professing English Today": An inaugural professorial lecture presented at University College, University of New South Wales, Australian Defence Force Academy, Canberra, on 27 May 1993. Canberra: University College, UNSW, 1993. Print.

Bradley, David. "Professor's vision shaped new era". *Australian* (2015). Print.

Brissenden, R.F. "The Rainbow Bird and Other Stories". Review of *The Rainbow Bird and Other Stories*, by Vance Palmer; selected by Allan Edwards. *Quadrant* 1.4 Spring (1957): 97–98. Web. 13 Jun 2015.

Brown, Daniel. "West Coast Correspondences: Randolph Stow encounters Thom Gunn's *The Sense of Movement*". *Australian Literary Studies* 26.1 May (2011): 33–50. Print.

Burrows, Leonard. Interview with Leonard Burrows by Julia Wallis. UWA Historical Society. Claremont: University of Western Australia Historical Society, 13 Sept. 2012 and 20 Sept. 2012. Web. 15 Mar. 2015. <http://oralhistories.arts.uwa.edu.au/items/show/5>

Carter, David. "Literary canons and literary institutions", in Delys Bird, et.al eds. *CanonOZities: The Making of Literary Reputations in Australia*. Spec. Issue of *Southerly* 57.3 (1997): 16–37. Print.

"Chair of English". *Monash Reporter* 3. 16 March (1966): 2. Monash University. Web. 12 Feb. 2015.

Collits, Terry. "Sydney revisited: Literary struggles in Australia (circa 1965 and ongoing)". *Australian Book Review* 210 May (1999): 23–28. *Informit*. Web. 11 Feb. 2015.

Cowan, Peter. Interview with Peter Walkinshaw Cowan (1914–2002) by Stuart Reid. OH 2501. Perth: State Library of Western Australia, Oct. 1991 – Aug. 1992. Transcribed by Sheana Masterson. Transcript. Print.

"Curtain up on UWA Theatre". *Uniview* 26. 2 Winter (2007): 23–25. *The University of Western Australia*. Web. 25 Oct. 2014.

Dale, Leigh. *The Enchantment of English: Professing English literatures in Australian universities*. Sydney: University of Sydney Press, 2012. Print.

———. *The English Men: England's colonial grip on Australian universities*. Canberra: ASAL Halstead, 1997. Print.

"Death closes literary era". *West Australian* 22 Aug. 1995. n.p. Biographical cuttings on William Allan Edwards, Emeritus Professor, containing one or more cuttings from newspapers or journals. National Library Australia. Print.

Dolin, Tim. "The literary regime and its knowledge institutions: Literary studies in Australian upper-school syllabuses, 1945–2005". Unpublished conference paper. Print.

——. "Modernism and modernist criticism in Australian upper-secondary English". *Required Reading*. Ed. Tim Dolin, Jo Jones and Patricia Dowsett. Melbourne: Monash University Publishing. 2016. 285–309. Print.

Dunstone, Bill, and Joan Pope. "University Theatre, drama and the community". *Seeking Wisdom*. Ed. Jenny Gregory. Crawley: University of Western Australia Publishing, 2013. 287–305. Print.

Education Department of Western Australia (EDWA). *ABC Radio and Television Annual Programme Guide: Secondary Schools 1970*. Perth: ABC, 1970. Print.

Edwards, Allan. "Australian Literature Courses". *Meanjin* 11.2 Winter (1952): 174–175. Print.

——. "Donne Not an Elizabethan: Review of *The Oxford Book of Sixteenth Century Verse* by E.K. Chambers". *Scrutiny*, June 1933: 82–85.

——. "Examiner's Report – "Leaving English 1950". University of Western Australia Archives. Consignment 116. Staff file P202. William Allan Edwards, 1941–1971 88–93. Print.

——. "Ideals and facts in adult education: Reviews of *Adult education in practice* by Robert Peers (ed), *English in Australia* by E.G. Biaggini with a foreword by F.R. Leavis, and *Reading and Discrimination* by Denys Thompson". *Scrutiny* June 1934 3 (1): 91–101.

——. Interview with Emeritus Professor William Allan Edwards by Anne Reid (with additional notes). OH 36. University of Western Australia Archives. Consignment 1486. Vas 793. Transcript. Print.

——. "Review: *The History of the Russian Revolution* by Leon Trotsky". *Scrutiny*. December 1932: 301–303.

Ewers, John K. Reply to letter of Mr Burrows. "Exam Syllabus". *West Australian* 20 Mar. 1952, p.15. *Trove*. Web. 22 Nov. 2014.

——. Reply to Letter of Mr King. "Study Courses". *West Australian* 27 Mar. 1952, p.17. *Trove*. Web. 22 Nov. 2014.

"Fay Zwicky (1933–)". n.d. *Australian Poetry Library*. Web. 17 Mar. 2015.

Geering, Ron. "Pattern and life". Review of *The Rainbow Bird and Other Stories* by Vance Palmer. *Southerly* 18.1 Mar (1957): 51–54. Web. 13 Jun 15.

Gregory, J.A. *Building a Tradition: a History of Scotch College, Perth 1897–1996*. Nedlands: University of Western Australia Press, 1996. Print.

Griffen-Foley, Bridget. *Changing Stations: The Story of Australian Commercial Radio*, UNSW Press, Sydney, 2009.

Haskell, Dennis. "News and tribute: Bruce Bennett remembered". *Asiatic* 6.1 June (2012): 7–9. Print.

Hay, John. "King, Alexander (1904–1970)", *Australian Dictionary of Biography, National Centre of Biography*. Web. 20 Dec. 2011. <http://adb.anu.edu.au/biography/king-alexander-10739>.

Hilliard, Christopher. *English as a Vocation: the Scrutiny Movement*. Oxford University Press, Oxford, 2012. Print.

Herrnstein-Smith, B. "What was 'close reading'?: A century of method in literary studies". Revised text of a talk presented 6 May 2015, Heyman Center, Columbia University, New York. Web. 15 Dec. 2015.

Heseltine, Harry. *In Due Season: Australian literary studies: A personal memoir*. North Melbourne: Australian Scholarly Publishing, 2009. Print.

Hewett, Dorothy. *Wild Card: An Autobiography 1923–1958*. South Yarra, Vic: McPhee Gribble, 1990. Print.

King, Alec. "Lecture notes – *The Control of Language*". University of Western Australia. Department of English. 5 Oct. 1942. Print.

——. "Poetry in school". *WA Teachers' Journal* July (1963): 172–74.

——. Reply to Letter of Mr Ewers. "Exam syllabus". *West Australian* 22 Mar. 1952, 10. *Trove*. Web. 22 Nov. 2014.

——. *Writing*. London: Longmans Green and Co, 1955. Print.

——, and Martin Ketley. *The Control of Language: A critical approach to reading and writing*. London: Longmans Green and Co, 1939. Print.

Kotai-Ewers, Patricia. The Fellowship of Australian Writers (WA) from 1938 to 1980 and its Role in the Cultural Life of Perth. PhD Thesis, Murdoch University, Murdoch, 2013. Murdoch University Research Repository. Web. 23 Aug. 2014.

La Nauze, John. *Walter Murdoch: A biographical memoir*. Melbourne: Melbourne University Press, 1977. Print.

"Leaving English papers". *West Australian* 12 Aug. 1950, 8. *Trove*. Web. 22 Feb. 2016.

Leavis, F.R. *Mass Civilisation and Minority Culture*. Cambridge: Gordon Fraser at St. John's College, Cambridge, at the Minority Press, 1930. Print.

Levis, Ken. Review of *The Rainbow Bird and Other Stories*, by Vance Palmer. *Meanjin*. 16.2 (1957): 209–212. Web. 13 June 2015.

Lewis, Clive Staples. *The Abolition of Man, or, Reflections on Education with Special Reference to the Teaching of English in the Upper Forms of Schools*. London: Fount Paperbacks, 1978. Web. 21 Feb. 2016.

McLean Davies, Larissa. "Building bridges: Classic Australian texts and critical theory in the senior English classroom". *English in Australia* 44.2 (2009): 7–15. Print.

——. "Magwitch madness: Archive fever and the teaching of Australian literature in subject English". *Teaching Australian Literature: From classroom conversations to national imaginings*. Ed. Brenton Doecke, Larissa McLean Davies, and Phillip Mead. Kent Town, SA: Wakefield in association with the Australian Association for the Teaching of English, 2011. 129–52. Print.

Moran, Rod. "Obituary: Bold voice of landscape". *West Australian* 28 June 2002. *Factiva*. Web. 19 Aug. 2012.

Murdoch, Walter. *Collected Essays*. Sydney: Angus and Robertson Ltd. 1938. Print.

Palmer, Vance. *The Rainbow Bird and Other Stories*. Sydney: Angus & Robertson, 1957. Print.

Peel, Robin. "'English' in England: its history and transformations". *Questions of English: Ethics, aesthetics, rhetoric, and the formation of the subject in England, Australia and the United States*. Ed. Robin Peel, Annette Patterson, and Jeanne Gerlach. London: Routledge Falmer, 2000. 39–115. Print.

Ross, Alan. "Isolated Men". Rev. of *The Rainbow Bird and Other Stories*, by Vance Palmer. The Literary Supplement Historical Archive. *The Times Literary Supplement*. Issue 1910. 6 Dec. 1957, 733. Web. 13 Jun 2015.

Ryan, Simon and Delyse Ryan. "Theory, 'F.R. Leavis 1895–1978'". *The Academy*. ACU National, n.d. Web. 28 Oct. 2014.

School Curriculum and Standards Authority (SCSA). *Western Australian Certificate of Education Examination, 2012. Question Paper – English. Stage 3*. Osborne Park, WA: School Curriculum and Standards Authority of Western Australia. Web. 15 Mar. 2015.

Serle, Geoffrey. "Australian literature". *Meanjin* 10.1 Autumn (1951): 69–70. Print.

Smith, Robert W. "Values, distances, cultures: Foundation of *Westerly*". *Westerly* 51 (2006): 7–15. Print.

Tomlinson, T.B. "Review of *Charitable Malice: An anthology of 18th century satire*, by Leonard Burrows and David Bradley". *Meanjin* 15.3 Spring (1956): 309–310. Web. 14 Jun 2015.
University of Western Australia. "Donations and major purchases". *Information Services Annual Report 2009*. Web. 18 Nov. 2014.
University of Western Australia. *Manual of Public Examinations held by the University*. Nedlands, WA: The University of Western Australia, 1926. Print.
——. *Manual of Public Examinations held by the University*. Nedlands, WA: The University of Western Australia, 1948. Print.
——. *Manual of Public Examinations held by the University*. Nedlands, WA: The University of Western Australia, 1950. Print.
——. *Annual Examination Papers 1955–1975*. Nedlands: University of Western Australia. Print.
University of Western Australia Archives. Consignment 268. Vol.1. Minutes of Meetings – Teachers and Examiners of English. 16/4/1942 to 28/4/1947.
——. Consignment 268. Vol.2. Minutes of Meetings – Teachers and Examiners of English. 1/5/1947 to 12/3/1952.
——. Consignment 268. Vol.3. Minutes of Meetings – Teachers and Examiners of English. 14/3/1952 to 29/3/1956.
——. Consignment 268. Vol.5. Minutes of Meetings – Teachers and Examiners of English. 24/2/1959 to 30/3/1962.
——. Consignment 268. Vol.6. Minutes of Meetings – Teachers and Examiners of English. 2/4/1962 to 26/4/1966.
——. Consignment 116. Staff file P202. William Allan Edwards, 1941–1971.
——. Consignment 394. Minutes of Meetings – Public Examinations Board. 3/5/1946 to 13/8/1954.
Willis, Ken. "The shaping of secondary English in Western Australia: The formative years, 1890s – 1915". *Teaching the English Subjects*. Ed. Bill Green and Catherine Beavis. Geelong: Deakin University Press, 1996. 96–117. Print.

Part III

Texts, Authors, Periods, Theories

Chapter Eleven

SHAKESPEARE AND THE CONDITIONS OF DISSENT

Jenny de Reuck

> Soul of the age!
> The applause, delight, the wonder of our stage!
> My Shakespeare, rise! I will not lodge thee by
> Chaucer, or Spenser, or bid Beaumont lie
> A little further, to make thee a room:
> Thou art a monument without a tomb,
> And art alive still while thy book doth live
> And we have wits to read and praise to give.
>
> From Ben Jonson, "To the Memory of My Beloved the Author, Mr. William Shakespeare", 1623)[1]

To answer the question, "Which of Shakespeare's plays were set on school syllabuses and why?" critics often resort to the notion of "relevance". In doing so they praise Shakespeare's ongoing contemporaneity, which is only a small step back to Ben Jonson's declaration that the Bard was "not of an age but for all time". Harold Bloom has argued in this manner for Shakespeare's universal relevance, claiming for the playwright nothing less than "the invention of the human", the title and central argument of the influential book in which he asserts that "Shakespeare will go on explaining us, in part because he invented us" (xviii). Scholars have contested this somewhat exaggerated claim from a variety of contemporary theoretical

---

1   www.poetryfoundation.org/poem/173731 Web. 28 May 2015.

perspectives, regarding it as simultaneously a problematic distortion and an essentialising of what "the human" might constitute. Bloom's views, however, are part of a long tradition. During the Restoration, Shakespeare's plays were among the first to be recovered from the obscurity that Puritanical oppression had inflicted upon the writers of the early seventeenth century, and adapted for re-awakened and insatiable audiences. The elevation of Shakespeare (the man and his work) continued through the eighteenth and nineteenth centuries, as first the neo-classicists and later the Romantics found much to admire in these memorable dramas of the late sixteenth and early seventeenth century. In short, it has become something of a truism to note, as I do at the outset of my own lecture series on Shakespeare, that his writings occupy the pinnacle in the hierarchy of literary value that has shaped the canon of English literature, specifically its manifestation and operation in secondary schools and university departments of English. The reasons for the continuing currency of the plays of this particular Elizabethan playwright are complex, and the origins of his status on English syllabuses perhaps even more politically layered. But I hope to be able to add something to the discussion here by suggesting why Shakespeare occupies so singular a position in the study of subject English and why we continue – the naysayers notwithstanding – to respond to the riches of his oeuvre, whether as actors, directors, readers or critics.

As Sarah Olive indicates in her analysis of Shakespeare's place in the English curriculum in the United Kingdom (where since 1989 his are the only texts every student is expected to have read upon the completion of their high school studies), the cultural value of Shakespeare is hotly debated in media and academic circles. The responsibility for what many "on the left" regard as "elitist" views of what should constitute an appropriate canon are still, after many decades, being laid at the feet of the "teacher and critic" (as his epitaph describes him), F.R. Leavis. Olive explores the impact of Leavis on contemporary curricula of "subject English" both in the United Kingdom and "the colonies" (she specifies New Zealand and Australia), noting that, paradoxically, despite Leavis being ascribed responsibility for the valorisation of Shakespeare in the canon (first articulated in and characterised by his concept of a "great tradition" of English literary works), "Leavis' own work was not primarily concerned with questions of the playwright/poet's place in the canon" (Olive). The canon of works that for Leavis comprised "the great tradition" in his well-known book of that name is primarily novels.[2]

---

2   Olive's analysis of Leavis' canon (and I am in agreement with her on this) is that it was a remarkably generous one, even prescient in some ways. She points out that

It is certainly true that Shakespeare's plays are not given a special place in Leavis's evaluative system but it is a fact, nevertheless, that no discussion of literary value in the present can be complete without some acknowledgement of the impact of his approach to the study of literature, which combined "close reading" (a mode of analysis refined by the American New Critics[3] after I.A. Richards's development of "practical criticism"[4]) with value-laden (normative) approaches to the study of literature. As Olive states further:

> Leavis' controversial attempts to delineate the value of specific literary genres and authors, demonstrated throughout his work, but especially prominent in titles such as *The Great Tradition* (1948) and "Valuation in Criticism" (1986), as well as to fix the value of education and culture has been most profoundly adopted by policymakers in relation to Shakespeare.

She is referring to policy-making in the United Kingdom, of course, but with the focus of the ALIAS database on the many different ways in which value was attached to forms of writing and modes of reading in senior school classrooms, Leavis's ghost is inevitably summoned – and if his predecessor, Matthew Arnold, is also discerned faintly in the background, I would suggest that we are in the presence, still, of powerful pedagogic influences that have their origins as far back as the nineteenth century when universal education was first mooted.[5]

A contemporary exploration of the ways in which literature syllabuses inform our ideas of what constitutes "good" or "great" writers and their work is one focus of the ALIAS study. As indicated above, the editors,

---

with Austen and Conrad among those selected for the status of canonical writers, his views regarding the value of works was neither gender-blind nor xenophobic. It would take until the 1980s for the voices of feminist and postcolonial theorist/activist critics to be heard and for the unquestioned domination of white, male writers on the syllabuses where English was studied to be challenged and renegotiated.

3   Among the most influential of them were John Crowe Ransom, W.K. Wimsatt and Cleanth Brooks.

4   Responsible for the idea of "practical criticism", Cambridge academic I.A Richards developed an essentially behaviourist reading model in the early twentieth century in an attempt to establish a more scientific basis for the study of literature.

5   The concept of "Universal Education" gained momentum in the United Kingdom in the nineteenth century, culminating in various Acts of Parliament. The first, in 1870, *The Elementary Education Act*, established the groundwork for ensuring that children from all walks of life were provided with the opportunity to achieve an education (www.educationengland.org.uk/documents/acts/1870-elementary-education-act.html)

drawing on the ALIAS data, seek to know whether syllabus lists represent an underlying mechanics of canon formation in New South Wales, Tasmania, South Australia, Victoria and Western Australia between 1945 and 2005. They also maintain that the ALIAS database presents "a picture of what many Australians were *obliged to read* [italics mine] in upper secondary school" (Chapter One above). As outlined in Chapter One of this book, the editors are correct, in my view, to suggest that these texts lists reveal conditional assent: "assent to the power of imaginative writing on condition that it serves the always changing needs and purposes at hand" (11). My point of contention, however – and what I am arguing here – is that such "conditional assent", granted ultimately by government bodies, is ill served to meet any conception of "the always changing needs and purposes to hand". Such conditional assent assumes that canon formation rests on the belief that (in this case) Shakespeare's work affirms parochial contemporary values, whether social or political. My argument suggests that such a position misconceives the radical nature of Shakespeare's "work ideology" (Ruthrof 136), which should be viewed not as merely adaptive (reflecting the mores and values of a specific historical moment) but as a process of endless self-creation.

A politically parochial perspective that contains the playwright in this way does violence to our understanding of the "genius" of Shakespeare that "bardolaters" with the academic prestige and authority of Harold Bloom, Jonathan Bate or Stanley Wells continue to affirm in our historical moment. Equally, to make Shakespeare's imagination conform to currently held values misconceives the ground notes of Shakespeare's extraordinary achievement. His work is profoundly more expansive than a single historical or social moment can constrain and thus must always escape the politically charged "changing needs and purposes to hand" that the editors offer as the reason for his presence in the formation of a canon of literary works within and for subject English. The "infinite variety" (*Antony and Cleopatra*, 2.2.241: 2648)[6] of character constructions projected onto our imagination by an encounter with Shakespeare's body of work emerges from his vision of the creative foundation of human manifestations. This vision sets our period's moral order in question as the tumult of Shakespearean characters continually escapes the boundaries of any particular age's moral theory.

While the ALIAS database provides scholars with a rich set of data that has never been collected or collated, my argument challenges an assumption

---

6   All references to the plays are taken from *The Norton Shakespeare*, 1997.

that remains embedded in Chapter One of this volume: namely, that Shakespearean texts hold a mirror up to nature, reflecting, in their capacity for adaptation, the spirit and structure of any given historical moment. Viewed from that perspective, this line of thinking suggests that his works offer readers and audiences versions of the current (dominant) ideological orientation that informs the reception aesthetics[7] of the reading/viewing moment. Shakespeare's oeuvre – particularly his plays (and given their prominence since 1945 on the literature syllabuses in Australia, his tragedies, more specifically) – provides a sounding that reveals nothing less than the "authentic" depths of the human psyche.

The historical moment's conditions of assent are, I suggest, contested dramatically by Shakespeare's affirmation of the almost infinite variability of the human condition. The hesitancy to proclaim a final ordering – evident in his writings – allows, in the flux of history, the unconditioned essence of humanity to express itself in the plastic "self-fashioning" (Greenblatt, *Renaissance*) of what may be termed the deep subjectivity characteristic of individual human beings living their diverse lives to the full under varying orders of power. That these orders of power are able to discipline Shakespeare's conception of the universal nature of the human spirit is a precept this chapter contests: and here my argument invokes elements of Harold Bloom's, where he states that "there is an overflowing element in the plays, an excess beyond representation that is closer to the metaphor we call 'creation'" (xviii). Shakespeare's works offer more than mere mimesis or representation: their "originality" is to be found in the typically destabilising dramatic impact of the world of his plays, which, if they do in fact hold a mirror up to society, it is to reflect not its beliefs, but rather the epistemic instability of its foundations.

A critical stance that locks Shakespeare into the ideological frameworks of a particular historical moment does the playwright less than justice, therefore, revealing not the "infinite variety" of his dramatic constructions but what might be characterised as the hollowed-out keel of his thought. I would argue that a deeper, more profound assessment of the "essence" of a Shakespeare for all time(s), is one that provides a more complex reminder of the conditionality of commitment – what one might perhaps, more appropriately, call the conditions of *dissent*. This conditionality, if the argument

---

7   Roman Ingarden's influence (*Renaissance*; *Learning*) is acknowledged here, as are the texts of Franz Stanzel, Mieke Bal, Gerald Prince and Horst Ruthrof. These theorists all address in different ways the question of reception by an audience/readership of a literary work and their insights inform the discussion above.

in this paper is sound, requires of the relevant syllabus committee that they have both the courage and critical values to defend their assent to the placement of a particular Shakespearean text on the syllabus in terms of the *challenge to contemporary thought such a text would engender.* Such a text would not endorse current literary or ethical orthodoxies and paradigms; rather, it would be chosen to challenge them. The conditions required for official endorsement (assent) now become those that best contest the assumptions of any given historical moment. What becomes clear is that determining the "spirit" of the Shakespearean oeuvre involves a creative critique of the historical moment.

The freedom of human cognition and expression, from this perspective, becomes the essential condition of dissent that stops what may be conceived of as a freezing or rigidifying of the human spirit dominated by the particular conditions of assent (Newman) and dictated and policed by the regimes of power. And this – the assertion of the right to dissent – is Shakespeare's gift to humanity. What grounds this freedom of expression in the world that Shakespeare constructs is his profound understanding of what constitutes the noumenal: namely, that the essence of humanity is its capacity for endless self-creation or (as I will suggest in a brief reading of *Hamlet* below) self-destruction. The characters he writes into being encompass in their individual realities qualities as disparate, and complex, as those we see in Iago on the one hand (who toys with his object of vengeance, Othello, without a discernible motive) and on the other those that comprise Cordelia (who expresses, without it being recognised by Lear, the essence of filial piety and love). Such oppositions are readily discernible in Shakespeare's plays but his characters more often than not exceed narrow, binarist readings, defying attempts to reduce them to terms in a "marked/unmarked" linguistic set.

Of course, each age can seek exemplars of their idealisations of humanity, but what I am suggesting here is that such self-affirming of the age ill serves our attempts to comprehend the creative genius (as Jonathan Bate has cogently argued) of Shakespeare. In the next section of this chapter, I will suggest, using the Polish philosopher Roman Ingarden's phenomenological interrogation of the literary work of art, the ways in which the ontological "being" of Shakespeare's plays contributes to their status as exceeding the socio-historical constraints of any given moment. Before doing so, however, I want to recall the discussion of Leavis earlier and briefly engage with an aspect of "value" that seems to me to illuminate our critical comprehension of some of the moral questions his works raise. My objective is to demonstrate that it is important to argue against any given set of external conditions that might validate a particular understanding of the ethics of Shakespeare's output.

Current bureaucratic conceptions of the contemporary moral order that satisfy their underwriting of the "conditions of assent" and that will warrant their preparedness to place certain of Shakespeare's plays on the school syllabus are vitiated by the degrees of relativity in current ethical and aesthetic thought. Greenblatt quotes Robert Weimann[8] as arguing:

> the process of making certain things one's own become inseparable from making other things (and persons) alien, so that the act of appropriation must be seen always already to involve not only self-projection and assimilation but alienation through reification and expropriation. (*Learning* 213)

He goes on to argue for an interpretative model that "will more adequately account for the unsettling circulation of materials and discourse that is … the heart of modern aesthetic practice." (214). He continues the argument against essentialism, maintaining that contemporary theory must position itself "not outside of interpretation, but in the hidden places of negotiation and exchange."

In the domain of ethics we also see that utilitarianism, virtue-based systems and deontological[9] theories vie for our intellectual alliance, but even in their most advanced formulations, they nevertheless admit no single universally recognised account. Marked aporias or relativities are generally acknowledged to hold between the contested epistemological claims to certainty that each of the above ethical stances advocates. These deep relativities undermine all political attempts to stabilise ethical theory around current perceptions of an authentic set of values, sufficient to satisfy their "conditions of assent".

Arnold Weinstein affirms that

> Shakespeare inherited a view of human inconstancy and indeterminacy from Montaigne, whose splendid term *ondoyant* (wavelike) perfectly captures the fluid nature of identity … The mad Ophelia

---

[8] This is a reference to the East German critic's work, *Shakespeare and the Popular Tradition in the Theater: Studies in the Social Dimension of Dramatic Form and Function*, 1987, edited by Robert Schwartz.

[9] See Chris W. Surprenant's *Kant and the Cultivation of Virtue*, 2014, where he suggests that Kant's argument for deontological theory is accompanied by a theory of the cultivation of virtue which aims at bridging the gap between knowledge of the good and the required desire to adhere to its dictates.

expresses it in folktale terms: "They say the owl was a baker's daughter. Lord, we know what we are, but know not what we may be". (IV.v.41–42)

Claudius, likewise, Weinstein continues, "expresses the same dark wisdom: "This we would do, / We should do when we would; for this 'would' changes / And hath abatements and delays as many / As there are tongues, are hands, are accidents / And thus this 'should' is like a spendthrift's sigh / That hurts by easing" (IV.vii.116–121) (380–81).

Though densely written (both Weinstein's analysis and the complex utterances that Shakespeare gives to his characters, Ophelia and Claudius), they reward our engagement as critics. Ophelia and Claudius occupy opposing poles of the drama's moral spectrum and yet each, in essence, is given the same insight about the human condition. They both recognise the dark wisdom to which Weinstein refers as they articulate, in their own way, the shifting opacity of ethical thought. Hamlet's insights into the human condition have been the chief focus of critical investigation and analysis and we are all familiar with such excerpts as the following, where he describes to Rosencrantz and Guildenstern his burgeoning ennui:

> I have of late, (but wherefore I know not) lost all my mirth, forgone all custom of exercises; and indeed, it goes so heavily with my disposition; that this goodly frame the earth, seems to me a sterile promontory; this most excellent canopy the air, look you, this brave o'er hanging firmament, this majestical roof, fretted with golden fire: why, it appeareth no other thing to me, than a foul and pestilent congregation of vapours. What a piece of work is a man! How noble in reason, how infinite in faculty! In form and moving how express and admirable! In action how like an Angel! in apprehension how like a god! The beauty of the world! The paragon of animals! And yet to me, what is this quintessence of dust? Man delights not me; no, nor Woman neither; though by your smiling you seem to say so. (*Hamlet*, 2.2.285–300:1697–98)

It is a timely reminder perhaps to recall the potent "play" of complex observation that even the secondary characters in his dramatic worlds are capable of eliciting.

Peter Dews in his *Logics of Disintegration* explores Adorno's notion of a "logic of disintegration" ("Logik des Zerfalls"). He outlines Adorno's argument

> that the historical process must be understood as advancing both towards less and less mediated forms of unity, and towards increasing antagonism and incoherence, because of the abstraction built into the instrumental use of concepts, which idealist philosophy overlooks. [...] The culmination of this process is a social world of which every aspect has become inherently contradictory, and therefore resistant to univocal interpretation. (224–5)

Adorno concludes, echoing the sentiments of Ophelia, that it is not "possible to grasp the totality of the real through the power of thought" (225). Relevant at this point is Weinstein's argument concerning Hamlet's melancholy, which he suggests is to be understood "in the light of this devastating view that time undoes self, ... dissolves simply by the act of living" (382). This resonates with Dews's insight that "the process of disintegration is manifested in the decline of the bourgeois individual, the breaking down of the autonomous ego" (225). This tragic fate underlies the despair expressed by Hamlet as well as by both Ophelia and Claudius. Hamlet's despair, though, emanates from a penetrating intellect coupled to a unique capacity for introspection that acknowledges the fluidity of that "quintessence of dust" that is the temporal self.

To conclude the argument I have advanced for the positioning of Shakespeare outside the boundaries of "assent" that would distort our apprehension of the scope of his creative capacity, the philosopher Roman Ingarden's (1973a) analysis of the constitutive elements of a literary work offers us a powerful theoretical model. He provides a phenomenological typology for understanding the literary work as a socio-cultural artifact and offers us insights into the ways in which we might access the complex meaning-making structure that the literary (dramatic) work and its cognition comprise. His interrogation of the nature and scope of the "mode of being" of a literary work is presented, schematically, as an ascending set of layers, each with their related aesthetic value. For Ingarden, the literary work of art is a stratified intentional object comprising the stratum of verbal sounds and phonetic formations, the stratum of semantic units, the stratum of "schematised aspects" where states of various kinds portrayed in the work come into appearance, and the stratum of the objectivities portrayed in the intentional states of affairs projected by the sentences.

A fifth, "metaphysical", stratum is discernible in some works of literature (Shakespeare's plays, given their canonical status, would qualify for inclusion in this category) but, possibly because of the contested nature of this somewhat rarefied arena with its capacity to mobilise subjective aesthetic value, Ingarden rules it out as being non-essential (though desirable) for his notion of what constitutes a literary work of art. Nevertheless, and because of the position Shakespeare occupies in contemporary culture, it is with this fifth, metaphysical, stratum that I am primarily concerned here. The field of contemporary reception aesthetics acknowledges the varying degrees of indeterminacy in the literary (dramatic) work of art and the co-creativity incumbent upon readers/audiences if the meanings of a work are to be apprehended.

Ingarden's metaphysical stratum is readily discernible in the (re)construction of the Shakespearean text: the writer's infinitely expansive self-creativity is evident in all his major works from *Hamlet* to *King Lear*, *Macbeth* and *The Tempest*. Hamlet's cry –

> We defy augury. There is a special providence in the fall of a sparrow. If it be now, 'tis not to come. If it be not to come, it will be now. If it be not now, yet it will come. The readiness is all. (5.2.157–60:1751)

– demands of directors, actors and audiences (not to mention readers) a layered grid of reception if the meanings in this speech are to be mobilised. Lear, on the heath, in extremis, prefigures Beckett's tramps in *Waiting for Godot* ("They give birth astride of a grave, the light gleams an instant, then it's night once more", says Pozzo, in Act 2, [89]) with his bleak construction of humanity as "… the thing itself; unaccommodated man […] no more but such a poor, bare, forked animal as thou art" (3.4.98–101: 2519). Then there are his words to Gloucester, blinded by Regan and Cornwall, in which the anguish of their condition – and that of humanity by extension – is interpellated: "We came crying hither; / Thou know'st, the first time that we smell the air, / We wail and cry …" (4.6.172–174: 2538).

Shakespeare's most profound constructions are an affirmation of self-creativity. If the ALIAS notion/project is to assess which texts of Shakespeare's are represented on the secondary school syllabuses, thereby creating a canon that reinforces the ideological needs or purposes that underwrite (or become) the conditions of assent that political agendas demand, then the argument advanced here is that such reification is undermined when the achievement of Shakespeare is understood in its fundamental nature.

Given the popularity of Shakespeare today and the number of adaptations that appear each year on the stage – from London to Taipei, Berlin to Mumbai – and in film, there is a great deal of discussion of the malleability of the works he created; that they can be massaged to fit the Zeitgeist of any age and represent any mood or trend (Hopkins 188–209). An early instance of this co-opting of Shakespeare for a specific political agenda was Laurence Olivier's (1944) film version of *Henry V*. It was produced as a conscious attempt to infuse British troops with the kind of patriotic fervour to be found in Henry's rallying cry on the eve of the Battle of Agincourt. The bleaker, more unsavoury elements (the killing of the prisoners, for example) in this dramatic exploration of what it means to wage war and who bears responsibility for its outcomes are elided. In Kenneth Branagh's 1989 version, however, there is no such shirking of the representation of the horrors of war, and events that are merely referenced in the stage play (the hanging of Bardolph for his miscreancy and the death of Falstaff before the start of the action) are graphically portrayed with some degree of poetic licence on the part of Branagh as adapter/director. Certainly, adaptations abound and have done since the recovery of Shakespeare's plays when the playhouses opened after the Restoration and the audiences – hungry for a diet of comedy after years under Puritanical constraint – were treated to re-worked versions of the tragedies in which, for example, Cordelia is saved and, in a rather tortuous twist of the plot, marries Edgar for the requisite happy ending.[10] Such appropriations and adaptations notwithstanding, the reality remains that this is to misconceive the deep conditions of Shakespeare's works, which actually defy and transcend the moment of appropriation no matter how subtle or "relatable" they may be deemed.

To return, finally, to the concept that Greenblatt has bequeathed the study of early modern drama, the "self-fashioning" of a specific "age" cannot "freeze-frame" itself as endorsed by Shakespeare's vision. The self-fashioning of humanity will always dissolve any particular age's conception of its correlation with the deeper insight of his artistic vision. There is no "essence" to our species that limits our construction of creativity (and our co-creativity) in the realisation of the dramatic or other literary work. Shakespeare's creations will free any future period's received self-image from fixity for, in interrogating the notion of "assent" posited as the way in which the canon is shored up – albeit conditionally – by the prevailing social currents, it is evident that, together with a theoretical notion such as Ingarden's metaphysical stratum for the literary work, the deep relativities in contemporary ethical theorising support the view of the fluidity of self-fashioning. Shakespeare's ontological positioning is one that is best

---

10   See Nahum Tate's adaptation of *King Lear*, in *Adaptations of Shakespeare: A critical anthology of plays from the seventeenth century to the present*, ed. Daniel Fishlin and Mark Fortier, London and New York: Routledge.

characterised as that of "dissent", as not contained or constrained by "an age". His celebration of humanity in all of its vitality and creativity – unconstrained by the self-fashioning of a particular socio-historical moment – is what we take away from an encounter with his work.

Works Cited

Bal, Mieke. *Narratology: Introduction to the theory of narrative*. Toronto: University of Toronto Press, 1997. Print.
Bate, Jonathan. *The Genius of Shakespeare*. Oxford: Oxford University Press, 1998. Print.
Beckett, Samuel. *Waiting for Godot*. 1953. London: Faber and Faber, 1978. Print
Bloom, Harold. *Shakespeare and the Invention of the Human*. New York: Pine-Head Books, 1998. Print.
Branagh, Kenneth. *Henry V*. BBC Films. 1989. Film.
Brooks, Cleanth. *The Well-Wrought Urn*. London: Harcourt, Brace, 1947. Print.
Dews, Peter. *Logics of Disintegration*. London: Verso, 1987. Print.
Dolin, Tim, Jo Jones and Patricia Dowsett. "Conditional assent: literary value and the value of English as a subject." *Required Reading: Literature in Australian schools since 1945*. Clayton: Monash University Publishing, 2017. 3–18.
Fishlin, Daniel and Mark Fortier (eds). *Adaptations of Shakespeare: A critical anthology of plays from the seventeenth century to the present*. London and New York: Routledge, 2000. Print.
Greenblatt, Stephen. *Renaissance Self-Fashioning: From More to Shakespeare*. Chicago: Univ. of Chicago Press, 1980. Print.
——. *Learning to Curse: Essays in early modern culture*. New York and London: Routledge, 1990. Print.
——, et al. (eds.). *The Norton Shakespeare, based on the Oxford Edition*. New York and London: W.W. Norton & Company. 1997. Print.
Hopkins, Lisa. *Beginning Shakespeare*. Manchester: Manchester University Press, 2005. Print.
Ingarden, Roman. *The Literary Work of Art*. Translated by George G. Grabowicz. Evanston: Northwestern University Press, 1973a. Print.
——. *The Cognition of the Literary Work of Art*. Translated by Ruth Ann Crowley and Kenneth R. Olson. Evanston: Northwestern University Press, 1973b. Print.
Jonson, Ben. "To the memory of my beloved the author, Mr. William Shakespeare". 1623. Web. 28 May 2015. <http://newramblerreview.com/book-reviews/literary-studies/after-close-reading>.
Leavis, F.R. *The Great Tradition*. 1948. London: Faber and Faber, 2011. Print.
——. *The Common Pursuit*, London: Chatto & Windus, 1952. Print.
Newman, John Henry. *An Essay in Aid of a Grammar of Assent*, edited by I.T. Ker. Oxford: Clarendon Press, 1985. Print
Olive, Sarah. "Shakespeare in the English national curriculum". *Alluvium*, Vol. 2, No. 1 (2013): 12 January 2013. <http://dx.doi.org/10.7766/alluvium.v2.1.01>. Web. 28 May 2015.
Olivier, Laurence. *Henry V*. Metro-Goldwyn-Mayer Studios Inc., 1944. Film.
Prince, Gerald. "Narratology". *The Cambridge History of Literary Criticism. VII: From Formalism to Postructuralism*. Ed. R. Selden. Cambridge: Cambridge University Press, 1995: 110–30. Print.
Ransom, John Crowe. *The New Criticism*, Norfolk, Conn.: New Directions, 1941. Print.

Richards, I. A. *Practical Criticism*, London: Kegan Paul, Trench, Trubner, 1929. Print.
Ruthrof, Horst. *The Reader's Construction of Narrative*. Boston Mass: Routledge & Kegan Paul Ltd., 1981. Print.
Stanzel, F. *Narrative Situations in the Novel*. Translated by James P. Pusack. Bloomington and London: Indiana University Press, 1971. Print.
Surprenant, Chris W. *Kant and the Cultivation of Virtue*, New York: Routledge, 2014. Print.
Weimann, Robert. [1978] "Shakespeare and the popular tradition in the theater: Studies in the social dimension of dramatic form and function". Ed. Robert Schwartz, Johns Hopkins University Press, 1987. Print.
Weinstein, Arnold. *A Scream Goes Through the House: What literature teaches us about life*. New York: Random House, 2003. Print.
Wells, Stanley. *Shakespeare in the Theatre: An anthology of criticism*. Oxford: Oxford University Press, 2000. Print.

Chapter Twelve

WHAT THE DICKENS?

Exploring the role of canonical texts in mediating subject English in Australia

Susan K. Martin and Larissa McLean Davies

Introduction

The ALIAS database shows that the novels of Charles Dickens, particularly the antipodean-inspired work *Great Expectations*, have retained an enduring presence on English and Literature syllabuses in Australia since 1948. *Great Expectations* appears on 119 syllabuses, equalling Emily Brontë's *Wuthering Heights* (119 syllabuses) and well overtaking the notionally similar (if "female") *Bildungsroman*, Charlotte Brontë's *Jane Eyre* (44), and Australian "classics" like Patrick White's *A Fringe of Leaves* (48), Miles Franklin's *My Brilliant Career* (18) and Marcus Clarke's *For the Term of His Natural Life* (9).

This chapter will draw on the rich resources of the ALIAS database and build on previous analytical and conceptual work on Dickens's circulation and uses in colonial Australia (Mirmohamadi and Martin), and his impact on texts set for study in senior secondary level (McLean Davies "Magwich Madness") in order to explore the changing role of Dickens's novels in Australian versions of subject English. Specifically, the chapter will investigate the ways in which Dickens's *Great Expectations* is increasingly placed in conversation with other novels from Australia and elsewhere, and the ways in which these practices contribute to negotiations of identity that are brokered by the intended English curricula.

In order to mobilise and investigate the ALIAS database in this way, we have put the text lists of the database in dialogue with a range of other texts and "data". State syllabus documents and accounts of teacher experiences in teaching *Great Expectations* are used to "read" the ALIAS database, and illuminate the changing way this text is used in the context of secondary school education. We start by considering the way in which Dickens was perceived as a cultural figure by colonial Australians. This provides a way of exploring the motivations behind selection of this text when the senior years of subject English were first established in the 1940s. This chapter then considers the shifting values of the texts as carriers of cultural value and national and international meaning, and their circulation in the field or economy of the school curriculum and the national marketplace.

Historical Dickens: the context of *Great Expectations* in subject English

Dickens's works already had a quite specific role in public education and in the dissemination of English and Englishness by the turn of the twentieth century (Mirmohamadi and Martin). The role of the teacher in the classroom, in the nineteenth and twentieth centuries, standing before a class and reading and explicating Dickens's works, had a more intimate connection than might be expected with the author's relationship to his works and his audience. Dickens was well known for his public readings and performances of his works. He commenced reading for charity in 1853, and for his own profit by 1858, and toured America and Britain extensively on reading tours (Ferguson 730). His practice was to both "stage" these readings with props and to dispense with the props as anything beyond symbolic. For instance he would include a lectern – a familiar item for a public lecturer but also for nineteenth-century teachers of a certain level – but would not remain behind it. Thus he registered the presence of such props partly by his abandonment of them – he always had a book with him, but often did not refer to it at all. As Susan L. Ferguson notes, other authors offered formal lectures, but Dickens's readings were a distinct performance of himself as writer, and, she argues, as reader.

The readings were also understood as educative experiences. In 1856 a letter from Samuel James to the *Port Phillip Herald* complained that the contents of the Public Library were not sufficiently accessible to the public, and did not contain novels, in particular those "moral teachers", Dickens and Thackeray (James 7). In James Bonwick's novel, *A Tasmanian Lily*

(1873), the character Tom's education is described as somewhat lacking, but its general moral soundness is affirmed in the account of his reading, and the incorporation of Dickens constitutes a guarantee of that morality:

> [h]e was not fond of reading for its own sake, and did not see any advantage in studying English literature outside of law-books, excepting Dickens and the newspapers. Dickens is pre-eminently adapted to the Colonial mind. His wit, his hearty mirth, his droll characters, his tender pathos …

What are described as "low, trashy" stories have no purchase on Australian boys, according to Bonwick, because there is "too much common sense, too just an appreciation of morals" (53).

The combined idea that Dickens's work was educative and that performance of Dickens might constitute an educational experience is further reflected in the widespread adaptation of Dickens readings by Dickens devotees. Actors, clergymen, teachers, elocutionists: amateurs and professionals across the latter half of the nineteenth century offered readings from Dickens after the style of the author. These were variously described as entertainments, charitable performances, and readings. *Great Expectations* featured in these readings, although it was by no means the most popular text.

Children were generally admitted at half price (which reinforced the notion that these were not solely adult entertainments). When lantern slides – glass slides made from photographs or painted images (the nineteenth-century precursor of contemporary data projection technology) – were introduced to readings, or even in place of readings of Dickens in some cases, these performances were marketed as of particular appeal to children, but not just as entertainments. Lantern shows were regarded as particularly instructional, despite, or because of, their spectacular appeal (Kember 63). Performances with light shows and readings from Dickens were regularly put on for children's instruction and entertainment, particularly "A Christmas Carol", and "Gabriel Grub" (Mirmohamadi and Martin 157–159). "Gabriel Grub", as William Main and Joss Marsh point out, was inspired by, and inspired, magic lantern productions (Main; Marsh 337–338). For schoolchildren, the pedagogical lessons of Dickens were reinforced by the "lessons" in the former, and the visit to the schoolroom and Scrooge's reading self, in *A Christmas Carol*. Older readers were also thought to benefit from Dickens's influence. Australian prisons and night schools were also stocked with Dickens's works (Mirmohamadi and Martin 19–21).

The very popular readings of the Reverend Charles Clark, which he toured around the capitals of the Australian colonies, included "teachings" derived from Dickens's life as well as his works, as if Dickens himself exemplified and provided a moral education. In a report on a Hobart presentation in February 1876, Clark outlined Dickens's time as a court reporter, "having pointed out that it was at this period that Dickens experienced his first love, [Clark] touched lightly upon his descriptions of that time, and added a few brilliant observations on the experiences and teachings of that peculiar stage in the program of a life." ("Rev. Charles Clark").

Along with the direct line between educational contribution and impact drawn between Dickens and Australian schooling, the connection also extended to relationships with the physical space. Some Dickens readings took place on school property and in school halls, which further reinforced the educational context of the readings/content. Readings in churches and church halls reinforced the almost sacred, and certainly wholesome flavour of Dickens, as the presentation of Dickens in public buildings reinforced the civic and national context of the Britishness of works like *Great Expectations*. Likewise the use of Dickens readings events as a fundraising opportunity for schools reinforced the connections between Dickens and education. Across the nineteenth century and into the twentieth, amateur readers donated their proceeds from Dickens performances to schools among other "good causes". The Hobart barrister dubbed the "Prince of Dickens's Entertainers", Charles Davenport Hoggins, toured his Dickens readings and renditions of *A Christmas Carol* extensively through Tasmania, Victoria and beyond, donating all his proceeds to good causes. A letter from Stella M. Cheeseman of "Benfrieze" in the Hoggins archive thanks the reader for his Charles Dickens entertainment, which raised £5 for the South Hobart "School Fair Funds" (Cheeseman to Hoggins).

Across all of these uses, Dickens's connection to Britishness was constantly affirmed. Many of the readers in Dickens performances were elocutionists. The implication of choice of Dickens, in nineteenth-century readings, and potentially in twentieth-century curriculum, is that Dickens's work carries correct Englishness – both culturally and linguistically. In a review of a Hobart performance of "A Christmas Carol" in 1878, the writer enthused that the reader's

> choice of subject matter was a good one, not only as being appropriate to the near approach of the festive season but also from the inherent value of the work and the hold it has always had upon English hearts

in all parts of the world where the tongue is spoken in which the great master of fiction wrote it. (Review of *A Christmas Carol*)

Thomas Padmore Hill, who published *The Oratorical Trainer* in 1862, publicised his book and his oratorical services through series of public readings of English authors, including Dickens. One reviewer commented on the nature of his "Elocutionary Entertainment" in the *South Australian Observer*, "The programme embraces the tragic and humorous powers of Hood – the poetry of Byron and Campbell – Shiel, and the oratory of the House of Commons – Shakespeare, and the idea of which his greatest conception, "Hamlet," is the embodiment – and the influence of the writings of Dickens upon the spirit of the age." ("Mr Hill's "). The distinction made here between Shakespearian genius and Dickens's encapsulation of "the age" arguably remains evident in curriculum choices into the twentieth century. Shakespeare is on the curriculum representing genius, and Dickens stands for both popularity and the essence of English (with place and language conflated).

By the early twentieth century, the transportation of these Dickensian lessons into schools had been effected. Pupils from Hunter College, Newcastle, performed a "Dickens entertainment" to raise money for the school tennis courts in November 1922, and the *Newcastle Sun* reported the praise of "Mr Ellis Price, the well-known Newcastle elocutionist" on the standard of their performance. Mr Price went on to urge a "greater appreciation of Dickens, both for his literary and dramatic value … When we are young" he said, "we read him because we must [and certainly this was the experience of most of the secondary students of Australia from the mid-twentieth century] … If young people can grasp the true value of his writing they have done much" ("Music and Elocution"). Elocution lessons and performances, within and outside schools continued to be popular in the 1920s, 1930s and into the 40s, and consistently featured Dickens, usually alongside Shakespeare and nineteenth-century poets, particularly Tennyson. The alignment of Dickens and elocution in these arenas suggests a particular understanding of proper language and value. Some of the elocution performances involved replicating Dickensian representations of regional or classed accents, rather than "proper English", but this in itself suggests that Australian elocution could be acquired through a mastery of the performance of Dickens's versions of British English, rather than any Australian equivalent. The formalisation of English curriculum in Australian schools in the second half of the twentieth century saw the ratification of Dickens essential place in English studies.

Setting expectations: mapping the uses of Dickens's text in subject English in Australia, 1948–2002

Given the pervasive and ubiquitous nature of Dickens in the new colonies, and his increasing marker as a way of bridging antipodean and imperial culture, it is unsurprising that Dickens, and specifically *Great Expectations*, appeared consistently on the New South Wales, Western Australian, South Australian and Victorian syllabuses, and to a lesser degree on the Tasmanian curricula over the period represented in the ALIAS database. In the following section we will offer a mapping and analysis of the patterns of the appearances and uses of this novel in Western Australia and South Australia, the states where *Great Expectations* has been most listed, and make some comments about the use of this text in Victoria. While the ALIAS database provides a comprehensive list of all texts studied in the Australian states listed above, it is when these lists are put in dialogue with syllabus documents and, most importantly, examination papers that the archival researcher can begin to discern the politics and ideology behind the setting of texts. As Annette Patterson notes, when undertaking similar work investigating the teaching of specifically Australian literature:

> Selecting texts for study is a process influenced by the interests of educators and of governments. Syllabus documents and examination papers provide a solid historical record of these influences over time. However, a text list is not something from which we can simply read off the ideology of an era, although it does provide a guide to the inclusion or exclusion of particular types of texts and of particular authors. Over time a text list can provide valuable historical information about identity formation, social values and ideological alignments. ("Australian Literature")

It is, of course, important to note the limitations of this aspect of inquiry, and of the data sets with which we work. While this assemblage of documents and data provides key insights, at the level of policy, into the ways in which *Great Expectations* has been used in English, the absence of data on the patterns of selection enforce some limitation to our analysis – for example, we do not know how many teachers set this text, what their pedagogical approach might have been, nor how many students choose to write on this text (which is always offered as one of several options). It is important to note that just because a text is set, even repeatedly, this does not mean that teachers will select it: indeed it is possible, even in states where Dickens and Shakespeare are set for decades, that students in those states may never study texts by these writers. Yet, the enduring presence of the text across the states indicates to some measure its popularity. The pragmatics of text selection (Jogie "Desperate Shadows", "Too Pale and Stale"; McLean Davies "What's the Story", "Auditing Subject English") mean that it is unlikely that any text would continue to be set if at least a critical mass of teachers were not teaching it, and students did not choose to focus on it in examination. Indeed, Teese's research with Victorian English teachers has shown the enduring place of canonical texts in high-stakes, post-compulsory English examinations (Teese). So, while the absence of assessment reports and data about local selection practices can, to some extent, be ameliorated, this inquiry is also limited by the absence of teacher and student voices that would provide insights into the ways in which this official "intended" curriculum has been enacted by teachers and experienced by students. As Patterson also contends, this is a vital aspect of any conversation about text selection ("Australian Literature") and will be the focus of the next stage of our research. As Guillory observes: "it is only by understanding the social function and institutional protocols of the school that we will understand how works are perceived, reproduced, and disseminated over successive generations and centuries" (Guillory viii).

With acknowledgement of its limitation and boundaries, then, the following analysis will show the changing ways in which *Great Expectations* has been put to use, in terms of the evolving models and purposes of subject English that unfolded in Australia in the twentieth century, and offers insights into the ways in which subject English has developed distinct characteristics in two different geographical locations. This analysis will contribute to an emerging body of work interested in the ways in which selecting literary texts for study in Anglophone secondary schools is not only about the moral development of students and subjects and citizens (cf. Hunter *Culture and Government*; Patterson "The Legacy of Ian Hunter's Work"; Patterson "Teaching Literature") but is also about contesting and negotiating particular national and international identities in these contexts, and the challenges of this negotiation (see for example: Green and Cormack; Goodwyn; Jogie; McLean Davies, "Magwitch Madness"; McLean Davies, Doecke and Mead; Yandell). As we will explain in what follows, our analysis of the traces of *Great Expectations* through syllabus and curriculum documents provides valuable insights into the changing perceptions of citizenship carried by subject English in different places and the ways in which, in undertaking this subject, Australian students were positioned to engage with conceptions of nation and world through literary texts.

In exploring the continued presence of *Great Expectations* in English curricula in Western Australia, South Australia and Victoria, and the ways in which this might be explained in terms of the negotiation of national identities and the purpose of subject English, it is important to acknowledge that, in part, these impacts are likely to be brought about by pragmatic considerations. Writing about the Victorian context, Teese et al. has shown that the enduring presence of canonical text has been sustained by both the notion that canonical texts will receive better marks in external, high-stakes examination (Teese et al.) – a notion that is supported by the greater range of resources produced to support the teaching of canonical texts, as opposed to the more contemporary texts that might be listed in curriculum documents. In her comparative investigation of the attitudes of teachers and English curriculum bureaucrats in both New South Wales and England, Jogie ("Too Pale and Stale") has observed that the apparent abundance of resources available for canonical texts is one of the key factors impacting on the repeated listing of these works by curriculum authorities in both countries (Jogie "Too Pale and Stale" 295, 303). While we acknowledge the pragmatic motivations for selection, both at the levels of policy and curriculum and school, nonetheless we argue that pragmatic decisions concerning text selection cannot be separated from their ideological outcomes (McLean Davies "Magwich Madness", McLean Davies, Doecke and Mead) and therefore while motivation for selecting texts is important, motivation and impact are not necessarily linked. It may indeed have been convenient for state curriculum authorities to set *Great Expectations* repetitively from 1948, and no doubt, with each year it was set, more teaching resources were produced; however, the impact of this commitment to Dickens's text also has implications for the national identity and consciousness. Australia is depicted as a place of exile and deprivation while the real business of life takes place in England; contemporary teachers and their students may contest and challenge this reading, and will undoubtedly have done so since postcolonial sensibilities began to impact on the English curriculum in the 1980s and 90s. Nonetheless, whatever reading is adopted, the text remains a powerful symbol of the ways in which national and international identities are negotiated in and through subject English in Australia.

Dickens over time and place in Western Australia, South Australia and Victoria

Before embarking on an analysis of the traces of Dickens in the three states mentioned, it is perhaps useful to briefly acknowledge the way curriculum is developed and functions in Australia, a country of 23 million distributed across six states and two territories. As Patterson ("Teaching literature") notes, the examinations and curriculum practices across the nation are diverse. Australia's federated system of government means that curriculum authorities (the term often used for bureaucratic curriculum-setting organisations) in the local jurisdictions write and administer curriculum documents.

The purpose of providing this account, as preface to the analysis of the ways Dickens's *Great Expectations* has been used in three states from the period 1948 to 2005, is twofold. First, the distributed, territorial and competitive nature of curriculum work in Australia supports an analysis that examines each state in turn: states have and continue to function as different representations of Australia and Australians, places where diverse national identities are negotiated and, at different times, advocated. In the following sections we will explore the ways that Dickens's text is used to negotiate national identities in these ways. Second, the Australian curriculum context serves to remind us that during the time period captured by the ALIAS database, state curricula, even states geographically "next door", developed separately and distinctly, and while there are commonalities, particularly with regard to the setting of Dickens's famous novel, across state jurisdictions, these commonalities were not mandated and therefore are perhaps more remarkable. This points to the important role of texts, and in the case of this inquiry, *Great Expectations*, in showing literary and educational archivists' unintended but shared assumptions and discourses about texts and subject English that form a vital part of the history of this subject in Australia.

Western Australia

According to the records available in the ALIAS database, Western Australia was the first state in Australia to set *Great Expectations* for study, in 1948. It was set for a single year, and then returned for a two-year and then four-year appearance (1961–2 and 1967–70), before being listed for 23 consecutive years (1975–98), a commitment which seems evidence of bureaucratic "Magwitch madness" (cf. McLean Davies). It is interesting to note, as will be discussed later, that while in Victoria Dickens's novel is passed between versions of mainstream and specialist English subjects, *Great Expectations* is firmly entrenched in the WA Literature subject, and only starts life in the English subject (1948–68) where it is located on the "literature" component of the exam. The endurance and longevity of the text is even more remarkable when one realises that it survived several syllabus changes during this long period – changes that, as we will discuss below, impact on the way this text is understood in the context of a literary education.

The Literature subject in Western Australia is a specialist study, traditionally taken by students who enjoy literary study and approach it with confidence, as opposed to the "mainstream" English subject. Understood in this context, the repetitive setting of *Great Expectations* can be seen not so much as location of a text that all students, i.e. those taking mainstream English, need to experience, but rather identifying it as belonging to a specialist literary coterie, and offering essential knowledge for those likely to pursue literature study at a tertiary level. This use of *Great Expectations* emphasises, from the outset, a Cultural Heritage model of English education (Locke "Constructing" 9). Locke notes that Cultural Heritage was the dominant model of literary studies at universities between 1930 and 1980. He writes:

> ... this approach asserted that there was a traditional body of knowledge (including a canon of precious texts and specialist literary knowledge) which was to be valued and inculcated as a means of "rounding out" learners so that they became fully participating and discriminating members of society. (Locke "Paradigms" 17)

Further to this, as Macken-Horarik notes, Cultural Heritage models continue to be privileged in examinations and by extension "privilege" those students who control them (10).

In order to explore the perspective on cultural heritage being offered by the early English syllabuses in Western Australia, it is useful to investigate the texts being set alongside Dickens for examination. It is worth noting that while the initial setting of Dickens on the "literature" paper of the single English study shows a distinctly British cultural bias, and thus an effort to claim an imperial education for Australian students – Dickens is accompanied by texts by Conrad, Wells, Austen and Brontë – among the options for the compulsory study is M. Barnard Eldershaw's *A House is Built* (1929), a collaboration by Australian writers Marjorie Barnard and Flora

Eldershaw. Although the setting of this text offers possibilities for students to explore one version of Australian experience, the fact that only one novel from this section can be chosen, and these texts are not placed in dialogue, prevents any affordances that could be achieved through comparison. While Barnard Eldershaw's novel does not enjoy longevity on the early lists for Leaving English, later text lists show that the practice of selecting one Australian text among an otherwise British offering is sustained. In 1961 Vance Palmer's *The Passage* is listed alongside works by British writers Dickens, Hardy and Golding. Yet by 1968, it becomes clear that a different perspective on cultural heritage was being offered to Australian students. *Great Expectations* is listed with Hardy's *The Mayor of Casterbridge* and Golding's *Lord of the Flies*, and these texts previously set for study are now accompanied by Twain's *Huckleberry Finn* and United States academic C.L. Cline's edited collection *The Rinehart Book of Short Stories*, which includes seminal stories by British and American writers.

The examination questions themselves offer additional insights into the ways in which these texts were being used within a Cultural Heritage framework. In the 1970 English Literature Leaving Examination, students in Western Australia were asked to "Consider the roles of TWO of the following in the working out of the themes of *Great Expectations*: Magwitch, Miss Havisham, Wemmick" (UWA, Leaving Examination 1970 English Literature 4), a question that tests close knowledge of the text and its possible meanings. In 1975, the importance of this text, as access to "insider" imperial culture is further reinforced:

> Wilkie Collins, a novelist who was a friend of Dickens, had a "recipe" for writing a novel: "Make 'em laugh, make 'em cry, make 'em wait." Would Collins have approved of Great Expectations in the light of this recipe? (Western Australia. Tertiary Admissions Examination 1975 English 6)

The "test" being offered in this examination is one of cultural membership: does the student have significant knowledge of this text to make assertions about its validity according to what has been determined by Collins – one who possesses "natural" cultural capital and represents the heritage to which the student might gain access through showing "appreciation of major forms of literature in English (Board of Secondary Education WA 1975 English syllabus 86).

The presentation of cultural heritage as indisputably British and North American, evident in the setting of texts and more specifically in the examination questions, shifts in the 1980s, when students are offered the possibility of comparing and juxtaposing novels from North America, England and Australia in this section of the exam. The 1980 Western Australian tertiary Entrance Examination for Literature offers students the possibility of drawing on one or more of Dickens, Faulkner (*As I Lay Dying*), Hardy (*The Mayor of Casterbridge*), Richardson (*Australia Felix*), Trollope (*Barchester Towers*) and White (*Voss*). Dickens (along with Hardy) remains a stable text of empire as contemporary Australian texts are added to the list of novels.

In 1989, a new structure for the examination is implemented which retains the focus on prose fiction, poetry and drama, and the opportunity to put texts such as Thea Astley's *A Descant for Gossips* (introduced in 1990) in dialogue with Dickens's text, and introduces a context section, which moves significantly away from literature as Cultural Heritage, or literature as "a study of culture" to literature as "cultural studies" (Patterson, "Teaching Literature" 311), drawing more on models of literature as critical practice, and to some extent personal growth (Locke, "Constructing", "Paradigms"; Macken-Horarik). The contexts listed for the period 1989–1991 (but retained until at least 1996) – Australian Studies, Women's Studies and Studies of Self and Society – indicate, explicitly and implicitly, that a study of nation, and the role of texts to produce or contest national identities, is a vital part of English literature. In answering context questions, students are required to put texts in dialogue. The examination explicitly tests "the cross generic range and depth of candidates' reading during the course", and requires candidates to provide "detailed reference to one of two of the texts set for detailed study, and the ability to draw appropriately on a wide range of reading" (SEA 1989 130). The examination paper from 1990 shows the increasingly open way students are able to engage with literature (SEA 1990 3). While one general question is listed for each context, a fourth question allows students to reflect on their own reading experiences over the subject studied. A shifting view of what constitutes literature is also present, over the 1990s, with more recent, late twentieth-century novels set as options for the 1996 exam than had previously been offered (ALIAS).

The difficulty of retrieving student examination responses and the boundaries of this inquiry mean that we are not able to ascertain to what extent *Great Expectations* was utilised in the context study, and how, if at all, it was used in terms of discourses around nation and society. We can assert, though, that from the 1980s, *Great Expectations* was no longer a stand-alone text that could provide access for candidates to a culture beyond their own. While still holding a significant place in the English Literature syllabus, the design of the course meant that teachers and students were positioned to approach *Great Expectations* in terms of its connection to other texts, which to some measure repositioned it as a text that could contribute to the values of societies more broadly.

South Australia

While Western Australia was the first state to list *Great Expectations*, and the one to list it for the longest consecutive period, South Australia, listing Dickens's novel for the first time in 1950, is the state to show the greatest commitment to this work, setting it for study for a total of 40 years out of the period surveyed. Dickens's novel is first located on the English Literature Leaving (fifth form) syllabus, where an aesthetic appreciation of literature is being developed. Like Western Australian students at this time, South Australian students show their knowledge of the literary canon through close analysis of the text and by responding to questions focused on character. The 1950 Leaving English Literature Examination question for *Great Expectations* is as follows:

> Take two characters from *Great Expectations*, one of which you find more convincingly depicted than the other. Describe both the characters and what part they play in the story. (UA 157)

Analysis shows that this subject is particularly focused on British texts and the cultural capital they carry. Other novels on the 1950 syllabus are Brontë's *Jane Eyre*, Hardy's *Under the Greenwood Tree*, Scott's *Ivanhoe* and Stevenson's *The Master of Ballantrae*. The mastery of English is clearly linked, in the English Literature Leaving Examination, with mastery of British literary forms. Students are being explicitly assessed on not only their knowledge of cultural heritage, but on their ability to become part of it. In the 1952 examination students (and teachers) are reminded: "Great importance is attached to the accuracy and aptness of expression ... Marks will be deducted for errors in grammar, spelling and punctuation, and for illegible handwriting" (UA 1952 82).

In the 1960s, *Great Expectations* is found on the Matriculation Examination for English – the subject taken by all wanting to achieve their Matriculation Certificate for the completion of high schooling, and to potentially qualify for university entrance. Here the novel represents the "traditional" literature study, while other sections of the exam indicate the expanded understanding of what mainstream English should entail. Interestingly, while *Hard Times*, arguably one of Dickens's more challenging texts, is set for the Leaving Examination for English in the same year, it is *Great Expectations* – the story of a young man's coming of age in a country far from Australia – that has the premier position on the final secondary school English syllabus. The 1967 Matriculation Examination outlines the range of responsibilities of subject English: "In addition to the study of prescribed books, training in English composition, English usage and the elements of clear thinking should be continued in the Matriculation year." (UA 1967 174) It is interesting to note that the 1967 matriculation syllabus includes a section on "recommended reading" – called "section d – where some specifically Australian texts are included such as: *Australian Idiom: An Anthology of Contemporary Prose and Poetry*, selected by H.P. Heseltine, and Peter Coleman's *Australian Civilisation*. Teachers are advised:

> The intention of Section d is twofold: firstly, that teachers should be able to recommend and candidates to choose, books relating to each candidate's special interests; and, secondly, that some pupils should be encouraged to read beyond their usual fields. In the examination, questions will not presuppose close and detailed study of the texts. (UA 1967 175)

This clarification is instructive. It both shows the ways in which subject English in South Australia at this time is shifting to have greater consideration for the development of the whole person, and that national identity is part of this; however, these recommended texts do not require close reading in the same way as the canonical texts on the syllabus, and therefore, given the high-stakes nature of this assessment, are perhaps less likely to be read with the same kinds of attention as a text like *Great Expectations*, which remains a marker of cultural capital, even within this examination designed to develop and test a range of "English" skills and knowledges.

In the 1970s, the English matriculation syllabus and examination further developed to include "extension" texts for each of the literary genres listed: prose, poetry and drama. In the examination, students could expect to write answers to four questions across these genres, including at least two questions on core texts (of which *Great Expectations* remained one) and at least one question on the extension texts. Thus while greater textual engagement is facilitated by the examination, *Great Expectations* continued to stand for core knowledge of canonical texts for South Australian students.

Great Expectations is listed throughout the 1970s and 1980s, but by 1983 there is evidence of a shift in approach to these canonical works from the texts to the authors themselves. Two texts are listed for each author represented. In 1983, students studying Dickens's novels selected both *Great Expectations* and *David Copperfield*. While it is not only nineteenth-century British and North American writers who are represented on this list – Ursula le Guin's *The Left Hand of Darkness* and *The Dispossessed* are among the offerings, as is Lawson's *While the Billy Boils* (two volumes), the list is still weighted towards established canonical texts. As in the 1970s, this examination positions discussion of national identity outside these prescribed canonical texts. See for example the questions from the prescribed list on Dickens, and an example from the extension section below for the 1985 English Matriculation Examination:

> "Dickens reveals the cruelty of individuals towards each other, even towards those they love". How far is this true of your readings of Dickens's novels? (SSABSA 1985 2)

> "Australians like to take things easy". To what extent does your reading this year support this view of Australians? (7)

This distinction between the ways different kinds of texts are used in this syllabus is worth further consideration. The syllabus and examination appear to imply that only some fiction can be generalised to personal experience, some can't. Dickens and other canonical texts are thus increasingly rarefied in this context, which positions "real" literature, that which requires sustained engagement, as mostly coming from "elsewhere".

In 1986, the Senior Secondary Assessment Board of South Australia administered the new final year English examination, no longer called matriculation (SSABSA English). Dickens and the weighty canonical texts remain on the list in the same way as previously – as an author study – however the new curriculum mandates that students write on one Australian text in the examination, indicating a national "personal growth" agenda for English in South Australia at this time.

A new syllabus for senior secondary English was introduced in 1991 (and retained until 2001). Similarly to the Western Australian syllabus in the 1990s, this syllabus, which retains *Great Expectations*, gives greater opportunity for students and teachers to pair and compare texts set on the list, while a poetry anthology and one other text must be studied as a 'single' text, four others must be selected as paired texts. As one would expect in this format, examination questions are necessarily broad. The examination from the year 2000 asks students, when drawing on their single texts study, to answer questions that focus either on responding to literature as if it were a means through which life could be better understood, or as an aesthetic work to be appreciated through an appraisal of form and technique:

> "Supportive or destructive? What view of family is presented in one of the core texts?"

> "Explain how the techniques used by the author were effective in shaping your understanding of the central ideas in one of the core texts" (SSABSA English Studies 5).

Paired questions also ask students to generalise from literature to philosophies about life and society, and are interesting in that they address the student in the second person, making the links between literature and personal growth more apparent: "To what extent are the two texts you studied this year similar in suggesting that making the right choices is often complex?" (5).

While the authority of *Great Expectations*, as it was initially presented in the 1950s, has been potentially ameliorated by the opportunity to pair texts, the enduring place of a single study means that it is possible for teachers and students to experience *Great Expectations* in a similar way to their predecessors engaging with the South Australian Leaving exam. Interestingly, the focus on Australian texts evident in the previous iteration of the curriculum is not evident here – an Australian text is no longer mandated. Indeed, in contrast to the specifically Australian-focused questions of the Western Australian syllabus in the 1990s, the paired text questions about society assume a homogeneous internationalism. *Great Expectations*, once clearly positioned to negotiate a British identity, therefore can now be used by teachers to either reinforce the importance of the canon, through single text study, or as a way of understanding society as it is being broadly defined.

Victoria

Melissa Jogie notes that "in Australia and England well-known texts are constantly repeated or reshuffled" ("Too Pale and Stale" 288), and this seems particularly the case for the way *Great Expectations* is used in the English subjects in Victoria. As in the South Australian example, Dickens's novel, introduced in 1959, starts in the specialist English Literature subject where it is listed on average every third year, and on one occasion (1966–7) for two years, until 1992. In the years it is not set in English Literature, it is taken up in English, where it is consequently set on average every three years, until it is taken off the list for a sustained period (1999–2002). In terms of the years covered by the ALIAS database, *Great Expectations* is listed for 19 years in Victoria. Unlike both Western Australia and South Australia, where *Great Expectations* is ultimately located in Literature (WA) or as part of mainstream subject English, the shifting between the English subjects in Victoria can be seen as an indication that the ubiquitous Dickens is considered suitable for all and any English study.

While mapping the traces of Dickens in the syllabuses and exam documents of Western Australian and South Australian courses show to different degrees the ways that English becomes more open, and that there is the option to place *Great Expectations* in dialogue with other texts, the Victorian examples shows the way different approaches to English, through the English/ESL Study Design and the Literature Study Design, are being explored. The early listings of *Great Expectations* in the English Literature subject show evidence of a personal growth approach (Locke, "Constructing English"). In 1966, *Great Expectations* is one of eight British or American canonical novels set for single study. Examination questions are general, and use personal pronouns "we" and "you" to indicate that it is the student's reading of the chosen text that is important. By 1980, specific and general questions are set which relocate the text in a Cultural Heritage paradigm:

> "The world of *Great Expectations* is peopled with foolish, proud and selfish characters. It is the disappointment of his expectations that saves Pip being like them. Is this a fair comment on the novel?" (VISE 1980 11)

Clearly resonating with Hunter's notion of subject English as invested in moral development of individuals (*Culture and Government*), this question positions students undertaking the exam as experts entering the discourse community, those who are able to assess the "expertise" of a world-famous writer.

While these specific questions return by 1985, in the early years of the 1980s, a more flexible structure is tried. In 1982, students can either study *Great Expectations* in the context of a Unit on 'The Individual in the nineteenth century novel', or have the option of an entire Unit on the works of Dickens. (1982 Victorian English Literature Syllabus Optional Units F and G) While a greater range of texts is included in English literature in the 1980s, Dickens clearly remains central to testing and working through new forms or approach and assessment in the Victorian Literature subject in the 1980s and early 1990s.

Like the Literature subject, the traces of *Great Expectations* in English show that this text is part of new innovations within the course, and is perceived as being able to add value to many kinds of text responses either when set as part of a thematic group (in the mid-1970s) or when listed a single study question (e.g. 1981, 1984). The egalitarian and democratic response to Dickens in Victoria is particularly evident in 1988, when it is set in as supplementary reading for a theme – such as "Growth" (VCAB 15). Theme studies, called List B, are set in addition to the texts set for close reading (List A). Given the role of *Great Expectations* in Western Australia and South Australia, where teachers always had the option to study Dickens's novel closely, this can be read as a somewhat radical de-centring of the text of empire. Not only is it not listed on Part A, understood as the key texts worthy of close study, but it is not listed in the Part B groups, and is only an optional text that may help illuminate those that are set. After being put to use in this capacity, *Great Expectations* returns to Part A in 1999 ('English' 16). The movement of Dickens's work both across and within English and Literature subjects in Victoria serves, to some extent, to both demystify this canonical text, and also to present each aspect of the courses as valid and significant, and as a talisman for what English can be.

Some observations across the states

This analysis of the ALIAS database and associated documents has shown that a mapping of Dickens's *Great Expectations* can also be understood as a mapping of the English subjects in Australia as they negotiate the changing focus of the subjects in the 1970s and 80s towards more textually inclusive personal growth models. While this mapping of *Great Expectations*, particularly in the 1988 Victorian example, shows a move towards seeing this text in the context of other (perhaps Australian works), and not simply as a marker of cultural capital, this understanding also remains, as we see in the listing of this text for Part A at the start of the twenty-first century. While the changing presentation of Dickens on these lists, and the various associated examination questions, shows possibilities for students to engage with Dickens increasingly as a way of negotiating national identity (shown most clearly in Western Australia in the 1980s), these choices are ultimately the jurisdiction of the teacher and so further research is required to ascertain the ways in which these curriculum documents were enacted in teachers' school-based practices.

Transcending English: *Great Expectations* as a marker of Australian educational experience

Arguably, the dominant role of Dickens and *Great Expectations* in early Australian colonial life, and the novel's central role on English syllabuses around Australia and the world, has impacted on the rhetorical and cultural narratives surrounding schooling and teachers. *Great Expectations* as text and cultural marker has become more than a text to be studied, one that moves the reader closer to the imperial centre or supports the negotiation of new "worlded" cultural identities in and through subject English. While the text continues to be set for study at senior levels, it has effectively transcended English, and has become a kind of shorthand to explain and locate the educational outlook, achievements, transformation and challenges facing students and teachers.

Indeed, an analysis of the research literature produced by teacher-researchers shows that "great expectations" has become a particularly popular phrase in discussions of educational experience. Many of these usages rely on at least an implied connection to Dickens's novel. They draw on the context of the novel as a text about education and the desire for knowledge as well as an educational text (one that teaches language, culture and moral lessons). In some cases the echo is more distant. "Great expectations" is also used as a literal term that hardly plays on the large expectations for/from teachers and students across a number of pedagogical areas. This latter usage has virtually nothing to do with the novel, beyond the fact that the high expectations do often circulate around literacy, linguistic capacity and related skills (cf. Smith and Hopkins).

The novel underpins a number of narrative explorations of the (early) teaching experience – as allegory or parallel as well as example. For instance, some "coming of age as an educator" stories around beginner teachers' experiences feature "growing up" with the novel, most explicitly Cohen and Hunt's "New Voices: Great Expectations and *Great Expectations*: A Young Teacher Grows up with Pip", which chronicles Cohen's trial-and-error methods as an inexperienced teacher experimenting on her students in order to find the best pedagogical methods of teaching the text *Great Expectations*.

Another form in this genre is the one in which *Great Expectations* is positioned as "growing up" text, from more experienced teachers, finding ways in which *Great Expectations* remains still relevant to young people. In this genre, articles by teachers such as Granata in "Pip's *Great Expectations* and Ours" (1965) make claims for its coverage of the big questions, as do much more contemporary articles by Bucolo ("Instalments" and "'Survivor"). Both of Bucolo's articles, like Granata's 35 years earlier, argue for the current relevance of *Great Expectations*, suggesting consecutively that it can easily be made accessible through a contemporary twist on traditional serial reading, and outlining a useful likeness to serial television viewing, and generic and thematic links to reality television. The latter article, for instance, compares Satis House to the *Big Brother* House (30). This mode seems more common for American teachers.

By contrast, and in relation to the Australian context, Jogie ("Too Pale and Stale"), as noted, while apparently agreeing that Dickens's themes are "timeless", takes issue with the perpetual curriculum setting of texts such as *Great Expectations*. In a discussion of the need to include a diversity of texts, including postcolonial readings, in the upper-secondary curricula in the UK and Australia (NSW), Jogie notes that *Great Expectations* has been on the curriculum for over fifty years, and implicitly includes it in the "pale and stale" irrelevant texts of her title, inaccessible to an ethnically and culturally diverse population of students (295–296). In her analysis Jogie argues that the repetition and context of the setting of *Great Expectations* constrains the extent to which it can be made relevant or properly studied.

Great Expectations, then, by the twenty-first century, features in curriculum discussions identified *both* as a text accessible to secondary level readers because they can make meaningful connections with their own contemporary culture and consumption practices, *and* as inaccessible and inappropriate for its reader cohort generally, and particularly non-Anglo readers or less engaged readers, as "a more challenging read because it speaks of a distant time, with norms and values far removed from those of a contemporary culturally diverse society". (Jogie, "Desperate Shadows" 346). Both attitudes occur nationally and internationally (McLean Davies, "Magwich Madness", "You are what you read"; Johnston and Mangat 19–20). The recurrence of *Great Expectations*, like Jogie's need to argue against such classic repetitions on the syllabus, indicates its continued value as a text with easily recognised cultural capital, however unstable that is. In the twenty-first century these texts are not only still embedded in the curriculum, they have become part of the narrative of the curriculum and subject English.

Works Cited

Analysis of Literature in Australian Schools Database (ALIAS). www.australiancommonreader.com/syllabus. Web. 3 September 2016.

Barnard Eldershaw, M. *A House is Built*. London: Harrap; Sydney: Australasian Publishing, 1929. Print.

Board of Secondary Education Western Australia. 1975 English Literature Syllabus. WA: Government Printer, 1975. Print.

Bonwick, James. *The Tasmanian Lily*. London: Henry S. King, 1873. Setis eBook. Web. 30 July 2015.

Bucolo, Joe. "Teaching *Great Expectations* in instalments". *The English Journal* 89.2 (1999): 33–39. *Jstor*. Web. 30 Aug. 2015.

——. "'Survivor: Satis House': Creating classroom community while teaching Dickens in a reality-TV world". *The English Journal* 100.5 (2011): 29–32. *Jstor*. Web. 30 Aug. 2015.

Cheeseman to Hoggins. 13 August 1915. "Image 1012". Hoggins Archive. Private collection, courtesy Hoggins family.

Cohen, Abby D., and Bud Hunt. "New voices: *Great Expectations* and great expectations: A young teacher grows up with Pip". *The English Journal* 97.4 (2008): 97–100. *Jstor*. Web. 30 Aug. 2015.

"English; English (ESL) Text List 1999". *VCE Bulletin February 1998*. Melbourne: n.p., 1998. Print.

Ferguson, Susan L. "Dickens's public readings and the Victorian Author" *SEL* 41.4 (2001): 729–749. Print.

Green, Bill. and Phil Cormack. "Curriculum history, 'English' and the New Education; or, installing the empire of English?" *Pedagogy, Culture & Society* 16.3 (2008): 253–267. *Informaworld*. Web. 24 Feb. 2011.

Guillory, John. *Cultural Capital: The problem of literary canon formation*, Chicago: University of Chicago Press, 1993. Print.

Goodwyn, A. "The status of literature: English teaching and the condition of literature teaching in schools". *English in Education* 46.3 (2012): 212–227. *Wiley*. Web. 1 July 2014.

Hunter, Ian. *Culture and Government: The emergence of literary education*. Basingstoke, Hampshire: Macmillan, 1988. Print.

Hill, Thomas Padmore. *The Oratorical Trainer: A system of vocal culture*. Melbourne: George Robertson, 1862. eBook. 30 July 2010.

James, Samuel. "The Public Library", [letter from Samuel James] *Port Phillip Herald*, 25 Feb. 1856, 7. *Trove*. Web. 25 Jan. 2010.

Jogie, Melissa Reshma. "Desperate shadows of 'Belonging': Revealing pedagogical issues with teaching prescribed English texts in the NSW Higher School Certificate (HSC)". *Australian Educational Researcher* 42 (2015): 335–352 *Springer*. Web. 21 July 2014.

——. "Too pale and stale: Prescribed texts used for teaching culturally diverse students in Australia and England". *Oxford Review of Education* 41:3 (2015): 287–309. *T and F online*. Web. 30 Aug. 2015.

Johnston, I. and J. Mangat. Reading Practices, Postcolonial Literature, and Cultural Mediation in the Classroom. Rotterdam: Sense Publishers, 2012. Print.

Kember, Joe. *Marketing Modernity: Victorian popular shows and early cinema*. Exeter: Exeter Studies in Film History, 2009. Print.

Locke, T. "Constructing English in New Zealand: A report on a decade of reform *L1*" *Educational Studies in Language and Literature* 7.2 (2007): 5–33. 14 *Springer*. Web. April 2011.

———. "Paradigms of English". *Masterclass in English Education: Transforming teaching and learning*. Ed. S. Brindley and B. Marshall. London: Bloomsbury, 2015. Print.

Macken-Horarik, M. "Making productive use of four models of school English: A case study revisited". *English in Australia*. 49.3 (2015): 1–13.

Main, William. "Charles Dickens and the magic lantern". *History of Photography* 8.1 (1984): 67–71. *T and F online*. Web. July 30, 2014.

Marsh, Joss. "Dickensian 'dissolving views': The magic lantern, visual story-telling, and the Victorian technological imagination". *Comparative Critical Studies* 6.3 (2009): 333–346. *Euppublishing*. Web. September 2, 2016.

McLean Davies, Larissa, Brenton Doecke and Phillip Mead. "Reading the local and global: Teaching literature in secondary schools in Australia". *Changing English: Studies in culture and education* 20.3 (2013): 224–240. Print.

McLean Davies, Larissa. "You are what you read: Text selection and cultural capital in the (globalising) English classroom". *International Perspectives on Teaching English in a Globalized World*. Ed. A. Goodwyn, L. Reid, and C. Durrant. New York: Routledge US, 2014: 235–244. Print.

———. "Auditing subject English: A review of text selection practices inspired by the national year of reading". *English in Australia*, 47.2 (2012): 11–17. Print.

———. "Magwitch madness: Archive fever and the teaching of Australian literature". *Teaching Australian Literature: From classroom conversations to national imaginings*. Ed. Brenton Doecke, Larissa McLean Davies and Phillip Mead. Kent Town, Australia: Wakefield Press, 2011: 129–152. Print.

———. "What's the story? Australian literature in the secondary English curriculum". *National Conference for Teachers of English and Literacy*. Adelaide, Australia: Australian Literacy Educators Association, 2008. 1–12. Print.

Mirmohamadi, Kylie, and Susan K. Martin. *Colonial Dickens: What Australians made of the world's favourite author*. North Melbourne: Australian Scholarly Publishing, 2012. Print.

"Mr Hill's elocutionary entertainment". *South Australian Register* Friday, 15 July 1853, 3. *Trove* Web. 1 July 2015.

"Music and elocution / Value of Dickens / Dramatic entertainment". The *Newcastle Sun* Saturday 18 Nov. 1922, 5. *Trove* Web. 1 July 2015.

Patterson, Annette. "Teach literature in Australia: Examining and reviewing senior English". *Changing English 15*.3 (2008): 31–322. *QUTePrints*. Web. 15 Sept. 2015.

———. "Australian literature: Culture, identity and English teaching". *Journal of the Association for the Study of Australian Literature* 12.1 (2012):1–14. *JASAL* Web. 12 Sept. 2015.

———. "The legacy of Ian Hunter's work on literature education and the history of reading practices: Some preliminary remarks". *History of European Ideas* 40.1 (2014): 89–95. *T and F online*. Web. July 1 2014.

"Rev. Charles Clark at the Town Hall". *Hobart Mercury* 1 Feb 1876, 3. *Trove*. Web. 1 July 2015.

"Review of *A Christmas Carol*". *Hobart Mercury*, 4 December 1878, 3.

[SEA]. Secondary Education Authority. *English Literature (Year 12) – E005*. Osborne Park: SEA. 1989. Print.

[SEA]. Secondary Education Authority. Tertiary Entrace Examination, 1990. Question Paper. English Literature. WA: n.p. 1990. Print.

[SSABSA]. Senior Secondary Board of South Australia. English. Year 12 Detailed Syllabus Statements for English and English P. 1986–1990. SA: SSABSA, 1986. Print.

[SSABSA]. Senior Secondary Board of South Australia. *Public Examination, 1985. English. Paper One.* SA: SSABSA, 1985. Print.

[SSABSA]. Senior Secondary Board of South Australia. *Public Examination, 2000. 2000 English Studies.* SA: SSABSA, 2000. Print.

Smith, Karen and Chris Hopkins. "*Great Expectations*: Sixth-formers' perceptions of teaching and learning in degree-level English". *Arts and Humanities in Higher Education* 4.3 (2005): 304–318 *Sage*. Web. July 30 2015.

Teese, R., S. Lamb, and S. Helme. "Hierarchies of culture and hierarchies of context in Australian secondary education" in Ed. Melzer, W. and R. Tippelt. *Cultures of Education: Proceedings of the 21st Congress of the German Society for Educational Research (DGfE)*, Verlag Barbara Budrich, 2009: 71–92. Print.

[UA] University of Adelaide. *Leaving Examination Papers, 1950. English Literature.* SA: Public Examinations Board, 1950. Print.

[UA] University of Adelaide. *Leaving Examination, 1952. English Literature.* SA: n.p., 1952. Print.

[UA] University of Adelaide. Syllabus for the Year 1967. *Leaving Examination. English.* SA: n.p., 1967. Print.

[UA] University of Adelaide. Syllabus for the Year 1967. *Matriculation Examination. English.* SA: n.p., 1967. Print.

[UWA] University of Western Australian. *Leaving Examination 1970 English Literature.* UWA, 1970. Print.

[VCAB] Victorian Curriculum and Assessment Board. "English Booklist for 1988". *VCAB Bulletin February 1987.* Melbourne: VCAB, 1987. Print.

[VISE] Victorian Institute of Secondary Education. *Higher School Certificate Examination 1980 English Literature.* VISE, 1980. Print.

Western Australia. Tertiary Admissions Examination, 1975. English Literature. WA: n.p. 1975. Print.

Yandell, J. "Agency and canon: Your Shakespeare, everybody's Shakespeare?" *Teaching Australian Literature: From classroom conversations to national imaginings.* Ed. Brenton Doecke, L.arissa McLean Davies and Phillip Mead. Kent Town, Australia: Wakefield Press, 2011: 213–230. Print.

Chapter Thirteen

GROWING UP WITH *TESS*

Contexts, close reading and theoretical analysis

Tully Barnett, Kate Douglas, Alice Healy-Ingram

I first read Tess of the d'Urbervilles *by Thomas Hardy in the summer between 1990 and 1991 because it was one of a number of books listed on the South Australian senior English curriculum list for 1991 – the year I was to undertake Year 12 English. For Christmas 1990, in the months between Years 11 and 12, my mother bought me all of the books on the Year 12 syllabus to prepare me for the year ahead, to get a head start on the reading and thinking for my favourite subject, to hit the ground running the following year. In all honesty, I only read about half of the books over the summer break and, as luck would have it, read almost none of the books I would actually face in the school year. But what I did read was* Tess of the d'Urbervilles *by Thomas Hardy. I recall that I also listened to it as an audiobook, on a CD series that was part of one of those series newsagents love to sell, and which was, I think, the first or second compact disc in the house as my family made the transition from vinyl to CD. I listened to parts of the audio as I was reading the words on the printed page, an experience that continues to inform my understanding of intermediality. I don't remember a great deal about my first reading of the novel, except for a general outrage over society's treatment of the kindly girl. I remember being a bit bewildered by Tess and her experiences. I mean, there is all that blood that poor Prince, the horse, sheds over the road early in the book. There is the loss of her baby that I, as a 15 year old, could not begin to comprehend. I cried when Prince died and again when*

Sorrow died and again when Alec d'Urberville died, not for the loss of him but for the loss of Tess whose way out of the misfortune of her life was barred completely now.

I next read Tess *20 years later when co-designing a course called Big Books – not our chosen title – a third-year capstone English class intended to allow students to study canonical literature in some depth. When I came to teach the text, my relationship with the book was complicated by those earlier recollections of it, but I also approached the classroom with excitement. What would students make of the symbolism? I found that* Tess *was a book that resonated with a large number of the students in the class. Where they had struggled to read* Moll Flanders *and to get through the bulk of* Middlemarch, Tess *offered them something they could read more readily. The trope of a series of unfortunate events and a young girl adrift in the world was familiar to them and the symbolism of the Maypole provided useful learning moments as students filled up the whiteboard with connections between the first few pages of the novel and the last few.*
(Tully Barnett)

Introduction

Reading lists and English syllabuses, whether secondary or tertiary, are always political, interrogated and contested. The teaching and learning of, and with, literary texts in education is cyclical: priorities such as teaching canonical literatures or Australian or postcolonial literatures, for instance, shift, change and cycle back as priorities. This is often the result of cultural trends, changing social and/or political conditions and, significantly, the backgrounds and personal experiences and agendas of teaching staff. Teachers bring their experiences of reading, in secondary and tertiary contexts, into university classrooms and look back on their own experiences of learning through literature with nostalgic frames. Our memories of the works we studied at earlier stages in our education are flowing with nostalgia, dread, boredom or struggle, or a combination of these, and this impacts not only on how we recall the reading of key texts of the literary canon but also how we then go on to teach those texts. At the same time, our re-reading of these literary texts can change with life experience, with situating the reading within new contexts or other theories and texts that we have read and taught, and with media frameworks and platforms – the networks of texts into which individual reading experiences are fitted. How we teach is heavily influenced by how and what we ourselves were taught at the various stages of our journeys towards becoming university literature teachers, and how we incorporate texts into our lives. But so often that journey goes unexamined.

The Analysis of Literature in Australian Schools (ALIAS) database builds a narrative of literary value and thematic concentrations over a 61-year period by listing the novels that have been taught in secondary education. It allows manipulation of the syllabus data to reveal frequencies of text, author, nationality, gender and so on. It places individual literary texts within a network of literary sources and approaches to those sources – no book is an island, to misquote John Donne. It provides insight into trends in literary studies education over time. Connecting this information with our teaching practices and our personal learning histories offers understanding of contemporary teaching and learning in literary studies. The books we set for students can tell us many things about how we see ourselves as a nation, what kinds of literature are valued, what role literature plays in secondary and tertiary learning environments and what gifts we want to pass on to future generations. Playing around with the ALIAS database, we discovered that the second most frequently set novel on syllabuses in South Australia, Victoria, New South Wales, Tasmania and Western Australia between 1945 and 2005 was Thomas Hardy's *Tess of the d'Urbervilles* (hereafter *Tess*) and this resonated with we three co-authors in ways we thought worth exploring. The enduring choice to teach *Tess* – across time, states, pedagogical periods – invites further examination.

Given the way the database reveals the enduring place of *Tess* in Australian secondary English education, we want to situate and explore this knowledge in relation to experiences of teaching *Tess* in university English contexts. We will draw on secondary material concerning pedagogies for teaching "difficult" texts, and our own reflections on reading, studying and teaching *Tess*. We argue that this novel illuminates some of the fascinating trajectories and tensions involved when we move or progress the analysis of a literary text from high school to university-level English. For example, what are the limits of a feminist literary analysis at high school level? What ground might be gained in employing such an analysis at university level? How does the school context affect teaching and reception of the work? Using the case study of *Tess*, this chapter sifts through the material offered by the ALIAS database and combines that with personal reflection and secondary material to consider how close, contextual and theoretical readings necessarily change even when texts do not.

How we approached the database

We three are teachers and researchers of literary studies and Australian studies at a university in South Australia. We are similar in age; two of us completed secondary studies in Adelaide (one at a public school and one at a Catholic school in 1991 and 1988 respectively) and one completed secondary studies at a Catholic school in Maitland, NSW, in 1992. Initially we used the database in a nostalgic manner – to prompt recollections about our own very different high school English experiences during the late 1980s and early 1990s, to reminisce about the works of literature we had encountered in formal learning environments, and to compare that with the ways we interact with required readings today. We wanted to see what was similar and different around the country within our time frames as well as across time. The database supported our personal pursuits of context for our own education. We see this reminiscence as a form of reflective practice that informs teaching critically and productively. It enables the teacher to think outside of the time pressures of the current moment and connect the study of literature across time. We wanted to connect our memories of senior secondary English with the official data and we used the combination to prompt reflections on our pathways to our current practices in teaching and researching literature.

Our experiences were at once similar in the way they were constrained by text choices and exam questions, and different in the contexts (for instance, the ideologies) from which the texts were taught. We gleefully looked up the texts that had been options for our senior English teachers and, as professionals in literary studies, analysed and second-guessed their choices. We noticed the frequency with which Hardy's *Tess* came up in the lists. Of course *Tess* is not the only novel that appears again and again on the Australian curriculum.[1] But we each have a relationship with the novel: whether having strong memories of reading it during Year 12 at a Catholic girls' school and then of picking it up again at a difficult life moment; having read it during university studies and noting the impact the intersection of intellectual and personal responses has upon our interpretation; or having introduced it to upper-level university students and observed its considerable affect and complicated reception.

These experiences and memories have prompted our inquiry here, persuading us that *Tess* would make a noteworthy case study for this book.

---

1   Various plays by Shakespeare repeatedly make an appearance such as *King Lear*, *Othello* and *Macbeth*. Dickens makes repeated appearances on the top texts list, as does Austen.

We are also motivated by the gap in the scholarship of teaching *Tess*. We hope that our research and reflections here will make a contribution to this scholarship in relation to teaching canonical literatures, teaching canonical literatures as "difficult" literatures, and teaching these literatures through contemporary lenses and preoccupations.

Teaching difficult texts; *Tess* as a difficult text

What constitutes a difficult text is, of course, a matter of debate and individual context. For some, the label of difficult text could be reserved for teaching *Ulysses* to first year undergraduates. Or it could be applied to teaching Chaucer where language and syntax complicate the instant comprehension we might expect when skim-reading a text. For others, a text's difficulty is more about the content of the work, about the confronting material or themes that make going from one page to another a challenge. The teaching of literature in secondary and tertiary contexts frequently includes exposure to fictional or non-fictional events that are provoking. But of course what one reader finds provoking, another will not (Douglas and Barnett). In a moment in which serious questions are being asked about the appropriateness of including on syllabuses works that have traumatic content, works in which characters may experience sexual assault or child abuse or similar, we think it is worth thinking through the role of confronting content in the teaching of literary studies. For instance, in 2014 and 2015 there was a great deal of discussion in the popular media and subsequently in the scholarly press about whether syllabuses should contain "trigger warnings" to alert readers that material on the text may not be safe to read.[2] Regardless of personal views on the appropriateness of trigger warnings on campus, merely raising the possibility of including them makes everyone slightly more concerned about what and how they teach, undermining the strength and stretch of English education. Literary studies is certainly not the only field to experience the problem of traumatic material, but it does experience it uniquely.

Tess contains such material, but the added challenge here is context: students read *Tess* from their early twenty-first-century perspectives (which offer very useful interpretive angles) but they must also be guided through

---

2   Greg Lukianoff and Jonathan Haidt. "The Coddling of the American Mind", *The Atlantic*, September 2015 www.theatlantic.com/magazine/archive/2015/09/the-coddling-of-the-american-mind/399356/; Kate Manne. "Why I use Trigger Warnings", *The New York Times*, September 19 2015 www.nytimes.com/2015/09/20/opinion/sunday/why-i-use-trigger-warnings.html.

the historical contexts that made and continue to make *Tess* a morally and intellectually challenging text. For example, *Tess* inaugurates the age of the banned or proscribed work of high literature. Hardy wrote a book that challenged Victorian morality and its treatment of women and the rural classes. His 1887 contract with W.F. Tillotson & Son to write a newspaper serial was cancelled after the publishers learned of "Tess's violation, an illegitimate baby, and its baptism" (Grindle and Gatrell xxix). Hardy later sent sections of the novel to two magazines: *Murray's Magazine* and the *Graphic*, both of which rejected the text because of the content (xxix). Juliet Grindle and Simon Gatrell, in their "Note on the Text" in the Oxford edition of *Tess*, argue that Hardy sent his manuscript to these magazines knowing they would reject it on the grounds of immorality. This gave him further evidence on which to base his famous essay "Candour in English Fiction", which denounces the "narrow blindness of magazine editors and proprietors of circulating libraries who dictated that thick veils should be drawn over truths of human behaviour" (xxx).

To ensure publication, Hardy did radically edit the text to offer more ambiguous representations, changing or deleting sections as the story was serialised and published in *The Graphic* and in *Harper's Bazar* in the USA (Grindle and Gatrell xxxi). And in the following years the novel was published (as a whole) in several different editions that brought back previously deleted sections (xxxii–xxxiii). As Penny Boumelha notes, *Tess* "has held in the imagination of generations of readers a deserved place in the great series of novels of sexual tragedy that nineteenth-century Europe produced" (Boumelha xiii). It is a novel about sexual violence, the tragic death of a child, emotional abuse, class disadvantage, inequality and prejudice, and the predestined but tragic death of Tess. Boumelha continues:

> It is important that the novel is set in the unspecific "once upon a time" of fairy tale, but embeds its folk elements squarely in the context of recognizable English society of the nineteenth century. The changing conditions of rural labour, factional disputes within the Church of England, the class structure of society, the National School movement, all take their place besides the mythological, biblical, and folk allusions to ensure that the novel bestows a challenging contemporaneity upon its tale of the maiden seduced and abandoned. Added to that realism is the strain of moral – even polemical –commentary which repeatedly insists to the reader that Tess has done nothing wrong. Given these elements of the novel, it is perhaps not surprising that it has, from the outset polarized its readers into supporters and detractors. (xiii)

This polarisation is as evident in faculty as it is in classrooms. Some colleagues prefer not to teach *Tess* because of its potential to be read as anti-feminist. Of course there is much scholarly debate around this question. As James A.W. Heffernan notes, Hardy added the subtitle "A Pure Woman" to the novel after reading page proofs. He wished to remove any ambiguity in the representation of Tess (5). However, much ambiguity has remained. For instance, critics are troubled by the ambiguous representation of Tess's rape (see Rooney). James Kincaid grapples with the novel's unending focus on Tess's suffering: Tess becomes "a titillating snuff movie we run in our own minds" (29). Boumelha concurs:

> Sometimes it can seem that there is no respite for Tess, no escape from the erotic gaze of the narrator whose fascination with her reduplicates that of her sexual pursuers. For many modern readers, the tightness of the narrative focus on the suffering, violated, bleeding Tess becomes a source of discomfort. The reader can feel implicated in a dialectic of desire and victimization. (xx)

But as Boumelha notes, this was a time when debates about gender and sexuality had become prominent in public discourse: "the introduction of civil divorce ... the rise of what is now called first-wave feminism ... campaigns against child prostitution" (xiv). Oliver Lovesey reminds us that *Tess* was written at a time when "the late Victorian obsession with virginity had turned into a mania due to revelations about child prostitution, an increase in prosecutions for child sexual assault, and a revival of the stereotype of the wicked, exploiting mother" (914). And Boumelha explains:

> Controversially, it showed a young woman whose feelings for her child were ambivalent, who sought recuperation rather than redemption, and dared to imagine that she could recommence her life, and who expected her new husband to react to her earlier sexual transgression exactly as she had responded to his ... The greatest challenge to contemporary sensibilities, however, came in the shape of the novel's subtitle: "A Pure Woman". This made it abundantly clear that the text was designed, not to set out Tess's story as a warning fable, but as a defence of her moral virtue. (xvii)

Tess is undoubtedly a complex and often ambiguous novel. Lovesey describes its "ideological unwieldiness" (913) because we are not always sure who is to blame for the tragedy – is it fate or unequal social structures affecting women and people without financial means? The representations of tragedy and trauma are presented in a way that challenges the reader; interpretations of the novel shift over time, as morality changes, and this is one of the reasons why this is a difficult text to teach.

A further point for consideration here is the extent to which students may or may not feel empowered in their interpretations of the novel based on the pedagogical approach (for instance, the assessment questions they are being asked to respond to). Regardless of one's response to this debate, as teachers we have a responsibility to scaffold learning; we must prepare students for what they may encounter in reading a text, help them to respond intellectually, and provide rich contextual information around which students are encouraged to build their interpretations.

The database, contexts and our findings

The discipline of English or English Literary Studies (as it is variously called around Australia) has traditionally been a central discipline for school students across year levels. It has often been a compulsory subject within high school curricula. As James S. Brown and Scott D. Yarborough summarise, there are various, commonly accepted reasons why Literature is a central subject for study at different levels of education. It is thought to "broaden the mind", "teach new ideas" and teach us "about our culture" (1). Though such ideas might seem a little presumptuous to those teaching at the coal face, they reveal the sorts of investments that have traditionally been made around the subject discipline. Brown and Yarborough argue that we are invested in canonical literatures because these are the texts which are perceived to have particular "aesthetic and cultural value" (2). But, as they note, literary canons are highly contextual and often contested, relying on "shifting, subjective, and potentially political standards". Thus, "the process of canonization is problematic in the extreme" (2). And, inevitably, such shifts in thinking are reflected in the way Literature has been taught in Australian schools in recent decades. John Yiannakis notes that subject English "has not been as stable or as singular as sometimes assumed, particularly given that the aims and content of the subject are continually contested" (98).

Looking at the deployment of Hardy in education in England, Peter Widdowson refers to the role of the institution of education in the "making" of a "classic author" (78). For Widdowson the institution of education sits alongside the institution of criticism as a force in canonisation of certain texts and authors (popular media being a third institution of influence). For Widdowson, a study of syllabus materials and examination questions over time tell us "what critical assumptions lie behind the teaching and examining of his work; and therefore to perceive that artificial construction, the 'great writer' Thomas Hardy, as constituted for the school student" (79). Widdowson sees a "profound pressure exerted by the ruling ideology of 'English' by way of its syllabus and its assessment" (80). Widdowson emphasises the constructedness of the author within educational institutional contexts by using scare quotes around Hardy's name so that we are thinking not about Thomas Hardy in education but "'Thomas Hardy' in education".

In looking at the documents, and Widdowson includes a couple of syllabus and examination documents from New South Wales in his analysis, he concludes that

> What becomes clear, I think, is the extent to which a particular literary ideology dominates GCE "English" – one which has particular notions of taste, of value, of fictional mode, and of what constitutes "the literary". By way of a restriction of possible texts and, within that, of the possible ways of perceiving those texts, this ideology constructs a "great writer" who conforms to and confirms that dominant ideology. (88)

Widdowson's analysis provides insight into different ways we can read syllabus and examination documents. The so-called controlling ideology of secondary education canon formation is not necessarily an organised institution consciously and cohesively driving a canon through syllabus and examination documents. Other factors influence text choice, including concerns with what students relate to and what texts serve as good vehicles upon which to develop conceptual knowledge. Widdowson concludes his chapter on "'Thomas Hardy' in Education" by arguing that "'Thomas Hardy' at tertiary level, then, is a bulkier and more diverse figure than in secondary education, but he is still constituted by the ceaseless forming and reforming processes of the major discourses in which he remains actively present in history" (92).

The changes in the way Literature has been taught reflect ideological shifts. Though not always major, such ideological shifts respond to broader cultural and political changes, but also new pedagogical knowledge around the value of certain teaching approaches and the benefits of including certain types of texts (genres, subjects). For instance, David Homer, writing about teaching literature in the 1970s in Australia, notes that in the early to middle part of twentieth century, literature was thought to be a "humanizing agent to counter the perceived ills of the mass industrial society" (343). The suggestion was that literary texts provided exemplars for moral and social development. Reading literatures was also important in the more general advancement of "good taste". These models of approaching English, supported by the likes of F.R. Leavis and David Holbrook, were, as Ken Watson notes, heavily influenced by particular nineteenth-century values around culture and its relationship to civilisation – for instance, those of Matthew Arnold (48). But in the 1960s, the perceived limitations of this model saw the rise of the Personal Growth or "experience-centred" approach to teaching English, which privileged a critical model where students related the themes of texts from different periods to their own lives (Homer 344; Watson 60). The Dartmouth conference of 1966 was instrumental in these shifts to "growth pedagogies", which became, "a subject model which opened up the possibility for young people to appropriate literary texts as a moment in the formation of their identities" (Howie 170). But contextual analysis and critical literary analysis tended to be sidelined in these modes (Homer 345).

Writing in 1977, Homer advocates what he describes as a "sociolinguistic" approach to teaching English, which would encompass a range of different methodological approaches. He also notes that Literature is a staple for all teacher training programmes (342), but that English was expanding to include other literatures beyond canonical works of prose: "journalism, biography, television and radio scripts, song lyrics, comics, advertisements" (342). Homer's ideas about text selection and wider theoretical approaches reflected the cultural studies turn, which reached its full impetus in the 1980s following its emergence in the work of Raymond Williams, E.P. Thompson and others in the 1960s. It offered an interdisciplinary model, "drawing on History and Sociology as well as English, thus placing literary ideas in the wider cultural context" (Peel in Watson 74). Approaches to subject English shifted from the "study of culture" to "cultural studies", a tension that still exists in public debates over the English curriculum (Patterson, "Teaching Literature" 311; Yiannakis 99).

Mark Howie suggests that, currently, English teaching sits between two models – the Cultural Heritage model which follows the importance of canonical literature (its aesthetic, intellectual and moral distinction) and Growth pedagogy (170). While the former model has its political implications, especially from more recent perspectives, the latter approach has endured since the 1960s and centres on the "language and experience of young people". Howie sees these two models as often "in contradistinction" to each other (170), and is aware of the positioning of such approaches in the classroom: "Student readers are not simply trained in ethics; rather, their lived experience of the classroom is ethically implicated and has ethical significance" (170).

Thus English has, as a discipline, undergone a range of significant changes during the period that we are looking into. Another example of this is the spread of 'levels' and the shift in modes for teaching English. Where once there might have been only one English subject on offer – setting a universal standard for English studies, over time – English has become split into different levels, most often three or four, designating different degrees of difficulty but also a commitment to different types of texts and learning activities. The highest levels of Year 12 English – for example, 3 Unit English in New South Wales and English Studies in South Australia – expose students to traditional literary genres (novels, plays, poetry) and tend to have a strong commitment to teaching canonical authors such as Shakespeare, Austen and Dickens. Other types of English tend to interpret literature more broadly and the result is often that students read fewer novels and a greater number of shorter contemporary texts – for instance contemporary fiction and non-fiction, young adult literature, film, television programs and, more recently, internet media. As Patterson notes (when discussing the NSW English curriculum), the differences that underlie different modes or levels of English relate to students' need to demonstrate particular skills and knowledge about literature. Patterson writes:

> The outcomes of the English (Advanced) course incorporate and extend beyond the English (Standard) course outcomes. It is especially through the unique section of the English (Advanced) course that students have the opportunity to demonstrate knowledge, skills and understanding beyond the outcomes established for the English (Standard) course. The English (Standard) course emphasises reflection on texts and demonstration of the effectiveness of texts for different audiences and purposes. The emphasis of the English (Advanced) course is on the analysis and evaluation of texts and the ways they are valued in their contexts. ("Teaching literature" 314)

Certain pedagogical agendas, ideologies, values and also politics underlie these decisions about how to deliver Literature and which texts to choose as teaching and learning tools. Such decisions are often based on the research of scholars and the experience of teachers, and are influenced by educational objectives and expected learning outcomes. English studies need to "do" or provide some core knowledge for students, and most commonly the expected skills are reading, interpretation and critical thinking, and writing skills. Arguably, many different types of texts could be deployed in the classroom to achieve these learning outcomes. The choice of texts is always significant, and the appearance or omission of canonical texts is often an intriguing and controversial issue.

The ALIAS database allows us to see what the most frequently taught English/Literature texts set for matriculation or Year 12 study across the Australian states were from the period 1945 to 2005. Over the 60-year period, the most popular (most frequently set as core texts) books were (in this order): *Hamlet*, *The Crucible*, *Wuthering Heights*, *Tess of the d'Urbervilles*, *Pride and Prejudice*, *The Adventures of Huckleberry Finn*, *King Lear*, *Othello*, *Macbeth* and *Antony and Cleopatra*. This selection of texts, when grouped together, has a particular flavour: "classic" works from English-language literatures emerging from Britain and the USA. Dominant themes include coming of age and/or moving towards knowledge. Tragedy also features strongly, and inevitably Shakespeare dominates the list.

Hardy makes 249 appearances on the syllabuses of the participating states, across 12 different texts (though three editions of the poems mean that there are actually nine works).

Table 13.1. Prevalence of Hardy's Writing on State Curricula (ALIAS database)

Work	Number of times on the syllabus	Earliest appearance	Latest appearance	States
Tess of the d'Urbervilles	41	1966 (SA)	2005 (SA, Tas, Vic)	NSW, SA, Tas, Vic, WA
The Mayor of Casterbridge	47	1949 (WA)	2005 (WA)	SA, Tas, Vic, WA
Jude the Obscure	4	1968 (SA)	1979 (Vic)	SA, Vic
Far From the Madding Crowd	16	1946 (WA)	1995 (Tas)	SA, Tas, Vic, WA
Hardy's poems (different editions)	22	1951 (WA)	2000 (Vic)	SA, Vic, WA
The Return of the Native	16	1947 (Vic and WA)	1974 (SA)	NSW, SA, Vic, WA
The Trumpet-Major	6	1945 (WA)	1961 (SA)	NSW, SA, Tas, WA
Under the Greenwood Tree	15	1945 (SA)	1959 (SA)	SA only
The Woodlanders	5	1972 (Vic)	1987 (Tas and Vic)	Tas, Vic

Table 13.1 reveals that New South Wales didn't set many Hardy novels in the period for which the data exists, constraining itself to only *Tess*, *The Return of the Native* and *The Trumpet-Major*. While *Tess* is set 41 times in that state during the period, sometimes more than once in the same year on its different courses, the other two books were set only three times combined. Meanwhile other states enjoyed a greater diversity of Hardy's work, though *Tess* still reigns supreme among them.

The earliest recorded appearance of *Tess* in the Australian curriculum is in Victoria in 1955;[3] it appears 14 times between then and 2005, though in different courses (English Literature, English, and Literature [Part B]). *Tess* is first recorded in the New South Wales curriculum in 1967 and is on the English curriculum more often than not until 2000.[4] It wasn't featured between 2001 and the end of the database data in 2005; we can only speculate upon why but perhaps it has reappeared more frequently on university subjects such as ours as a consequence. *Tess* made its first appearance in South Australia in 1966, featured on the syllabus there eight times, and is still listed at the end of the database data in 2005. Tasmania first features the book on its 1968 syllabus and it appears 15 times between then and 2005 (where it features consistently from 1998 to 2005). In Western Australia it appears 15 times between its first appearance in 1971 and its last in 1997. Yiannakis notes that between 1991 and 2005, *Tess* was "the most regularly listed novel" around the country for both English and Literature reading lists and the "second most popular novel", following Joseph Conrad's *Heart of Darkness*, for Literature (108). These facts seem to confirm our earlier remarks that the teaching of Literature in Australia has involved diverse and changing content. However, the recurrence of *Tess* is quite notable and marks it as a text that has often been invested in to teach students something valuable about literature.

If we look in particular at the decade of 1985–1995, during which time we co-authors studied senior secondary English, *Tess* is still the third most popular novel across the curricula after *Wuthering Heights* and *Great Expectations*.[5] A decade later, 1995–2005, the more general picture starts

---

3   Peter Widdowson reports that *Tess* makes its first appearance on the UK English curriculum in 1961, pointing out that "(for many years the novel was proscribed by the Vatican Index – which may help to account for its only recent provenance as an 'acceptable' text in schools) and then intermittently up till about 1979" (82).

4   *Tess* appears on the syllabus during 20 of the years during this time and is not featured in 14 of the years.

5   The full list is, in order: *Hamlet, Wuthering Heights, The Crucible, Great Expectations, Tess of the D'Urbervilles, Antony and Cleopatra, A Streetcar Named Desire, Heart of Darkness, Pride and Prejudice* and *Summer of the Seventeenth Doll*.

to change. While canonical texts formed the centrepiece of English during the 1940s through to the 1980s, as new English subjects emerged in the 1990s and 2000s different texts emerged in the curriculum to challenge the centrality of canonical literatures. In particular, this period saw a rise in the representation of Australian authors in the Australian curriculum, and a rise in the number of contemporary texts. This is in line with changing notions of Australian textuality. The Australian Bicentenary of 1988 plays a role here, as does the growing mobilisation of a national literature in school contexts. *Tess* remains in the top five, and is the second most common novel on the syllabus after *Cloudstreet*, and is the fourth text, with 35 appearances on collected syllabuses in the period. The top 10 texts during this period are: *Cloudstreet, Diving for Pearls, Hamlet, Tess of the d'Urbervilles, Othello, A Doll's House, The Crucible, King Lear, Selected Poems by Gwen Harwood* and *The Penguin Henry Lawson Short Stories*.[6] So, even with changing politics and agendas around inclusions and exclusions in the English curriculum, *Tess* remains (alongside Shakespeare) as a representative of the "traditional" canon.

Tess in a Catholic classroom

> Tess *seems to appear in my adult life in every decade, when personal situations and learning contexts have affected my response to the narrative. My first encounter with the novel and its ill-fated heroine was at a strict Catholic girls' school in 1980s Adelaide. It is relevant to describe the learning environment of this school to explain how I formed an understanding of the novel's themes and characters. I recollect that learning was driven by a confusing mix of guilt, female empowerment and rote learning. Year 12 English was taught by a militant nun who was the Principal of the senior school at the time. In retrospect, the nuns had their own version of feminism and were rigorous academic*

Focusing on the decade of 1985–1995, a decade that covers our senior secondary school and undergraduate study for the most part, we note that *Tess* appears frequently across the dates: in NSW in 1987 (2 unit and 3 unit), 1988 (2 unit and 3 unit), 1989 (2 unit and 2A general course, 3 unit) 1990 (3 unit, 2 unit and 2A) and 1991 (2A general course). In South Australia, it was on the English P syllabus in 1985, 1986, 1987, 1988, 1989, 1990, 1991, 1992, 1993, 1994, 1995. In Tasmania, it appears in 1992 and 1993. In Victoria, it appears in our decade of investigation only in 1987. In Western Australia in 1989, 1990, 1991, 1992, 1993, 1994 and 1995.

6 What this frequency analysis reveals is that there is much more diversity in novel titles than in play titles.

teachers, but their methods of teaching were often driven by Catholic moral discipline and discouraged individuals students' questioning and interpretation – the Personal Growth model was nipped in the bud, so to speak! The school itself seemed to encourage class-based female empowerment (if you're bright, study law) and conventional materialism (marry the lawyer or doctor, and you will be right), rather like a modern (Catholic) version of Henry Handel Richardson's PLC in The Getting of Wisdom. *Of course, this is my memory of it and it could be tainted by subsequent life experiences – relationships, novels I have since read, feminist theory, late motherhood.*

Such a middle-class Catholic school was expected to achieve outstanding Matric results. Extensive worksheets invited close readings of the texts and the periods in which they were written, and this was a valuable part of their teaching. These worksheets helped to consolidate our knowledge of Hardy's world view, the Victorian period and our understanding of plot, theme and character. They were presented as a series of finite facts and there was no opportunity to elaborate on Hardy's critique of Christianity in the novel.

Sister had a pragmatic agenda in her classes – students were to learn key quotes for the exams and this would provide a solid basis for good academic results. These quotes were selected by Sister – I don't remember her asking students for their suggestions. We thumped them out on our desks and repeated them several times in each class. One could question the method used to select these quotes – was it to honour what she saw as the essential themes of these works, or to enhance certain moral teachings that the school endorsed? Was literature then used as a mirror to our own lives, warning us to adopt certain social and gender codes if we wished to keep our agency? Twenty-six years later, a call on social media revealed that many of my classmates still remembered these quotes: Tess was "a fresh and virginal daughter of nature"; "a mere vessel of emotion untinctured by experience"; "Beauty lay not in the thing, but in what the thing symbolized"; "'It was to be'. There lay the pity of it." Beauty, purity, fate, emotion, nature ... there could have been a good opportunity to delve into the messiness of female adolescence here, but the teacher didn't allow for such discussions.

Older scholars of the school (my mother's generation) told me that they were not allowed to study Tess *because it had been banned on the Vatican index. Widdowson (82) confirms that the ban wasn't lifted in the UK until 1961. I don't remember an open discussion about the rape/seduction scene, but I do remember that* Tess *was used as a warning fable about our sexuality. My memory of senior English classrooms, especially the classes on* Tess, *appear in my mind alongside more overt warnings about sex in "compulsory" sessions on "saying no" and avoiding pregnancy. There was also an emphasis on Hardy's subtitle, "A Pure Woman, Faithfully Presented", implying that her gender was "part of nature" and her moral values were violated.*

Eleven years later, I read Tess *again in order to prepare a lecture for the Matric English Revision conference at the University of Adelaide. My reading of the novel was tinged with more than a bit of emotional confusion in a difficult life moment. My school notes had emphasised Tess's purity as something to be idealised and told the story of a violated victim. Much of the interpretation was given to us by the teachers, rather than guiding us into looking at it from various perspectives. My re-reading of* Tess *yielded a very strong response: I saw Hardy's presentation of a misogynistic society – the narrator's objectification of Tess, the erotic gaze, the presentation of a woman with little to no agency. I found the notion of "purity" to be an offensive value. I offered the Matric students a feminist reading of the text and compared Tess's situation to those of heroines from contemporary popular culture. I asked the students to think about Tess's situation in terms of the Victorian society that Hardy was portraying, but also contrast his portrait of Tess with representations of heroines today. Whereas previously my reading of* Tess *was restricted to "prepping for the exam", my re-reading of the novel was affected by personal experience, a growing sense of identity and subsequent reading in literature and theory.* (Alice Healy-Ingram)

There's something about *Tess*

Tess has long been taught; but the database unfortunately cannot reveal the different approaches to *Tess* in the classroom. This is a limitation of this discussion. As Patterson comments, an analysis of exam papers does not adequately reflect "the ways in which teachers interpret the curriculum and syllabus documents or the subject more broadly" ("Teaching literature" 317). However, an analysis of the exam questions does reveal something of the perceived cultural and pedagogical value of *Tess*. As a novel, what is *Tess* thought to do or show to our students, both in terms of literary skills and knowledge, and perhaps also cultural work? What might teachers hope to achieve by including this novel in their teaching?

Looking at exam questions is useful because they reveal another set of relationships to the text in question. English pedagogies have changed through the years, yet the exam questions for Year 12 English Studies are suggestive of a much slower uptake of the changing agenda for teaching literature. Drawing on Hunter's work (1997), Annette Patterson analyses the differences in commentaries across exam papers in three states, suggesting that they offer very different uses of the "traditional territory covered by English: ethics, aesthetics and rhetoric" ("Teaching literature" 314). She speaks of the more recent questioning of the model that holds literary texts as the most ideal location for developing students' engagement with these three areas: "in recent years the emphasis has shifted to an engagement with 'real-world' social issues and a focus on social and cultural 'contexts'" (314). She claims that this debate about "good literature versus popular texts, critical theory versus functional literacy, and relativism (particularly in relation to 'postmodernism') versus reasoned debate" is apparent in the examination papers and commentary (314).

Looking at the questions set for English examinations over the decades covered by the ALIAS database, we can identify three pedagogical themes:

General questions asking for literary evaluation

From the 1940s through 1960s the trend across the states was to ask general evaluative question in exams that could be applied to different set texts.[7] By the 1970s, more text-specific questions were being asked that allowed for a stronger assessment focus on the particulars of the text and provided a more clear indication of why the text was chosen – what knowledge about literature it was expected to impart. We can speculate on why this shift occurred; as literary studies established itself differently over time, as certain texts became more canonically entrenched and new texts were emerging strongly (for instance, feminist and postcolonial literatures), literary scholars became increasingly aware and more reflexive in their scholarship on the diversity of literature and its multifarious cultural, political and literary functions.

---

7   "Make lists", "which writers excel … ?" or questions about "effectiveness". There were also a variety of general questions around literary subgenres, such as tragedy (which could be applied generally to different texts on the syllabus). Questions about a text's relationship to "life" were also very common during this period, including questions asking for students' view on texts and issues.

Questions about tragedy and fate and how these work in *Tess*

This was an enduring approach to teaching *Tess*, as is evident from the exams. For example, in WA in 1975 this was an exam question for the subject English Literature:

> Early in *Tess of the d'Urbervilles* the following dialogue takes place:
>
> 'Did you say the stars were worlds, Tess?'
>
> 'Yes.'
>
> 'All like ours?'
>
> 'I don't know, but I think so. They sometimes seem to be like the apples on our stubbard-tree. Most of them splendid and sound – a few blighted.'
>
> 'Which do we live on – a splendid one or a blighted one?'
>
> 'A blighted one.'
>
> Discuss the significance of this in relation to Hardy's purpose in *Tess*. (Western Australia. Tertiary Admissions Examination 1975 English 6)

In New South Wales in the 1970s the following questions were asked:

> "Few people will deny the terrible dreariness of the tale, which, except for a few hours spent with cows has not a gleam of sunshine anywhere." Do you consider this a relevant criticism of *Tess of the d'Urbervilles*?[8] (Department of Education NSW HSC Examination 1970. English Second Level, Second Paper 3)

and,

> "There is no room for Tess in the shabby world into which she was born." What light does this comment throw on Hardy's presentation of Tess? (Department of Education NSW HSC Examination 1980. English 3 Unit Course, First Paper 5)

Such questions allowed for discussions not only of tragedy and fate but also class, religion, and gender.

---

[8] Q.D. Leavis quotes this as being from a "Saturday Reviewer" in her article, "Hardy and Criticism" (1943), republished in *A Selection from Scrutiny* Volume 1. Compiled by F.R. Leavis, Cambridge University Press, 1968: 295.

Questions about characters and their experience of in/justice in the novel

> Hardy added the subtitle *A Pure Woman* to *Tess of the d'Urbervilles*. What does this phrase reveal of the author's attitude towards the characters and events of his novel? (Department of Education NSW HSC Examination 1975. English Second Level, Second Paper 4)

and,

> Who is to blame for Tess's difficulties? Argue your point of view. (Board of Studies NSW 1990 HSC Examination English 2 Unit General 1990 2; incidentally a very similar question was asked in 1995)

and,

> In *Tess of the d'Urbervilles* there is punishment but no justice. Discuss. (Board of Studies NSW HSC Examination 2000 English 2/3 (Common) 6).

Through the formulation of exam questions we can see something of the changing trends and agendas influencing the teaching and learning of English. Literary texts such as *Tess* are highly amenable to ambiguities in style and subject and to changing emphases in teaching literature, and contain such complexity that teachers can focus on practically any aspect of literary studies. This is a valuable commodity when teaching English and it allows teachers not only to focus on a particular trend but also to remain agnostic to that trend, that is, to teach close reading and traditional elements of literary studies in balance with theoretical approaches to understanding novels. This demands a more complex and nuanced reading. Recent scholarship has been preoccupied with the skills, values and knowledge often associated with English studies at high school level. For example, to what extent is the primary role of English to share ideas about ethics, aesthetics and rhetoric? As we have mentioned above, more recently English has been tasked with connecting students to their social world but there is significant crossover between the two approaches, creating a mutually beneficial relationship between aesthetics and a sociological approach to literary studies. The exam questions on *Tess* that we have looked at confirm that there has always been a mutually beneficial approach to English that brings in both ethics/aesthetics/rhetoric and the social/political contexts for reading literature.

The exam questions reveal ways the sanctioned interpretations, or interpretation strategies, opened up the text for students to enter and inhabit. The questions required students to apply knowledge about the characteristics of tragedy, most commonly studied, for students, in the works of Shakespeare and then to apply that to other works of literature, genres, and formats and from there into studies of culture more generally. And it is in this work that the ALIAS database and its broader project can make an intervention.

Conclusion

> Tess *is an important novel, but it is also a "difficult" novel. Its difficulty may be academic, but it may also be personal or moral. Our experience, of late, teaching university Literature in the 2010–2015 classroom is that our students are not very experienced readers and may not bring a diversity of reading experiences into their studies.*[9] *This impacts on how we approach* Tess; *there are limits to what we can achieve, but these limits also motivate us to take students to a challenging place with their reading and interpretation.*
>
> *We are discovering that one of the enduring (though not endearing) features of our students' literary analysis is the curious notion of "relatability". When we asked students to offer a preliminary or general response to a novel, their response so often includes whether or not they "related" to or understood the characters or events in the novel, or whether or not they "liked" the characters. This is particularly challenging when we introduce students to pre-twentieth-century literatures (especially those students who have read mostly twentieth and twenty-first-century texts in South Australia's English Studies).* Tess's *world is not their world and we want them to understand the characters and events regardless of whether they relate to them, and to comprehend and be able to talk/write about Hardy's literary techniques with confidence and sophistication, even if the language and style is unfamiliar.*
>
> *So when we taught* Tess *in our third-year capstone subject, we were surprised and impressed with the students' commitment. This was the final book for the semester; fatigue was setting in, and the*

---

9   Douglas, Kate, and Tully Barnett. "Teaching traumatic life narratives: Affect, witnessing, and ethics." *Antipodes* 28.1 (2014): 46–61; Poletti, Anna, et al. "The affects of not reading: Hating characters, being bored, feeling stupid". *Arts and Humanities in Higher Education* October (2014).

break was just around the corner. The students had struggled with other nineteenth-century novels, but likely developed as literary scholars because of this struggle. But there was something about Tess *that captured the students' minds and energies. Those who had been quiet all semester contributed to discussion. The debates around heroes and villains were thoughtful and informed by evidence and mature perspectives. Students offered feminist and Marxist perspectives without even knowing it, so we were able to bring these theories to the table through secondary readings and general theoretical readings. Influenced by contemporary perspectives and ideologies, the students struggled to accept Hardy's notions of fate and determinism in favour of explanations along class and gender lines. Mature-aged students and younger students alike were vehemently defensive of Tess and equally angry at Angel Clare and Alec d'Urberville.*

The students' literary analysis was also highly competent – being willing to engage in close textual analysis because they understood the relationships between thematic and theoretical-based analysis, and textual and contextual analysis. Tess *is a text that is conducive to making such connections and we can only speculate why. It seems to us that it is a text that allows us to exercise many skills and much knowledge relevant to literary studies all at once.* (Kate Douglas)

What happens when a text written in a certain period is read in very different times and places and studied in classroom settings? The late Victorian society that Hardy depicts is a far cry from Australia in the late twentieth century, in which we three authors first studied the novel, and the early twenty-first century, in which we set the book for our students to read. This is a society in which significant and ongoing social shifts including industrialisation alter forever the relationship between individuals and the land, class changes cause conflicts between old and new money, both at the expense of the impoverished, and where notions of gender and the changing role of women are caught up in the above issues of class and land like wheat in the threshing machine at Flintcomb-Ash. Here women are represented as internal to the natural world, and yet at the same time, they have increasing access to education. These ambiguities and contradictions offer a rich opportunity for modern readers to locate their interpretations in the context of an ever-changing world. Furthermore, the network of interpretation alive in reading the book in one's teen years is very different to that at work in one's forties, and it has been the pleasure of working on this paper to discover some of the intricacies of that statement.

What is it about Tess Durbeyfield that makes her story so amenable to senior secondary education? The novel's presence on the curriculum in many states consistently, for the most part, between 1945 and 2005, as evidenced by the ALIAS database, is quite extraordinary. Whether it is the abundance of symbolism in the novel to be unpacked in the reading or the classroom or whether it is the challenges that beset Tess Durbeyfield as she grows into womanhood in a changing England, it is hard to say. Above all, *Tess* is teachable. Coursework designers are always looking for the texts that are important not only for their positions in the canon but for what work they can be put to in a classroom and how the students – themselves an incredibly diverse set of persons with very different life experiences – will respond to it, so that syllabus formation is equally about determining a canon determining appropriate vehicles for the learning of literary concepts.

The ALIAS database is a tool for teaching and learning. It reflects back and reflects forward as we navigate cycles of teaching. Can *Tess*'s continual presence on the curriculum lists for senior English across the nation and across decades be accounted for by patterns of passivity in the text, allowing for its interpretation to grow and change with the learning outcomes of the curriculum or the theory trends of the day? Perhaps *Tess*'s enduring presence has something to do with how passively the book resists appropriation. Is it that *Tess* is a text that embraces ambiguity, serving as a blank slate upon which various readings can be placed? In this way, the ALIAS database opens up many more questions than it answers and that is its gift to literary studies and to the scholarship of teaching and learning. And as our daughters enter various levels of education from kindergarten to Year 12, and as some of our students become postgraduate students and teachers of undergraduates or teachers of secondary English, our continued fascination with and feeling for *Tess* takes on new dimensions.

Works Cited

Analysis of Literature in Australian Schools Database (ALIAS). www.australiancommonreader.com/syllabus. Web. 28 March 2015.

Board of Studies NSW. 1990 Higher School Certificate Examination English 2 Unit General Responses to Literature. Board of Studies. Government Printer. NSW, 1995. Print.

——. Higher School Certificate Examination 2000 English 2/3 Unit (Common) Paper 2: Poetry-Fiction-Drama. Board of Studies. Government Printer. NSW. 2000. Print.

Boomer, Garth, Margaret Gill, and Ian Reid. "The crisis in English studies". *English in Australia*, 49.2 (2014): 35–43. Web. 28 Mar 15.

Boumelha, Penny. "Introduction". *Thomas Hardy's* Tess of the d'Urbervilles. Eds. Juliet Grindle and Simon Gatrell. Oxford: Oxford University Press, 2008. xii–xxvii. Print.

Brady, Kristin. "Thomas Hardy and matters of gender". *The Cambridge Companion to Thomas Hardy*. Ed. Dale Kramer. Cambridge: Cambridge University Press, 1999. 93–111. Print.

Brown, James S. and Scott D. Yarborough. *A Practical Introduction to Literary Study*. Upper Saddle River: Pearson, 2005. Print.

Davis, William A., Jr. "Hardy and the 'deserted wife' question: The failure of the law in *Tess of the d'Urbervilles*". *Colby Quarterly* 29.1 (1993): 5–19. Print.

Department of Education NSW. Higher School Certificate Examination, 1970. English Second Level. Second Paper: Drama and Novel. Board of Senior School Studies. Government Printer. NSW. 1970. Print.

——. Higher School Certificate Examination, 1975. English Second Level. Second Paper: Drama and Novel. Board of Senior School Studies. Government Printer. NSW. 1975. Print.

——. Higher School Certificate Examination, 1980. English 3 Unit Course. First Paper: Poetry-Novel-Drama. Board of Senior School Studies. Government Printer. NSW. 1980. Print.

Dolin, Tim. "Melodrama, vision, and modernity: *Tess of the d'Urbervilles*". *A Companion to Thomas Hardy*. Ed. Keith Wilson. Malden, Mass.: Blackwell Publishing Ltd, 2009. 328–344. Print.

——. "Reading history and literary history: Australian perspectives". *Modern Australian Criticism and Theory*. Eds. David Carter and Wang Guanglin, Qingdao, China: China Ocean University Press, 2010. 127–138. Print.

Douglas, Kate, and Tully Barnett. "Teaching traumatic life narratives: Affect, witnessing, and ethics". *Antipodes* 28.1 (2014): 46–61. Web. 22 Feb. 2016.

Gelder, Ken. "Proximate reading: Australian literature in transnational reading frameworks". *Journal of the Association for the Study of Australian Literature* (JASAL). Special Issue: Common Readers. 2010. Web. 22 Feb. 2016. <www.nla.gov.au/openpublish/index.php/jasal/article/view/1535/2082 >

Hardy, Thomas. *Tess of the d'Urbervilles*. Ed. Juliet Grindle and Simon Gatrell. Oxford: Oxford University Press, 2008. Print.

Hardy, Thomas. "Candour in English fiction". New Review, January, 1890, 15–21. Web. <http://people.stfx.ca/rnemesva/hardy/candour.html>. 7 Feb 2016.

Heffernan, James A. W. "'Cruel persuasion': Seduction, temptation and agency in Hardy's *Tess*". Thomas Hardy Yearbook 35 (2005): 5–18. Print.

Homer, David. "The teaching of literature". K.D. Watson and R.D. Eagleson (Eds.) *English in Secondary Schools: Today and tomorrow*. Ashfield: English Teachers Association of NSW, 1977. 342–360. Print.

Howie, Mark. "Authenticity was never really the question". *Literary Praxis*. 2011. 169–187. Print.

Kincaid, James. "You did not come: Absence, death and eroticism in *Tess*". *Sex and Death in Victorian Literature*. Ed. Regina Barreca. Bloomington and Indianapolis: Indiana University Press (1990): 9–31. Print.

Leavis, Q.D. 'Hardy and criticism". 1943. *A Selection from* Scrutiny *Volume 1*. Ed. F.R. Leavis. Cambridge: Cambridge University Press, 1968. 291–298. Print.

Lovesey, Oliver. "Reconstructing *Tess*". *SEL: Studies in English Literature, 1500–1900* 43.4 (2003): 913–38. Web. 22 Feb 2016.

Patterson, Annette. "Teaching literature in Australia: Examining and reviewing senior English". *Changing English: Studies in culture and education* 15:3 (2008): 311–322. Web. 15 March 2015.

Rooney, Ellen. "'A little more than persuading': *Tess* and the subject of sexual violence". *Rape and Representation*. Ed. Lynn A. Higgins and Brenda Silver. New York: Columbia University Press, 1991. Print.

Watson, Ken. *English Teaching in Perspective*. Sydney: St Clair. 1981. Print.

Western Australia. Tertiary Admissions Examination, 1975. English Literature. n.p. WA. 1975. Print.

Widdowson, Peter. *Hardy in History: A study in literary sociology*. London and New York: Routledge. 1989. Print.

Yiannakis, John. "A possible literary canon in upper school English literature in various Australian states, 1945–2005". *Issues in Educational Research* 24.1 (2014): 98–113. Web. 15 March 2015.

Chapter Fourteen

MODERNISM AND MODERNIST CRITICISM IN AUSTRALIAN SENIOR SECONDARY ENGLISH

Tim Dolin

Introduction

The upper-school Literature classroom is often characterised as a battleground between two opposed critical practices: on one side, text-centred close reading; on the other, reader-centred cultural critique. These practices, and the longstanding antagonism between them, are associated with specific historical moments, critical movements and theoretical approaches: Anglo-American New Criticism, reader-response theory, and cultural studies respectively. Whenever close reading is invoked, so too is a contentious and fractious history of disciplinary struggle that saw a conservative imperialistic hermeneutics supplanted by a progressive postcolonial hermeneutics in many Australian schools about three decades ago. The term "close reading" was coined simultaneously with the term "New Criticism" by John Crowe Ransom in 1941 (Ransom), and since then the practice of close reading – "stylistic analysis in a formalistic mode rooted in aesthetic appreciation of technique" (Leitch 46) – has been intimately associated with a North American theoretical worldview and pedagogic practice. Ransom, Cleanth Brooks, Allen Tate and Robert Penn Warren belonged to "a group with its own distinctive intellectual roots in the American South" (Menand and Rainey 7). The "gradual establishment of the New Criticism as a powerful critical orthodoxy within American universities, [was] epitomised by Brooks's move from Louisiana State University to Yale in 1947" (7). Within a decade New Criticism was dominant, but the success of its "increasingly ossified formalism ... as represented by W.K. Wimsatt (*The Verbal Icon* was published in 1954)" (7) in the large liberal arts programs of the 1950s and 60s (where students needed only to bring a short poem to class) was soon its undoing.

There are significant differences between American New Criticism and what is better known (and more often vilified) in Australia as Leavisism, but they are frequently bundled together as Anglo-American New Criticism. Both were associated with close reading, called "practical criticism" in Britain, but American New Criticism's signature disregard for context (the main reason for its portability) was completely at odds with Leavisite cultural criticism, which was effectively an engaged critique of the here and now, and fed into Marxist cultural materialism on the one hand and British cultural studies on the other. (The Birmingham School was started by left-Leavisites.) What both share, however, is an origin in modernist literature and critical practice: T.S. Eliot first of all, then I.A. Richards and William Empson at Cambridge in the 1920s. F.R. Leavis founded the *Scrutiny* enterprise on the cultural critique contained in Richards's empirical *Practical Criticism* (1929). In this book Richards reports on an experiment in which Cambridge students were set to evaluate and interpret 13 poems, some of them insignificant, with all information about author and context removed. The aim of the experiment was to show that students were not willing or able to risk interpreting or evaluating what they read but relied slavishly on the insights and judgements of external critical authorities. What the New Critics took from Richards was in fact mediated through his student Empson, who developed the idea that "form is meaning" and that literature is "ultimately metaphorical and symbolic" (Eliot 1104). What resulted was a form of critical practice in which readers were urged to inspect texts very closely, bracketing them off from their surrounding political, social and cultural contexts and analysing them as self-sufficient verbal artifacts that cannot be paraphrased. Literary language was held to be radically specific and characterised by complex semantic relationships and formal tensions and paradoxes, and by ambiguity and irony. New Critical readings rigorously subordinated content and theme to form, and were hypersensitive to textual repetitions and patterns, multiple meanings, puns, etymologies, figurative language (especially metaphor) and literary allusion. Most of all, they sought to reconcile any complexity and irresolution with a sure sense of the unity and wholeness of the text.

Modernist poetry, the highest expression in literature of the autonomy of the avant-garde, was a touchstone for the mission – openly militant in Leavis, more subtle in New Criticism – to "undo in students of English the effects of the almost universal dissociation of sensibility" (Samson 77) by training them in close reading. In large part, New Criticism remade literature in the image of modernist literature, although there are dangers in assimilating them – treating New Criticism "as if it were merely a more systematic, more philosophical, or more academic articulation of formalist undercurrents within modernism" (Menand and Rainey 3). As Brooks wrote in *The Well-Wrought Urn* (1947), the question of "what poetry communicates, if anything, has been forced upon us by the advent of 'modern' poetry" with its special interpretive challenges for readers. But in truth, "modern poetry .... communicates whatever any other poetry communicates" and it is "difficult for the reader simply because so few people, relatively speaking, are accustomed to reading poetry as poetry" (Brooks 67). And Leavis remade the criticism of modern culture by counterposing poetic discourse to the rationalist technologico-Benthamist discourse of efficiency and instrumentalism in industrial modernity (also a concern of Ransom, Warren, and Brooks). Like Eliot before him, Leavis's keynote is "mordant disapproval" and a missionary dedication to criticising modern culture "for its lack of a coherent moral ground, and for the idiosyncratic and makeshift value systems it produced to compensate for that lack" (Menand "Eliot" 17).

The rise and decline of New Criticism coincides with the rise and decline of literary modernism, and the significance of modernism in the development of pedagogy in English studies cannot be underestimated. Yet it has been. Consider Ian Hunter's influential thesis about criticism and schooling, for example. The primary function of close reading in school education, Hunter wrote, was originally to deny students "immediate instructional or pleasurable access to literature" (Hunter "Aesthetics" 357). Literary works were essentially devices "in a practice of self-problematization" in which the density and difficulty of literary discourse, converted into the "instituted incomprehensibility" of close reading, put into question individuals' "'ordinary' relation to all spheres of existence" and reconstituted them as "sites of aesthetic incompletion" (358). This was above all "an ethical technique" aimed at compelling individuals to experience themselves as divided or alienated. Significantly, the term Hunter uses for this subjective state is one he borrows from T.S. Eliot: the "dissociated sensibility" (351). For Eliot, however, the dissociation of sensibility – the abandonment or loss of a uniquely poetic form of thought, uniting intellect and feeling, some time in the late seventeenth century in England – had precisely the opposite effect of inducing the poetic *facility* of Gray and Collins, Tennyson and Browning. To overcome it, modern poetry was obliged to become difficult again, Eliot contended, in the way that Donne had been difficult: to reject the allure of poetic refinement and be "more and more comprehensive, more allusive, more indirect, in order to force, to dislocate if necessary, language into … meaning" (Eliot 1100). The debt to Eliot is not explicitly acknowledged by Hunter; understandably, perhaps, since it would relocate aesthetic difficulty as a technique of subject formation from German Romantic thought to twentieth-century literary modernism, and backwards via Eliot to the sixteenth century. The designation of difficulty as the chief characteristic of literary discourse helped to secure Literary Studies as a professional academic discipline: "the difficulties of modernism brought criticism to the fore as an important source of assistance for the 'plain reader'" (Hickman and McIntyre 106). Modernism, with its unique demands on trained readers, became essential to the emergence of English as an autonomous university discipline, and ultimately, in the promise of producing critical readers of culture, to the continuing centrality of English in the school curriculum.

This chapter re-examines historical narratives of modernism and modernist criticism in Australia, and traces out some lines of influence between European modernism and Australian school English that have become faint with time. Most of the historical evidence suggests that school English did not really embrace modernism until the second half of the 1960s, when Australian modernism was moving into the mainstream – not only in the paintings of Arthur Boyd and Sidney Nolan or the novels and plays of Patrick White but in cinema, fashion, graphic design and the design of buildings, appliances and so forth. Many of the leading modernist texts (and especially Australian modernist texts) first appeared on upper-school syllabuses at this time, and the theoretical precepts and critical practices of the *Scrutiny* group and American New Criticism began filtering down from the universities. If this history sounds familiar, it is because it closely follows the familiar narrative of Australia's belatedness in taking up modernism itself (see Williams, Carter, Stephen et al. *Modern*, Stephen et al. *Documents*). The object of this chapter is to sketch out a context for thinking about modernist criticism/s in the plural, in the same way that we now think about multiple modernisms.

Modernism/s and Australian modernity

For a long time modernism was regarded singularly as an invention of the metropolitan centre: a product of Euro-American modernity exported to the rest of the world along with modern institutions and social structures, modern ideas and forms of knowledge, and modern identities and subjectivities. Even then it was dogged by problems of definition and demarcation. Was it a period or a style, or both? If a period, then *when*? If a style, then *what*? Answers to those question took three main forms. First, a list of names:

> a body of major writers (James, Conrad, Proust, Mann, Gide, Kafka, Svevo, Joyce, Musil, Faulkner in fiction; Strindberg, Pirandello, Wedekind, Brecht in drama; Mallarmé, Yeats, Eliot, Pound, Rilke, Apollinaire, Stevens in poetry) whose works are aesthetically radical, contain striking technical innovation, emphasize spatial or "fugal" as opposed to chronological form, tend towards ironic modes, and involve a certain "dehumanization of art." (Bradbury 145)

Second, a list of formal features:

> Modernist art is ... experimental, formally complex, elliptical, contains elements of decreation as well as creation, and tends to associate notions of the artist's freedom from realism, materialism, traditional genre and form, with notions of cultural apocalypse and disaster. (145)

Modernism can be recognised by its

> fragmenting unities (unities of character or plot or pictorial space or lyric form), the use of mythic paradigms, the refusal of norms of beauty, [and] the willingness to make radical linguistic experiment, all often inspired by the resolve (in Eliot's phrase) to startle and disturb the public. (Levenson *Companion* 3)

And third, genealogical claims: when and where modernism started, what its origins and antecedents were, and whether or not it has ended (see, for example, Levenson *Genealogy*; S. Smith). Getting the genealogy right has always been imperative since modernism set itself apart from other cultural periods by the very violence of its rupture with the artistic past and its traditions, conventions, aims, concerns and aesthetic forms. It was about starting anew: it was the art of the cultural condition of the modern, "in which the seemingly absolute necessity of innovation becomes a primary fact of life, work, and thought" (Terry Smith; Turner).

Increasingly since the 1980s, however, the view of modernism as a branching line of descent from Paris in the nineteenth century to the rest of Europe, thence to New York and out to the wider world with the twentieth-century spread of modernisation, has been challenged by a new view. Modernisms are stylistically diverse and variably occurring "responses to problems posed by the conditions of modernity" (Whitworth 3). For T.J. Clark modernity means contingency: "It points to a social order which has turned from worship of ancestors and past authorities to a pursuit of a projected future – of goods, pleasures, freedoms, forms of control over nature, or infinities of information. This process goes along with a great emptying and sanitizing of the imagination" (Clark 7). Weber's phrase for this, borrowed from Schiller, was "the disenchantment of the world". Secularisation, Clark goes on, is "a nice technical word" for the blankness that is our experience of this disenchantment: "It means specialization and abstraction; social life driven by a calculus of large-scale statistical chances, with everyone accepting (or resenting) a high level of risk; [and] … the de-skilling of everyday life [leading to an] available, invasive, haunting expertise" (7). For Clark, its cause is "the accumulation of capital, and the spread of capitalist markets into more and more of the world and the texture of human dealings" (7). The "truly new, and disorienting, character of modernity", he writes, "is its seemingly being driven by merely material, statistical, tendential, 'economic' considerations", producing "a new form of life, in which all previous notions of belief and sociability have been scrambled" and which is "ruled – and obscurely felt to be ruled – by sheer concatenation of profit and loss, bids and bargains: that is, by a system without any focusing purpose to it": a system that makes visible its hiddenness (8).

The change to "modernisms" has gone along with the politicised pluralisation of modernity as the alternative "modernities". It is now common to speak of multiple histories of multiple modernisms: the "vernacular modernism" of popular art forms like cinema (Hansen); modernist women's writing (Felski *Gender*; Scott); "modernisms at large" (Huyssen); "peripheral" or "minor" modernisms, those modern "aesthetic forms generated beyond capitalism's cores" (Parry; Caplan); and "postcolonial modernisms". These last, which concern us here, offer alternatives to "literary-historical narratives predicated upon notions of cultural belatedness – or, more drastically, the absence of cultural modernity" (Irvine 7). They enable a model of historical cultural analysis that does not have to "reproduce narratives that correlate these emergent, marginal, or peripheral modernisms with a dominant cultural centre" (7).

Yet a glance at recent volumes of the most prestigious scholarly journals in the area (*Modernism/Modernity*, for example) reveals that although literary modernism has been pluralistically opened up to popular and minority literatures, the field is still dominated by the inner circle of Euro-American high-modernists who produced the formal style that everyone still recognises as "modernism". This is no doubt partly because the cultural centre remains hegemonic in modernism studies and perpetuates against its revisionary best self the idea of a normative originary modernism. But there is more to it than that, for modernisms are subject to a common paradox. They all share a desire "to wipe out whatever came earlier, in the hope of reaching at last a point that could be called the true present" (de Man 148), even if they find different modes of expression for the true art of this true present. In newly postcolonial societies like Australia, this "will to modernity" – a "desire to seek a place outside of the tradition that enables it" (Meisel 4) – took two main forms initially: a fierce avant-gardist rejection of European modernism, and a nationalist indifference to it. In the 1920s Australia produced its own adversarial art of the new in such avant-garde ventures as the Lindsays' *Vision* magazine, which expressed the arch-modernist desire to awake from the nightmare of history: to forge a radical break with the Australian cultural past. That past was dead Europe. As old-fashioned, vulgar and schoolboyish as Norman Lindsay's rampant nudes and fauns might look to us now, this was one Australian version of the shock of the new. A symptom of the widespread cultural pessimism that descended from Nietzsche to Spengler's *Decline of the West*, its enemy was the decadent new art of the decadent past: the art that was itself a symptom of those same forces in Europe. Nietzschean thought was absorbed simultaneously into Futurism and the *Vision* aesthetic, which, if its avant-gardism was at one with its cultural conservatism, nevertheless sent shockwaves through the reactionary institutions of its own country: the church, the art establishment, the garden suburbs. The Lindsays were, as the European modernists were, challenging "unfreedom, the oppressions of journalism, of genteel audiences, of timid readers, of political and religious orthodoxy" (Levenson *Companion* 2; see also Carter).

It does not follow, therefore, that the violent reaction against European modernism in Australia in the inter-war years amounted to the backlash of a "quarantined culture" (Williams). This argument – that "an improvised, unstated but de facto cultural quarantine existed in Australia [which] was propagated by an inchoate grouping of racial supremacists, anti-Semites, anti-bolsheviks, protectionists, anti-industrialisers, and the leaders of an élitist and conservative art-world Establishment" (Williams 5) – understands modernism unambiguously as a threatening cultural import resisted by philistine gatekeepers (if finally and belatedly submitted to). Rather, European modernism expressed a European response to the conditions of modern life that did not offer Australians a way to be subjects of their own modernisation. In early twentieth-century Australia, the local conditions of modernisation were so tied up with processes of national formation and consolidation that mainstream aesthetic responses to modernity were inevitably going to take the form of a cultural nationalism.

So it is worth pointing out that the Australian experience of modernism, and the experience of modernism in the Australian upper-school literature syllabus, were not simply outcomes of our postcolonial situation – extreme forms of the cringe, direct or inverted – although the relationship between centre and periphery is certainly implicated. With our own version of genealogical anxiety we have worried that Australia finally succumbed to Euro-American modernism with the slavishness of colonials and junior allies in the Cold War. We have staked claims for Australian forerunners (Furphy's *Such is Life*) and scrapped around for evidence that we were right there with Eliot and Joyce in 1922 (Slessor's "Nuremberg"). Even now we are not done with Ern Malley, or what his example seems to tell us about the endurance of the quarantined culture. Yet there are very good reasons why the revolutionary aesthetics of the late-industrial, late-capitalist northern hemisphere should emerge in a new environment like Australia when it did, in the 1940s. As Peter Beilharz argues, this was when modern Australia began:

> It is posited by Federation, the Great War and the earlier reconstruction, but it emerges only with war, planning, federal powers, Postwar Reconstruction, and the latent local Fordism that develops into Holdenism and the Lucky Country, the Australian version of the American dream. (Beilharz 50)

So we should not suppose that modernism occurred belatedly in Australia. Modernisms, like modernities, can (in Beilharz's words) "be so varied and mixed as to mean, via the principle of uneven development, that the less developed [cultural] economies of the peripheries (so to say) show the future to those of the centres" (Beilharz 47). It is nothing more than a sign of the modernism of Australian modernist writing that it should, like Euro-American writing before it, be characterised by an acute, indeed an often crippling, self-consciousness about art and its relation to the world, a sense of crisis and a highly conflicted attitude towards the cultural past. Modernism, after all, can be understood as "a defensive response to the increasingly intolerable burdens of coming late" in that tradition (Meisel 2). The condition of belatedness, in other words, belongs not just to peripheral or postcolonial modernisms, but also to Euro-American modernism understood in this way as "a structure of compensation, a way of adjusting to the paradox of belatedness that is its precondition" (Meisel 5).

Where is modernism in the history of English in Australian schools?

The field known as the "history of English" was a product of the British New-Left revisionism of the 1970s, and that project underlies still-dominant narratives about the history of subject English in schools, which typically trace a colonialist transmission of ideas from the centre to the peripheries: from Eliot, to Richards, to Leavis and American New Criticism – to Australia. These narratives are oddly complicit in the perpetuation of the big story of the discipline, a fable of origins and struggles that obscures and reshapes the very evidence that is adduced in contradiction of it, short-circuiting any serious inquiry into the "speculative, ideological functions of English literary study" in Australian schools, or their relation to "the larger sociopolitical economy" (Court 4). The continuing authority of this story may be seen in this précis of it, from as recently as 2008:

> There seem strong grounds for arguing that secondary English has undergone a significant shift over the past four decades, from a 'study of Culture' in the Arnoldian–Leavisite tradition to 'cultural studies' in the Williams–Eagleton tradition. These two traditions appear to be on opposing sides in the battle for the minds and hearts of the English student. Each brings into sharp relief the type of person that English teachers would like their students to become: on the one hand, a cultured individual, with a heightened appreciation of great literature, capable of articulating the contribution of that literary heritage to the development of civil society; and on the other hand, the sensitive, reflective citizen capable of creatively expressing his or her own experiences in the context of textual understandings, who also is able to deconstruct the role of culture in the creation of meaning within modern societies. (Patterson 311)

This account of English's self-appointed role in civic subject formation is now so familiar as hardly to warrant questioning, and the history of Literary Studies in Australia appears to bear it out. Schools are generally perceived to have followed, at varying distances, the directions set by university departments, from belletrism and philology to New Criticism and Leavisism. And school teachers, trained in universities rather than teachers' colleges since the post-Dawkins 1980s, are perceived to have followed their lecturers in reconceptualising the object and aims of Literary Study in the age of theory, challenging and abandoning the ideals of aesthetic education under the aegis of poststructuralism, Marxism, feminism and cultural studies.

Yet it is significant that the shorthand version cited above ends with Eagleton, because it is a caricature of his chapter on "The Rise of English" in *Literary Theory: An Introduction* (1983). Eagleton's account was important and influential (although it was not the first: see Palmer; Widdowson; Baldick);[1] but it is now more than 30 years old, and many important qualifications, corrections and alternative histories of English have appeared in the meantime (e.g. Graff; Kearney; Hunter *Culture*; Viswanathan; Court; Guy and Small; Reid). They demonstrate that there were many other factors and many other conflicts in the emergence of the discipline, and that the moment of theory was not its first moment of critical self-consciousness, or its last. In fact, the "paradigms structuring the teaching of 'English' were *always* in transition and conflict" (Jones et al.). Despite all these advances in historical knowledge, however, the same old story of English is perpetuated, unexamined, especially in Australia, where it has its own history (Docker, Frow). It is so useful in curriculum history, too, because school English has a profound investment in the "critical textual studies" approaches that established themselves in the 1980s, and which have been so effective in transferring the work of socialisation – the production of an ethical subjectivity in students – from aesthetic to political reading practices. This has locked school Literary Studies into trench warfare with a non-existent Oedipal antagonist, "traditional" Literary Studies, the spectre of which is routinely and unhelpfully conjured up by the conservative newspaper press, for whom subject English is a battleground for the future of the free world.

The transition from the Arnoldian (i.e. high-Victorian) "cultured individual, with a heightened appreciation of great literature" to the "sensitive,

---

1   Baldick's book was based on his 1981 D.Litt thesis under Eagleton.

reflective citizen" of cultural studies can only be achieved, of course, by pretending modernism never happened in between – or perhaps only by assuming, in the tradition of John Docker's *In a Critical Condition*, that modernism is already consecrated as the great humanist art of "the metaphysical ascendancy" (Docker 83–109) by the time it finally gets into Australian classrooms. As the ALIAS data show, the canonical texts of Anglo-American modernism – most of them written before World War Two (see Table 14.1) – did not enter the school syllabus in Australia until the mid-1960s, and then did so almost all at once. There were good reasons for this.

Modernism and modernist criticism in the upper-school syllabus

If modernism goes together with economic modernisation (as in the 1940s in Australia), modernism studies become visible at the moment of disciplinary modernisation (which happened in Australia in the 1960s). The most significant historical detail to emerge from the ALIAS data is that Anglo-American modernism and Australian modernism both enter the upper-school Literature syllabus at exactly the same time in Australia: when forces of disciplinary transformation and professionalisation, entrenched in Britain and the USA and intimately tied up with modernism, were consolidated in the universities to the degree that they could influence the shaping of the school syllabus.

Consider briefly the evidence from ALIAS. As Tables 14.1 and 14.3 show, modernism arrived with a bang not a whimper in the mid-1960s, most controversially in the crusading, programmatic syllabus initiated by S.L. (Sam) Goldberg in New South Wales in 1967, but also elsewhere. In Victoria T.S. Eliot's *Murder in the Cathedral* (1935) was first set in 1955 and remained on the syllabus for much of the subsequent decade, and Joyce's *Portrait of the Artist* (1916) appeared in 1969. Beckett's *Waiting for Godot* (1953), pioneered on the Goldberg syllabus in 1967, was also set in South Australia, Victoria and Western Australia in 1971 and was a staple for much of the next two decades in two of those states. Of Lawrence's fiction, only the relatively approachable (and adolescent-friendly) *Sons and Lovers* (1913) was widely selected, and as early as 1963 – in Victoria it remained on the syllabus virtually until the end of the twentieth century. Lawrence's more challenging novels were, understandably, taboo for schools – although *Kangaroo* (1923) was set in Tasmania on a single occasion, in 1984. By the 1970s, students in a number of states could study Eliot, Woolf, Joyce, Conrad and Faulkner.[2]

The arrival of modernist criticism in Australia is often assumed to correspond roughly with this history. Students of Leavis arrived or returned from Cambridge in the 1960s, bringing with them a social mission for English criticism, an organicist view of form and tradition, and techniques of close reading derived from Richards and Empson. American New Criticism found its way here with the professionalisation of the discipline, in the rapid expansion of postwar scholarly journals and the wide circulation of Norton Anthologies and college English textbooks like Brooks and Warren's *Understanding Poetry*. In Australia the advent of New Criticism in the universities in the 1960s is often associated with Docker's "metaphysical ascendancy" (83–109). In an attempt to legitimise Australian literature as a disciplinary field worthy of being admitted to the syllabus, Australianists were determined to raise it onto a level with the European literatures. A generation of critics therefore set about expelling the old radical nationalist Australian canon (exemplified by Lawson and Furphy) and instating a metaphysical canon (a "great tradition" from Christopher Brennan to Patrick White). In this specific context, New Critical close reading was brought into the service of a project to "reveal a text's true metaphysical presence, authority and value" (Docker 95).

The original for this project was F.R. Leavis's vitalist great tradition, which admitted Lawrence as a modernist but neither Woolf nor Joyce. Australian English departments in the 1960s and 70s were likely to combine the technical vocabulary and "How-to-read-a-poem" pedagogic methods of American New Criticism with the metaphysical-moral vocabulary of Leavisism. This influence can be seen in senior secondary Literature

---

2   The engagement with Anglo-American modernism in upper schools in Australia occurred about 10 years later than it did in Britain, where by 1955 A-level English Literature teachers could select a unit on Modern Literature, which included Joyce's *Portrait* and Eliot's *Waste Land* (1922), but also the less formally confronting *Clayhanger* by Arnold Bennett (1910), Hardy's poetry, Forster's *A Passage to India* (1924) and G. Lowes Dickinson's *A Modern Symposium* (1905). By 1975, this unit in the A-level syllabus had become more demanding, but the interspersion of modernist and non-modernist writers continued. It included Woolf's *To the Lighthouse* (1927) but also Bennett's *The Old Wives' Tale* (1908), famously the target of Woolf's criticism; the modernist T.S. Eliot as well as the Georgian Edward Thomas; Forster, but also Beckett's formidable *Malone Dies* (1951). Overall, though, the British A-level syllabuses remained highly traditional in their structure through the 1960s and 70s, with the Modern Literature unit tacked onto a survey syllabus that covered the major authors from Chaucer and Shakespeare to Milton, the Romantics and the Victorians.

most clearly in one of those "moments of high ideological visibility" (Carter 16) and rupture in the system when Goldbergian Leavisism rose to prominence in New South Wales in the late 1960s. As Tables 14.2 and 14.3 show, S.L. Goldberg's idiosyncratic Leavisite syllabus (although Goldberg was himself a Joycean, significantly) transformed the HSC at a stroke. The text lists for 1963–66 are, coincidentally, not without certain Leavis authors – *Macbeth* and *The Tempest*, Conrad and some of the poets in the standard school anthologies. But these old text lists are pretty outworn: belletristic essays, nationalist Australian works, broad-survey anthologies, and novels by Thackeray and Wells. Their pre-1960s world is summarily swept away in the Goldberg text lists by the arrival of modernism – represented in proto-modernists like Hardy and Hopkins, Irish modernists (Beckett and Cary, Shaw), metaphysical modernists like Eliot (and his rediscovery, Donne) and Patrick White – and a constellation of figures around leading figures in the organicist moral tradition in English literature: Austen and Lawrence. The abandonment of anthologies for single poems signals the primacy of New Critical close reading and Leavisian discrimination – and the whole list is imbued with the sense of urgency and moral seriousness attached by Leavisites to literary reading.

On the evidence of past papers, however, a form of modernist criticism was actually being practised in Australia much earlier: one directly influenced by T.S. Eliot, which sprung up in parallel with developments in England. At least that is what seems to be happening in the 1925 NSW Honours Paper in English, co-written by E.R. Holme and John Le Gay Brereton, the first Australian-born and educated Professors of English to be appointed to an Australian university. Both were students and protégés of Mungo MacCallum at the University of Sydney and owe their positions to the patronage of the influential Chair of Modern Language and Literature (Dale 77–89). When MacCallum retired, his Chair was divided into four new Chairs. Holme took up the McCaughey Chair of Early English Literature Language (in 1920) and Brereton the Challis Chair of English Literature (in 1921), a split that reflects the emerging discrimination in the discipline between primarily philological and primarily literary-critical practitioners.

It is likely that much of the work on the exam paper was Brereton's. Holme had a background in Anglo-Saxon and middle-English language and literature, and although he regularly taught into the Literature program at Sydney he was, as A.G. Mitchell observes, "a university man first and a teacher of English second" (Mitchell). In the 1920s he was Dean of Arts and Fellow of the Senate, and a regular traveller to Britain on university business. Brereton, on the other hand, was "among the leading humanist scholars of his day", whose "[a]cademic responsibilities occupied most of his time and energies" (Heseltine "ADB"). To H.P. Heseltine, Brereton's life and writing were to provide the first significant link between two major traditions of Australian literary culture (Heseltine *John Le Gay Brereton* 15). Brereton was a nationalist and a social democrat – the friend and champion of Lawson in the 1890s. He was also an internationalist, a humanist and a scholar of English and European literature – the friend and champion of Christopher Brennan, "a poet in almost every respect the reverse of Lawson" (*John Le Gay Brereton* 15). A specialist in the Elizabethan drama, Brereton lectured on English Literature from the sixteenth to the nineteenth centuries, and (with H. M. Green) "taught at least some Australian literature" at Sydney in the 1920s and 30s (Dale 229), although as Dale points out no Australian books were set as texts before 1940.

The 1925 paper ought to be a high point in the old orthodoxy, when the discipline was characterised by a scholarly mix of generalist literary history, biography, genre description and impressionistic evaluation. This paper certainly has many of those characteristics, but is also on its way somewhere else, and for reasons that cannot confidently be explained by biography or institutional history (of the University of Sydney English Department, for instance). It is divided into three untitled sections, which may fairly be described as literary history (Section A), literary criticism and theory (Section B) and practical criticism (Section C). The examination is demanding: candidates were required to answer five questions in three hours, two each from Sections A and B, and the Section C close reading. The five questions in Section A assume candidates will possess detailed knowledge of individual set works and be able to engage in sophisticated analysis of historical periods and literary movements from the fifteenth to the twentieth century. They are expected to explain the underlying causes of literary-historical change, make connections between genre and history, and undertake comparative analysis. Question 1 calls for "a brief critical account of any four of the following", indicating "the period of which they are characteristic products". The syllabus (which is not limited to "the following", as witnessed below) is significant for its unexpectedness. Whether it is a reflection of Brereton's outré mystical interests (he was brought up a Swedenborgian and was a follower of the fashionable cult of Pan in the 1890s) as well as his special expertise in early modern literature is an open question. Texts included Chaucer's long dream-poem, *The Parlement of Foules* (1478?); Edmund Spenser's courtly satire, *Prosopopoia, or Mother Hubberd's Tale* (1591); Ben Jonson's satirical drama of greed, *The Alchemist* (1610); the (uniquely challenging) spiritual autobiography of Sir Thomas Browne, *Religio Medici* (1643); Congreve's Restoration comedy, *The Way of the World* (1700); the first gothic novel, Horace Walpole's *The Castle of Otranto* (1764); Shelley's radical verse drama, *The Cenci, A Tragedy, in Five Acts* (1819); George Eliot's political novel, *Felix Holt* (1864); and Francis Bacon's *The Advancement of Learning* (1605).

In the remaining four questions of Section A, candidates are asked to delineate "the causes of the decline of English drama during the first 40 years of the seventeenth century"; "explain why satire was so dominant in the eighteenth century"; compare the novels of the nineteenth century "with those of the present day", noting the differences (Dickens and Thackeray are given as suggested examples); and describe what the Romantic revival was, naming "the chief romantic poets at the close of the eighteenth century". These are the kinds of conventional literary-historical questions that might be expected to appear on final year English exam papers in Australia during this period. They are relatively straightforward, and only the question on the Victorian novel invites, but does not demand, a critical response.

Before discussing Section B, I want to skip to the final section, where students were confronted with a de-identified poem they were unlikely to have encountered in their studies: Donne's Holy Sonnet, "Death, Be Not Proud". The examination rubric is open-ended:

> Comment critically upon the following poem, pointing out what you consider meritorious in it, discussing the thought and feeling which it may be the author's aim to elicit, the effect of the imagery and of the verse form, and whatever else you think to the purpose.

This is a piece of practical criticism just *avant la lettre*. Here is an excerpt from the Cambridge Faculty of English "Virtual Classroom" lesson on practical criticism:

> Practical criticism is, like the formal study of English literature itself, a relatively young discipline. It began in the 1920s with a series of experiments by the Cambridge critic I.A. Richards. He gave poems to students without any information about who wrote them or when they were written. In *Practical Criticism* of 1929 he reported on and analysed the results of his experiments. The objective of his work was to encourage students to concentrate on "the words on the page," rather than

relying on preconceived or received beliefs about a text. For Richards this form of close analysis of anonymous poems was ultimately intended to have psychological benefits for the students: by responding to all the currents of emotion and meaning in the poems and passages of prose which they read the students were to achieve what Richards called an "organised response." This meant that they would clarify the various currents of thought in the poem and achieve a corresponding clarification of their own emotions. ("Faculty of English")

The 1925 NSW Paper does exactly this: it encourages students to concentrate on the words on the page so that they can respond to the poem's swiftly moving currents of emotion and feeling without distraction. Equally to the point, however, is the examiners' choice of this particular poem. School students in 1925 would almost certainly never have encountered the sonnet because Donne's reputation was only beginning to be revived in 1925 (A.J. Smith 1).[3] Herbert Grierson's anthology, *Metaphysical Lyrics and Poems of the Seventeenth Century*, had only appeared in 1921, and was reviewed by T.S. Eliot in October of that year. His essay review famously introduced the idea of the dissociation of sensibility discussed above, linking Donne with the temper of the modern age and reconnecting the problem of modernism's difficulty with a broken tradition. Here are all the signature features of New Critical interpretation: wit, ambiguity, paradox, irony (see Guillory 169–70). Encountered as an unseen examination text, a candidate's reading of "Death, Be Not Proud" would likely pick up on the sonnet's high poeticism (its archaic pronouns, for example), but would be quickly engaged by the immediacy of its strenuous, even dogged, argumentation, and react feelingly to the ingenious conceit that it is death that suffers and dies. What the examiners were seeking were answers that responded to the desperate intensity in the speaker's cleverness, and recognised how emotion was carrying the argument to its clinching thought: "Death, thou shalt die."

The six questions in Section B are similarly in tune with contemporary problems of literary theory, critical practice, discrimination, and genre in 1925:

---

[3] Smith points out that Donne's fluctuating reputation was a far more complicated matter: "People still make it an article of faith that Donne's poems had a fashion in his own day and just after, then fell wholly into neglect until recent times when our like predicament showed us ourselves *in* them" (A. J. Smith 1); but he concedes that general readers (of anthologies etc.) would be unlikely to have encountered Donne before his revival by Grierson and Eliot.

6. "A literary work is always the expression of its author's personality." Discuss this.

7. What is meant by comedy? Should a comedy always be realistic?

8. What do you understand by "sincerity" in poetry? (Can a fictitious narrative be sincere, for example? Is Shakespeare sincere in the cruel speeches of Iago or the cheerful lies of Falstaff?)

9. In criticising Australian poetry, would you or would you not adopt the same standard as if you were discussing English poetry? Why?

10. A French critic has called the admiration of Shakespeare "an English superstition." Do you consider there is any justification whatever for this view?

11. If a story has been well told in prose, why should a poet retell it in verse? Illustrate your answer by reference to English poetry.

Three of these, questions 6, 8 and 11, come within the scope of theoretical problems that would become central to modernist criticism in the decades after 1925. The first, on personality, raises an issue best known from Eliot's seminal essay, "Tradition and the Individual Talent", published in 1919 and again in Eliot's *The Sacred Wood* in 1920. In this essay Eliot put forward his theory of impersonal poetry. He repudiated the accusation that modernism was a rejection of poetic tradition, arguing that any "really new" work of art was shaped by that tradition and at the same time remade that tradition (Lewis 27). A great poem emerges from the encounter of the new and the old, and is not primarily the expression of the individual poet's personality but of the tradition that is altered by the existence of the poem. What happens in the creation of a poem is exactly what, for Richards, is being reconstructed in its reading: not the representation of the poet's emotions and ideas but the surrendering of those ideas and emotions to the intensity of poetry, which fuses them under pressure into something independent of the poet. The rejection of the intentional fallacy by American New Criticism is the inverse of this rejection by Eliot of the poet's personality. Psychology, biography, cultural history – anything external to the poem clouds what is essential to it, and clouds that view of the past that is only possible through its close reading.

Question 8 takes up the problem of sincerity and literary value. Sincerity remained central to the thought of Richards and Leavis, and is one of the ideas that links them back to Arnold and the Victorians. In Arnold's famous "The Study of Poetry" he predicts that religion and philosophy will eventually be replaced by poetry, and argues for the vital importance of the evaluative critical study of poetry. For Arnold the mark of great poetry is "the high seriousness which comes from absolute sincerity" (184). Leavis's great tradition may be described as the tradition in which this high seriousness – for Leavis it is framed as maturity – is allied with absolute sincerity. Yet for the Richards of *Practical Criticism* (1929), the concept of sincerity survived from the nineteenth century predominantly as an unexamined cliché of students, who used it unselfconsciously as a vague term of critical appreciation (Ball 8). Its presence in this examination as a term to be put under question is notable.

It would be absurd, finally, to imagine that the 1925 examiners were anticipating the New Critical "heresy of paraphrase" in question 11, but the question does once again gesture towards issues central to modernism – this time the idea, put so compactly by Eliot in his Metaphysicals essay, that "form is meaning" (1104). Poetry, even when it retells old stories (Orpheus or Eve or the Fisher King), transforms them into something that cannot be reconverted into prose without losing what was essential to the poem's meaning. The question here, more straightforwardly, asks students to explain what, if anything, poetry adds to narrative: is it anything more than an embellishment or a mnemonic, and if so what?

This early exam paper suggests counter-intuitively that modernism arrived in New South Wales schools first as a profound shift in the way criticism was done, and only much later in the setting of modernist texts on the syllabus. Whether the new directions of the 1925 paper were followed in subsequent years or are found also in other states is a question for further research. In any case I would not want to argue, even provisionally, that "Australia got there first" (Carter 2) – one more time. This evidence does, however, take issue (in Robert Dixon's words) "with the assumption that modernity is first invented in the metropolitan centre and then exported to the colonial peripheries, which are always, by definition, belated." Like modernism itself, modernist criticism was a "world system ... a set of interdependent sites, ... a network of relations rather than a one-way transfer of culture and authority" (Dixon xxiii–xxiv). Just as there were multiple modernisms, so were there multiple modernist criticisms, which are worthy of more detailed investigation.

Table 14.1: Modernism in Australian schools

CONRAD, JOSEPH	ELIOT, T.S.	FAULKNER, WILLIAM	SLESSOR, KENNETH	WHITE, PATRICK
Heart of Darkness	*Selected Poems*	*As I Lay Dying*	*Selected Poems*	*The Tree of Man*
NSW 1984–94	NSW 1967–85, 92–94	SA 1974–75	NSW 1986–89, 1995–2000 (2 Unit A)	NSW 1972, 77–78, 81–82, 84–85, 96–98
Tas 1974, 76, 82, 86, 2004–05	SA 1983–90	WA 1979–1995	NSW 1976–78 (2 Unit)	SA 1971–73, 83–90
Vic 1980, 86, 89, 92, 2004–05	Tas 1972, 82, 88	*Intruder in the Dust*	SA 1964–67	Vic 1977, 82
WA 1981–2005	Vic 1985	SA 1970–74	Tas 1968–69, 90, 98–99	*Voss*
Lord Jim	WA 1983–2005	*YEATS, W.B.*	Vic 1988, 92–94	NSW 1967–71, 74–76, 79–80
NSW 1972, 87–89	*Murder in the Cathedral*	*Selected Poems*	WA 1981–88	Tas 1970, 72, 74, 76
SA 1945	NSW 1967–72, 82	NSW 1972, 86, 1994–2000	*STOW, RANDOLPH*	Vic 1972, 75, 80, 82
Tas 1948–50, 61–62, 66–67	SA 1970–82	SA 1983–90	*The Merry-Go-Round in the Sea*	WA 1979–80
Vic 1969, 72	Tas 1983	Tas 2004–05	NSW 1972, 77–79, 84–86	*Riders in the Chariot*
WA 1948	Vic 1955, 57, 59, 62, 65, 70, 81–82	Vic 1986, 89, 2003–05	SA 1968–74, 83–90	SA 1970, 74–75, 83–90
Youth	WA 1968–88	WA 1996–2005	Tas 1978–80, 83, 85, 88	*A Fringe of Leaves*
SA 1945–56			Vic 1982, 87, 90, 92, 97–99	NSW 1990–92
WA 1945, 58–59			WA 1974–95	SA 1980–82

LAWRENCE, D.H.	BECKETT, SAMUEL	JOYCE, JAMES	To the Islands	Tas 1981, 83, 90
Sons and Lovers	Waiting for Godot	Portrait	NSW 1985–86	Vic 1983–84, 86–87, 91–92, 2002–04
NSW 1967–83	NSW 1967–95	NSW 2000	Tas 1976	WA 1983–2005
SA 1968–90	SA 1971–90	Vic 1969	SA 1983–90	The Eye of the Storm
Tas 1969–70, 75, 81, 94–95	Tas 2004–05	Dubliners	Vic 1965, 75	Vic 1986, 89
Vic 1963, 65, 68, 70, 72, 74, 76–77, 80, 83, 86, 92, 97–99	Vic 1971–78, 84, 87, 97–99	NSW 1977–78	WA 1990–2005	The Burnt Ones
WA 1969–88	WA 1971–80	SA 1970–73, 77–90	CRAIG, ALEXANDER (ED.)	Vic 1992
Kangaroo	Happy Days	Vic 1984, 2004–05	12 Poets 1950–1970	WA 1994–2005
Tas 1982	SA 1983–90	WALLACE-CRABBE, CHRIS (ED.)	SA 1974–78	WOOLF, VIRGINIA
Selected Poems	All That Fall	Six Voices	Tas 1980–87	Mrs Dalloway
SA 1966–69, 76–82	Tas 1980, 83	NSW 1965–72	Vic 1976	NSW 1969–71
Tas 1993–2003		Tas 1967–84	WA 1974–85	To the Lighthouse
WA 1962–63, 1981–88		Vic 1966–69		WA 1996–2005
		WA 1965–68		

Table 14.2: HSC 1963–1966

1963			1964		
Australia Felix	Richardson, Henry Handel	Fiction	Australian Short Stories	Murdoch, W.M. and Drake-Brockman, H.	Fiction
Fire on the Snow, The	Stewart, Douglas	Fiction	Henry Esmond	Thackeray, William	Fiction
History of Mr Polly, The	Wells, H.G.	Fiction	Wuthering Heights	Brontë, Emily	Fiction
Modern Short Stories	Merson, A.	Fiction	Book of Poetry, A	Smyth, W.	Poetry
Modern Poets' World, The	Reeves, James	Poetry	Galaxy of Poems Old and New, A	Parker, Ernest	Poetry
Poets' Quest, The	Southwell, Elsie	Poetry	Macbeth	Shakespeare, William	Drama
Tempest, The	Shakespeare, William	Drama	She Stoops to Conquer	Goldsmith, Oliver	Drama
Selections from the English Essay	Merson, A.	Non-fiction	Essays Old and New	Barnes, H. (Ed.)	Non-fiction
Topics and Opinions	Scott, Arthur	Non-fiction	Spoken Word, The	Scott, Arthur	Non-fiction

1965

Fire on the Snow, The	Stewart, Douglas	Fiction
Modern Short Stories	Merson, A.	Fiction
Nigger of the Narcissus, The	Conrad, Joseph	Fiction
Passage, The	Palmer, Vance	Fiction
Modern Poets' World, The	Reeves, James	Poetry
Six Voices	Wallace-Crabbe, Chris	Poetry
Julius Caesar	Shakespeare, William	Drama
Eight Essayists	Cairncross, A.S.	Non-fiction
Nine Twentieth Century Essayists	Gardiner, Harold	Non-fiction

1966

Australia Felix	Richardson, Henry Handel	Fiction
Australian Short Stories	Murdoch W.M. and Drake-Brockman, H.	Fiction
History of Mr Polly, The	Wells, Herbert	Fiction
Boomerang Book of Australian Poetry, The	Moodie, Heddle E.	Poetry
Galaxy of Poems Old and New, A	Parker, Ernest	Poetry
Man for All Seasons, A	Bolt, Robert	Drama
Richard II	Shakespeare, William	Drama
Selections from the English Essay	Merson, A.	Non-fiction
Speaking of the Famous	Scott, Arthur	Non-fiction

Table 14.3: The Goldberg HSC 1967

FICTION		DRAMA	
Emma	Austen	Waiting for Godot	Beckett
The Horse's Mouth	Cary	Murder in the Cathedral	Eliot
Joseph Andrews	Fielding	The Crucible	Miller
The Power and the Glory	Greene	Look Back in Anger	Osborne
Tess of the d'Urbervilles	Hardy	King Lear	Shakespeare
Sons and Lovers	Lawrence	Othello	Shakespeare
The Adventures of Huckleberry Finn	Twain	Saint Joan	Shaw
Voss	White	Oedipus the King	Sophocles
POETRY			
The Anniversarie	Chaucer	Journey of the Magi	Eliot
The Apparition	Donne	The Love Song of J. Alfred Prufrock	Eliot
The Good Morrow	Donne	Carrion Comfort	Hopkins
Hymne to God my God, in my Sicknesse	Donne	God's Grandeur	Hopkins
The Pardoner's Tale	Donne	Hurrahing in Harvest	Hopkins
Satyre: Of Religion	Donne	Pied Beauty	Hopkins
The Sunne Rising	Donne	Spring and Fall	Hopkins
A Valediction: Forbidding Mourning	Donne	The Windhover	Hopkins
The Hollow Men	Eliot	Paradise Lost	Milton
Portrait of a Lady	Eliot	Epistle to Burlington	Pope
Preludes	Eliot	An Epistle to Dr Arbuthnot	Pope
Rhapsody on a Windy Night	Eliot	The Rape of the Lock	Pope

Works Cited

Arnold, Matthew. "The study of poetry". *English Literature and Irish Politics*. Ann Arbor: University of Michigan Press, 1973. 161–88. Print.

Baldick, Chris. *The Social Mission of English Criticism, 1848–1932*. Oxford English Monographs. Oxford: Clarendon Press, 1983. Print.

Ball, Patricia M. "Sincerity: The rise and fall of a critical term". *The Modern Language Review* (1964): 1–11. Print.

Beilharz, Peter. *Thinking the Antipodes: Australian essays*. Clayton, Vic.: Monash University Publishing, 2015. Print.

Bradbury, Malcolm. "Modernism". *The Routledge Dictionary of Literary Terms*. Eds. Childs, Peter and Roger Fowler: Routledge, 2006. 145. Print.

Brooks, Cleanth. *The Well-Wrought Urn: Studies in the structure of poetry*. New York: Reynal & Hitchcock, 1947. Print.

Caplan, Marc. *How Strange the Change: Language, temporality, and narrative form in peripheral modernisms*. Stanford University Press, 2011. Print.

Carter, David. *Always Almost Modern: Australian print cultures and modernity*. Melbourne: Australian Scholarly Publishing, 2013. Print.

Choo, Suzanne S. "On literature's use (ful/less) ness: Reconceptualizing the literature curriculum in the age of globalization". *Journal of Curriculum Studies* 43.1 (2011): 47–67. Print.

Clark, T. J. *Farewell to an Idea: Episodes from a history of modernism*. New Haven: Yale University Press, 1999. Print.

Court, Franklin E. *Institutionalizing English Literature: The culture and politics of literary study, 1750–1900*. Stanford, Calif: Stanford University Press, 1992. Print.

Dale, Leigh. *The Enchantment of English: Professing English literatures in Australian universities*. Second edition. 2012. Print.

de Man, Paul. *Blindness and Insight: Essays in the rhetoric of contemporary criticism*. Minneapolis: University of Minnesota Press, 1983. Print.

Dixon, Robert. *Photography, Early Cinema, and Colonial Modernity: Frank Hurley's synchronized lecture entertainments*. London; New York: Anthem Press, 2012. Print.

Docker, John. *In a Critical Condition: Reading Australian literature*. Ringwood, Vic.: Penguin, 1984. Print.

Eliot, T.S. "The Metaphysical Poets". *The Norton Anthology of Theory and Criticism*. Ed. Leitch, Vincent B. New York: Norton, 2001. 1098–1105. Print.

Faculty of English, University of Cambridge. "Introduction to Practical Criticism". <www.english.cam.ac.uk/classroom/pracrit.htm> Web. Accessed 14 April 2016.

Felski, Rita. *The Gender of Modernity*. Cambridge, Mass.: Harvard University Press, 1995. Print.

——. "Modernist studies and cultural studies: Reflections on method". *Modernism/Modernity* 10.3 (2003): 501–17. Print.

Graff, Gerald. *Professing Literature: An institutional history*. Chicago: University of Chicago Press, 1987. Print.

Guillory, John. *Cultural Capital: The problem of literary canon formation*. Chicago and London: University of Chicago Press, 1993. Print.

Guy, Josephine M., and Ian Small. *Politics and Value in English Studies: A discipline in crisis?* Cambridge: Cambridge University Press, 1993. Print.

Hansen, Miriam. "The mass production of the senses: Classical cinema as vernacular modernism". *Modernism/modernity* 6.2 (1999): 59–77. Print.

Heseltine, H. P. "Brereton, John Le Gay". *Australian Dictionary of Biography*. 1983. Web. 25 May 2015.

——. *John Le Gay Brereton*. Melbourne: Lansdowne Press, 1965. Print.

Hickman, Miranda B., and John D. McIntyre. *Rereading the New Criticism*. Columbus: Ohio State University Press, 2012. Print.

Hilliard, Christopher. *English as a Vocation: The* Scrutiny *movement*. Oxford: Oxford University Press, 2012. Print.

Hunter, Ian. "Aesthetics and cultural studies". *Cultural Studies*. Eds. Grossberg, Lawrence, Cary Nelson and Paula A. Treichler. New York: Routledge, 1992. 347–72. Print.

——. *Culture and Government: The emergence of literary education*. Basingstoke: Macmillan, 1988. Print.

Huyssen, Andreas. "Geographies of modernism in a globalizing world". *New German Critique* (2007): 189–207. Print.

Irvine, Dean. "Spectres of modernism". *Canadian Literature* 209 (2011): 6–10. Print.

Jones, K., et al. "Investigating the production of university English in mass higher education". *Arts and Humanities in Higher Education* 4.3 (2005): 247–64. Print.

Kearney, A. "The first crisis in English Studies 1880–1900". *British Journal of Educational Studies* 36.3 (1988): 260–68. Print.

Leitch, Vincent B. *Literary Criticism in the 21st Century*. London: Bloomsbury, 2014. Print.

Levenson, Michael H. *The Cambridge Companion to Modernism*. 2nd ed. Cambridge

University Press, 2011. Print.

———. *A Genealogy of Modernism: A study of English literary doctrine, 1908–1922*. Cambridge; New York: Cambridge University Press, 1984. Print.

Lewis, Pericles. *The Cambridge Introduction to Modernism*. Cambridge Introductions to Literature. Cambridge; New York: Cambridge University Press, 2007. Print.

Meisel, Perry. *The Myth of the Modern: A study in British literature and criticism after 1850*. New Haven: Yale University Press, 1987. Print.

Menand, Louis. "T. S. Eliot". *The Cambridge History of Literary Criticism: Modernism and the New Criticism*. Eds. Litz, A. Walton, Louis Menand and Lawrence Rainey. Cambridge: Cambridge University Press, 2000. 17–56. Print.

Menand, Louis, and Lawrence Rainey. "Introduction". *The Cambridge History of Literary Criticism: Modernism and the New Criticism*. Eds. Litz, A. Walton, Louis Menand and Lawrence Rainey. Vol. 7. Cambridge: Cambridge University Press, 2000. 1–14. Print.

Mitchell, A. G. "Holme, Ernest Rudolph". *Australian Dictionary of Biography*. 1983. Web. 25 May 2015.

Palmer, D. J. *The Rise of English Studies: An account of the study of English Language and Literature from its origins to the making of the Oxford English School*. London; New York: Oxford University Press, 1965. Print.

Parry, Benita. "Aspects of peripheral modernisms". *ARIEL: A review of international English literature* 40.1 (2009). Print.

Patterson, Annette. "Teaching literature in Australia: Examining and reviewing senior English". *Changing English* 15.3 (2008): 311–22. Print.

Ransom, John Crowe. *The New Criticism*. Norfolk, Conn.: New Directions, 1941. Print.

Reid, Ian. *Wordsworth and the Formation of English Studies*. Burlington, Vt.: Ashgate, 2003. Print.

Richards, I.A. *Practical Criticism: A study of literary judgement*. London: Kegan Paul, Trench, 1929. Print.

Samson, Anne. *F.R. Leavis*. Modern Cultural Theorists. London: Harvester Wheatsheaf, 1992. Print.

Schryer, Stephen. "New Criticism". *The Princeton Encyclopedia of Poetry and Poetics*. Ed. Roland Greene. 4th ed. Princeton: Princeton University Press, 2012. 936–37. Print.

Scott, Bonnie Kime. *Refiguring Modernism*. 2 vols. Bloomington: Indiana University Press, 1995. Print.

Smith, A.J. *John Donne: The critical heritage*. London: Routledge and Kegan Paul, 1975. Print.

Smith, Stan. *The Origins of Modernism: Eliot, Pound, Yeats and the rhetorics of renewal*. Hemel Hempstead, Hertfordshire; New York: Harvester Wheatsheaf, 1994. Print.

Smith, Terry. "Modernity". *Grove Art Online*. Web. 11 Jan 2017. <http://www.oxfordindex.oup.com>

Stephen, Ann, Andrew McNamara, and Philip Goad. *Modernism & Australia: Documents on art, design and architecture 1917–1967*. Miegunyah Press Series. Carlton, Vic.: Miegunyah Press (Melbourne University Publishing), 2006. Print.

Stephen, Ann, Philip Goad, and Andrew McNamara. *Modern Times: The untold story of modernism in Australia*. Carlton, Vic.: Miegunyah Press, 2008. Print.

Turner, Jane. *The Dictionary of Art*. 34 vols. New York: Grove, 1996. Print.

Viswanathan, Gauri. *Masks of Conquest: Literary study and British rule in India*. New York: Columbia University Press, 1989. Print.

Whitworth, Michael H. *Modernism*. John Wiley & Sons, 2008. Print.

Widdowson, Peter, ed. *Re-Reading English*. New Accents. London: Methuen, 1982. Print.

Williams, John F. *The Quarantined Culture: Australian reactions to modernism, 1913–1939*. Studies in Australian History. New York: Cambridge University Press, 1995. Print.

Chapter Fifteen

"ONE OF THE WORST THINGS YOU CAN DO TO IT"

The teaching of Judith Wright's poetry

Georgina Arnott

The Analysis of Literature in Australian Schools (ALIAS) database was created to further our understanding of the precise way in which literature has been taught in Australia and of the nature of literary canonisation. It provides confirmation that Judith Wright's poetry was part of this canon; in this chapter I ask what her record in the database reveals about the process of canonisation.[1] Specifically, I seek to test a not-uncommon complaint among creative writers, made strongly by Wright herself, that school curricula too closely direct the reading of literature, dictating interpretations and thereby creating canons of receptivity, rather than simply of the texts themselves. Frank Kermode's influential supposition in *The Sense of an Ending* (1967) that modern readers approach literature with an eye to its social "usefulness", tolerating a text as long as it conforms to the uses for which it is intended, appears to support this proposition, though from a perspective less critical of this process. Within the classroom, both Wright and Kermode might have agreed, the teacher and the curriculum board's interpretation of the text dominates, based as it is on their understanding of its "usefulness". But is this really how Wright's poetry was used in Australian classrooms in the second half of the twentieth century? Are we

---

1   The ALIAS database shows that Wright's poetry was first listed on Australian curricula in 1964 and that between 1966 and 1975 it was included in four out of five states. It remained on curricula until the end of the period, in 2005, with frequent listings in the 1990s, making her poetry amongst the most popular of Australian writers.

able to ascertain this on the basis of quantitative data such as that produced by ALIAS? And should Wright's criticisms about pedagogical standardisation give pause for thought when seeking to approach literary history in this statistically driven way?

"If there's one thing that does make me sick", wrote Wright, "it is the way poetry is used in examinations and in schoolrooms, still one of the worst things you can do to it" (Wright, *With Love* 402). Wright's letters reveal her frustration, spanning several decades, at the attempts of teachers, researchers and publishers to get her involved in what she considered a parasitic and coercive enterprise pedalled by "those damn idiots of English teachers" (*With Love* 159). In a life of much intellectual development and flux it was a constant. She would not engage in their interpretations of her poetry, advance her own, or participate in cassette productions to be used as classroom aids. Wright believed the teaching of poetry, in anything other than a purely minimal way, forced meanings onto poems and ways of thinking onto young people, assaulting a natural, human process of creative interplay between poem and individual. She seemed not to consider that some teachers may have had these concerns themselves and sought to minimise the impact they had on the poem's effect. When discussing teachers and their methods, Wright used language that evoked aggression, even violence: she "recoiled" from those who taught poetry in schools, "however innocent their intentions" (*With Love* 385). The teaching of poetry had become another means of applying "Authority" in schools (226). That poetry had been "theorised and objectified and subjectified and pontificated over" had led to its "present plight" within society: that is, its slow death (448–449). The teaching of creative writing, similarly, was tantamount to "coercion" (246). Wright's biographer Veronica Brady noticed the way Wright linked the teaching of poetry with violence, claiming that Wright said "teachers murdered poems by dissecting them line by line" (Brady 245).[2]

Kermode also perceived a violence within modern reading practices. Like Wright he imagined that the text is now obliged to comply, or assent, to the conditions dictated for it. In a real-life setting, this might be realised in a classroom in which a poem describing some aspect of colonial experience is presented by the teacher within a particular narrative of national development. The poem is "forced" to illuminate, like a performing

---

[2] These are Brady's words, not Wright's, though Brady does cite a source for the idea with the following details, included in the body of the text: "Schools Don't Help, Says Australian Poet". *West Australian* 27 February. Correct reference is as follows: Gillian Ranson. "Schools Do Not Help, Says Australian Poet". *The West Australian* 26 February 1968, 10.

monkey, this greater narrative, proffering moral lessons that support the teacher's narrative, and if it fails it will be swiftly cast aside, neglected or dumped, in Kermode's language, having lost its "operational effectiveness" (Kermode 40). But, despite this, and bearing in mind that Kermode was as alarmed by the prospect of systemic violence as Wright (born four years apart, their early adult years took place when totalitarian regimes excited a world war), their responses to the brutality of modern approaches to reading differ fundamentally. Whereas Kermode viewed this process as a positive demonstration of the reader's freedom to critique, modify and control the text, rather than the more threatening possibility that texts control us (as myth traditionally did), Wright considered that a text carried its own meanings, truth, *life* even, and that to extinguish this was to condition readers towards brutality and fabrication.

Wright's theory of reading emerged from a deep valuing of human individuality. "To Younger Poets", published the year before her death, was a stark enunciation of her philosophy of writing, and offered a guide to reading too: "A light comes off the Object, called Relation. / It connects the maker with what is made, / and illuminates both" (Wright, *Overland* 4). Creativity occurs when the external world speaks to the writer's unconscious, making it consciously difficult to control or even understand: "I wish I knew where creative ideas come from ...", she once wrote (*With Love* 402). Proper reading was a reversal of this process, whereby the illumination of the world present in the poem is unconsciously related to the reader. The reader might take meaning from the poem, but perhaps only semi-consciously, making it difficult to put into words. Maybe the meaning of a poem necessarily resides in a non-verbal place, she wondered: "It's the individual response that counts; the more talk there is about poetry, the less you get of that ..." (226).

It might have been a lamentation for the loss of reading texts as myths, in Kermode's terms. Kermode contended that modern readers no longer tolerated the world created by myth, which "presupposes total and adequate explanation of things as they are and were", collapsing one's origins and endings within a grand scheme (Kermode 39). Though Wright used the language and form of modernism, particularly in *The Moving Image* (1946), and even once defended her criticism of the teaching of poetry on the basis that unlike English teachers she understood "the principles of modern poetry", much of her thinking might be termed "pre-modern" (*With Love* 159). Some have noticed the influence of a Romantic sensibility in her work, and argued that this works to constrain the political challenge posed by poems such as "At Cooloolah" and "Nigger's Leap, New England" (McCann). Brady believed that "from the beginning of her career Judith was to appeal away from history, experienced as a growing series of disasters threatening the very continuance of life, to the world of myth, of the archaic and so-called 'primitive'" (Brady x). Wright's approach to the text appears to support this claim. To read the poem without imported, abstracted scaffolding, from a mental posture of openness, free from any demand to explain one's reading experience, was to read it in terms that, for most modern intellectuals in the West, were not only naïve but potentially dangerous.

The notion that the text and author be spared interrogation – of responding to the poem with silence – is reminiscent of how sacred texts, within traditional and usually radically hierarchical societies, have been treated, often for tyrannical purposes. Certainly this was the case for Kermode, who considered that it was a positive development that texts were no longer treated as myths. Texts are, for modern readers, "not myths, and they are not hypotheses; you neither rearrange the world to suit them, nor test them by experiment, for instance", he wrote tellingly, "in gas-chambers" (Kermode 41). Wright might have countered that we should be prepared to be rearranged by the text because the text is simply the world speaking through the poet. To believe this requires faith in her theory of creativity and of the individual's ability to absorb meaning correctly. From her point of view, a subjugation of the poem's true meaning was tyranny of a different kind.

Wright's valuing of the individual's response had its basis in her personal experience. Until the age of 13 she was home-schooled. Mornings she spent dashing off the work set by Blackfriars Correspondence School; afternoons she spent reading. The experience cultivated within her, like other graduates of this system, including Dorothy Hewett, an independence of mind and originality of interpretation. In a 1985 letter to the Principal of a correspondence school, Wright suggested that her unconventional outlook existed before any schooling ("I have never been conventional in my ways of thinking and working – the freedom I had as a correspondence student was just what I needed"), but also acknowledged that home-schooling furthered her unconventionality, applauding other parents who home-schooled, thereby allowing their "children to take their own tract in their own way and at their own time" (*With Love* 406–7).

At 13 Wright was cast into a more regimented society, becoming a boarder at New England Girls' School. It worked to dampen her interest in literature because she was not able to experience it independently. She told Douglas Stewart in 1971 that "I don't think I myself would ever have been attracted to writing if I hadn't been introduced to poetry before I went to school, and happened luckily to like the stuff from my own point of view". At NEGS she was not "able to read much – there seemed always to be a bell ringing to signal a move to another lesson in another classroom … I had to adjust my learning speed to that of the rest of the class instead of taking my own way through the text" (*With Love* 226). At university she had a similar experience, quitting second-year English honours when she discovered that the entire course consisted of reading part two of *Beowulf*, something she had already done (Wright, "An Interview" 2.1.16). That the lecturer might have framed the text with an abstract body of knowledge did not impress her in the slightest. It merely drew her further from the text, and this intimacy was for her both the real function and only pleasure of reading. Her aim at school became always to retreat and "spend happy hours alone" reading (Wright, *Half* 111). At university, she afterwards reflected, her main mentor was the Fisher library ("An Interview" 2.1.24).

Wright's beliefs about the link between independent thought and independent reading should be seen in the context of her family's mistrust of city-based education. Although her father, Phillip Wright, went on to become Vice-Chancellor of the University of New England, none of the family members she grew up around had been to university, prominent within their society though they were. The basis for Phillip Wright's involvement in UNE was his concern that young people faced "almost certain subsequent absorption" by the city when they went there for education. He referred to absorption that was beyond the bodily; many country people, especially those involved in the Country Party like himself, believed that tertiary education lent their children city views, characterised by an immorality and inability to think clearly. When Wright told her father she wanted to go to the University of Sydney, he was "reluctant to consider Sydney, let alone university" (*Half* 117). Elsewhere she said he was "terrified that going to university was going to be the ruin of me" ("An Interview" 1.1.25). After spending a year attempting to change her mind, eventually Phillip agreed. Acknowledging the depth of Phillip's misgivings, Judith's daughter Meredith McKinney has observed that this was "pretty enlightened for a pastoralist" (McKinney).

Perhaps he need not have worried, for Wright carried with her to the University of Sydney a suspicion of university learning and the student who was an exemplar of it. While there she became a columnist for the student newspaper *Honi Soit*. Her 13 columns reveal a sensibility and set of concerns largely at odds with those of her older self, which only makes more conspicuous the continuity that existed on one issue: her profound concern with individuality and suspicion that education promoted conformity (Arnott 134–9). Already a savvy writer, Wright knew her audience; anything serious had to be couched in campus humour as it was then: jolly, carefree, mocking. In her first column she included an original poem entitled "University Specimens: No. 1: The Perfect Student", in which she caricatured the "lousy frowsy dastard / With a self-contented kink / Whose head is stuffed with paper / And whose humour smells of ink". The ideal student, who by her contemporaries was imagined as highly literate, well-informed, verbally dexterous and analytical, became, in her hands, evasive, performative, overly-critical, time-wasting and unprincipled:

> He works and sports and frivols
> In an ostentatious way.
> He's aware of current happenings
> And discusses them all day.
> He's a very model student,
> But whatever he may think,
> He's a lousy frowsy dastard
> With a self-contented kink.

The final refrain creates a circularity reminiscent of the student who constantly discusses "current happenings", but never does anything about them (Wright, *Honi* 14:3). There is a strong continuity between "The Perfect Student" and many of Wright's later poems, including "To Hafiz of Shiraz" (1966), in which the speaker perceives that knowledge about the world – how "each star has its path" – should not, as it does for some, make "the night sky any less strange". To her mind, the miracles of the world are "over and over repeated but never yet understood". Knowledge gained from reading intellectually, critically, analytically, does not necessarily lead to greater comprehension of the world. Moreover, as the Perfect Student unwittingly demonstrated, such knowledge risks creating a deep passivity and lack of wonderment about it.

The university columns Wright wrote were foremost performance but from behind her mask she submitted the very radical suggestion that formal education does not lead to one's liberation but to a kind of castration and constriction of selfhood. A frequent refrain was that students should study less. One story she introduced with the lament that just as we "were beginning to think it was worth coming to Law lectures ..." (*Honi* 16:3). Around her, she saw autonomous minds, bodies and books subjugated to the will of a greater authority: "there must be someone, somewhere, under some obscure bushel, who doesn't merely creep about this bright, young University, blinking like an earthworm dragged from its hole and carrying Aristotle's Ethics under its paralytic arm" (*Honi* 17:3). Judith Wright might be remembered for her earnestness, but it was not always so. She lamented that no student had made "a little printable whoopee"; that they seemed all so frustratingly proper, perfect, same-ish (*Honi* 22:3).

Throughout her life Wright perceived a creeping conformity within Australian life and a gradual dissolution of selfhood, of feeling, of independent thought. In "Computers" (1966), she began: "those things make me nervous". Humans, she said, were becoming more like them: "we're ashamed to fall in love / because They don't do it. / We analyse poems instead of reading them / because that's what computers do". Such analysis formed knowledge that was cold, inhumane, incomplete. Similarly, in "Advice to a Young Poet" (1970), Wright asked her subject: "your mind's gone electronic / and your heart can't feel? / but listen, your teachers tell you, / it's not to worry." Teachers, those symbols of authority and knowledge, were no figures of comfort or wisdom in Wright's imagination. In a society that provided ever fewer opportunities for exercising one's imagination and strengthening one's individuality, Wright found it sinister that young people were ushered away from experiencing poetry as a tangle of sounds, images and possible meanings; an unmeasurable, personal, sensory pleasure.

Basic acquaintance with Australian English curricula suggests that students have not been introduced to literature as Wright would have them. But have they been schooled to read as Kermode argues modern readers do, in an almost directly oppositional way to that which Wright advanced? To approach the text as a fiction? To test it constantly against their own historical "reality", believing in its value only on when it assented to that reality? Does the use of her poetry in Australian curricula reveal this?

Data produced by ALIAS on Wright's poetry shows that six selected or collected publications and 15 individual poems were used in curricula between 1964 and 2005. (This does not include any of Wright's poetry that may have been studied using one of the many school poetry and literature anthologies in which she had, and continues to have, a significant presence.) The decision by state curriculum boards to list specific poems, instead of books, may have been economic. Forty of the 52 instances of such listings took place in New South Wales between 1969 and 1972. In contrast, Western Australia and South Australia never listed individual poems, obliging students to buy books or schools to stock multiple copies. Wright understood that the publication of her work was closely tied to the realities of the student market. Despite preferring to publish a longer collection of her work, she told Tom Thompson at Oxford University Press in 1991 that a smaller, selected edition "could just about pay for itself through settings for educational syllabuses, while students couldn't have afforded a Collected!" (*With Love* 471).

Before considering the listing of individual poems, what does the more substantive listing of collections and selections of poetry reveal? Are there, for instance, differences in selection which perhaps indicate a preference on the part of curriculum boards for particular poems, or periods in her poetic output?

Wright's record in the ALIAS database points to some of the challenges of quantitative research. It is difficult to know exactly which publications were used or how significant their differences were to the teaching of her work. The database shows many listings under a fictive title, "Selected/Collected Poems", which potentially describes six separate publications, some with multiple editions. Although the sheer quantity of data in quantitative research sometimes necessitates unsubtle categorisation and prevents an assembler from knowing when such categorisations are limiting, papering over distinctions such as this can mean it is difficult to interpret data in a meaningful way. In the humanities, where "data" often contain complex formulations and require interpretation, the demand for meaningful granularisation of compiled data is a continuing challenge.

Another risk is that what becomes definitively true when we pursue the data may not be all that illuminating. The only discernible trend revealed by the listing of book titles in Wright's record is that smaller publications were used in the early decades whereas mainly larger ones were used in the latter.[3] While there were some differences of selection between the three

---

3   *Five Senses* (1963), *Australian Poets: Judith Wright* (1963) and *Judith Wright: Selected Poems* (1963), each between 87 and 192 pages long, were the most common choices in curricula

publications chosen in the first half of the period, it seems more likely *Judith Wright: Selected Poems*, at 87 pages, was chosen over *Five Senses*, at 170 pages, for its brevity rather than because particular poems were chosen above others. Costs and availability, of varying consequence in each state, were as likely to be factors as the small variation in selections of poems, none of which appears controversial. Could we legitimately make an argument around the privileging of certain poems by curriculum boards when we cannot eliminate the influence of material realities in their decision-making? The increasing preference by curriculum boards for longer works over the entire period can similarly be explained by a number of pedestrian facts, including that Wright had produced more poetry; that because of this, and her growing reputation, publishers were more willing to publish collected and large selected books; that these were what were in stock over the period; and that the cost of printing became relatively cheaper for publishers over the period, making longer books more commercially viable.

In spite of this, when considered alongside ancillary material the data does appear to illuminate something of the way in which Wright's poetry, and perhaps the work of other poets, has been taught in Australia. It is noteworthy that her poetry was not included in curricula until 1964, despite her first collection, *The Moving Image*, being published in 1946. Certainly it would not be normal (or perhaps reasonable) for the work of a newly published poet to be included in a school curriculum, but Wright's arrival on the Australian literary scene was not entirely normal, making the 18-year delay significant. *The Moving Image* received 12 reviews in its first two years, according to another database, *AustLit*, many of which were in major publications. Several poems from it had been published in important periodicals already, especially *Meanjin*. Shirley Walker, in her study of Wright, reflected: "it is difficult to overstate the impact" on Australian writing of that first collection (Walker 2). This ensured that the five single volumes of poetry that followed, before 1964, were taken seriously by periodicals and critics. In the decade before her first inclusion in a school curriculum, South Australia in 1964, her work was reviewed a hefty 95 times according to *AustLit*. In the first decade in which it was included, it was reviewed an

---

from 1964 until 1980. Wright's record in ALIAS includes two texts called *Australian Poets: Judith Wright* but my research has uncovered only one such work. I believe one was confused with *Judith Wright: Selected Poems* (1963), which was part of the Australian Poets Series, and so have used this title. Two publications, *Collected Poems* (1971 and 1994 editions) and *Human Pattern: Selected Poems* (1990), each between 242 and 436 pages, were the most common choices in curricula from 1980 until 2005.

even higher 110 times. In the following two decades there were significantly fewer reviews of her work (40 and then 64), suggesting that once a writer becomes a "critical success", to put it simply, it is not important to the setting of their work on curricula that they continue to be critically evaluated to the same extent. They have, in short, proved their canonical status and do not need to do so again.

There may be other, material reasons, though, why Wright was not included in curricula until almost 20 years after her first volume of poetry was published. It was only in 1963, the year before South Australia included her in their curriculum, that her first selected poems was published, which became the set text. This might suggest that publishers influence the curriculum, for it is their choice when to publish such a compilation, the only practical way of teaching across a poet's oeuvre. Publishers, however, would likely counter that market demand is the major factor in their decision. And so we might deduce from this that the public has to buy a poet's work in sufficient quantities before it can be set in any practical way on a school curriculum; this seems as potentially democratic a means of deciding which writers should be included as any.

But could it have been that her status as an Australian woman poet, and one who wrote explicitly about these two facets of her identity, influenced the delay? It has been noted elsewhere in this book that women writers were as popular as men between 1945 and 1955 on Australian curricula, so her gender provides no obvious explanation (Yiannakis). Relatively few Australian writers, however, were set in this same period, especially compared to the period 1966 to 1975, when the number "grew dramatically" (Yiannakis 30). Being Australian may have been a factor in the delay of her work being included. And yet, if the delay indicates a sense of national cultural inferiority on the part of Australian intellectuals, this is hardly a groundbreaking observation today.

The listing of single poems, used when curricula specified them, is more helpful than those of collected or selected works in the ALIAS database, and helps build a case for the way in which Wright's poetry has been taught in Australian schools. Although the data relating to them is small (single Wright poems were used overwhelmingly in New South Wales between 1969 and 1972), if treated as a sample this sample indicates that Wright's early work was favoured over her later work by curricula. Of the 13 poems used in New South Wales in that period, three were from *The Moving Image* (1946); three were from *Woman to Man* (1949); four were from *The Gateway* (1953); and three were from each one of the following collections: *The Two Fires* (1955), *Birds* (1962) and *Five Senses (The Forest)* (1963).[4] The curriculum board chose no poems from *The Other Half* (1966), although it was published three years before the start of the period, and none from *The Shadow* (1970), once it was published. In other words, despite Wright having published several volumes in the most recent decade, the curriculum board mostly chose poems that had been published 16 or more years earlier. Together with other data already mentioned, we might deduce from this that every volume, perhaps every poem, which the poet produces has to prove its canonical status, critically, before it can be included in an Australian curriculum, and this takes time. More contemporary work, which has not been extensively evaluated, tested and approved, cannot easily sidestep canonical barriers. The poems become canonical, not the poet.

Of course, the time lag may not exist simply to allow for the testing of "quality" (leaving aside the problems this raises). Time enables the construction of an elaborate and comprehensible scaffolding to be produced around the poem. Such scaffolding, or "discussion points" in the classroom, usually includes the historical period from which the poem has emerged, the dialogue created by critical works, and the poet's biography, which becomes longer, possibly more interesting (certainly in Wright's case) and usually more public with time. That such significant time lags exist between the production and teaching of Wright's work is further evidence for Wright's claim that such scaffolding is what is really being taught in poetry class. If, conversely, the teacher presented a poem written recently by a relatively unknown poet, which had received little or no critical attention, would the teacher have anything to say about it? Or, more to the point, would they have anything to say which might be considered authoritative in the eyes of an educational institution, and therefore of the students who have been schooled in its ways?

The ALIAS data on specific Wright poems indicates that such scaffolding was central. Poems included, such as "Bullocky", "South of My Days", "Remittance Man", "Woman to Man", "Woman to Child" and "Metho Drinker", all from her first two volumes, were some of her most critically evaluated, and elicit discussion relating to the formal elements of poetry, Wright's biography as a pastoral girl and a woman poet, and popular issues such as Australian colonial history, non-Indigenous responses to the land,

---

4   Poems used in NSW curricula between 1969 and 1972: "Bullocky", "Remittance Man", "South of My Days", "Metho Drinker", "Woman to Child", "Woman to Man", "Legend", "Old Man", "The Cedars", "Cicadas", "Sanctuary", "Black Cockatoos" and "Sports Field".

and second-wave feminism. Throughout those poems the sure-footed voice of a young woman tackles complexities but is rarely broken by them.

In contrast, her most recently published collection in 1969, *The Other Half* (1966), is dark and troubling at an elementary level. The poet herself is insecure, fearing for herself, humanity, and the world's dim prospects for survival. "Destruction", "Power" and "Pro and Con", and many other poems in the collection wonder at our ability to live in the face of certain death. Yet others, including "The Encounter", "City Sunrise" and "Turning Fifty", point to humankind's apocalyptic drive, that last poem noting "... granted life or death, death's what we're choosing". "Wishes", "Beside the Creek", and "Prayer" raise doubts about her own ability to write, love and be wise in the face of this despair. And of course other poems in the collection, including "Naked Girl and Mirror", "Eve to her Daughters", and "To Another Housewife" suggest that socially acceptable roles for women crush their idealism, independence of mind, sexuality: the very things that make them human. Various biographical events might explain the collection's dark, foreboding tone. There are rare moments of hope, when she conjures the possibility of renewal, such as "Snakeskin on a Gate", "Cleaning Day", and in the final lines of the collection: "I raise my cup— / dark, bitter, neutral, clean / sober as morning— / to all I've seen and known— / to this new sun", but these are both rare within, and feeble against, the gloom generated throughout. Brady observed that Wright "was becoming increasingly radical" in the years preceding the publication of *The Other Half* (Brady 219). Certainly she was despairing and increasingly intolerant of mainstream society.

It may be that the time lag between poems being written and included in curricula allows the politics of mainstream society to catch up with a poet's "progressive" politics. Wright made the point in 1988, indicating that setting texts within a curriculum was increasingly about enforcing politics of the mainstream:

> It has been a matter of setting acceptable standards – whose application then has lately been in the devising of school and university syllabuses and lists of recommended reading. Naturally, the writers of the "underground", the advocates and protestors of causes unpopular with authority, or not yet so far absorbed by the critical establishment as to be safely acceptable, are left on one side or dealt with gingerly (Wright, "The Writer" 132).

Poems from the 1960s which had at the time been left on one side by curriculum boards in New South Wales seem to have become safe by the

1990s. "To Another Housewife" and "Eve to her Daughters", both from *The Other Half* (1966), constituted two of the six poems used in examinations (NSW Government). By then, the political challenges raised by these poems, very broadly feminist and environmental, were more widely accepted. Furthermore, some of their political potency may have been diluted in the intervening 30 years, making them safer still. For students, whose whole lives had taken place in the interval, the urgency with which "Eve to her Daughters" warns of environmental collapse may have been hard to appreciate.

It might be argued that interest in Wright's early work during the 1960s was more about its style than its politics. Certainly, throughout the 1960s and 1970s the increasingly abstracted nature of her work was cited as the reason why critics overwhelmingly preferred her earlier collections. Although, as stated above, this was the period in which Wright received most reviews, much of the reviewing was busily noting a decline in quality within her poetic output. In 1972 Frank Kellaway noted that "Australian critics have often expressed a growing doubt and uneasiness about the quality of her later achievements" and singled out the influential critic Vincent Buckley who, in 1968, complained of a "false simplicity", a "growing portentousness", an "increasing impersonality" in recent collections, and added that such poetry "does not seem to mean very much either to us or to herself", a comment which Kellaway believed "betrayed malice". And yet even Kellaway contended that "few serious critics would disagree with the view that there was a slackening of poetical intensity and a failure sometimes to communicate her vision in a concrete way" in most work after her 1949 volume *Woman to Man* (Kellaway 90–91). The inclusion of poems from *The Other Half* in examinations of the 1990s demonstrates that even widely derided stylistic indulgences or idiosyncrasies can become "acceptable". It also reminds us that poetry is intrinsically awkward subject matter for the classroom. Whereas poetry tends to lead its audiences towards new aesthetic possibilities, prowling around the edges of our linguistic range, educational institutions can prefer forms of knowledge – including ways of speaking – that have already been tested. Wright knew this too well.

While sympathetic to criticisms of Wright's latter work, Kellaway still could not shrug the notion that there was something disproportionate in this reception, and said it was as if critics wanted to "silence" her, an observation the poet might have agreed with. Such claims about the reception of her work – which raise the prospect that it was informed by her gender, or her politics – are another example of the scaffolding created by a time lag.

When a poem such as "Woman to Man", originally published in 1949, was presented to a 1972 classroom, not only were there feminist questions arising from the poem to discuss, albeit questions posed more than 20 years earlier, but questions around the possibly gendered reception of her work also.

Further ancillary data from the New South Wales curriculum board's website suggests that time lags continued to be important, but that there may have been an increasingly open approach to the teaching of her poetry in the final years of the century. In 1996 the 242-page collection of selected poems, *A Human Pattern*, was put on that state's curriculum, which appears to have been linked to its republication.[5] English exam papers from 1996 to 1998 identified six poems from it which students should discuss in their response, two from her 1946 collection, one each from her 1949 and 1953 collections, and two, as already mentioned, from her 1966 collection (NSW Government).[6] The time lag between publication and inclusion in the curriculum was now even wider, suggesting that the scaffolding for the poetry continued to be important. However, in the 1999 and 2000 NSW exam papers, the last to list Wright's poetry, specific poems were not chosen, suggesting a less directive approach. Also suggesting this is the actual exam questions for the five-year period, which are remarkably open: "In what ways is time important in Judith Wright's poems?"; "The most effective poems vividly convey the poet's ideas and feelings"; "Poetry makes nothing happen. What is the point of poetry?"; "The achievement of Judith Wright's poetry is that it shows us how we learn from others"; "Show to what extent Wright's poetry balances the concerns of the past with those of the present" (NSW Government).

If these questions were all that were asked of the student then it is hard to see even Wright finding fault with them, but of course any familiarity with classrooms of the 1990s and the requirements of teachers suggests students had already been schooled in a particular method of interpretation before they arrived at the exam. To prove or disprove Wright's fears categorically, we need more data, including whether curriculum boards issued schools

---

5   *A Human Pattern: Selected Poems* was first published in 1990 by Angus and Robertson. As noted above, Wright acknowledged in a letter to Tom Thompson at OUP that a selected edition of her work would sell more successfully to students than a more expensive collected edition. *A Human Pattern*, however, was not listed on any curriculum, according to the ALIAS database, until 1996. That same year it was republished by Tom Thompson, who had bought the rights from A&R three years earlier, under his ETT imprint and with the consent of Wright.

6   Poems specified in NSW 1996, 1997 and 1998 exams were "Remittance Man", "South Of My Days", "Woman to Man", "Legend", "To Another Housewife" and "Eve to her Daughters".

teaching directives, advice about appropriate framing devices which they might encourage their students to use in the face of an open exam question, and even, prior to examinations, lists of preferred poems for students to draw on.[7] This is where qualitative data, such as interviews with teachers, curriculum boards members or even students of the period, would further our understanding of the way in which literature has been taught.

* * *

In 1986 Wright became so frustrated that the continuing interest in "Bullocky", now 40 years old, was predicated on an interpretation with which she disagreed that she withdrew it from further publication in anthologies. She told Stephen Murray-Smith: "it was all too clear from the outraged responses from teachers that that was just what they wanted – a hymn to the pioneers. *But I hadn't written it*" (*With Love* 411). It was the pinnacle of her frustration with the teaching of her poetry, for it was clear to Wright through their use of "Bullocky" that teachers, and by extension curriculum boards, sought poetry to fit their realities, rather than being receptive to the realities presented by poetry. An unusual act among creative writers, it was cast by some as extreme, even censorious. In Wright's terms, she was saving the poem – and perhaps her own reputation – from being brutally misconstrued, from a big lie being inflicted on students. It went against her own rule that she wouldn't comment on her poetry but leave others to interpret freely (*With Love* 226). And, ironically, this incident underscores the judiciousness of that position, for the publication of her letters in the last decade reveals that she changed her interpretation of that poem based on her changing outlook. Her own scaffolding shifted, substantially, to suit her changed reality.

In 1963 Wright told friend and literary critic Dorothy Green that while the historical figure on whom she based the bullock-driver was "probably a kind of religious maniac", whether or not he was mad was not significant: "Let me emphasise", Wright wrote to Green, that "this hasn't anything to do with the poem". The poem was meant to "justify old men like him, and in fact to justify the human race, I suppose, or certain of its actions and pursuits" (*With Love* 152). Then, in 1986, when her thinking on Australian

---

7   The membership of NSW subject curriculum boards and teaching guides are not publicly available, except possibly via a Freedom of Information request (Clarke).

history had developed, she explained to Murray-Smith that she objected to the way critics had read the poem "shorn of context": "the fact is, the old man in question ... was mad insofar as he was a religious maniac, though of a gentle order as I personally knew him. Yes, the pioneers were mad all right, and often wicked too" (*With Love* 410). His madness became relevant, and so the poem went from being the "justification" of a universal character, to the condemnation of colonialism, represented by the bullock-driver's deranged and morally suspect state-of-mind. The poem, in Kermode's terms, became "useful" in a new way.

Furthermore, Wright acknowledged that context, even if just that provided by other poems in the collection, was necessary to the correct interpretation of the poem. Her defence of her decision to withdraw it, made at length in major newspapers, suggests that the poem required further, more instructive context to be interpreted correctly – at least for teachers. It substantiates Kermode's point that as modern readers we rearrange the text according to our realities – here even the writer did – but also, in some senses, the desirability of this, for it surely makes art more interesting if new meanings are created by new contexts, be they historic or intellectual. Wright might even have approved of the contexts that have been increasingly used in relation to her work in the years since her death in 2000. As English curricula, and society as a whole, catch up with her politics, poems such as "Nigger's Leap, New England" and "The Dark Ones" are, among others, framed within explicitly anti-national, postcolonial narratives, and her work is often taught in tandem with Oodgeroo Noonuccal's, prompting new and possibly challenging dialogues for students and teachers alike.

And yet, to accept that poetry contains no intrinsic reality, carries no unchanging and inherent meaning which an individual can recognise via poetry's various and unique modes of communication, modes which are not always easily explained or quantifiable, seems also to abandon its very singularity, and this was Wright's point: how, in this case, does it differ from any text? In the end, the fact that poetry continues to be taught suggests that its special function continues, at least to some extent, to be recognised.

* * *

The ALIAS database reveals, with a clarity that has not been apparent before, that context matters in the process of canonising poems. Context, which requires time to develop, gives curriculum boards and teachers more material with which they can provide an interpretation of a poem, an interpretation which assents broadly with the "reality" they want to teach. At the same time, there's much that ALIAS cannot tell us about how poetry functions in the classroom. And this points to the grain of truth in Wright's suspiciousness towards attempts to impose interpretive frameworks on poetry, her insistence on the illimitable nature of poetic language and the individual nature of poetic experience.

Works Cited

Arnott, Georgina. *The Unknown Judith Wright*. Crawley, WA: University of Western Australia Publishing, 2016. Print.

Brady, Veronica. *South of My Days: A biography of Judith Wright*. Sydney: Angus and Robertson, 1998. Print.

Clarke, Rhonda. Principal Project Officer, Board of Studies, Teaching and Educational Standards New South Wales. Telephone interview by the author. 18 February 2015.

Kellaway, Frank. "The collected poems of Judith Wright". *Overland* 50/51 (1972): 90–92. Print.

Kermode, Frank. *The Sense of an Ending: Studies in the theory of fiction with a new epilogue*. 3rd ed. New York: Oxford University Press, 2000. Print.

McCann, Andrew. "The literature of extinction". *Meanjin* 65.1 (2006): 48–54. Print.

McKinney, Meredith. Interview by the author. Tape recording. Braidwood, NSW, 8 August 2008.

NSW Government. "NSW Higher School Certificate (HSC) Examination Papers 1995–2000". *Board of Studies Teaching and Educational Standards NSW*. Web. 15 Jan. 2015. <www.boardofstudies.nsw.edu.au>

Ranson, Gillian. "Schools do not help, says Australian poet". *West Australian* 26 Feb 1968: 10. Print.

Walker, Shirley. *Flame and Shadow: A study of Judith Wright's poetry*. St Lucia, QLD: University of Queensland Press, 1991; reprint 1996. Print.

Wright, Judith. *A Human Pattern*. Sydney: Angus and Robertson, 1994. Print.

———. An interview with Judith Wright McKinney". By Heather Rusden. ORAL TRC 2202. Transcript of tape recording. Oral History and Folklore collection, National Library of Australia, Canberra. Numbers in parenthesis indicate tape, tape side, page, in that order.

———. Author record. Austlit database. University of Queensland, n.d. Web. 15 Jan. 2015.

———. "Computers". *Sydney Morning Herald*. 18 June 1966, 15.

———. *Collected Poems*. Sydney: Angus and Robertson, 1994.

———. *Half a Lifetime*. Melbourne: Text Publishing, 1999; reprint, 2001.

———. "Quadrangles". *Honi Soit*. 14, 16, 17, 22 (1936).

———. "The writer as activist". *Born of the Conquerors*. Canberra: Aboriginal Studies Press, 1991: 127–136.

———. "To younger poets". *Overland* 154 (1999): 4.

———. *With Love and Fury: Selected Letters of Judith Wright*. Ed. Patricia Clarke and Meredith McKinney. Canberra: National Library of Australia, 2006.

Yiannakis, John. "An overview of the ALIAS data and findings". *Required Reading: Literature in Australian Secondary English since 1945*. Clayton: Monash University Publishing, 2017. 19–37.

Chapter Sixteen

THE CONDITIONS OF ASSENT AND ASCENT

Cloudstreet as classroom classic

Claire Jones

I was a fourteen-year-old high school student in 1991 when *Cloudstreet* was published. My first memory of the novel is accompanying my sister to the bookshop at the University of Western Australia at the beginning of the 1992 academic year. She was going into her first year of an Arts degree and *Cloudstreet* was on the English text list. She was the first person in our family to go to university so this expedition was a big deal. The university sits on the banks of the Swan River across the road from Matilda Bay, the opening and closing setting of the novel, a place that we had often visited for Sunday family picnics. Growing up, my sister and I used to talk about the university and imagine life inside the lush grounds and sandstone buildings. It seems my life keeps circling back to this location and this novel – familiar sites within my life.

Throughout her first year my sister would talk to me about the things she was studying, giving me an overview of the books and lectures. When it came to *Cloudstreet* she told me parts of the story but would linger over the eerie playing of middle C (which she would play on our family piano for added effect) and speculate on where in Perth's inner suburbs Cloud Street could be. I was determined to read it and once she was finished I did. Since that initial reading I have revisited this novel many times, no longer as a way of satisfying curiosity but as a professional requirement. As a senior school English teacher for ten years, Winton's work occupied for me a constant place in the specialised educational canon and in my first years of teaching I was charged with teaching it. Later I was asked to write a teaching resource for Copyright Agency Limited to satisfy the requirements of the then incoming Australian curriculum. In the process of researching the syllabus and curriculum histories of English it became clear that *Cloudstreet* had played a critical role in the classroom since its first publication. So as I write this essay from the sandstone Arts building of the University of Western Australia, overlooking Matilda Bay and the Swan River, I can hear the opening chords playing: "Shall we gather at the river?" While I know the words, unlike many others, I have some concerns about joining in with the singing.

Assent and ascent

The circumstances of *Cloudstreet*'s incorporation into the educational canon are unique. It appears that the novel's ascent to this guarded space was connected to its popularity as one of our "best-loved" literary works. Almost from the moment of its publication it was adopted in tertiary and secondary syllabuses, and it has remained firmly embedded in secondary text lists. When considering the novel's dominance in this field it has been difficult to separate its popularity with the general reading public from its dominance in the secondary English classroom. Penguin's branding of *Cloudstreet* as "the modern Australian classic" has little opposition within popular culture. The novel has been awarded numerous literary prizes, including the Miles Franklin award, and has been voted the favourite Australian novel by the reading public in numerous polls since its publication. When the scope of the ABC's 2004 literary poll extended beyond the national domain, Winton's work was equally as impressive in the eyes of Australians, achieving fifth place behind *The Lord of the Rings*, *Pride and Prejudice*, the *Bible* and *To Kill a Mockingbird*.[1] These top five texts raise interesting questions about the conditions of assent (see Chapter One). They are a mixture of literary classics, ethical handbooks, fantasy teachings and foundational epics. Perhaps this provides some indication of what *Cloudstreet* means in Australian schools?

The cultural reputation and popularity of Winton's family saga might not be the sole reason for its position in an educational canon, but it cannot be dismissed. It seems ascent and assent may be connected here. Reflecting on the ALIAS database John Yiannakis finds that the inclusion of Australian

---

1   See www.theage.com.au/news/Books/Tolkien-is-spellbound/2004/12/05/1102182155661.html.

works was "the biggest change to have taken place since 1945" in senior secondary syllabus selections (Yiannakis 108). Since *Cloudstreet*'s 1991 release it has held an unprecedented position in Australian senior secondary classrooms. First included for secondary study on the Western Australian Literature text list in 1993, it has since remained on this recommended list, as well as being added to the state's English recommended text list; in states where there is a compulsory or set list, such as New South Wales, Victoria and Tasmania, it has appeared and reappeared on a regular basis. The ALIAS data shows that from 1995 to 2005 it was the most popular novel on school syllabuses. In this it does not meet the conventional requirements of literary canonisation. *Cloudstreet* has no long history of consecration and Winton is no Nobel Laureate. Moreover, the novel was not part of teachers' own educational experiences, and it would not initially have been an available text within the English department storeroom (McLean Davies, "Auditing" 11). It does appear that ascent and assent were simultaneous.

Great Australian Novel

One reason often given for *Cloudstreet*'s general popularity, and also for its presence in the Australian classroom, is that it is a "Great Australian Novel". But what are the elements of a Great Australian Novel? The criteria for the Miles Franklin prize – a novel that "is of the highest literary merit and which must present Australian life in any of its phases"[2] – seem to sum it up. But what does "highest literary merit" mean? A panel discussion about *Cloudstreet* on the Australian Broadcasting Corporation's *First Tuesday Book Club* gives some idea of what readers mean by literary value in relation to this novel. Popular Australian cultural figure and one-time politician, Peter Garrett, comes right out with it: "I think it's a true classic. And to be honest, it's great literature which is very readable, and it touches chords deep inside all of us, I suspect, and difficult to find the words, really."[3] Host Jennifer Byrne's follow-up question gives the game away: "Did you cry?" she asks. Garrett replies:

> Oh, yes, and ... Look, it's community, it's the community of these people and their character ... and the characters that he draws out of them and it's the way in which they confront their own humanity and their limitations, and it's ultimately about the fact that this thing

---

2   www.milesfranklin.com.au/about_history.
3   www.abc.net.au/tv/firsttuesday/s2795575.htm.

goes on. The young boy is born and they have the barbecue and the picnic down by the river, but there's so much more in it. The writing is extremely powerful, imaginative, evocative, but not showy. It's got a really gutsy sort of Australianness to it, I think in a real sense, without being corny or clichéd, and, yeah, I think it's going to be one the great books of all time.

So it is not simply the representation of "Australian life", but the way in which this life is expressive of a "gutsy sort of Australianness" that makes it worthy of literary merit: its power to evoke particular emotive responses with a voice, rhythm and location that is recognisably connected to the national mythology.

But still, the popularly determined labels "greats" or "classics", or whether a text makes you cry, are not generally considered reasons for educational popularity or assent to canonicity. If we return to the top five of ABC's poll we can see this is not always the case. Indeed the work of Patrick White, our 1973 Nobel Laureate, has been an important part of the Australian literary canon, continually appearing on secondary and tertiary syllabus lists, but his work has never been widely popular. Popularity and canonicity are not always companions, particularly in relation to Australian literature, so why has this novel become one of the most widely studied novels in secondary English and Literature classes in Australia? To explore this question it is helpful to consider John Guillory's *Cultural Capital*, with particular reference to his explanation of "canon formation" (vii). If we apply Guillory's findings to *Cloudstreet* the novel's dominance in secondary English is in part explained. Guillory argues that canonicity is a measure of the "usefulness" of literature in relation to cultural capital. In his exploration he seeks to construct a "sociology of judgement in relation to canonicity", explaining that the "institutional forms of syllabus and curriculum", or "the school", has a "historical function of distributing, or regulating access to, the forms of cultural capital" (vii).

Applying a generic and linguistic matrix, Guillory demonstrates the process by which texts are accorded canonical status within vernacular curricula. Calling on Samuel Johnson's assessment and praise of Thomas Gray's *Elegy Written in a Country Churchyard*, Guillory explains that its power lies "in the evocation of the 'common'" (90), that the poem "seems to be uttered by the *Zeitgeist*, as though it were the consummate expression of a social consensus" (91). In this way, the commonplace becomes a significant aspect of style as well as a critical component of ideological and thematic expression (91). This is what Garrett recognises and admires in *Cloudstreet*. With reference to Benedict Anderson, Guillory goes on to argue there is an interconnection between linguistic and nationalist agendas since the bourgeois voice shifts from being the voice of international connections, removed from literature through previous canonised classical expression, to being the voice of a national vernacular that can sustain a literary culture. This process, explained through the 1751 poem and the schooling system, we can translate to the Australian working-class ethos at the centre of the cultural mythology of *Cloudstreet* – a common vernacular recognised in a literary text by a "common reader" (118).

Central to this discussion is Guillory's argument that "there can be no general theory of canon formation that would predict or account for the canonisation of any particular work, without specifying first the unique historical conditions of that work's production and reception" (85). This is also the case made by Australian academic Ken Gelder. In his response to questions over canonisation and Australian works he explains that Great Australian Novels are possible at times "when literary culture invested heavily in a nationalist project that could stand alongside the best elsewhere in the world."[4] While for Gelder *Cloudstreet* is no literary masterpiece, it appeared at a moment when it can have popular appeal and an important function within the school. If we follow Guillory's argument, the aspects of the text that cause such a response in the general reading public are indeed the same conditions for ascent into the school canon at this moment in time.

The Bicentennial novel

Robert Dixon describes *Cloudstreet* as Tim Winton's Bicentennial novel (Dixon). In doing so he places it in the context not only of that historical moment, but as a production of the arts machine that was funded by Australia's cultural heritage investment. It has been well documented that Winton wrote the novel away from Australia, funded by the Arts Council and living in Greece and Paris. While many have speculated on the influence that distance can have on the sharpness of the image created of Australia, this context of governmental production and national retrospection brings into greater focus the national mythology associated with *Cloudstreet* as a timely demonstration of Australian history and landscape, and most importantly the Australian national character.

---

[4] http://newsroom.melbourne.edu/news/n-206.

In his essay "Australian Literature and the Bicentenary", Patrick Buckridge deliberates over a critical question about literature and its employment for national purposes. In a time of heightened nationalist sentiment, literature like other cultural forms was invited to share in the process of national re-self-definition. As a result, Buckridge argues, literature became a site of "undisguised conflict" (69–70). In his assessment of canon formation he identifies the "Bicentenntial Effect" (which he describes as "an impact study of sorts"), where this national moment precipitated "a sudden and temporal change of ideological pressure on an established feature of the Australian cultural environment" (70). This celebration exposed a fundamental conflict in the Australian literary system, and as a consequence Australian literature as an institution emerged from the "bicentenarising" treatment more fragmented. In a system in which canon formation has never been entirely detached from national sentiment, it was in the 1990s openly at odds with itself as it attempted to reconcile the "popular/egalitarian/democratic meaning attributed to Australian Literature and the hierarchical and exclusive nature of 'canon form'" (73).

The *Bicentennial Australian Studies Schools Project* was a critical aspect of this process of national self-definition, and evidence of governmental intervention in this cultural moment. This project was a government-commissioned education series that sought "ways of encouraging innovative approaches to teaching on Australian society". The discussion papers that accompanied this project (with the institutional name of "bulletins") formalised a general movement in the literary field towards the inclusion of Australian literature. This had been gathering pace since the 1970s and was predicated on poststructuralist and cultural studies paradigms. However, in the subsequent curriculum changes in many states this was to become a formal requirement of English subjects. By this point Tim Winton's work had already established an important presence in secondary education and in 1988 his short story "Neighbours" was used in the TEE English Examination paper, Western Australia's final year examination.

While this movement was indicative of a number of factors in the general field of English (or literary and cultural studies, by this stage), *Cloudstreet* does not occupy the same position in the education canon. My sister's first year English course in 1992 was clearly an early adopter of the novel, but tertiary English courses have not retained *Cloudstreet* to anything like the same extent as the secondary English subjects. Winton's work does appear on many university English reading lists but, according to the *AustLit* "Teaching Australian Literature" resource, *Dirt Music* and *Breath* are more popular Winton works at this educational level. Other Australian writers such as David Malouf, Alexis Wright, Kate Grenville, Kim Scott and Miles Franklin figure more prominently on tertiary courses than Winton. This difference can be easily explained through the greater flexibility of university text selection and individual institutional autonomy over teaching. It is also apparent that governmentality, while critical to the overall functioning of tertiary institutions and the awarding of research funding, does not have the same degree of influence over curriculum matters as it does in the secondary space. In returning to Guillory's explanation of "the school" and canon formation, the conditions that he describes are amplified at secondary level.

Classroom confusion and *Cloudstreet*

Building on the Cultural Heritage traditions of Arnold and Leavis, the altered perspective of the Growth model and the critical literacy pedagogy, the 1990s English secondary curriculum and the classroom were conflicted sites. Add to this the cultural studies movement of the 1980s and the influential figure of Terry Eagleton in critical theory, as well as the growing awareness that the English classroom had for a long period been serving as a cultural arm of colonialism, and you realise that English syllabus documents and classroom teachers were attempting to reconcile a number of conflicting theoretical imperatives. In their article "Producing Readings: Freedom versus Normativity", Patterson and Mellor characterise this moment of English teaching through the paradox: "To teach and yet not to teach" (2). Their meaning here is that the capabilities demanded of students require a substantial amount of literary and contextual knowledge if students are to produce responses based on the principle of "self-realisation". They explain that, "in order to achieve the goal of 'critical consciousness', for example, the reader must already possess the faculty which enables 'critical scrutiny' which produces critical consciousness" (3). In his discussion from 1991 Terry Eagleton explained that "confusion might seem to come from the vast number of influences at this moment between so many frameworks, but it is actually the similarities and closeness that cause the most confusion" (cited in Patterson and Mellor 3). What are the influences and how are they similar?

This was a moment of curricular instability in English, when academic discussion around disciplinarity and pedagogical approaches became crowded and conflicted. Aside from the bicentenary, for which *Cloudstreet* was a useful companion in the classroom, there are a number of additional factors that need to be considered around the formation of the educational canon. *Cloudstreet* also satisfied a number of other criteria that secondary English teachers and authorities were seeking to embed in classroom practice. Without constructing a detailed curriculum history of this period, I believe it is most useful to refer to the works of Ian Hunter and Graeme Turner to explain what happened. Through his 1997 essay *After English* Hunter defends English as the "study of aesthetic, ethics and rhetoric" in direct response to the dominance of "critical literacy" in Australian English teaching (315-334). Hunter represents the increased influence of this pedagogical practice as problematic in that it distances secondary English from the disciplinary fields of Literary and Cultural Studies in the tertiary zone, and complicates the approach of secondary teachers who are seeking to satisfy the competing pedagogical forces in the discipline. Turner explains: "critical literacy in Australia is a mode of discourse analysis developed by theorists from the discipline of Education and enthusiastically taken up by state education bureaucrats influenced by the branch of systemic linguistics identified with the University of Sydney professor, M.A.K. Halliday" (159). He also comments that this "critical literacies approach has, improbably, been placed at the centre of every senior English syllabus in the country" (Turner on Hoggart 159).

Turner also explains that while the early efforts of Richard Hoggart democratised English and empowered readers to respond to a wide variety of texts so as "not to be conned", it has also resulted in a secondary English field where the skills of close reading associated with literary criticism are diminished and students instead learn to become experts in what Threadgold calls "ventriloquism" – they "learn to mimic the discourses of the master" (365) – and Marnie O'Neill calls "Right Readings". Critical literacy drew wide criticism in the national press during this period from figures like Luke Slattery, who accused "teachers of pretending to be intellectuals" and treating the politics of texts reductively (Turner 365). In this confused context, Hunter's call for subject English to be a balance of aesthetics, ethics and rhetoric is an attempt to return literary and cultural studies to the centre of the subject, and while not dismissing critical literacy, it does diminish its importance. In this contested space, *Cloudstreet* is still relevant and teachable, for while it is highly accessible to critical literacy, the novel also has significant literary value. And, as Annette Patterson comments, "if English is to be counted as a serious intellectual subject, capable of providing a discriminating measure of students' abilities to engage intellectually as well as personally with the big questions and issues of our time, then it will need to re-introduce an emphasis on the missing pedagogical elements: rhetoric and aesthetics" (Patterson, "Teaching Literature" 313–4).

Cloudstreet's "usefulness"

Returning to Guillory's argument about the "usefulness" of literature in relation to cultural capital, it is clear that *Cloudstreet* remains extremely useful as a text that mediates between critical literacy (ethics) and aesthetics/rhetoric, which is why it remains a part of the school canon. *Cloudstreet* is not widely accepted in the academy as a literary masterpiece. Indeed, it has never really been the subject of much literary criticism. This raises questions about the different criteria for literary merit in secondary English and the discipline of Literary Studies – and about the problem of reintroducing the aesthetic into secondary English without reifying an unwelcome liberal humanism. Hunter's emphasis on rhetoric – the study of the devices through which aesthetic effects are achieved – is salutary. Reading *Cloudstreet* for the formal sources of its "literariness" is a valuable classroom approach, and proves its usefulness in satisfying curriculum demands. Exploring the form of the family epic or Australian saga, the literary trope of coming of age or the thematic approach of man versus nature allows for an appreciation of the aesthetic that is rich and rewarding. Reading the novel as an example of magic realism or for the duality of the hero that is Quick/Fish are all methods of engaging with complex and demanding literary aspects of the text.

Considering some examples of how students are required to respond with reference to this novel helps us to understand how it is in fact taught. In 2010 the New South Wales HSC examination posed this question to students:

> "Winton's *Cloudstreet* continues to engage readers through its narrative treatment of hardship and optimism."
>
> In light of your critical study, does this statement resonate with your own interpretations of *Cloudstreet*. In your response, make detailed reference to the novel.

Here the code-words "hardship" and "optimism" connect the student to traditional elements of the "Australian legend", reading the novel as an exploration of national myths, and identifying a nostalgia for an Australian experience that has passed. A sample VCE English question –

"Tim Winton's *Cloudstreet* depicts a changing Australia with ambivalence and regret." Discuss.

– demonstrates how this text functions as a scene of reading for ongoing national introspection. It encourages students to engage with a national discourse, or if not engage, perhaps to demonstrate "ventriloquism" in discussing a wider ideological framework about nation and identity. This form of reading, however, cannot escape the novel's resolution and the ideological reconciliation that occurs at the conclusion of the novel through Wax Harry's birth and Fish's reunification. There is a national "usefulness" within this text that is about more than providing material for literary, cultural or critical discussion: studying *Cloudstreet* has become more an experience of studying national sentiment than literary aesthetic or rhetoric.

A study guide prepared by Rod Quin, a significant figure in Western Australian English teaching, explains:

> But *Cloudstreet* can also be read as marginalising Aboriginal people, stereotyping them, constructing them as "other" and endorsing European displacement of Aboriginal people. ... The novel is silent on or marginalises the real social conditions of Aboriginal people during the period of its setting, such as the reasons why an Aboriginal man is selling or why Aboriginal people cannot vote". ... Lester's comment on the latter, "Jesus that's a bit rough. They need a union" and Rose's laughing response can be seen as "trivializing the oppression of Aboriginal people". (http://englishteachingresources.typepad.com/english_study_resources/files/representation_of_aboriginality_in_cloudstreet.pdf)

This suggests that *Cloudstreet* could also be "useful" in the classroom as a site of resistant reading. This novel can provide an experience of interrogating our national past in relation to traditional and conservative representations of certain social issues and ideological positions related to race, class and gender. Resistant reading is an important critical reading practice that is certainly highlighted in more recent syllabus documents, and *Cloudstreet* is a text that can be relatively easily challenged without requiring complex understandings of reading theories. While we might hope that this reading practice is widely explored in the teaching of the novel, and this teaching resource example would indicate that it is sometimes part of some classroom experiences, most assessment tasks focus on the sentimental reading explored above.

While we can certainly track the usefulness of Winton's novel in terms of satisfying syllabus concepts, and as a text to refer to when answering examination questions, the greatest "usefulness" of *Cloudstreet* appears to be through its cultivation of cultural capital – that is, the greatest importance of the text is how the wider reading public recalls and values it. The unapologetic sentimentality of the *Tuesday Night Book Club*'s panel in recollections of their reading; the importance placed on decoding and interpreting national representation through the novel in the school curriculum: the same nostalgic experience has been provided to at least one generation of Australian readers. If we understand the implication of Guillory's connections between popularity and canonisation, which are clearly operating in relation to this text, we can assess the power of the school canon to act as an apparatus for national sentimentality and the collective experience. It seems this collected panel of Australian cultural figures are all gathering at the river, singing along with the Lambs and the Pickles', and Winton.

MARIEKE HARDY: … It's just … [*Cloudstreet*] is Australian … But reading it felt like coming home. It feels like looking through the plane window when you're flying back into the country. It really does. I mean, it feels like … Bugger the citizenship test, know Don Bradman's birthday, get everyone to read *Cloudstreet* before they enter the country.

PETER GARRETT: It's a really good suggestion.

MARIEKE HARDY: I think so. Because maybe if it is how we want to be, then why not aspire to that sense of community and maybe that's all we are yearning for. And I think to have that heart and that sense of family coming first, I mean, that's no small feat. That's something for us all to aspire to.

Works Cited

Bicentennial Australian Studies Schools Project. *Australian Literature. Bulletin 5.* Canberra: Curriculum Development Centre, 1988. Print.

Buckridge, Patrick. "Canons, culture and consensus: Australian literature and the Bicentenary". *Celebrating the Nation: A Critical Study of Australia's Bicentenary*. Ed. Tony Bennett and Patrick Buckridge. St Leonards: Allen and Unwin, 1992: 69–86. Print.

"Cloudstreet". *The First Tuesday Book Club*, Australian Broadcasting Corporation, Sydney. 2 March 2010. Television.

Dixon, Robert. "Tim Winton, *Cloudstreet* and the field of Australian Literature". *Westerly*, 50(2), (2005): 240–260. Print.

Guillory, John. *Cultural Capital: The problem of literary canon formation*. Chicago: University of Chicago Press, 1993. Print.

McLean Davies, Larissa. "Auditing subject English: A review of text selection practices inspired by the national year of reading". *English in Australia*, 47(2) (2012): 11–17. Print.

"No chance in contemporary culture for Great Australian Novel – literary commentator". *University of Melbourne: The Melbourne Newsroom*. 2 Dec 2009. Web. 25 July 2016. <http://newsroom.melbourne.edu/news/n-206>

Patterson, Annette J. "Teaching literature in Australia: Examining and reviewing senior English". *Changing English*, 15(3) (2008): 311–322. Print.

Patterson, Annette. and B. Mellor. "Producing readings: Freedom versus normativity?" *English in Australia*, vol. 109 (1994): 42–46. Print.

Quin, Rod. "The representation of Aboriginal people in *Cloudstreet*". *English Curriculum: Resources for teachers*. Web. 25 July 2016. <http://englishteachingresources.typepad.com/english_study_resources/files/representation_of_aboriginality_in_cloudstreet.pdf>

Steger, Jason. "Tolkien has us spellbound". *The Age* 6 December 2004. Web. 25 July 2016 <http://www.theage.com.au/news/Books/Tolkien-is-spellbound/2004/12/05/1102182155661.html>

The Miles Franklin Award Website. Web. 25 July 2016. <https://www.perpetual.com.au/MilesFranklin>

Turner, Graeme. "Critical literacy, cultural literacy and the English school curriculum in Australia". *Richard Hoggart and Cultural Studies*. Ed. Sue Owen, London: Palgrave, 2008. 158–170. Print.

Yiannakis, John. "A possible literary canon in upper school English literature in various Australian states, 1945–2005." *Issues in Educational Research*, 2014, Vol 24(1): 98–113. Print.

Chapter Seventeen

LITERATURE'S GHOSTS

Cultural heritage and cultural analysis in subject English

Tim Dolin

The social and the aesthetic

It comes as no surprise to find that two literary works were set more frequently than any others in Australian senior secondary schools between 1945 and 2005. Both are studies in extremity, and therefore exemplary texts with which to engage adolescent readers. Their heroes (in one of them female and the other male) are anguished, rebellious, misunderstood outsiders who will never reconcile themselves to the corrupt values and dead conventions of the societies in which they struggle, and fail, to survive. The worlds represented in these works are so pervaded by the evils of death, pain, cruelty, violence and injustice that everything is overshadowed – characters and events, places and people, institutions and systems of property and power: the whole material real – by a wild, dark, terrifying metaphysical reality, of storms, ghosts and hauntings, monsters, superstitions and devil-possessions. One of these works, *Hamlet*, is often described as the greatest tragedy of the greatest writer the world has ever known. It is the arch-canonical work of the arch-canonical figure of "Eng. Lit". The other, *Wuthering Heights*, has been on school syllabuses and best-loved books lists for so long that it is also pigeon-holed as "an enduring classic", forgetting what a "rude and strange production" (C. Brontë xvii) it is, and how it was "in a great measure unintelligible, and – where intelligible – repulsive" (xvii) to its first readers.¹ We also forget that, although the Brontës are now a constant in nineteenth-century literary history, one sister is always "valued above the others and then sinks as public tastes change" (Stoneman 214). Thus, Charlotte Brontë, who single-handedly rescued her sisters' reputations (and founded the Brontë myth) in her "Editor's Preface" to the posthumous edition of *Wuthering Heights and Agnes Grey* in 1850, nonetheless found much of *Wuthering Heights* puzzling, distasteful and embarrassing. She had to explain away the novel's glamorous but odious hero and heroine by mythologising her sister as "a native and nursling of the moors" (xx) whose bizarre creations were "hewn in a wild workshop, with simple tools, out of homely materials" (xxiv). Having "formed these beings, she did not know what she had done" (xxi).²

Wuthering Heights has stayed on Australian upper-secondary syllabuses for more than 60 years, but not just because it is "a canonical work", which explains nothing.³ The novel's greatness was once defended in the organicist New Critical and Leavisite terms of its author's "Shakespearean ability to keep opposites in suspension" (Knoepflmacher 106); and Brontë's "special appeal to the twentieth-century imagination" was explained by our acute need for "union in a destructive world" (107). As long ago as 1975, however, Terry Eagleton began *Myths of Power: A Marxist Study of the Brontës* by remarking that it was "no longer fashionable to see the Brontës as a marooned, metaphysical trio, sublimely detached from their historical milieu" (1), and since then studies have tended to focus on the violent disturbances of class, gender and race boundaries in the novel (on the last, see Eagleton's own later essay, "Heathcliff and the Great Hunger"). Nowadays, by contrast, *Wuthering Heights* is more likely to be valued for its relevance to post-humanism and relativistic postmodernism. It is admired for its exploration of the "radical instability of behaviour, judgement and point-of-view" (Rylance 167):

> Instead of the psychologically stable world of "character", based on the authority of the will and the security of agreed values, *Wuthering Heights* depicts a world, psychologically, of compulsion, obsession,

---

1 On the novel's popularity see, for example, "Emily Brontë hits the heights in poll to find greatest love story". *Guardian*. Friday 10 August 2007. Web. Accessed 22 February 2016.

2 Even if we accept Catherine's "perverted passion and passionate perversity" (xxii), Brontë wonders whether "it is right or advisable to create beings like Heathcliff, I do not know: I scarcely think it is" (xxiii).

3 ALIAS shows it has been set semi-regularly in the SA syllabus since 1948, NSW since 1955, Victoria since 1956, Tasmania since 1957, and WA since 1971.

sadism, fanaticism, self-harm and addiction. The very sources of this behaviour are as obscure as they are powerful. (168)

Where this novel is concerned, at least, "literariness" is no longer bound to New Critical unities (or Cold War anxieties). Latterly critics are preoccupied with the novel's undecidability and its unsettlement of settled categories, its blunt critique of the delusions of civilisation and the innate violence of the social order, and its out and out animosity towards liberal humanism and its shibboleths. This makes *Wuthering Heights* an ideal text for the critical literacy approaches that presently dominate Australian school English classrooms. It also makes it an ideal text for a discipline (and subject) in which literature itself has become a bit of a problem. *Wuthering Heights* expresses an unmistakable hostility towards capital-L Literature, as represented, for example, in its dull metropolitan interloper-narrator, Lockwood, whose stiff pretentious literary style ("she waxed lachrymose") is engulfed by the suddenly released (unlocked, as it were) vernacular energy of Catherine's diary: "How little did I dream that Hindley would ever make me cry so!" (E. Brontë, 23). That energy is so direct and powerful that it calls up her very ghost, scaring Lockwood out of his wits and dispensing him unceremoniously from the centre to the sidelines of the narrative.

The history of literature is full of such gestures in which worn-out literary language and form are swept away: by the vitality of ordinary speech as it is wrought into new kinds of art, by the comic spirit, by a somatic sensationalism, or by surprising intertextual alliances.[4] But rarely in the history of literature does this happen in a way that is so strange, *fauve*, and excessive, so apparently artless, and so aggressively anti-literary. *Wuthering Heights*, a novel concerned with the violence of language and the social and sexual politics of writing and reading, was not written in ignorance of the literary culture that produced it, as Charlotte Brontë pretended in 1850,[5] but in angry defiance of that culture and its dead hand. How could the fortunes of such a book change as quickly they did, so that what was coarse and repulsive in 1847 was being hailed as an extraordinary work of art after 1850?[6] And is it really possible that *Wuthering Heights* could ever have

---

4   Think of Becky Sharp tossing Miss Pinkerton's gift of Johnson's *Dictionary* from the carriage at the end of chapter one of Thackeray's *Vanity Fair*, for example.

5   See Juliet Barker on the 1850 edition, 655.

6   "[*Wuthering Heights*] will live a short and brilliant life, and then die and be forgotten … The public will not acknowledge its men and women to have the true immortal vitality. Poor Cathy's ghost will not walk the earth forever; and the insane Heathcliff will soon rest quietly in his coveted repose." (G.W. Peck, *American Review*, June 1848; Allott 241.)

been treated with hushed reverence as a monument of "cultural heritage", a repository of significant meaning to be appreciated and preserved from the corruptions of the present – like a display in a gallery of the best that has been thought and said?

The answer to these questions lies in the history of the institution of literature, which emerged in the late eighteenth century in Europe and reached its apogee in the period of European and Anglo-American modernism (c.1880–1950). As Alain Badiou observes, literature is "an exception in the field of art" because as a term it "cuts across literary genres" (135). This "raises it above classical genres and puts it entirely beyond the scope of the empirical world" (135). "Literature" is not the same category of entity as "tragedy": literature is a signifier of symbolic value or what Badiou calls the "literary conscience, a conscience not exactly comparable to artistic judgement, since it relates not to rules of taste but to the conviction of the existence of an entirely separate phenomenon: the literary fact, as compact and distinct as an Idea" (136). The emergence of literature corresponded with the emergence of the nation-state and served what became a liberal myth of culture. It functioned, as institutions like law and the family did, to minimise harm in post-Christian societies comprised of self-serving individuals. But at the other extreme literature also dallied in the Nietzschean glamour of the beyond-good-and-evil. If it could promote reason, tolerance and pluralism, therefore, it could also be offensive, indecorous, irrational and perverse. Yet it could do so without offending the powers that be: like the licensed fool, its "deviance and subversion" were tolerated, even protected (Angenot 227).

Literariness might not be determined by rules of taste, as Badiou proposes, but to understand it as an effect of framing that sets apart certain texts across a range of disparate and variable genres is surely to understand it in the context of the historical rise and fall of the aesthetic attitude. By the term "literary conscience", however, Badiou imputes a moral dimension to the inward knowledge or consciousness of literature's value – aesthetic judgement is aligned with virtue – that helps to explain the significance of literature, as distinct from art in general, in education. As we know from studies of the influence of Romantic notions of aesthetic education on the emergence of English, literature's putative separateness rests on its claim to disinterestedness. Literary study is a highly effective form of civic training because it conjoins the experience of aesthetic pleasure, which does not serve the experiencer's self-interest, and the development of ethical literacy, which relies on the reconciliation of competing ideological interests.

It is well known that in Australia upper-secondary English, with its long-established program of engaged cultural critique, played an important role in redefining what constituted the literary, and in transforming how Literary Studies was done. Long before that, however, the idea of literature had determined what constituted subject English, and how it would be taught and go on being taught even when literature was no longer a major component of it. We might describe this as the extrication of the literary conscience from the embarrassments of the aesthetic. This was what drove the "crisis in English studies" of the 1980s, when English started falling apart, as John Frow approvingly put it in 1990 ("Production" 359). For Frow, English originally formed as a discipline "in a context of political and cultural colonialism, and of the teaching of a high culture that was specifically that of the English ruling class." As such it had no claim to its self-avowed "ethical superiority and ... disinterested neutrality in relation to social struggles." He continued:

> It has claimed to be a critical discipline, but its critique has often been of a purely spiritual order. It has until recently been blind to the ways in which the high culture it disseminates has worked as an instrument of class legitimation. Until recently it has systematically slighted – with certain honorary exceptions – the work of women and of non-European writers, and indeed has hardly noticed the paradox of the self-disqualification this entails. Despite its close connection with the secondary schooling system it has rarely taken seriously the realities of its roles in ethical regulation and in the training of students in functional literacy – indeed, it has been associated with a rigidly normative teaching of language skills. (358–59)

This view of Literary Studies as it was (and as certain conservative groups wanted it to remain) dominated debates about English in Australia for decades. An enduring version of it can be found in the polemical history of "the rise of English", which emerged almost simultaneously in Britain and Australia and in literary theory and the theory and practice of school English teaching. It saw English as an outmoded institution committed to "a fetishized object of study" grounded in "normative 'unreflected discourses of value'" (Frow "On Literature" 44), and is most widely known through Terry Eagleton's entertaining chapter on "The Rise of English" in his bestselling *Literary Theory: An Introduction* (1983), and to Australian school teachers through Ian Reid's influential *The Making of Literature* (1984). In Chapters 3 and 14 of this book I discuss why I think the narrative of a revolutionary transformation of English from "the study of culture" to "cultural studies" is historically inaccurate. In this chapter I want to examine the return of the aesthetic in the Australian national curriculum as an awkward appendage to syllabuses dedicated to teaching skills in ethical judgement. I will argue that this revenant of the aesthetic is kept in its place by reverting to the language of cultural heritage, which still calls up memories of reactionary regimes of reading dedicated to producing "a cultured individual, with a heightened appreciation of great literature, capable of articulating the contribution of that literary heritage to the development of civil society" (Patterson 311). The chapter concludes by arguing that we must change our attitude towards literature as cultural heritage.

The aesthetic in the Australian curriculum and the WACE syllabus

There are about 400 works on the 2016 Western Australian Certificate of Education (WACE) "Prescribed Texts" list for the Literature subject. Inclusive to a fault, the list is a declaration of victory in the long emancipatory war fought by subject English against the rule of the pale, male and stale (SCSA). On the face of it there seems to be no limit to what can be taught as literature (within the limits of the "literary": see below). What *is* taught as literature, however, suggests something very different. Less than 10 per cent of these works have been taught or examined since the list was first authorised more than a decade ago, and that 10 per cent constitutes a de facto teaching canon that is every bit as narrow and ideologically circumscribed as the canon it displaced so long ago. Every Lit. teacher in the state knows it well. It includes *Othello* and *The Tempest*, and still occasionally *Hamlet*, but not much else by Shakespeare, as well as Jack Davis's *No Sugar* and Ibsen (usually *Ghosts*). Its big novels are *Frankenstein, Heart of Darkness*, and *The Handmaid's Tale*; its big poets Gwen Harwood, Seamus Heaney, and T.S. Eliot. Why do teachers choose these works year after year? In part it is because they are familiar to overworked, under-resourced English departments, and because they are proven with students. But they are also particularly well suited to the syllabus as it has evolved and adapted over the past 20 years in Western Australia. A brief examination of the syllabus documents and the official teaching support materials provided by the State Government's School Curriculum and Standards Authority shows very clearly what Literary Study is in the Western Australia upper-secondary syllabus and how it is inseparable from the wider project of subject English as it has developed in this state.

The 2016 WACE Literature syllabus is structured on the Australian curriculum, which in English consist of three strands: language; literature; and literacy. It reproduces the four basic learning units of the national senior secondary curriculum, which are broadly focused on the following:

> how language, structure and stylistic choices are used in literary forms, and how contexts shape meaning
>
> how literary texts connect with each other, and with different audiences and contexts
>
> how language, culture and identity are related in literary works
>
> how literary interpretation is always changing, how values and ideas are represented in texts, and how aesthetic considerations influence their reception. (Australian curriculum, "Structure")

In the literature strand students "develop interest and skills in inquiring into the aesthetic aspects of texts, and develop an informed appreciation of literature". Noting that there are "many different ways to engage with literature", the Australian curriculum quickly focuses its attention on just one: the way literature provides "mediated experiences and truths that support and challenge the development of individual identity". By engaging with literature "students learn about themselves, each other and the world". By the term "literature", moreover, the curriculum authors mean "texts from across a range of historical and cultural contexts that are valued for their form and style and are recognised as having enduring or artistic value". At the same time,

> While the nature of what constitutes literary texts is dynamic and evolving, they are seen as having personal, social, cultural and aesthetic value and potential for enriching students' scope of experience. (ACARA "Key Ideas")

This is not the aesthetic as Coleridge imagined it – the "coincidence of form, feeling, and intellect" (254). Literary texts are, primarily, texts of personal, social and cultural value, "chosen because they are judged to have potential for enriching the lives of students, expanding the scope of their experience" and (secondarily) "because they represent effective and interesting features of form and style" (ACARA "Key Ideas"). In line with the Australian curriculum the WACE Literature course:

focuses on the study of literary texts and developing students as independent, innovative and creative learners and thinkers who appreciate the aesthetic use of language; evaluate perspectives and evidence; and challenge ideas and interpretations. (SCSA "Support")

The aesthetic here is the occasion for an unexpected rehabilitation of that old bogey word in English, "appreciation", with all its connotations of indebtedness and deference to, even reverence for, cultural heritage. In practice, however, the WACE course is pre-eminently interested in the way literary texts do or do not align with the dominant values and attitudes presented in the syllabus – values and attitudes that may be broadly described as left-liberal: tolerant, pluralistic, inclusive. It is also interested in the way the texts' contexts of production – both the original conditions of literary production and contemporary reading practices – do or do not align with those values and attitudes. It is less sure what to do with the aesthetic, since it is intent on distancing itself from ideas of literature as aesthetic practice, because of their powerful historical associations with contrary values and attitudes (exclusiveness, inequality, literature as a form of cultural power).

As a consequence, teachers, students and examiners struggle to integrate aesthetic analysis and social/cultural analysis (see Misson and Morgan). Examination questions call for knowledge of language techniques, generic conventions, historical contexts, intertextuality and reading practices, and the texts being examined – that 10 per cent of the syllabus list – are highly amenable to readings that bring those elements into dialogue with themes and representations of class, race/ethnicity, gender, social power relations and cultural identity (including nationhood). A few examples from recent papers indicate how this works:

- Explore how a writer uses language and literary devices to invite audiences to change how they view identity and nationhood.
- Examine the ways in which writers shape and adapt generic conventions to reflect and expose particular value systems.
- In their treatment of ideologies, literary texts are complex, even contradictory. Discuss this statement in the light of your reading of at least one literary text.
- Discuss how the relationship between the aesthetic and contextual functions of setting is necessary to an appreciation of at least one literary text.
- Discuss how a writer's style might serve an ideological purpose.

- How do different reading practices prioritise particular elements of a text, enabling alternative interpretations?
- Omissions or silences in a text can be as important to a text's meaning as the things that are included. Evaluate this statement by referring to at least one text you have studied. (SCSA "Past Papers").

Literature as cultural heritage

In the WACE Literature course, literary study is cultural analysis. In the syllabus's terms, aesthetic value is detached from any questions about endurance. Works do not endure; it is rather that some are valued for their relevance to the syllabus and to contemporary students. There can be no question of those students being the inheritors of a vast body of English-language written culture from the past. The idea of literature as cultural heritage is fundamentally at odds with the student-centred personal growth agenda at the heart of subject English. Indeed, the term Cultural Heritage was first used in relation to the study of literature in schools (as far as I know) in John Dixon's *Growth through English* (1967), where it was opposed to "personal growth". But the term gained currency in this context only in the 1980s when two things happened. The word "heritage" came into common usage in Britain as a shorthand for a Thatcherite fantasy of national nostalgia and pride in a country being decimated by post-industrialism (Wright 1985, Hewison 1987). At the same time the word "culture" underwent a profound semantic shift: "culture is not a residual category ... it is the very medium through which social change is experienced, contested and constituted" (Cosgrove and Jackson 95). The word once referred to the "refinement of mind, taste, and manners; artistic and intellectual development [and hence] the arts and other manifestations of human intellectual achievement regarded collectively" (OED), valued for that achievement, and passed down from previous generations. But by 1980 culture-as-high art was being subordinated to a far more inclusive idea of culture as the habits, practices, values, discourses and representations that comprise the whole way of life of a people, and the social relations and power that create and transform their personal experiences and everyday life.

This was also the period of the "heritage industry", when the material preservation of the past served the ideological interests of the cultural industries growing rapidly in late-industrial consumer economies, particularly heritage tourism and the heritage film industry. In Britain both sought to profit from a narrow idea of the national past that was represented by a nostalgic inflection of certain canonical literary works of the nineteenth and early twentieth centuries that were set in visitable landscapes or great houses. The green past of the "Merchant Ivory" aesthetic stretched from Austen's Regency England to Forster's Edwardian England, and included the Brontës as well as Trollope, Hardy and Henry James (see Higson). The assertion of an affinity between literature and tangible heritage was a compelling one because it implied that canonical works were like heritage sites: they were chosen and protected by official or semi-official bodies (National Trust, English Heritage, University Presses, and so on). They were to be treated with a kind of ritualised respect, and preserved from the depredations of the present.

Against this background, the 1989 Cox Report in the UK revived the idea of a Cultural Heritage view of literature. Where Dixon, in line with the Dartmouth conference consensus, had opposed Cultural Heritage to Skills and Personal Growth, the Cox Report presents it as one of five "views", including a personal growth view ("emphasises the relationship between language and learning in the individual child, and the role of literature in developing children's imaginative and aesthetic lives" [Cox 2.21]); cross-curricular view ("to help children with the language demands of different subjects on the school curriculum" [2.22]); and adult needs view ("to prepare children for the language demands of adult life" [2.23]). For Cox the Cultural Heritage view, which "emphasises the responsibility of schools to lead children to an appreciation of those works of literature that have been widely regarded as among the finest in the language" (2.24), sits alongside the cultural analysis view, which

> emphasises the role of English in helping children towards a critical understanding of the world and cultural environment in which they live. Children should know about the processes by which meanings are conveyed, and about the ways in which print and other media carry values. (2.25)

In Australia, where literary theory had been in conversation with subject English pedagogy for much of the 1980s, the polite division of intellectual labour between cultural heritage and cultural analysis views of literature in the Cox Report did not hold. Five years earlier, Ian Reid had written *The Making of Literature* with the aim of freeing students and teachers of English from the pedagogic culture of deference and passive aesthetic appreciation that arose around this Cultural Heritage understanding of literature. He wanted to empower them instead, so that they could engage with literature on equal terms, and collaborate actively and creatively in the "exchanges of meaning that occur through the medium of the text" (7). By changing the nature of that engagement – from the "gallery" to the "workshop", in the book's leading metaphors – we can enlarge "our concept of literature" and recognise "value in a wider range of writings" (6). The literary workshop as Reid conceives it is thus inclusive and active. Committed to a student-centred Personal Growth approach, Reid envisions students exploring verbal texts alongside texts in other media, analysing literary and non-literary texts together, writing literature as well as reading it,[7] and studying literary works through an examination of their conditions of production. This "polemical opposition" between the gallery and the workshop mobilises some familiar binaries when it opposes the old idea of literature (demanding passive appreciation) and the new (inviting the reader's active participation in meaning-making). It also opposes unity to diversity (formal and cultural), dominant to dominated, top-down to bottom-up, teacher to pupil, absolute value to relative value, past to present, author to reader, and (in Barthes's well-known terms) *lisible* to *scriptible*. In so far as literature (a narrow, self-serving category of value) is preserved from the past – part of our cultural heritage, that is to say – our relation to it will be deferential and passive. Only when it is absorbed into writing can our relation to it become active and truly critical.

There are several distinct but related arguments in play in *The Making of Literature*. First, literature's meaning and value are constituted by specific social relations, and literary works are therefore not specially immune to, or transcendent of, ideology. As a consequence they are equally prone to unenlightened attitudes (22), and are open to the same kind of critique as other texts. Literary analysis must therefore situate itself within a wider analytical practice: of social relations of textuality. Because literature is not "formally discontinuous with other verbal activities" (16), the study of literature should be part of general English and not ceded to a separate entity ("English Literature", "Advanced English"), because that

---

7   Interestingly, as early as 1913, the first Professor of English at Cambridge, Sir Arthur Quiller-Couch, announced in his inaugural lecture: "English Literature being (as we agreed) an Art, with a living and therefore improvable language for its medium or vehicle, a part—and no small part—of our business is *to practise it*. Yes, I seriously propose to you that here in Cambridge we *practise writing*."

"powerfully and perniciously" reinforces the idea that literary language is special and different. Second, literature is a category of value – all literature is by definition good literature – but the notion of what constitutes "good literature" is continuously contestable (12). Third, it is contestable because meaning is not inherent in literary texts but is produced in interactions between texts and readers, and the meaning that is produced thereby is not special by virtue of some mysterious "literariness" in the text. A work of literature is not "an object possessing special properties but ... an act performed in a special context" (17). "Literature" is a way of "specifying how to use [a] text, what one can expect to happen at different stages, and what to do if these expectations are not confirmed" (Frow, "Marxism" 221). The workshop is therefore a space in which teachers can separate literary texts from the "special contexts" that frame them as literature, and recontextualise or reframe them.

Returning to Badiou, because "literature" is not a genre there can be no empirically verifiable, historically consistent criteria for dividing the universe of written culture into the literary and the non-literary. Nor are there any properties of language that are unique to literary works: every technical or rhetorical effect in a literary work is as likely to be found in advertising, or journalism or propaganda. What the word "literature" describes, rather, is what phenomenologists call an *intentional relation* to certain written or written-down texts (which are also most likely to be printed texts, incidentally). Phenomenology limits its inquiry to the study of phenomena passing through the mind, insisting that as experiencing subjects we must always be framing, limiting and defining the objective world. Two closely similar Greek words are used in phenomenological thought to designate the interdependence of the experiencing mind, the *noetic*, and the experienced object-world, the *noematic*. These are two sides of the same thing: we often cannot distinguish between objects "out there" and our experience of them, so there is no primary phenomenal/noetic or real/noematic. We do not recognise ourselves framing, limiting and defining the literary, because, in the words of the French philosopher Jacques Derrida, the "literary character of the text is inscribed on the side of the intentional object, in its noematic structure, one could say, and not only on the subjective side of the noetic act". Literariness is not just present in the consciousness of readers, therefore, but is also present as "an intentional layer" in the texts themselves. This intentional layer expresses a "more or less implicit consciousness of rules which are conventional or institutional – social, in any case" and it is those rules that frame, limit and define the literary.

The interdependence of noetic acts and noematic structures feels inevitable and benign, but as Reid's own work on framing shows, the interpretive act is not always as generously collaborative, nor the work so obligingly amenable, as his metaphor of the workshop implies. Interpretation is "necessarily an interactive process, an ongoing struggle between text and reader" (MacLachlan and Reid 108): "a struggle (frequently unacknowledged, even unconscious) for semantic control, as different framings compete with one another" (85). That struggle between text and reader presupposes that literary texts, if they do not have special properties, at least assert a special identity (one that readers can always resist). The semantic control for which the two struggle in competing acts of framing is control over the way the text is used (a frame is "that metacommunicative space where messages about how to interpret the message are encoded" [106]). If there is nothing inherently literary about literary language, there is none the less something in a literary text that declares and defends its specialness – its difference from ordinary or other uses of language.

So if a work of literature is not "an object possessing special properties but ... an act performed in a special context" (Reid 17), what happens when it is removed from that context? What happened back then, when English rejected "literature" and dedicated itself to textuality instead (without, of course, rejecting those works that were still named as literature, pre-eminently in those upper-school specialist literature subjects that broke away from general English, some of which indeed called themselves "Literature")? While books like *The Making of Literature* were successful in encouraging students to develop ethical reading practices by encouraging in them an "increased sensitivity to the way in which the dual power of language to confine or to liberate is registered in literary texts" (21), they also succeeded in decreasing students' sensitivity to the power of language to do other things in texts: things that "non-literary" texts (and a good many texts that declare themselves to be "literary") are actually not very good at doing. The revisionism of recent decades has attempted to rescue literature from the classist and colonialist motives behind the "civilising project" that was English in the classroom. In doing so, however, it has had to confine literature to a realm of ethical discourse, consigning the aesthetic to the dustbin of the Enlightenment. The outcome, paradoxically, has been to give support to an ever-growing scepticism and indifference towards literature, on one hand, and on the other to reduce literature to a kind of ethical commodity, directed to "the generation of pre-experienced sensations, sensations known in advance, guaranteed to affect in particular sad or joyful ways" (Grosz 4).

An ethical alternative can be found in Derek Attridge's well-known argument for the singularity of literature: "to find oneself reading an inventive work is to find oneself subject to certain obligations – to respect its otherness, to respond to its singularity, to avoid reducing it to the familiar and the utilitarian even while attempting to comprehend it by relating it to these" (130). Attridge has been a cogent critic of "the diminishing of careful attention to the specificity of the literary within the textual domain, and to the uniqueness of each literary object" (10). For him, culture is a critical determinant of habitus. Authorship happens inside

> a changing array of interlocking, overlapping, and often contradictory cultural systems ... a complex matrix of habits, cognitive models, representations, beliefs, expectations, prejudices, and preferences that operate intellectually, emotionally, and physically to produce a sense of at least relative continuity, coherence, and significance out of the manifold events of human living. (21)

Yet literary works are never completely reducible to those systems and matrices. Attridge argues that the other "brought into being in a creative event is ... at once implicit in the cultural field and wholly unpredictable from it" (25). Thus, "the other is that which is not knowable until by a creative act it is brought into the field of the same". This otherness of literature is also associated with the more familiar politico-ethical sense of otherness in Attridge's argument: he is careful to distinguish it from that which "is other because its substance, its centre of consciousness, its ethical claim upon me, or some such fact about it is wholly beyond my grasp, wholly foreign to me and my experience" (32). The otherness of literature "is other only in so far as it has not yet come into being, as long as existing modes of thought or language, whose complexities, containments and overdeterminations are its breeding ground, are incapable of bringing it to birth" (32).

For Attridge literature is not an object from the past but an event in a succession of presents – an event "that can be repeated over and over again and yet never seem exactly the same" (2). This conception of literature-as-event usefully accommodates the objection that the literary cannot be defined as an a priori category of writing but only as an act of "historical actualization in particular texts and under particular institutional conditions" (Frow "On Literature", 50). To think of aesthetic form as something produced exclusively by a framing act of this kind is to foreclose the kind of ethical reading that can arise when readers, properly trained, open themselves to the irreducibility of language in the literary event, producing readings in which they are conscious of the "resistance that aesthetic form raises against a 'translation back to knowledge'" (McGann 106).

"The future is its provenance"[8]

Wuthering Heights is an outstanding example of a work that is "implicit in the cultural field and wholly unpredictable from it". No matter how strange it is, how outlandish or extreme its emotional registers, it can still be resolved dialectically into the field of nineteenth-century fiction – as a key text of anti-realism, for instance, which is its necessary other. Similarly, it can be explained intertextually through its gothic and Romantic codes, or through its suffocating, semi-incestuous, self-enclosed distortion of the dynastic conventions of narrative. Yet the novel's arch-singularity – and what else is even remotely like *Wuthering Heights*? – is surely also in need of explanation. Whether the language of explanation available to social critical discourse is sufficient for the kind of attention we must give to the work in its specificity, however, is open to question.[9] For if literature is a form of social discourse it is also a form of art, and "art does not produce concepts, though it does address problems and provocations. It produces sensations, affects, intensities as its mode of addressing problems" (Grosz 1). Unlike the plastic arts, the arts of language appear to "function under the regime of signs" (3) but they do so in order to "produce and generate intensity" (3). Elizabeth Grosz's Deleuzian account of artistic production as a framing of chaos which "enables matter to become expressive, to not just satisfy but to intensify – to resonate and become more than itself" (4) situates art not in high civilisation but in elementary nature, where a constant "becoming-artistic" is in play in all life forms when they do anything that exceeds "the bare requirements of existence" (6). Art arises with sexual selection and sexual attraction, which "affirm the excessiveness of the body and the natural order, their capacity to bring out in each other what surprises, what is of no use but nevertheless attracts and appeals": "the production of the frivolous, the unnecessary, the pleasing, the sensory for their own sake" (7):

> This roots art not in the creativity of mankind but rather in a superfluousness of nature, in the capacity of the earth to render the sensory

---

8   "The future is its provenance" Derrida, "Exordium," xix, *Specters of Marx*.
9   The history of Literary Studies is a history of change in the kinds of attention readers are expected to give to certain works: in this regard, Reid's assertion that a work of literature is "an act performed in a special context" (17) is absolutely right.

superabundant, in the bird's courtship song and dance, or in the field of lilies swaying in the breeze under a blue sky. It roots art in the natural and the animal, in the most primitive and sexualized of evolutionary residues in man's animal heritage. (10)

You can see where I'm going with this, and you might object that, yes, in *Wuthering Heights* (as later in D.H. Lawrence) there is undoubtedly a fascination with "the chaotic indeterminacy of the real" (8) and the role of art in establishing and exploring the strange couplings of chaos and order in nature. This novel is excessive, and it is about the value of the excessive, but a reading that explains it through the "most primitive and sexualized of evolutionary residues in man's animal heritage" is hardly surprising when (for example) critical animal studies are so fashionable in literary studies right now. My response to this would be: my job as a reader, and as a teacher of reading, is to acknowledge that an act of reading and a text coincide as an event that is at once completely predictable (it can be predicted from the habitus of the reader and from the state of the critical field at present) and, if properly attentive, completely surprising. To read the novel aright I must avoid reducing *Wuthering Heights* to "the familiar and the utilitarian" – social power relations as they express themselves in class, gender, sexuality, ethnicity, age or species – knowing all the time that I can only comprehend it, here and now, "by relating it to these" (Attridge 130). As Raymond Williams pointed out in *The Country and the City* (1973), "class and property divide Heathcliff and Cathy" (176) but no social alteration of any kind could recover what has been lost:

> What is created and held to is a kind of human intensity and connection which is the ground of continuing life. ... This tragic separation between human intensity and any available social settlement is accepted from the beginning in the whole design and idiom of the novel. (176)

Literature is trapped in the school syllabus by the absolute imperative for interpretation to lead in one direction only: towards an ethically acceptable social settlement. In this context the aesthetic must always be an accessory of privilege: a hermeneutic luxury over and above the essential social, cultural, political and economic interpretive modes (which is also a sign of the privilege and social inequality that produced the work in the first place). What we need to return to is a sense of writing as a means to "human intensity and connection which is the ground of continuing life"; and to view "heritage" in the same terms.

Presently in Australia the term "cultural heritage" presupposes that works of literature were once (in the past) treated as monuments inherited from some golden age (in the past), which were in reality assertions of the durability of a powerful social order (now also thankfully in the past). Not only that, *The Making of Literature* and the many other influential arguments that invoke the Cultural Heritage model of Literary Study disparagingly, assume not only that readers before about 1980 were critically immobilised by the power of the canon, but that our relation to heritage is and must be passive. The assumption that faithfulness to heritage entails the surrendering of critical thought is one that must be challenged.

The legacy of the cultural past is not "received passively", Derrida writes, but "as a heritage one calls upon to form new questions and new propositions".[10] Heritage carries with it "a double injunction": to learn and to reaffirm; "the passivity of the reception and the decision to say 'yes'".[11] With this "decision to accept our heritage comes the necessity to make choices, the necessity to 'select, filter, interpret, and therefore transform, to not leave intact, unscathed'" (Egéa-Kuehne 39).[12] This is for Derrida a familiar "tension between memory, fidelity, the preservation of something which has been given to us, and at the same time heterogeneity, something absolutely new" ("The Villanova Roundtable", Derrida and Caputo 6). It means that "one can be faithful to one's heritage only in as much as one accepts to be unfaithful to it, analyze, critique, and interpret it, relentlessly" (Egéa-Kuehne 40), and more: "it is precisely within this heritage that one can find the 'conceptual tools' which will enable one to challenge the very limits of this heritage as traditionally defined and imposed" (40).

English students have very restricted access to the conceptual tools needed to comprehend and challenge the limits of this heritage, and it is a heritage likely to be lost to future generations. As Derrida contends, the responsibility we have to those who are no longer part of the "living present" (*Specters* xix) is also a responsibility to those who are not yet part of that present. In safekeeping the past we are also being accountable for the future: "the ghosts of those who are not yet born or who are already dead" (*Specters* xviii). Derrida uses the example of Hamlet's father's ghost, in which "the voice of the past ... [summons Hamlet] to his future" (Kearney

---

10 "Cultures et dépendences" France 3 Television, May 2002. Qu. Egéa-Kuehne 38.
11 Derrida and Elizabeth Roudinesco *De quoi demain ... Dialogue* Paris 2001. 16. Qu. Egéa-Kuehne 39.
12 Derrida and Elizabeth Roudinesco, *De quoi demain ... Dialogue* Paris 2001. 16. Qu. Egéa-Kuehne 39.

174) – an injunction he must obey. The ghost of literature, I suspect, may be more like the ghost of Cathy in Lockwood's dream:

> I listened doubtingly an instant; detected the disturber [the branch of a fir tree that … rattled its dry cones against the panes], then turned and dozed, and dreamt again; if possible, still more disagreeably than before.
>
> This time, I remembered I was lying in the oak closet, and I heard distinctly the gusty wind, and the driving of the snow; I heard, also, the fir-bough repeat its teasing sound … it annoyed me so much, that I resolved to silence it, if possible …
>
> "I must stop it … !" I muttered, knocking my knuckles through the glass, and stretching an arm out to seize the … branch: instead of which, my fingers closed on the fingers of a little ice-cold hand! …
>
> … As it spoke, I discerned, obscurely, a child's face looking through the window. Terror made me cruel; and, finding it useless to attempt shaking the creature off, I pulled its wrist on to the broken pane, and rubbed it to and fro till the blood ran down and soaked the bed-clothes: still it wailed, "Let me in" and maintained its tenacious grip, almost maddening me with fear. (E. Brontë 25–26)

Many critics have hesitated over this famous passage, almost too well known to be readable ("Yes it's me, I'm Cathy, I've come home again …"), in which a violent, a cruelly violent, struggle is enacted at the threshold between – what? Genteel metropolitan culture (inside) and wild nature (outside)? The novel constantly disturbs the "polarity that opposes nature to culture, or the inhuman to the social, or the energetic to the placid" (Stevenson 60), so that we never quite know which belongs on which side of the window.[13] This scene gives us a startling glimpse of the "unacknowledged recesses of Lockwood's fantasy life" (Armstrong 251). Although Cathy is wailing to be re-admitted, it is Lockwood who smashes the glass, ostensibly to silence the fir tree, but as though he is trying desperately to escape. Subject English has not yet expelled literature, as the Australian curriculum demonstrates and WACE syllabus shows, but it has expelled everything about literature that is not identical to its own image of itself. And, as Patricia Parker observed of *Wuthering Heights*, "once expelled, the 'outside' functions as a ghost: the identical is haunted by what it excludes" (181).

---

13 "Trembling between internality and externality, wuthering becomes a movement of othering: a passing of boundaries that takes the outside in and the inside out, where the familiar is made strange (the domestic interior Lockwood encounters is riven by the storms it should exclude) and the strange comes to inhabit the familiar" (Vine 340).

Works Cited

ACARA (Australian Curriculum, Assessment and Reporting Authority). Australian Curriculum. "Literature: Structure of Literature". <www.australiancurriculum.edu.au/seniorsecondary/english/literature/structure-of-literature> Web. Accessed 8 April 2016.

——. Australian Curriculum. "English: Key Ideas". <www.australiancurriculum.edu.au/english/key-ideas> Web. Accessed 8 April 2016.

Angenot, Marc. "What can literature do? From literary sociocriticism to a critique of social discourse". *Yale Journal of Criticism* 17 2 (2004): 217–31. Print.

Armstrong, Nancy. "Emily's ghost: The cultural politics of Victorian fiction, folklore, and photography". *Novel: A forum on fiction* 25.3 (Spring 1992): 245–67. Print.

Attridge, Derek. *The Singularity of Literature*. London and New York: Routledge, 2004. Print.

Badiou, Alain. *The Age of the Poets: And other writings on twentieth-century poetry and prose*. Trans. Bruno Bosteels. London and New York: Verso, 2014. Print.

Barker, Juliet. *The Brontës*. New York: St Mark's Press, 1995.

Brontë, Charlotte. "Editor's preface". Ellis and Acton Bell, *Wuthering Heights and Agnes Grey*. London: Smith, Elder & Co., 1850. vii–xxiv. Print.

Brontë, Emily. *Wuthering Heights*. Ed. Pauline Nestor. London: Penguin, 2003. Print.

Coleridge, Samuel Taylor. "Letter to Mr. Blackwood". *Blackwood's Edinburgh Magazine*, 10: 253–255. Print.

Cosgrove, Denis and Peter Jackson. "New directions in cultural geography". *Area* 19.2 (June 1987): 95–101. Print.

Cox Report. "English for ages 5 to 16". *Education in England*. <www.educationengland.org.uk/documents/cox1989/cox89.html> Web. Accessed 8 April 2016.

Derrida, Jacques. *Specters of Marx: The state of the debt, the work of mourning, and the New International*. New York: Routledge, 1994. Print.

——, and John D. Caputo. *Deconstruction in a Nutshell: A conversation with Jacques Derrida*. Perspectives in Continental Philosophy. New York: Fordham University Press, 1997. Print.

Dixon, John. *Growth through English: A report based on the Dartmouth Seminar 1966*. National Association for the Teaching of English, 1967. Print.

Eagleton, Terry. *Heathcliff and the Great Hunger: Studies in Irish culture*. London: Verso, 1995. Print.

——. *Literary Theory: An introduction*. Oxford: Blackwell, 1983. Print.

——. *Myths of Power: A Marxist study of the Brontës*. London: Macmillan, 1975. Print.

Egéa-Kuehne, Denise. "Right to humanities: Of faith and responsibility". *Deconstructing Derrida: Tasks for the new humanities*. Ed. Peter Pericles Trifonas and Michael Peters. New York: Palgrave Macmillan, 2005. 37–51. Print.

Frow, John. *Marxism and Literary History*. Oxford: Blackwell, 1986. Print.

——. "On literature in cultural studies". *The Aesthetics of Cultural Studies*. Ed. Michael Berubé. Oxford: Blackwell, 2005. 44–57.

——. "The social production of knowledge and the discipline of English". *Meanjin* 49.2 (1990): 353–67. Print.

Grosz, Elizabeth. *Chaos, Territory, Art: Deleuze and the framing of the Earth*. New York: Columbia University Press, 2008. Print.

Hewison, Robert. *The Heritage Industry: Britain in a climate of decline*. London: Methuen, 1987. Print.

Higson, Andrew (2003) *English Heritage, English Cinema: Costume drama since 1980*. Oxford: Oxford University Press. Print.

Kearney, Richard. "Spectres of *Hamlet*". *Spiritual Shakespeares*. Ed. Ewan Fernie. Accents on Shakespeare. London and New York: Routledge, 2005. 157–185. Print.

Knoepflmacher, U. C., *Emily Brontë: Wuthering Heights*. Landmarks of World Literature. Cambridge: Cambridge University Press, 1989. Print.

MacLachlan, Gale L., and Ian Reid. *Framing and Interpretation*. Interpretations. Carlton, Vic.: Melbourne University Press, 1994. Print.

McGann, Jerome J. *Radiant Textuality: Literature after the world wide web*. New York: Palgrave, 2001. Print.

Misson, Ray, and Wendy Morgan. *Critical Literacy and the Aesthetic: Transforming the English Classroom*. Urbana: National Council of Teachers of English, 2006. Print.

Patricia Parker, "The (self-)identity of the literary text: Property, proper place, and proper name in *Wuthering Heights*", in *Wuthering Heights*. Ed. Patsy Stoneman. London: Macmillan, 1993: 175–84. Print.

Patterson, Annette. "Teaching Literature in Australia: Examining and reviewing senior English". *Changing English* 15.3 (2008): 311–22. Print.

Reid, Ian. *The Making of Literature: Texts, contexts and classroom practices*. Australian Assoc. for the Teaching of English, 1984. Print.

Rylance, Rick. "'Getting on': Ideology, Personality and the Brontë characters". *The Cambridge Companion to the Brontës*. Ed. Heather Glen. Cambridge: Cambridge University Press, 2002. 148–69. Print.

SCSA (School Curriculum and Standards Authority). "Literature ATAR Syllabus Year 12". 2015. <http://wace1516.scsa.wa.edu.au/__data/assets/pdf_file/0016/8620/Literature_Y12_Syllabus_AC_ATAR_pdf.pdf> Web. Accessed 8 April 2016.

SCSA (School Curriculum and Standards Authority). "Literature ATAR Support Materials". <http://wace1516.scsa.wa.edu.au/syllabus-and-support-materials/english/literature> Web. Accessed 8 April 2016.

SCSA (School Curriculum and Standards Authority). "Literature Past Examination Papers". <www.scsa.wa.edu.au/internet/Publications/Past_WACE_Examinations/English> Web. Accessed 8 April 2016.

Stevenson, John Allen. "'Heathcliff is me!': *Wuthering Heights* and the question of likeness". *Nineteenth-Century Literature* 43.1 (1988): 60–81. Print.

Stoneman, Patsy. "The Brontë myth." *The Cambridge Companion to the Brontës*. Ed. Heather Glen. Cambridge: Cambridge University Press, 2002. 214–41.

Vine, Steven. "The wuther of the other in *Wuthering Heights*". *Nineteenth-Century Literature* 49.3 (1994): 339–59. Print.

Williams, Raymond. *The Country and the City*. London: Chatto and Windus, 1973. Print.

Wright, Patrick. *On Living in an Old Country: The national past in contemporary Britain*. London: Verso, 1985. Print.

INDEX

AATE *see* Australian Association for the Teaching of English
ABC Schools Broadcasts 202–3
access to education 176, 192
Achebe, Chinua. *A Man of the People* 164, 170
   Things Fall Apart 56, 172
Addison, Joseph 86
aesthetic, in national curriculum 344
aesthetic practice xvi, 346, 351, 352–3, 354
aesthetic value, of canonical texts 268, 335, 345–6
aesthetics, of English 200, 206
Albee, Edward. *Who's Afraid of Virginia Woolf?* 143
Alcott, Louisa May 86
ALIAS 4, 19–35, 227–8
   database 21–2, 61, 71, 80, 159, 177, 228, 263, 264, 282, 317
alternative programs 180–1
Althusser, Louis 174
American cultural influence 24, 28, 42
American writers 25, 27, 206
Analysis of Literature in Australian Schools *see* ALIAS
Anderson, Jessica. *Tirra Lirra by the River* 63, 143, 152, 182
Andrich Report 31
Arnold, Matthew 26, 86, 99
   and literary theory 52, 53, 84, 227, 270, 294–5, 302, 333
   see also Cultural Heritage model
assessment, alternative approaches 181
assessment tasks, increasing range of 73–4
Astley, Thea 153
   A Descant for Gossips 249
ATAR 19
Attenborough, David. *Zoo Quest in Paraguay* 54
Attridge, Derek 352
Atwood, Margaret 181
   The Handmaid's Tale 32, 33, 344
Auden, W.H. 210
Austen, Jane 26, 30, 31, 33, 86, 125, 143, 160, 247, 297
   Emma 25, 32, 115, 127, 307
   Northanger Abbey 127
   Persuasion 26
   Pride and Prejudice 25, 27, 31, 99, 127, 143, 272
Australia, depiction by Dickens 245
Australia Council 163
   Literature Board 63

Australian Association for the Teaching of English 47, 73, 150
Australian Bicentenary 163, 166, 274, 331–2
   see also Bicentennial Australian Studies Schools Project
Australian cultural preoccupations 162–3, 166
Australian film 166–7
Australian Film Commission 163
Australian Idiom 251
Australian literary canon 163, 330
   see also national canon
Australian literary journals 49, 205–6
   see also names of journals, e.g. Meanjin
Australian literature, in school curriculum 7–8, 49–50, 72–7, 86, 89, 117, 152–3, 162–3, 165, 168, 183, 203–6, 274, 296
   research 62–4
   in universities 49, 203–6
Australian Short Stories 26, 205, 216, 305, 306
Australian Tertiary Admissions Rank *see* ATAR
Australian writers 25, 26–7, 31, 32, 319
Australia's Language, 1991 175
Bacon, Francis 86
   The Advancement of Learning 299
Badiou, Alain 342–3, 350
Ballard, J.G. *Empire of the Sun* 168, 172
Bantock, G.H. xv
Barnard Eldershaw, M. *A House is Built* 247–8
Barnes, H. *Essays Old and New*
Barnes, John 203, 206
Barthes, Roland 3
Bate, Jonathan 228
Baynton, Barbara 181
Beazley Report 30
Beckett, Samuel 216, 297
   All That Fall 304
   Happy Days 304
   Waiting for Godot 115, 295, 304, 307
Bennett, Bruce 201, 216
Bernstein, Basil 61–2, 76
Biaggini, E.G. 209 fn8
Bicentennial Australian Studies Schools Project 73, 332
biographies, decline in popularity 34
   South Australia, 1945 23
Blackburn Report, 1985 53, 69, 176
Blainey, Geoffrey. *The Tyranny of Distance* 50, 171, 172
Blake, William 100
Bloom, Harold 225–6, 228, 229

Board of Secondary School Studies (NSW) 101, 113
Board of Senior School Studies (NSW) 113
Board of Studies (NSW) 119
Board, Peter 83, 85
Boldrewood, Rolf. *Robbery under Arms* 25, 49, 204 fn5
Bolt, Robert. *A Man for All Seasons* 171, 182, 306
Bonwick, James. *A Tasmanian Lily* 239–40
Boomer, Garth 65–7
Boswell, James 100
Bouras, Gillian. *A Foreign Wife* 168, 171
Boyd, Arthur 288
Boyd, Martin. *Outbreak of Love* 180
Bradley, David 200, 214–5, 217
Bradley, Jeana *see* Tweedie, Jeana
Brautigan, Richard 181
Breaker Morant (film) 158–9, 167–8, 169, 171
Brecht, Bertolt. *Caucasian Chalk Circle* 33
Brennan, Christopher 296, 298
Brereton, John Le Gay 297–8
Briggs, Raymond. *When the Wind Blows* 182, 186, 189
British literary canon 348
    dominance 86, 91, 101, 107, 114, 129, 153, 160, 199, 250
Britton, James 48, 179
Brontë, Charlotte 25, 31, 33, 247, 340, 341
    Jane Eyre 27, 127, 238, 250
Brontë, Emily 60
    Wuthering Heights 25, 31, 32, 115, 127, 238, 272, 273, 305, 339–42, 353–4, 356
Brooks, Cleanth 285, 287
Browne, Sir Thomas. *Religio Medici* 299
Browning, Robert 100, 125
Bullock Report, 1977 50
Bunyan, John 100
Burke, Edmund 86
Burrows, Len 198, 200, 202, 214–5, 217
Butterfield, Herbert xv
Byron, Lord 86, 100, 125
Cairncross, A.S. *Eight Essayists* 306
Cambridge English 111, 113, 115, 123, 199, 214, 217, 286, 296
Camus, Albert, *The Outsider* 170, 182
canon formation 5, 8, 11, 101, 228, 268, 269, 320, 325, 330–1, 337
canon wars 53
canonical literature *see* literary canon
canonicity 38, 330
Careful He Might Hear You (film) 53
Carlyle, Thomas 86
Carter, Don, and curriculum policy 82
Cary, Joyce 297
    The Horse's Mouth 307
Cataldi, Lee 118

Catholic schooling 274–6
CATs *see* common assessment tasks
Centre for Studies in Literary Education (Deakin University) 63
The Chant of Jimmie Blacksmith (film) 167
Charitable Malice 214–5
Chaucer, Geoffrey 30, 32, 33, 86, 115, 125, 127, 211
    The Nun's Priest's Tale 32
    The Pardoner's Tale 127, 307
    The Parlement of Foules 298–9
    Prologue to The Canterbury Tales 23, 26, 27, 32, 34
Chekhov, Anton 33, 215, 216
child-centred education *see* student-centred pedagogy
Churchill, Caryl. *Top Girls* 32
circumtextual framing 61, 75–6
citizenship, perceptions of 244–5
Clark, Brian. *Whose Life is it Anyway?* 171
Clark, Reverend Charles 241
Clarke, Marcus. *For the Term of His Natural Life* 50, 238
class sets, reliance on 10, 64
Classic Australian Short Stories 170
classroom discussion 151–2
classroom practice 137–8, 154, 186–9
close reading 139, 141, 143, 144, 146, 154, 206–7, 227, 285, 286, 297 287, 296, 334
    see also textual intimacy
Cold War 25, 164, 341
Coleman, Peter. *Australian Civilisation* 251
Coleridge, Samuel Taylor 25, 86, 100, 125, 143
common assessment tasks 73, 190
communication, arts of 41
communism, fear of 24
compulsory subject, English as 45, 69, 79, 120, 175, 268
conditions of assent 229, 230, 231
conditions of dissent 229–30
Congreve, William. *The Way of the World* 299
Conrad, Joseph 23, 25, 31, 33, 100, 160, 247, 295, 297
    Heart of Darkness 31, 32, 33, 273, 303, 344
    Lord Jim 303
    The Nigger of the Narcissus 306
    Youth 303
conservatism, of curriculum 133
consumerism 28
context, and study of literature xvi, 351
Cook, Kenneth. *Wake in Fright* 180
Cormier, Robert. *After the First Death* 172
Corwin, Norman 27
Courses of Study for High Schools (NSW), 1911 83
    1945 91–2

Index

Court, Franklin 6
Cowan, Peter 215–6, 217
   Short Story Landscape 206, 216
Cox Report, 1989 348
creativity, Wright's theory of 312–3
critical literacy, and English syllabuses 39–40, 52, 333, 334, 335, 341
critical self-consciousness 44
critical thinking 53, 355
   capacity for 41, 42
CSLE *see* Centre for Studies in Literary Education
cultural analysis, emergence in UK 46
cultural capital, of texts 250, 251, 255, 257, 334, 337
cultural critique 44, 286
cultural diversity 175, 176, 179, 183, 184
cultural heritage, and critical thinking 355
Cultural Heritage model 45, 50, 85, 91, 97, 101, 107, 115, 117, 124, 128, 247–8, 254, 270, 333, 344, 347, 348, 355
cultural materialism 11, 286
cultural nationalism 30, 292, 332
cultural pessimism 291
cultural studies xv–xvi, 50–1
   foreshadowed by school English 54
   impact on curriculum 39, 55, 56, 160, 166, 249, 270, 285, 293, 333
   impact on university English 54, 55, 56, 160, 166
cultural value, of canonical texts 268, 345–6
culture, changing definition of 347, 352
Curie, Eve. *Madame Curie* 23
curriculum, development in Australia 246
   history 4
   redesign, teacher involvement 188
      in Victoria 68–74, 174–93
   reform 68, 180
   renewal, New South Wales 81
curriculum boards 42, 317, 318, 320, 321, 323–4
Curriculum Policies Project (University of Melbourne) 68–9
Cusack, Dymphna. *Caddie* 163
Dark, Eleanor. *The Timeless Land* 26, 27, 49, 71, 205
Daviot, Gordon 23, 33–4
Davis, Jack 118
   No Sugar 32, 33, 172, 344
Dawe, Bruce 31, 118, 181
   Condolences of the Season 180
Day Lewis, Cecil 210
Deleuze, Gilles 52
Delves, Tony 177–8
Derrida, Jacques 52, 350, 355
Desai, Anita. *The Village by the Sea* 168, 172
Dettman Report 30

Dews, Peter 232–3
Dickens, Charles 23, 25, 26, 30, 31, 33, 86, 100, 125
   in English syllabuses 238–57
   as moral teacher 239–40
   public readings 239, 240–2
   A Christmas Carol 240, 241
   David Copperfield 23, 252
   Great Expectations 31, 32, 238–57, 273
   Hard Times 251
difficult texts, teaching 265–8, 280–1
disciplinary crisis 52
dissociated sensibility 287–8, 300
distant reading 159, 160–1
diversity, of text lists 192
   see also gender diversity; set texts, broadening range of
Dixon, John 178, 179, 348
Dobson, Rosemary 118, 129
Doctorow, E.L. 181
Donne, John 115, 125, 127, 143, 297, 299, 300, 307
Donnelly, Kevin. "In Praise of Literature" 190
Dos Passos, John 215
Drake-Brockman, Henrietta 205, 216
drama, promotion of 199–202
   see also plays; radio plays; screen plays
dystopian narratives 163–4, 165
Eagleson, R.D. 47
Eagleton, Terry xvi, 53, 166, 333
   Literary Theory 52, 294, 343
   Myths of Power 340
economic change, 1980s–1990s 118, 165–6, 180
economic prosperity, 1950s–1960s 24, 28
Edge of Darkness (film) 53
Education Act (NSW) 1961 41, 109
Education and the Ideal 123
Education Department of Victoria 179
educational theory, history xv
educative system change, 1980s–1990s 160, 165–6
Edwards, Allan 196–209, 210–1, 212, 214, 217
Eldershaw, Flora *see* Barnard Eldershaw, M.
Eliot, George 23, 25, 31, 33, 86, 100, 125
   Felix Holt 299
   The Mill on the Floss 99
   Silas Marner 99
Eliot, T.S. 115, 127, 197, 210, 215, 216, 286, 287–8, 296, 297, 300, 301, 307, 344
   Murder in the Cathedral 26, 115, 210, 295, 303, 307
   Selected Poems 303
Elisha, Ron. *In Duty Bound* 172
elocution lessons and performances 242
Emerson, Ralph Waldo 86
Empson, William 286, 296

English, as a school subject 3–11, 19–20, 159–60, 268, 293
    conservatism of 133
    and literary studies 38–56
    and modernism 288, 295
    New South Wales 78–9, 82–9, 91–4, 109–11, 116–24, 138–9
    see also Year 12 English courses
English, as progressive subject 164, 169, 192
    division into two subjects 28–30, 42, 45–6, 159
    history of 52, 343
English (VCE subject) 69–70, 174–93
English curricula, Australia, 2005 inquiry 38–9
English curriculum, Australia 3–4
English Examiners' Report for WA, 1950 32
English Expression (school subject) 45
English in Australia (journal) 177, 179
English Study Design (Victoria) 186–7, 189, 192
    press response to 189–90
    significance of 193
English syllabuses, South Australia 250–3
    Victoria 253–5
    Western Australia 196–217, 246–50
English teachers, and curriculum design 125, 133
    motivation 153
    associations 47
    see also Australian Association for the Teaching of English; English Teachers' Association (NSW); English Teachers' Group; Victorian Association for the Teaching of English
English Teachers' Association (NSW) 138, 139–40, 141, 144, 146–7, 150
English Teachers' Group (NSW) 96–7
English textbooks 93
English Verse: Old and New 23
Ern Malley hoax 292
essays, 1945 23
    decline in popularity 32, 34
Essays of Today 99
ETG *see* English Teachers' Group
ethical function, of literature 10–1, 38, 335, 342, 351
Euripides 33
    The Bacchae 32, 182
    Medea 33
Evans, Edward R.G.R. *South with Scott* 23
Ewers, John K. 204, 205
exam-based assessment 190, 244, 245
examination answers, analysis 63–4
examination boards 42
examination format 99
examination papers, and interstate difference 42–4

examination questions 248–9, 250, 252, 253, 254, 298–302, 323, 335–6, 346–7
    analysis of 276–80
examinations, restructure 131–2, 249
    strictures of 89, 91, 99, 101, 108, 115–6, 130, 132, 150, 151, 180
examiners' reports, New South Wales 89, 91, 96
    Western Australia 31, 32, 33
Facey, A.B. *A Fortunate Life* 166, 171
Farmer, Beverley. *Home Time* 64
Faulkner, William 295
    As I Lay Dying 249, 303
Fellowship of Australian Writers in Western Australia 205, 206
Fielding, Henry. *Joseph Andrews* 115, 307
film study 53, 165, 167–8
Fish, Stanley 5, 154
Fitzgerald, F. Scott 181
Five Radio Plays 27, 49, 202, 204 fn5, 209
Flaubert, Gustav 44
Foucault, Michel 52
Fowles, John. *The Collector* 31
Franklin, Miles 181, 333
    All That Swagger 99
    My Brilliant Career 238
Friel, Brian. *Freedom of the City* 184
Frost, Robert 26, 206
Furphy, Joseph 296
    Such is Life 292
Futurism 291
Gardiner, Harold. *Nine Twentieth-Century Essayists* 306
Gardner, Helen. *The Metaphysical Poets* 32
Gaskell, Elizabeth 86
gender, of authors 23, 25, 27
gender diversity, of text lists 183
genocide, Australian 168, fn4
The Getting of Wisdom (film) 167, 171
Gibbon, Edward 86
Gilbert, Pam 68
Goldberg, Sam 113, 295, 297, 307
The Golden Book of Modern Poetry 23
Golding, William 33–4, 248
    Lord of the Flies 115, 248
Goldsmith, Oliver 25
Goldsworthy, Peter 18
    Maestro 148
Gow, Michael. *Away* 148
The Grapes of Wrath (film) 165
graphic novels 186–7
Gray, Robert 118
Green, Bill 68
Greenblatt, Stephen 231, 235
Greene, Graham. *The Power and the Glory* 164, 170, 307
Grenville, Kate 333

INDEX

The Secret River 168 fn4
Grierson, Herbert 300
Growth model of English 47–9, 50, 64–7, 98, 118, 179, 252, 254, 270, 333, 349
Guillory, John 5, 38, 192
   Canon, Syllabus, List 55
   Cultural Capital 330–1, 337
Hardy, Thomas 23, 25, 26, 31, 33, 215, 216, 248, 297
   in English syllabuses 272–3
   poetry 272
   Far from the Madding Crowd 272
   Jude the Obscure 272
   The Mayor of Casterbridge 31, 248, 249, 272
   The Return of the Native 272, 273
   Tess of the d'Urbervilles 31, 32, 115, 127, 261–82, 307
   The Trumpet-Major 272, 273
   Under the Greenwood Tree 250, 272
   The Woodlanders 272
Harwood, Gwen 344
   Selected Poems 32, 33, 153, 274
Hay, John 216
Heaney, Seamus 33, 344
Heller, Joseph. *Catch-22* 164, 170
Hemingway, Ernest 34, 181, 215, 216
heritage industry 347–8
Hewett, Dorothy 118, 200, 206, 210, 216, 313
Hibberd, Jack 181
Higher School Certificate (NSW) 107, 109, 116–26
Higher School Certificate (Victoria) 178, 179–82
Hill, Thomas Padmore 242
historical perspective, value of xv
Hoggart, Richard 52, 166, 334
   The Uses of Literacy 42
Hoggins, Charles Davenport 241
Holbrook, David 270
Holme, E.R. 297–8
Holmes, Oliver Wendell 86
Holt, Ronald. *The Strength of Tradition* 171
Homer 26, 27
Hope, A.D. 7, 47, 206
Hopkins, Gerald Manley 100, 115, 125, 297, 307
Horne, Donald. *The Lucky Country* 114
Howard, John, criticism of syllabuses 123
HSC *see* Higher School Certificate
Hughes, Ted. *Birthday Letters* 128
Hungerford, Tom. *Stories from the Suburban Road* 171, 172
Hunter, Ian 287–8, 334
Huxley, Aldous. *Brave New World* 164, 170, 171, 172
Ibsen, Henrik 33, 344
   A Doll's House 56, 274

An Enemy of the People 26
ideology of texts 192–3
   see also literary ideologies
ideology politics 10–1
Idiom (journal) 177, 179, 184, 185, 190
Idriess, Ion. *Flynn of the Inland* 23, 49, 204 fn5
immigrant stories 168
inclusivity xv, 344
Indigenous rights 30
Indigenous writers 168
Ingarden, Roman 229 fn7, 230, 233–4
Institute of Education, University of London 48
Intermediate Certificate (NSW) 88
International Forum: Contemporary Essays 171
interpretation, as interactive process 351
intertextuality 51
iterability 10
James, Clive. *Unreliable Memoirs* 171
Jhabvala, Ruth Prawer. *A Backward Place* 184
Johnson, Colin. *Wild Cat Falling* 168, 169, 172
Johnston, George 163
   My Brother Jack 162, 167, 168, 170, 172
Johnston, Jennifer. *How Many Miles to Babylon?* 184
Jones, Barry. *Sleepers Wake* 171
Jonson, Ben 100
   The Alchemist 299
Joyce, James 296
   The Dubliners 304
   Portrait of the Artist 295, 304
Keats, John 25, 100
Kellaway, Frank 322
Keneally, Thomas. *The Chant of Jimmie Blacksmith* 140, 163, 170, 171
Kenna, Peter. *A Hard God* 172
Kermode, Frank 310, 311–2, 313
Kesey, Ken. *One Flew Over the Cuckoo's Nest* 171, 172
The Killing Fields (film) 53, 168, 172
King, Alec 197, 198, 202, 203, 204–5, 209–15, 217
   Writing 213
   and Martin Ketley. *The Control of Language* 212
King, Catherine 202, 209
Kingsley, Charles 86
Kipling, Rudyard 23, 86
Knowles, John. *A Separate Peace* 170
Koch, Christopher, criticism of education 123
Kramer, Leonie 7, 47
Kristeva, Julia 51
Lamb, Charles 86
Lampedusa, Giuseppe di 33
   The Leopard 170, 184

A Language for Life 50
Language-study requirements, NSW 92, 94
lantern-slide shows 240
Lawler, Ray 33
  Summer of the Seventeenth Doll 31, 50, 64, 140–142
Lawrence, D.H. 30, 31, 296, 297
  Kangaroo 295, 304
  Selected Poems 304
  Sons and Lovers 115, 182, 295, 304, 307
Lawson, Henry 100, 127, 128, 143, 181, 296, 298
  The Bush Undertaker and Other Stories 184
  The Penguin Henry Lawson Short Stories 274
  While the Billy Boils 252
Le Guin, Ursula. *The Dispossessed* 252
  The Left Hand of Darkness 252
Leaving Certificate (NSW) 41, 88, 91, 101, 107
Leavis, F.R. 42, 44, 52, 55, 197–8, 203, 208, 209 fn8, 226–7, 270, 287, 302
Leavisism 207, 208–9, 217, 286, 287, 293–4, 296, 297, 333
Leavisite ascendancy 10, 44, 111, 113
Leavisite critical method 128
Leavisite understandings 54–5
left-wing origins, of Australian literature 163
Lessing, Doris. *Five* 181
Levertov, Denise 146–7
Lewis, C.S. 212
Life is Beautiful (film) 127
Lindsay, Norman 291
literary canon 6, 27, 31, 55, 244, 245, 268, 274
  definition 5
  see also Australian literary canon; British literary canon; canon formation; national canon
literary conscience 342
literary criticism, self-aware approaches 44
literary ideologies 269
literary language 286, 350, 351
literary regime, Frow on 2 fn1
literary sociability 151–2, 192
literary studies 4, 6, 288, 294
  curriculum 62–76
  and ideological shifts 46, 294–5
  interstate differences 42–4
  shifts in purpose 75
Literary Studies, and English as a school subject 38–56, 294, 343
literary study, as cultural analysis 347
literary value 3–11, 329
literary work, constitutive elements 233–4
literature, as art 353–4
  in Australian schools 3–4, 56
  as civilising force 52, 78, 79, 84–5, 91, 97, 107–8, 132, 269–70, 342, 351

as cultural heritage 347–52
democratising powers of 97
emergence of 342
ethical function 10–1, 38, 335, 342, 351
moral values of 206, 269–70, 342
nature of 8, 350–1
in the NSW curriculum 84–5, 93, 137–55
self-aware approaches 44
social function xvi, 310, 345–6, 354
student responses to 141–2, 147–8, 149–50, 154, 180, 183, 280–1, 345
  see also reader-response pedagogy
Literature (school subject) 45, 160, 268
  Western Australia 247, 344–7
Literature (VCE subject) 69–70, 71–2
Literature (WACE subject) 344–7
literature-as-event 352
literature teaching, ideological shifts 269–71
  research into 185, 263–5, 282
Liverani, Mary Rose. *The Winter Sparrows* 170
London Institute of Education 209, 210 fn9
London School 48
Longfellow, Henry Wadsworth 86
Lowell, James Russell 86
Lyotard, Jean-Francois 52
MacCallum, Mungo 297
Mack, Amy. *A Bush Calendar* 86
Mackaness, George and Joan. *The Wide Brown Land* 25, 49, 204 fn5
Mackellar, Dorothea 7
Mainly Modern 170
Malamud, Bernard. *The Fixer* 172
Malouf, David 33, 118, 333
  Antipodes 64
  An Imaginary Life 127–8
  Remembering Babylon 33
Manuel, Jacqueline, and curriculum policy 82
Mares, Peggy 64–5, 67–8
Marlowe, Christopher 100
Marquez, Gabriel Garcia 53
Martin, Nancy 48
Marx, Karl. *The Communist Manifesto* 54
Mason, Bobbie Ann 183
  In Country 184
Masters, Olga 183
  Amy's Children 184
matriculation rates, 1957 41
McAuley, James 7, 47
McGaw reforms, 1999 81
McGaw Report, 1984 31
McGaw Review, 1996 119
McRae, D. 180–1
Meanjin 204
media studies, impact on curriculum 39
Melbourne Declaration on Educational Goals for Young Australians, 2008 174
Melbourne Declaration, 1991 53

INDEX

Melbourne State College 181
Melville, Herman. *Moby Dick* 25
Merson, Alick. *The English Essay* 305, 306
   Modern Short Stories 305, 306
   Still Lighter Essays 27
metaphysical canon 296
Metaphysical poets 160
migration, postwar 24, 178
Miller, Arthur 31, 215, 216
   The Crucible 31, 114, 164, 170, 172, 272, 274, 307
   Death of a Salesman 114, 171, 172, 206
   A View form the Bridge 10
Milton, John 30, 86, 100, 115
   Paradise Lost 307
Misson, Ray 185, 193
modernisation, in Australia 292, 295
   of secondary education 41
modernism, in British schools 296 fn2
   definition 289
   origins 289–93
   and subject English 44, 285–307
modernist criticism, and subject English 285–307
modernist poetry 287, 288
modernity 290
Moodie Heddle, E. *The Boomerang Book of Australian Poetry* 306
moral values of literature 206, 269–70, 342
Moretti, Franco 159, 164
Morgan, Sally. *My Place* 168, 172
Morrison, Toni 53
multiculturalism 30, 33
Murdoch, Walter 198, 199, 201, 202, 205, 209, 216
Narayan, Rasipuram 33
nation-building 292
   and subject English 101, 244–5, 249, 251, 255
national canon 7, 274, 296
   see also Australian literary canon
national curriculum 22, 345
national identity, and *Cloudstreet* 335–6, 337
nationalism, and Australian literature 163, 164, 166, 331–2
neo-liberal policy 175
New Criticism 207, 285–7, 288, 294, 296, 300, 341
New Education Fellowship approach 199
New English *see* Growth model of English
Newbolt Report, 1921 84–5, 97, 109
Nietzschean thought 291, 342
Nolan, Sidney 288
non-British writers, 1945 23
non-print media 184
   see also film study
non-white authors 53

novels 22–3, 25, 26, 32
   and nationhood 164
Nowra, Louis 118
Oates, Joyce Carol xvi
Olive, Sarah, on Shakespeare 226–7
Ondaatje, Michael. *In the Skin of a Lion* 127
One Flew Over the Cuckoo's Nest (film) 165
Orwell, George 181
   1984 158, 164, 170, 171
Osborne, John. *Look Back in Anger* 307
Owen, Wilfred 31, 128, 148
Paley, Grace 181
Palmer, Vance. *The Passage* 248, 306
   The Rainbow Bird 206, 213–4
Park, Ruth. *The Harp in the South* 163, 170, 171, 182
Parker, Ernest. *A Galaxy of Poems Old and New* 305, 306
   A Pageant of English Verse 25, 26
Parsons, Philip 200
pedagogical canons 5–6, 9–10, 344
The Penguin Book of Modern Australian Verse 50
personal engagement, pretence of 67
personal growth agenda, and literary study 345, 347
personal growth pedagogy *see* Growth model of English
Perspectives Two 216
pervasive personalism 67
Petch, James A. 28, 45–6
Petch Report, 1964 45–6
Petrov Affair, 1954 24
phenomenology 350
Picnic at Hanging Rock (film) 53
Plath, Sylvia 128, 146–7
   The Bell Jar 171, 172
Plays for Radio and Television 206, 209
Plays of the Sixties 170
plays 22, 23, 25, 26, 32
   as scripts for performance 141, 142, 144
   see also drama; radio plays; screen plays
Poe, Edgar Allan 23, 33–4
   Tales of Mystery and Imagination 25
poetry 23, 25
   changing interpretations of 324–5
   compulsory in NSW 112
   decline in popularity 32, 34
   performance of 202
   promotion of 210
   teaching of 311
Poetry Writing Club 210
political criticism xvi
Pope, Alexander 115, 307
popular culture criticism 44
post-lapsarianism xv
poststructuralist critiques 52
postwar curricula 24–5

postwar expansion of education 178
Potok, Chaim. *The Chosen* 170, 171
   My Name is Asher Lev 171, 172
practical criticism 299–300
prescribed texts *see* set texts; text lists
Price, Ellis 242
Prichard, Katharine Susannah. *Coonardoo* 162, 167, 170
   Haxby's Circus 49, 204 fn5
professors *see* university professors
Public Examinations Board (WA) 198, 203
The Purple Rose of Cairo (film) 53
radio plays 202
Ransom, John Crowe 285
reader-response pedagogy 150–1, 154, 285
reading, across the curriculum 50
   assumptions about 64
   emphasis on 199, 207
   Wright's theory of 312–3
   see also close reading; resistant reading
reading lists *see* text lists
Reeves, James. *The Modern Poets' World* 305, 306
Reid, Ian 4, 68
   The Making of Literature 75–6, 343, 348–50, 355
Reinecke, Ian. *Micro Invaders* 171
related texts, chosen by students 129–31
Remarque, Erich. *All Quiet on the Western Front* 170
Representative English Poems 100
resistant reading, and *Cloudstreet* 336
retention rates *see* school retention
Rich, Adrienne 33
Richards, I.A. 198, 203, 208, 227, 286, 296, 299–300, 302
Richardson, Henry Handel 26, 206
   Australia Felix 25, 249, 305, 306
   The Getting of Wisdom 50, 71, 163, 170, 206
The Rinehart Book of Short Stories 248
Robinson, Marilynne 183
   Housekeeping 184
Rohan, Criena. *The Delinquents* 148, 172
Romance fiction 181
Rorabacher, Louise. *Two Ways Meet* 50
Rosen, Harold 178
Royal tour, 1954 24
Rushdie, Salman 53
Ruskin, John 86
Russell, Willy 183
   Educating Rita 168, 169, 171, 172, 184
Ruttledge, Hugh. *Everest 1933* 23
Salinger, J.D. *Catcher in the Rye* 114, 171
Scales of Justice (TV script) 148–9, 171
school libraries 64
school retention 44, 176, 180
school subjects as social systems 6

school-based assessment 131–2, 187, 190, 191
school-based decision-making 69
schooling, purposes of 174
science fiction 181
Scott, Arthur. *Speaking of the Famous* 306
   The Spoken Word 305
   Topics and Opinions 305
Scott, Kim 333
Scott, Ridley. *Blade Runner* 56, 158
Scott, Walter 86
   Ivanhoe 250
screen plays 182
Scrutiny movement 42, 52, 114–5, 197, 208, 209 fn8, 286, 288
Secondary Schools Board (NSW) 113
secularisation 290
Seddon, George 198
Senior Secondary Assessment Board of South Australia 252
Serle, Geoffrey 204
set texts, authority of 132, 133
   broadening range of 72–3, 148, 165, 179, 180, 182
   most frequently used 160, 170–3, 272, 339
   see also text lists
Seymour, Alan. *The One Day of the Year* 50, 54, 114, 140
Shaffer, Peter. *Equus* 143, 171
Shakespeare, William 30, 31, 33, 125, 160
   adaptations and appropriations 235
   in English syllabuses 225–36, 242
   and the historical moment 229–30
   in NSW curriculum 112
   relevance 225, 226, 228
   self-creativity 228, 230, 234
   Antony and Cleopatra 22, 272
   As You Like It 86, 99, 201
   Coriolanus 22, 86, 201
   Hamlet 25, 26, 27, 31, 32, 127, 232–3, 272, 274, 339, 344
   Henry IV 22, 31, 201
   Henry V 86, 235
   Julius Caesar 25, 26, 27, 86, 127, 306
   King Lear 22, 32, 34, 127, 143, 201, 234, 272, 274, 307
   Macbeth 23, 27, 86, 99, 128, 170, 272, 297, 305
   The Merchant of Venice 86
   A Midsummer Night's Dream 31, 32, 86
   Much Ado about Nothing 22, 201
   Othello 25, 32, 33, 55, 143–5, 272, 274, 307, 344
   Richard II 26, 27, 201, 306
   Richard III 127
   Romeo and Juliet 32, 171
   The Tempest 27, 32, 33, 86, 127, 297, 305, 344
   Twelfth Night 25, 201

Index

A Winter's Tale 86
Shaw, George Bernard 33–4, 100, 297
   Arms and the Man 26
   Caesar and Cleopatra 26
   The Devil's Disciple 26
   Saint Joan 26, 115, 307
Shelley, Mary. *Frankenstein* 32, 344
Shelley, Percy Bysshe 86, 100
   The Cenci 299
Sheridan, Richard Brinsley 25, 100
short stories 26, 32, 34, 64, 216
Skills model 50
Skrzynecki, Peter 148
Slessor, Kenneth 50, 143, 292
   Selected Poems 303
Small, K. *Break into Day* 170
Smyth, W. *A Book of Poetry* 305
social change 41, 118, 160, 165–6, 281
social function of literature xvi, 310, 345–6, 354
social justice, diminished concern for 175
social mission, of subject English 42, 269–70
socially disadvantaged youth 175, 191
sociolinguistic approach, to English 270
Sophie's Choice (film) 53
Sophocles. *Antigone* 127
   Oedipus the King 307
Southwell, Elsie. *The Poets' Quest* 305
Spark, Muriel. *The Prime of Miss Jean Brodie* 140, 164, 170
specialist teachers, need for 46–7
Spectrum One 216
Spectrum Two 170, 171, 216
Spenser, Edmund 100
   Prosopopia 299
Spiegelman, Art. *Maus* 186–7
SSABSA *see* Senior Secondary Assessment Board of South Australia
standards-based testing 189
standards-driven students 48, 175
Steinbeck, John. *The Grapes of Wrath* 171
Stevenson, Robert Louis 23, 25, 33–4, 86
   The Master of Ballantrae 27, 250
Stewart, Douglas 27
   The Fire on the Snow 305, 306
   Ned Kelly 71
Stoppard, Tom 33
Stow, Randolph 31, 216
   The Merry-Go-Round in the Sea 162, 167, 168, 170, 216 fn21, 303
   To the Islands 216 fn21, 304
Stratton, David. *The Last New Wave* 166
A Streetcar Named Desire (film) 165
student-centred pedagogy 87–9, 93
Study Designs (Victoria) 69–74
Sykes, Bobbi 183
   Love Poems and Other Revolutionary Actions 184
syllabus choice 22–3, 25, 30, 33, 72, 88, 94, 100, 129–31
TAFE college programs 187–288
TAFE colleges 180–1
Tate, Allen 285
teaching canons *see* pedagogical canons
teaching practice *see* classroom practice
technological change 30, 165
Teede, Neville 200, 203
Tennyson, Alfred 25, 26, 86, 99, 100, 242
tertiary entrance ranking 19, 20, 30
Tertiary Orientation Program 187–8
text essay, increasing emphasis on 188–9
text lists 3, 4–5, 10, 21, 22–3, 25–27, 30–4, 61, 62–3, 70, 71
   and curriculum history 79–80
   New South Wales 78–83, 85–9, 95–101, 111–5, 124–33, 297, 306–307
   Victoria, 1990 176–7
   Western Australia, 2016 344
   see also set texts; classroom sets
text response assessment 187
text selection, principles 161, 169, 321
   process 153–4, 174–93, 196–217, 243–4, 269, 270, 317–8
   student-centred 51, 88
textual intimacy, and English teaching 158–9, 161
Thackeray, William 100, 297
   Henry Esmond 26, 305
themes, in syllabuses 161
Thompson, E.P. 52, 270
Thompson, H.S. 197, 217
Thomson, Jack 185, 193
Thomson, Katherine. *Diving for Pearls* 274
Tickell, Gerry 178, 179
Tomlinson, T.B. 214
TOP *see* Tertiary Orientation Program
Tranter, John 118
trigger warnings, about texts 265
Trollope, Anthony. *Barchester Towers* 249
Turner, Graeme 39, 56, 334
   National Fictions 162, 166
Twain, Mark 31, 33
   The Adventures of Huckleberry Finn 26, 31, 32, 114, 127, 170, 206, 248, 272, 307
Tweedie, Jeana 200, 203, 217
Twelve Poets, 1950–1970 170, 180, 304
universal education 227
university English, literary criticism models 101
university expansion 49
University of Sydney 297–8, 314–5
   and school English curriculum 83, 90, 101, 112–3, 125
University of Western Australia, and school English curriculum 196–217

university professors, as AATE presidents 47
value criteria 9
VATE *see* Victorian Association for the Teaching of English
VCAA *see* Victorian Curriculum and Assessment Authority
VCAB *see* Victorian Curriculum and Assessment Board
VCE *see* Victorian Certificate of Education
Victorian Association for the Teaching of English 177, 188
Victorian Certificate of Education 62, 69–74, 175–93
Victorian Curriculum and Assessment Authority 186–7
Victorian Curriculum and Assessment Board 69, 190
Victorian Education Department 69
Victorian morality, Hardy's challenge of 266
video technology 53
Vietnam conflict, Australian troops 24
Vision (journal) 291
Vonnegut, Kurt 181
   Player Piano 182
WACE *see* Western Australian Certificate of Education
Wallace-Crabbe, Chris. *The Golden Apples of the Sun* 182
   Six Voices 304, 306
Walpole, Horace. *The Castle of Otranto* 299
Ward, Russel. *The Australian Legend* 162
Warner, Rex 210
Warren, Robert Penn 285
Waugh, Evelyn. *The Loved One* 170
Weinstein, Arnold 231–2
Wells, H.G. 25, 247, 297
   The History of Mr Polly 305, 306
Wells, Stanley 228
West Australian (newspaper) 204
Western Australian Certificate of Education 344–7
Western Australian English Literature Examiners' Report, 2005 33
Western Australian Examiners' Report for Literature, 1988 31
Whig interpretation of history xv
White, Patrick 31, 33, 129, 143, 215, 216, 288, 296, 297, 330
   The Burnt Ones 304
   The Eye of the Storm 63, 64, 304
   A Fringe of Leaves 32, 182, 238, 303–304
   Riders in the Chariot 303
   The Tree of Man 7, 303
   Voss 50, 114, 249, 303, 307
Whitlam, Gough 163
Widdowson, Peter, on Hardy 268–9
Wieland, Jim 207
Wilde, Oscar 33, 44
Wilkes, G.A. 112
Williams, Raymond 52, 166, 270
   The Country and the City 354
   Culture and Society 53
   The Long Revolution 46
Williams, Tennessee. *The Glass Menagerie* 31
   A Streetcar Named Desire 171
Williamson, David 118, 181
   The Removalists 148, 168, 172
Wimsatt, W.K. *The Verbal Icon* 286
Winterson, Jeanette 53
Winton, Tim 118, 153
   and university reading lists 332–3
   Breath 332–3
   Cloudstreet 31–2, 33, 56, 127, 158, 274, 327–37
   Dirt Music 332–3
Women of the Sun (TV series) 168, 172
women writers 25, 27, 33, 168, 319
women's liberation 30
Woolf, Virginia 296
   Mrs Dalloway 304
   A Room of One's Own 170
   To the Lighthouse 304
Wordsworth, William 25, 86, 100, 125, 127, 145–6, 210
working-class background, of students 48, 166, 178
Wright, Alexis 333
Wright, Judith 33, 50, 114, 125, 181, 206, 310–6
   critical reception 318–9, 322–3
   in English syllabuses 316–26
   Birds 319
   Five Senses 318, 319
   The Gateway 319
   A Human Pattern 323
   The Moving Image 318, 319
   The Other Half 320, 321, 322
   Selected Poems 318
   The Shadow 320
   The Two Fires 319
   Woman to Man 319, 322
Wright, Phillip, and University of New England 314
Wyndham Report, 1957 26, 41–2, 109
Wyndham Scheme 81, 109, 116, 132
Year 12 English courses 35
The Year of Living Dangerously (film) 53, 168, 171
Yeats, William Butler 100, 125
   Selected Poems 303
youth unemployment 180
Zwicky, Fay 216